ALSO BY ERICA MELTZER

. . . .

The Ultimate Guide to SAT® Grammar & Workbook

SAT® Vocabulary: A New Approach (with Larry Krieger)

The Complete Guide to ACT® Reading

The Complete Guide to ACT® English

The Complete GMAT® Sentence Correction Guide

GRE® Vocabulary in Practice

The Critical Reader

The Complete Guide to SAT® Reading

Third Edition

Erica L. Meltzer

◪ THE CRITICAL READER

New York

ISBN-13: 978-0-9975178-7-3

ISBN-10: 0997517875

Dedication

To Ricky, who pestered me to write this book until I finally acquiesced.

Table of Contents

Preface

Eight years elapsed between my last SAT®, which I took as a senior in high school, and the first time I was asked to tutor reading for the SAT. I distinctly remember sitting in Barnes & Noble, hunched over the *Official Guide*, staring at the questions in horror and wondering how on earth I had ever gotten an 800 at the age of 17. Mind you, I felt completely flummoxed by the SAT after I had spent four years studying literature in *college*.

Somehow or other, I managed to muddle through my first reading tutoring sessions. I tried to pretend that I knew what I was doing, but to be perfectly honest, I was pretty lost. I had to look up answers in the back of the book. A lot. I lost count of the number of times I had to utter the words, "I think you're right, but give me one second and let me just double-check that answer..." It was mortifying. No tutor wants to come off as clueless in front of a sixteen-year-old, but I was looking like I had no idea what I was doing. Grammar I could handle, but when it came to teaching reading, I was in way over my head. I simply had no idea how to put into words what had always come naturally to me. Besides, half the time I wasn't sure of the right answer myself.

Luckily for me, fate intervened in the form of Laura Wilson, the founder of WilsonPrep in Chappaqua, New York, whose company I spent several years writing tests for. Laura taught me about the major passage themes, answer choices patterns, and structures. I learned the importance of identifying the main point, tone and major transitions, as well as the ways in which that information can allow a test-taker to spot correct answers quickly, efficiently, and without second-guessing. I discovered that the skills that the SAT tested were in fact the exact same skills that I had spent four years honing.

As a matter of fact, I came to realize that, paradoxically, my degree in French was probably more of an aid in teaching reading than a degree in English would have been. The basic French literary analysis exercise, known as the *explication de texte linéaire*, consists of close reading of a short excerpt of text, during which the reader explains how the text functions rhetorically from beginning to end – that is, just how structure, diction, and syntax work together to produce meaning and convey a particular idea or point of view. In other words, the same skills as those tested on the SAT – the old test as well as the new version. I had considered *explications de texte* a pointless exercise (Rhetoric? Who studies *rhetoric* anymore? That's so nineteenth century!) and resented being forced to write them in college – especially during the year I spent at the Sorbonne, where I and my (French) classmates did little else – but suddenly I appreciated the skills they had taught me. Once I made the connection between what I had been studying all that time and the skills tested on the SAT, the test made sense. I found that I had something to fall back on when I was teaching and, for the first time, I found that I no longer had to constantly look up answers.

I still had a long way to go as a tutor, though: at first I clung a bit too rigidly to some methods (e.g., insisting that students circle all the transitions) and often did not leave my students enough room to find their own strategies. As I worked with more students, however, I began to realize just how little I could take for granted in terms of pre-existing skills: most of my students, it turned out, had significant difficulty even identifying the point of an argument, never mind summing it up in five or so words. A lot of them didn't even realize that passages contained arguments at all; they thought that the authors were simply "talking about stuff." As a result, it never even occurred to them to identify which ideas a given author did and did not agree with. When I instructed them to circle transitions like *however* and *therefore* as a way of identifying the key places in an argument, many of them found it overwhelming to do so at the same time they were trying to absorb the literal content of a passage. More than one student told me they could do one or the other, but not both at the same time. In one memorable gaffe, I told a student that while he often did not have to read every word of the more analytical passages, he did need to read all of the literary passages – only to have him respond that he couldn't tell the difference. He thought of all the passages as literary because the blurbs above them all said they came from books, and weren't all books "literary?" It never occurred to me to tell him that he needed to look for the word *novel* in the blurb above the passage in order to identify works of *fiction*. When I pointed out to another student that he had answered a question incorrectly because he hadn't realized that the author of the passage disagreed with a particular idea, he responded without a trace of irony that the author had spent a lot of time talking about that idea. Apparently, no one had ever introduced him to the idea that writers often spend a good deal of time fleshing out ideas that they *don't* agree with. And this was a student scoring in the mid-600s!

Eventually, I got it. I realized that I would have to spend more time – sometimes a lot more time – explaining basic contextual pieces of information that most adult readers took for granted and, moreover, I would have to do so at the same time I covered actual test-taking strategies. Without the fundamentals, all the strategy in the world might not even raise a student's score by 10 points. My goal in this book is to supply some of those fundamentals while also covering some of the more advanced skills the exam requires.

I would, however, like to emphasize that this book is intended to help you work through and "decode" College Board material. It is not – and should not be used as – a replacement for the *Official Guide*. To that end, I have provided a list of the Reading questions from the tests in the *College Board Official Guide, 2018 Edition* (also available through the Khan Academy website), corresponding to the relevant question type at the end of each chapter.

As you work through this book, you will undoubtedly notice that some of the passages are reused in multiple exercises. Although you may find it somewhat tedious to work through the same passages multiple times, that repetition was a deliberate choice on my part. This book is not designed to have you whiz through passage after passage, but rather to have you study the workings of a limited number of passages in depth. As you work through the exercises, you may also notice that different questions accompanying the same passage are targeting the same concepts, merely from different angles. Again, that is a deliberate choice. The goal is to allow you to solidify your understanding of these concepts and the various ways in which they can be tested so that they will leap out at you when you are taking the test for real.

In addition, I have done my best to select passages that reflect the content and themes of the redesigned SAT. The new exam focuses much more heavily than the old on science and social science topics, with a notable focus on the recent onslaught of new technologies (the Internet, the rise of social media, "green" energy) and new business models (flexible and individual vs. company-based and traditional), as well as the consequences of those developments. While some passages will address their downsides, you can assume that the overwhelming emphasis will be on their positive aspects.

That said, this book can of course provide no more than an introduction to the sorts of topics you are likely to encounter on the SAT. While the College Board has been very vociferous (to invoke an "irrelevant" term) about proclaiming that the redesigned test will reflect exactly what students are studying in school, the reality is of course a good deal more complex. Common Core or no Common Core, American high schools have nothing even remotely resembling a common curriculum, with the result that a student at High School A might emerge from AP US History having read dozens of primary source documents from the eighteenth and nineteenth centuries, while a student at High School B the next town over might emerge from what is nominally the same class having read only a few such documents. No short-term SAT prep program can easily compensate for knowledge gaps built up over a dozen years or more. So while some of the passages you encounter on the test may indeed seem familiar and accessible, others may seem very foreign. A list of suggested reading resources is provided on the following page, and I strongly encourage you to spend 15 minutes or so a day exploring them.

Unfortunately, there is no such thing as a "pure" reading test. To some extent, your ability to understand what you read is always bound up with your existing knowledge. Research shows that when students whose overall reading skills are weak are asked to read about subjects they are highly familiar with, their comprehension is *better* than that of students with stronger general reading skills.[1] The more familiar you are with a subject, the less time and energy you will need to spend trying to understand a passage about it, and the faster you'll move through the test. You'll also be familiar with any vocabulary associated with the topic, which means you won't have to worry as much about keeping track of new terminology.

Moreover, you will probably find it much easier to identify correct and incorrect answer choices. While it is true that answers that are true in the real world will not necessarily be right, it is also true that correct answers will not be false in the real world. If you see an answer that you know is factually true based on your pre-existing knowledge of a topic, you can potentially save yourself a lot of time by checking that answer first.

Finally, encountering a passage about a subject you already know something about can be very calming on a high-pressure test like the SAT because you will no longer be dealing with a frightening unknown. Instead of trying to assimilate a mass of completely new information in the space of a few minutes, you can instead place what you are reading in the context of your existing knowledge.

Provided that you have solid comprehension skills and contextual knowledge, success in Reading is also largely a question of approach, or method. Because the test demands a certain degree of flexibility – no single strategy can be guaranteed to work 100% of the time – I have also tried to make this book a toolbox of sorts. My goal is to provide you with a variety of approaches and strategies that you can choose from and apply as necessary, depending on the question at hand. Whenever possible, I have provided multiple explanations for questions, showing how you might arrive at the answer by working in different ways and from different sets of starting assumptions. The ability to adapt is what will ultimately make you unshakeable – even at eight o'clock on a Saturday morning.

~Erica Meltzer

---

[1] Daniel Willingham, "How Knowledge Helps," *American Educator*, Spring 2006. https://www.aft.org/periodical/american-educator/spring-2006/how-knowledge-helps

How to Use this Book

As you may have noticed, this book contains a fair amount of material, and you might be wondering just how to go about using it. If that's the case, here's a quick guide:

Step 1: Take a full-length diagnostic test from the <u>Official SAT Study Guide</u>.

I recommend choosing from among Tests 5-8 in *The Official SAT® Study Guide, 2018 Edition*, because those exams were actually administered. (Tests 1-4 were written as samples before the first administration of the redesigned SAT.)

Step 2: Identify what you need to focus on.

Mark your right and wrong answers. Then, use the index of questions by test on p. 340 to determine the types of questions you answered incorrectly.

Step 3: Work through the relevant chapters.

If your errors are primarily concentrated in a few specific categories, you can start by focusing on the corresponding chapters. If you want to practice with authentic questions in those categories, you can also use the list of questions by category on p. 335 to locate relevant items in the *Official Guide*.

If your errors are more random or encompass a wider range of question types, or if you have a significant amount of time before the exam, you will probably be best served by working through all of the chapters in order.

You may want to take practice tests periodically to gauge your progress, or you may prefer to work through the entire book before taking another complete test.

Step 4: Build a "bridge" to the test.

When you do the end-of-chapter exercises in this book, the strategy information will usually still be fresh, and you will also know in advance the concept that every question is testing. When you take full-length practice tests, however, all of the question types will be mixed together in unpredictable combinations. You will also need to recall a wide variety of strategies and, without any prompting, recognize when to apply them. That's a big strain on your working memory, and you may initially notice a gap between your performance on the individual exercises and your performance on practice tests.

If you find yourself in that situation, you must essentially create a "bridge" between the book and the test. Select a Reading Test from the *Official Guide*, and forget about time. Go through every question and label its category, e.g., function, tone, inference. Make sure to mark the supporting evidence pairs – for reasons discussed in Chapter 4, you must be prepared for these questions. (Note: it's probably slightly easier to mark the questions before you read the passage so that you're primed to look for specific information as you read, but you can also start by marking the questions if you prefer.)

Now, before you answer each question, stop and review the specific strategy it requires. For example, you can remind yourself to read before and after line references, play positive/negative, or focus on the conclusion. If you find it helpful, you can even write yourself notes in the margins of your test. The goal is to practice identifying which strategies are most appropriate in a given situation, and to become accustomed to applying them when no one (me) is holding up a sign telling you where to start. (As I used to tell my students when they stared at me pleadingly, "Don't give me that look – I'm not going to be sitting there when you take the test. You tell *me* what you need to do to answer the question.")

To reiterate, it does not matter how much time you spend on this step. If you find it helpful, you can sit with this book next to your test and flip to the corresponding chapter for each question, reviewing the relevant sections as you work. At this point, it is much more important to work carefully than to work quickly, particularly if you have a tendency to lose points for careless errors. If necessary, you can even do a second test this way – however long it takes for the process to become automatic. When things seem to be coming together, take a timed test and see what holds.

Step #5: Review your mistakes.

I cannot stress how important this step is. Do not move on from a test until you have reviewed every mistake and understood where things went awry, as well as what you need to do to avoid similar errors in the future. Note that working this way also reduces the chance that you will use up all of the *Official Guide* tests early on.

Step #6: Repeat as necessary until you are consistently scoring in your desired range.

To be sure, there is no way to control for every possibility. Reading is inherently less predictable than Math, and there may indeed be times when a correct answer genuinely hinges on something you do not fully understand and could not have foreseen. In many other instances, however, getting the right answer is likely to be a matter of slowing down, making sure you know exactly what you're looking for, and going step by step. If you control for everything you can reasonably control for, you can usually get pretty far.

So yes, working this way is not always pleasant. Yes, it is more involved than simply crashing through practice test after practice test, hoping that somehow things will just work themselves out. But ultimately, it tends to be pretty effective. And when your scores come back, you're a lot more likely to be happy – and possibly even done with the SAT for good.

Suggested Reading

The New York Times (particularly the Science section)

The Economist, www.economist.com

Scientific American, www.scientificamerican.com

National Geographic, www.nationalgeographic.com

Newsweek, www.newsweek.com

Time Magazine, www.time.com

Smithsonian Magazine, www.smithsonianmag.com

The Atlantic Monthly, www.theatlantic.com/magazine

Wired, www.wired.com

For links to many additional resources, Arts & Letters Daily: www.aldaily.com

Also see: Gerald Graff, Cathy Birkenstein, and Russell Durst: *They Say/I Say: The Moves that Matter in Academic Writing,* 2nd Edition. New York: W.W. Norton and Company, 2009.

Fiction, suggested authors: Julia Alvarez, Jane Austen, Charlotte/Anne Brontë, Michael Chabon, Charles Dickens, Jhumpa Lahiri, Toni Morrison, George Orwell, Edith Wharton

Key Topics and Controversies, Natural and Social Science:

Renewable Energy (Wind and Solar Power)

Big Data: Good or Bad?

Reliability of Scientific Findings

The Sharing Economy

Will New Technologies Create or Destroy Jobs?

Genetically Modified Foods

String Theory

The Higgs Boson/the Large Hadron Collider

Disappearing Coral Reefs

Declining Bee Populations

Science and Social Science Authors: Daniel Kahneman, Malcolm Gladwell, Adam Grant, Daniel Levitin, Brian Greene, Stephen Hawking, Lisa Randall

Note: If you are seeking additional resources for graphic-based questions, you may want to work with Science sections from released ACTs. Although somewhat more challenging than SAT data analysis questions overall, they nevertheless require many of the same skills tested on the SAT. In addition to the tests in *The Official ACT Prep Guide,* several more authentic exams are available online.

Key Historical Movements and Figures:

The Revolutionary Period: Benjamin Franklin, Thomas Jefferson, John Adams, Alexander Hamilton

The Abolitionist Movement: Frederick Douglass, William Lloyd Garrison, Henry Ward Beecher, Harriet Beecher Stowe

Transcendentalism: Ralph Waldo Emerson, Henry David Thoreau

The Civil War: Abraham Lincoln, Stephen Douglass, Daniel Webster

The Women's Rights Movement: Susan B. Anthony, Elizabeth Cady Stanton, Lucretia Mott, Angelina and Sarah Grimké (also active in the Abolitionist Movement)

The Progressive Movement and Muckrakers: Upton Sinclair, Jane Addams, Ida Tarbell, Jacob Riis, WEB DuBois, Booker T. Washington

World Wars I and II: Woodrow Wilson (WWI), Franklin D. Roosevelt (WWII)

The Civil Rights Movement: Martin Luther King, Jr., Malcolm X, Fannie Lou Hamer, John F. Kennedy

Historical Documents, Sources:
http://www.ushistory.org/documents/

Introduction to SAT Reading

The redesigned SAT contains one 65-minute reading section that will always be the first section of the exam. It consists of four long single passages and one set of shorter paired passages, accompanied by a total of 52 questions (9-11 questions per passage or paired passage set) covering a wide range of topics.

The breakdown of passages is typically as follows:

- Fiction (1 passage, always first)

- Social science (1 passage)

- Natural science (2 passages)

- Historical Documents (Usually 1 set of paired passages)

Each passage or set of paired passages ranges in length from 500-750 words. Science and social science passages may also include 1-2 related graphs or charts. In some instances, the graphic(s) will clearly support an idea or phenomenon discussed in the passage. In other cases, the relationship will be less clear-cut.

The majority of the Reading questions are text-based, but each test typically contains around five graphic-based questions. Some of these questions are based on the graphic alone, while others ask you to integrate information from the passage and the graphic.

What Does SAT Reading Test?

The SAT reading test is a literal comprehension test, but it is an *argument* comprehension test as well. **It tests not only the ability to find bits of factual information in a passage, but also the capacity to understand how arguments are constructed and the ways in which specific textual elements (e.g., words, phrases, punctuation marks) work together to convey ideas.** The focus is on moving beyond what a text says to understanding how the text says it. In other words, comprehension is necessary but not sufficient.

The skill that the SAT requires is therefore something called **"rhetorical reading."** Rhetoric is the art of persuasion, and reading rhetorically simply means reading to understand an author's argument as well as the rhetorical role or **function** that various pieces of information play in creating that argument.

Reading this way is an acquirable skill, not an innate aptitude. It just takes practice.

While the primary focus of the redesigned SAT is on having students use so-called "evidence" to justify their responses – that is, requiring them to identify which section of a passage provides the information necessary to answer a given question – the exam does still test a number of other skills. The most important of these include drawing relationships between specific wordings and general/abstract ideas; distinguishing between main ideas and supporting evidence; understanding how specific textual elements such as diction (word choice), syntax, and style convey meaning and tone; keeping track of multiple viewpoints and understanding/inferring relationships between arguments and perspectives; and recognizing that it is possible for an author to agree with some aspects of an idea while rejecting others.

That might sound like an awful lot to manage, but don't worry; we're going to break it down.

These skills are tested in various ways across a variety of different question types:

- **Vocabulary-in-context** questions test your ability to use context clues to identify alternate meanings of common words.

- **Big-picture** questions test your understanding of the passage as a whole. They may ask you to summarize, identify main points, or determine the purpose of a passage.

- **Literal comprehension** questions ask you to identify what the passage directly states.

- **Inference** questions ask you to identify what the passage suggests or indirectly states.

- Both literal comprehension and inference questions will frequently be followed by **supporting evidence** questions, which require you to identify the specific lines in the passage that provide the answer to the previous question.

- **Extended reasoning** questions ask you to apply ideas discussed in the passage to new situations.

- **Function** or **purpose** questions ask you to identify the **rhetorical role** (e.g., support, refute, criticize) that various pieces of information play within a passage.

- **Rhetorical strategy** and **passage organization** questions test your understanding of passage structure and point of view.

- **Tone** and **attitude** questions test your understanding of how specific words or phrases help establish an author's perspective.

- **Paired passage** questions test your ability to compare texts with different, often conflicting, points of view, and to infer how each author would likely react to the other's point of view.

- **Data analysis** questions test your ability to interpret information presented in graph or table form, and to determine whether and how it supports various pieces of information in a passage.

Each chapter in this book is devoted to a specific type of question and is followed by exercises that allow you to practice that particular skill.

Managing the Reading Test as a Whole

The 65 minutes you are given to complete the 52 questions on the Reading Test are both a blessing and a curse. On one hand, you have more than an hour to read and answer questions for just five passages. On the other hand, reading passage after passage for more than an hour without interruption can start to feel like a slog. Even though you have a good amount of time, you still want to use it as efficiently and effectively as possible. Regardless of whether you're aiming for a 600 or an 800, your goal is simple: to correctly answer as many questions as possible within the allotted time. You are under no obligation to read the passages and/or answer the questions in the order in which they appear. In fact, you can divvy up those 65 minutes and 52 questions in any way you wish.

If you're a strong reader across the board, or if you simply have a very strong aversion to jumping around, you may find it easiest to read the passages and answer the questions in the order they're presented (skipping and possibly coming back to anything that seems too confusing). If you have very pronounced strengths and weaknesses or consistently have difficulty managing time on standardized tests, however, keep reading.

One way to ensure that you use your time most effectively is to **do the passages in order of most to least interesting** or **easiest to hardest**. Working this way ensures that you'll pick up easy points – points that you might not earn as easily if you encountered those questions after struggling through a passage you hated. You won't get tired or frustrated early on, then spend the rest of the section trying to make up for the time you lost struggling through a difficult passage at the start. You might even finish the first couple of passages quickly, giving you additional time to spend on more challenging material.

It's true that this strategy requires you to spend about 10-15 seconds upfront skimming the beginning of each passage and seeing which ones seem least painful, but that can often be a worthwhile tradeoff.

If you don't want to spend time trying to figure out which passages to start and end with, you can come in with a plan of attack based on your strengths and weaknesses. **If there's a particular type of passage that you consistently find easy, do it first.** That way, you automatically start with your strongest passage without having to waste time. Likewise, **if there's a type of passage you consistently have trouble with, leave it for last.** When you're struggling through those last few questions, you can at least console yourself with the knowledge that you're almost done.

Let's look at some possible sequences for working through passages.

If you excel in science and graph reading but dislike more humanities-based passages, for example, you might prefer the following order:

1. Science
2. Science
3. Social Science
4. Paired Passages (usually Historical Documents)
5. Fiction

On the flip side, if you are strong in the humanities but find science passages and graphs challenging, you might choose to read the passages in this order:

1. Fiction

2. Paired Passages (usually Historical Documents)

3. Social Science

4. Science

5. Science

There are, of course, many possible combinations, and you will most likely have to spend some time experimenting to determine which order feels most comfortable to you.

Just as you should read the passages in an order that works to your advantage, you should also answer questions in an order that allows you to leverage your skills to maximum effect. **To reiterate:** although you should never leave questions blank, you do not need to devote significant time to every question. In fact, you may be better off planning from the start to guess on a certain number of questions. If you are not aiming for a perfect score, answering all of the questions may actually make it *more* difficult for you to achieve your goal.

Think of it this way: most time problems come about not because people spend too much time answering every question but rather because they spend too much time answering a small number of very challenging questions. Then, they feel pressured and rush. As a result, they miss easier questions they otherwise could have gotten right. If they were to eliminate those five or so time-consuming questions completely, they would have far more time to answer the remaining questions, and thus be considerably more likely to get them right. The goal then becomes to ensure that all of the easier questions are answered first.

One factor that can make implementing this strategy challenging, however, is that there is no way to predict where easy vs. hard questions will fall. A very difficult question may follow a very straightforward one. You must therefore practice recognizing which questions you are normally able to answer easily and which ones give you trouble so that you already have a clear sense of where to focus your attention when you walk into the test.

While "easy" and "hard" are somewhat subjective, **there are some types of questions – most notably combined passage/graphic and Passage 1/Passage 2 relationship – that tend to be both challenging and time consuming.** If you are not aiming for a tippy-top score, you may want to skip them and focus on more straightforward questions instead.

Unless you are absolutely set on trying to score 1600, keep in mind that you probably have more wiggle room than you think. You do not need to answer every question correctly to obtain a score that will make you a serious candidate at any number of selective colleges.

Furthermore, a high score on the somewhat more straightforward Writing and Language Test can offset a so-so showing on the Reading Test. If you answer 41/44 questions correctly on the Writing and Language Test, for example, you can incorrectly answer about 6 questions on the Reading Test and still obtain an overall Verbal score of 750. And you can miss about *12* questions and still end up around 700.

The Answer Isn't Always *In* the Passage

One of the great truisms of SAT prep is that "the answer is always in the passage," but in reality this statement is only half true: **the information necessary to answer the questions is always provided in the passage, but not necessarily the answer itself.** It's a subtle but important distinction.

The SAT tests the ability to draw relationships between specific wordings and general ideas, so while the correct answer will always be *supported by* specific wording in the passage (which you are sometimes responsible for identifying), the whole point is that you must make the connection. That, in essence, is the test.

As a rule, therefore, the correct answers to most questions will usually not be stated word-for-word in the text. In fact, **if an answer repeats phrasing from the passage word-for-word, you should approach that option very cautiously.** The correct answer will usually refer to an **idea** that has been discussed in the passage and that has simply been **rephrased**. Your job is to determine that idea and identify the answer that rewords it using **synonyms**. Same idea, different words.

Understanding Answer Choices

Although one or more incorrect answers may sound convincing, there is always a specific reason – supported by the passage – that wrong answers are wrong. Often, they describe a situation that *could* be true but that the passage does not explicitly indicate *is* true. They may also employ relatively abstract language that many test-takers find confusing or difficult to comprehend. That said, incorrect answers typically fall into the following categories:

- Off-topic

- Too broad (e.g., the passage discusses *one* scientist while the answer refers to *scientists*)

- Too extreme (e.g., they include words such as *never*, *always*, or *completely*)

- Half-right, half-wrong (e.g., right words, false statement)

- Could be true but not enough information

- True for the passage as a whole, but not for the specific lines in question

- Factually true but not stated in the passage

On most questions, many test-takers find it relatively easy to eliminate a couple of answers but routinely remain stuck between two plausible-sounding options. Typically, the incorrect answer will fall into either the "could be true but not enough information" or the "half-right, half-wrong" category. In such cases, you must be willing to read very carefully in order to determine which answer the passage truly supports.

Understanding Line References

A line reference only tells you where a particular word or phrase is located – it does **not** tell you that the answer will necessarily be in that line or set of lines. So, for example, a question that reads, "The author uses digital and video offerings (line 35) as examples of..." is telling you the phrase *digital and video offerings* is in line 35. The answer could be in line 25, but it's just as likely to be in line 23 or in line 27, or even in line 35.

In addition, **the most important places in the passage, the ones that you need to pay the most attention to, are not necessarily the ones indicated by the questions.** Focusing excessively on a particular set of lines can make you lose sight of the bigger picture.

At the other extreme, only a small section of a line reference may sometimes be relevant. In fact, **the longer the line reference, the lower the chance that all of it will be important.** There's no sense spending time puzzling over eight or ten lines that you've carefully marked off if all you need to focus on is the first sentence or a set of dashes.

Strategies for Reading Passages

One of the major challenges of SAT reading is that questions are arranged in two ways: first, in rough chronological order of the passage (although you should note that answers to supporting evidence questions may be found *after* the line reference in the following question); and second, in non-chronological order for graph and chart questions.

In addition, some big picture (main idea) questions that appear either at the beginning or in the middle of a question set may not provide line references. As a result, some jumping around is unavoidable. If you can understand the gist of the author's argument, though, you will likely be able to identify some correct answers – even those to detail-based questions – without having to hunt through the passage. You will also find it easier to answer supporting evidence questions because in many cases, you will already have a good idea of the information the correct lines must include.

There are essentially two major ways to read passages. Regardless of which strategy you choose, you should read the passage as quickly as you can while still absorbing the content. Do your best to focus on the parts you understand, and try to avoid spending time puzzling over confusing details (which may or may not ultimately be relevant) and repeatedly rereading sections you do not immediately grasp.

The **first option** is to read the entire passage with the goal of understanding the big picture, then answering the questions in one block after you are done reading. This strategy tends to work best for people who have excellent focus and comprehension, and who are strong at identifying and summarizing arguments.

Read the passage slowly until you figure out the **point – usually at the end of the introduction** – and underline it. Then, focus on the first and last sentence of each paragraph carefully, skimming through the body of each paragraph and circling major transitions, "interesting" punctuation (e.g., colons, semicolons, dashes), and strong language. Finally, read the conclusion carefully, paying particular attention to and **underlining the last sentence or two because the main point will often be restated at the end of the conclusion.**

Working this way will allow you to create a mental map of the passage: the introduction and conclusion will most likely give you the main point, and each topic sentence will generally provide you with the point of the paragraph, allowing you to understand how it fits into the argument as a whole. Then, when you're asked to think about the details, you'll already understand the ideas that they support and have a sense of their purpose.

If you consistently spend too much time reading passages, you can try another version of this approach. Read the introduction slowly until you figure out the point; then, read the first and last sentence of each body paragraph carefully, skipping the information in between. Finally, read the conclusion slowly and underline the last sentence or couple of sentences. That way, you'll get the major points without losing time.

If your comprehension is outstanding, you can simply move on to the next section of the passage (the place where the idea clearly changes) once you've grasped the point of any particular section of the passage you happen to be reading – regardless of how long that section may be. You can worry about the details when you go back.

The **second option** is to read the passage in sections, say a paragraph or two at a time, answering the more straightforward line-reference questions as you read. When you turn to a new passage, start by skimming through the questions. Notice which ones have specific lines references, then go to the passage and mark off those lines in the passage. (Note: bracketing lines is generally faster and more efficient than underlining.) Then, as you read the passage, you can answer those questions as you come to them, **keeping in mind that the answers to some questions will not be located directly in the lines referenced, and that you may need to read before or after in order to locate the necessary information.**

This is often a good approach for people who difficulty recognizing main ideas, or who have difficulty maintaining focus when they are confronted with too much information. Breaking passages down into smaller chunks can make them seem more manageable.

This can also be a helpful strategy for people who are concerned about spending too much reading and not having enough left over to comfortably answer all the questions. Knowing that you've answered even three or four of the questions by the time you get done with the passage can allow you to work more calmly through the remaining questions.

An important note about supporting evidence questions: If you choose to answer some of the questions as you work through the passage, you need to be careful with supporting evidence questions. They come in two types: ones in which the first question of the pair contains a line reference, and ones in which the first question of the pair does not contain a line reference.

When the first question of the pair does contain a line reference, you can probably answer both questions as you read the passage. Pay close attention to the lines you use to determine your answer to the first question; assuming you understand the passage, those lines will likely be cited in the correct answer to the second question, allowing you to answer both questions simultaneously. (Don't worry, we're going to look at some examples of how to do this a little later on, in Chapter 4.) For this reason, **you should make sure to mark both questions in this type of pair as you look through the questions.** If you overlook the supporting evidence question initially, you'll end up having to backtrack after you're done with the passage and re-locate information you've already found.

On the other hand: **when the first question of a supporting evidence pair does not contain a line reference, you should not normally try to answer both questions as you read, and you should not mark the line references in the second question.** If you attempt to pay attention to all those various places and connect them to the first question as you read, you will almost certainly become confused.

Answering the questions as you read the passage can work well if you are a strong reader, but it does have some potential drawbacks. Reading passages in bits can cause you to get lost in the details and lose sight of the argument. So while this method can be effective if you tend to have trouble understanding the big picture, it cannot fully compensate for that weakness. Strategies allow you to leverage the skills you do have, but they cannot substitute for the ones you don't. To be sure, it is possible to get many – or even all – of the questions right working this way. It's just that the process will be much more tedious and open to error.

You might be wondering why we're not going to seriously address the possibility of skipping the passage entirely and just jumping to the questions. If time is a serious problem for you, you might think that this option represents your best shot at finishing on time. After all, those passages are long! While I don't dispute that this strategy can be effective for the right person, I do not normally recommend it. The main problem is that it does not take into account what the SAT is actually testing, namely relationships between ideas – particularly between main ideas and supporting details. In order to determine relationships between ideas, you need context for them, which is very difficult to determine if you're reading isolated bits and pieces. You therefore run the serious risk of misunderstanding the entire passage.

Moreover, unless you are able to split your attention and glean main ideas at the same time you are hunting for answers to detail-based questions (an extremely sophisticated skill), you will have no way of using the big picture to "shortcut" detail-based questions. You are likely to spend considerable time hunting through the passage, rereading aimlessly as you try to figure out where to look. What is intended to be a time-saving strategy thus ends up requiring more time than would have been involved in simply reading the passage.

If you have a serious time problem, you are much better off simply reading a few key places – introduction, topic sentences, conclusion – so that you at least have a gist of what the passage is talking about when you look at the questions.

Skimming Effectively Means Knowing What to Focus On

If you ask those rare lucky people who can race through the Reading test in half an hour how they finish so quickly, they'll probably shrug and tell you that they're just reading the passages and answering the questions. What most highly skilled readers often do not recognize, though, is that their "naturally" fast reading is actually the result of a combination of specific skills. But because expert readers generally perform those skills subconsciously, they can't explain how they do what they do or teach someone else to do it. The good news is that those skills can be learned. You probably won't become a champion speed-reader overnight, but you can learn to read more quickly and effectively.

Brute speed, no doubt, is a useful thing to have, but it is not the whole story. In reality, **the key is to read efficiently.** If you understand main ideas, you can often use a general "bird's eye" view to answer some questions without even looking back at the passage, leaving you plenty of time to worry about questions that require more time.

One of the most common mistakes students make is to read as if every sentence were equally important. As a result, when they encounter something they don't understand, they assume it must be crucial and read it again. And if they still don't understand it, they read again. And then again, and again. Before they know it, they've spent almost a minute rereading a single sentence. When they finally move on, they're not only confused and frustrated (which makes it harder to concentrate), but they've also lost sight of what the passage is about.

What's more, when most people skim through a passage, they simply try to read *everything* faster, with the result that they don't understand the passage as more than a string of vaguely related sentences. When they look at the questions, they have only a fuzzy idea of what they just read. They haven't focused on the key places indicating main ideas and concepts, so they're often perplexed when they encounter big-picture questions that ask about the passage as a whole. And because they've just been worrying about each individual piece of information, they have difficulty thinking about where information would logically be located when confronted with questions without line references.

Effective skimming involves reading <u>selectively</u>. Some sections are read very slowly, while others are glanced over or even skipped. Reading this way requires a lot more focus, but it is also much faster and, when done properly, improves comprehension. But in order to know what to read slowly and what to skip, you must be able to recognize what is important.

As a general rule, authors are pretty clear about the parts of their writing that they want you to pay attention to. If they're really generous, they'll even come right out and tell you what the point is. Even if they're not quite that blatant, they usually make a decent effort to tell you what's important – if not through words, then through punctuation.

So first, **you should circle any words or phrases that indicate the author is making a** point, e.g., *the point, goal,* or *intention,* along with the word *important* and any of its synonyms (*significant, crucial, key*) and any italicized words. If you see one of these terms in the middle of a paragraph as you're racing through a passage, slow down, circle it, and read that section carefully. **If the author says it's important, it's important.** There's no trick.

Second, you need to learn to recognize when an argument changes or when new and important information is introduced: transitions such as *however, therefore, in fact;* "unusual" punctuation such as dashes, italics, and colons; strong language such as *only* and *never;* and "explanation" words such as *reason* are "clues" that tell you to pay attention. If one of these elements appears in or near a line reference, **the answer will typically be located close by.**

If you are able to do so while still absorbing the meaning of the passage, you should mark these key elements as you read so you'll know what to pay attention to when you go back. To be clear, you don't need to circle every last *and* and *but.* Rather, the goal is to use the author's "clues" to identify the major points of the argument.

If, on the other hand, you feel that looking for transitions will interfere with your comprehension, then you should not worry about them when you read through the passage for the first time. It is far more important that you understand what you are reading. When you go back to answer the questions, however, you do need to take transitions into account because correct answers will frequently be located right around them.

In the passage on the following page, key elements are in bold. **The chart on p. 205 provides a full list of key words, phrases, and punctuation, as well as their functions.**

The following passage is adapted from "Makerspaces, Hackerspaces, and Community Scale Production in Detroit and Beyond," © 2013 by Sean Ansanelli.

During the mid-1980s, spaces began to emerge across Europe where computer hackers could convene for mutual support and camaraderie. In the past few years, the idea of fostering such shared, physical spaces
5 has been rapidly adapted by the diverse and growing community of "makers," who seek to apply the idea of "hacking" to physical objects, processes, or anything else that can be deciphered and improved upon.

A hackerspace is described by hackerspaces.org as
10 a "community-operated physical space where people with common interests, often in computers, technology, science, digital art or electronic art, can meet, socialize, and/or collaborate." Such spaces can vary in size, available technology, and membership structure (some
15 being completely open), but generally share community-oriented characteristics. **Indeed, while** the term "hacker" can sometimes have negative connotations, modern hackerspaces thrive off of community, openness, and assimilating diverse **viewpoints – these**
20 often being the only guiding principles in otherwise informal organizational structures.

In recent years, the city of Detroit has emerged as a hotbed for hackerspaces and other DIY ("Do-It-Yourself") experiments. Several hackerspaces
25 can already be found throughout the city and several more are currently in formation. **Of course**, Detroit's attractiveness for such projects can be partially **attributed** to cheap real estate, which allows aspiring hackers to acquire ample space for experimentation.
30 Some observers have **also** described this kind of making and tinkering as embedded in the DNA of Detroit's residents, who are able to harness substantial intergenerational knowledge and attract like-minded individuals.
35 Hackerspaces (or "makerspaces") can be found in more commercial forms, **but** the vast majority of spaces are self-organized and not-for-profit. **For example**, the OmniCorp hackerspace operates off member fees to cover rent and new equipment, from laser cutters to
40 welding tools. OmniCorp also hosts an "open hack night" every Thursday in which the space is open to the general public. Potential members are required to attend at least one open hack night prior to a consensus vote by the existing members for **admittance; no**
45 prospective members have yet been denied.

A visit to one of OmniCorp's open hack nights reveals the **vast variety** of activity and energy existing in the space. In the main common room alone, activities range from experimenting with sound installations and
50 learning to program Arduino boards to building speculative "oloid" shapes – all just for the sake of it. With a general atmosphere of mutual support, participants in the space are continually encouraged to help others.
55 One of the **most** active community-focused initiatives in the city is the Mt. Elliot Makerspace. Jeff Sturges, former MIT Media Lab Fellow and Co-Founder of OmniCorp, started the Mt. Elliot project with the aim of replicating MIT's Fab Lab model on a smaller, cheaper
60 scale in Detroit. "Fab Labs" are production facilities that consist of a small collection of flexible computer-controlled tools that cover several different scales and various materials, with the **aim to make "almost anything"** (including other machines). The Mt. Elliot
65 Makerspace now offers youth-based skill development programs in eight **areas: Transportation,** Electronics, Digital Tools, Wearables, Design and Fabrication, Food, Music, and Arts. The range of activities is meant to provide not only something for everyone, but a well-
70 rounded base knowledge of making to all participants.

While the center receives some foundational support, the space also derives significant support from the local community. Makerspaces throughout the city connect the space's youth-based programming directly to
75 school curriculums.

The growing interest in and development of hacker/makerspaces has been **explained**, in part, as a result of the growing maker movement. Through the combination of cultural norms and communication
80 channels from open source production as well as increasingly available technologies for physical production, amateur maker communities have developed in virtual and physical spaces.

Publications such as *Wired* are noticing the
85 **transformative potential** of this emerging movement and have sought to devote **significant** attention to its development. Chief editor Chris Anderson recently published a book entitled *Makers*, in which he proclaims that the movement will become the next Industrial
90 Revolution. Anderson argues such developments will allow for a new wave of business opportunities by providing mass-customization rather than mass-production.

The **transformative potential** of these trends goes
95 beyond new business opportunities or competitive advantages for economic growth. **Rather, these trends demonstrate the potential to actually transform economic development models entirely.**

Using Key Words: Managing Questions Without Line References

Just as you must be able to recognize key words and phrases within passages, so must you be able to recognize key words and phrases within questions.

This is a crucial skill for questions that are not accompanied by line references. Although many of these questions will be accompanied by supporting evidence questions that direct you to look at specific places in the passage, you will also encounter detail-based questions in which line references are **not** provided in either the question or the answer choices. In such cases, you must be able to locate the necessary information efficiently by using the wording of the question for guidance.

For example, a passage about sustainable energy could contain a question like the following:

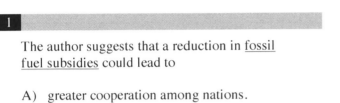

1

The author suggests that a reduction in <u>fossil fuel subsidies</u> could lead to

A) greater cooperation among nations.
B) decreased economic stability.
C) higher transportation costs.
D) more sustainable infrastructure.

This question is relatively straightforward, but it gives no indication of where in the passage the answer might be located. If you happen to remember the answer, you're in luck. If you don't remember it, however, you must know how to find the information in a way that does not involve staring at the passage and aimlessly (and increasingly nervously) skimming random parts of it.

The first step is to identify and **underline** the key word(s) or phrase in the question. That word or phrase indicates the specific focus of the question, i.e., the topic, and almost always follows *indicates/conveys* or *suggests/implies*. Here, the key phrase is *fossil fuel subsidies*.

Then, you should go back to the passage to skim for that word or phrase, **pulling your index finger down the page as you scan.** This may seem like a minor detail, but in fact it is extremely important: your finger establishes a physical connection between your eye and the page, keeping you focused and reducing the chance that you will overlook key information.

As you skim, you should **pay particular attention to the first (topic) and last sentence** of each paragraph because they are most likely to include key points. Even if they don't provide the information you need to answer a question, they will often provide important clues about where the necessary information *is* located.

Each time the key word or phrase appears, stop and read a sentence or two above and below for context. If that section of the passage does not answer the question, move on and check the next place the key word/phrase shows up. **Your goal is to avoid falling into a loop of reading and rereading a section, searching for information that isn't there.**

How to Work Through Questions with Line References

While your approach will vary depending on the specific question, in general I recommend the following strategy:

1) Read the question <u>slowly</u>.

Put your finger on each word of the question as you read it. Otherwise, you may miss key information, and every letter of every word counts.

When you're done, take a second or two to make sure you know exactly what the question is asking. If it is is phrased in an even slightly convoluted manner, rephrase it in your own words in a more straightforward way until you're clear on what you're looking for. If necessary, jot down the rephrased version.

This is not a minor step. If, for example, a question asks you the purpose of a sentence, you must reread it with the goal of understanding what role the sentence plays within the argument. If you reread it with a different goal, such as understanding what the sentence is literally saying, you can't work toward answering the question that's actually being asked.

2) Go back to the passage and reread the lines given in the question. If the question seems to call for it, read from a sentence or two above to a sentence or two below.

Purpose/function questions often require more context and, as a result, you should be prepared to read both before and after the line reference. The answers to most other question types are usually found within the lines referenced, but there are exceptions. **If the line reference begins or ends halfway through a sentence, however, make sure you back up or keep reading so that you cover the entire sentence in which it appears.** If a line reference begins close to the beginning of a paragraph, you should automatically read from the first sentence of the paragraph because it will usually give you the point of the paragraph.

There is unfortunately no surefire way to tell from the wording of a question whether the information necessary to answer that question is included in the line reference. If you read the lines referenced and have an inordinate amount of difficulty identifying the correct answer, or you get down to two answers and are unable to identify which one is correct, that's often a sign that the answer is actually located somewhere else. Go back to the passage, and read the surrounding sentences.

For long line references: a long line reference is, paradoxically, a signal that you don't need to read all of the lines. Usually the information you need to answer the question will be in either the first sentence or two, the last sentence or two, or in a section with key punctuation (dashes, italics, colon). Start by focusing on those places and forgetting the rest; they'll almost certainly give you enough to go on.

3) Answer the question in your own words, and write that answer down.

This step is not necessary on very straightforward questions, but it can be a big help on questions that require multiple steps of logic, particularly Passage 1/Passage 2 relationship questions. Writing things down keeps you focused, reminds you what you're looking for, and prevents you from getting distracted by plausible-sounding or confusing answer choices.

The goal is not to write a dissertation or come up with the exact answer in the test. You can be very general and should spend no more than a few seconds on this step; a couple of words scribbled down in semi-legible handwriting will suffice. The goal is to identify the general information or idea that the correct answer must include. Again, make sure you're answering the question that's actually being asked, not just summarizing the passage.

If you do this step, you should spend **no more than a few seconds** on it. If you can't come up with anything, skip to step #4.

4) Read the answers carefully, A) through D), in order.

If there's an option that contains the same essential idea you put down, choose it because it's almost certainly right. If it makes you feel better, though, you can read through the rest of the answers in order to be certain. Just make sure you don't get distracted by options that sound vaguely plausible and start second-guessing yourself.

If you can't identify the correct answer...

5) Cross out the answers that are absolutely wrong.

Try not to spend more than a couple of seconds on each answer choice. If an option clearly makes no sense in context of the question or passage, get rid of it.

When you cross out an answer, put a line through the entire thing; do not cross out the letter alone. As far as you're concerned, it no longer exists.

Leave any answer that's even a remote possibility, even if you're not quite sure how it relates to the passage or question. **Remember: your understanding of an answer has no effect on whether that answer is right or wrong. You should never cross out an answer because you're confused or haven't really considered what it's saying.**

If you get down to two answers, go back to the passage again and start checking them out. Whatever you do, do not just sit and stare at them. The information you need to answer the question is in the passage, not in your head.

When you're stuck between two answers, there are several ways to decide between them.

First, go back to the passage and see if there are any major transitions or strong language you missed the first time around; you may have been focusing on the wrong part of the line reference, or you may not have read far enough before/after the line reference. If that is the case, the correct answer may become clear once you focus on the necessary information.

The correct answer will usually contain a synonym for a key word in the passage, so if a remaining choice includes this feature, you should pay very close attention to it.

You can also pick one specific word or phrase in an answer to check out when you go back to the passage. For example, if the lines in question focus on a single scientist and the answer choice mentions *scientists*, then the answer is probably beyond the scope of what can be inferred from the passage. Likewise, if an answer focuses on a specific person, thing, or idea not mentioned in the lines referenced, there's also a reasonable chance that it's off-topic.

Remember: the more information an answer choice contains, the greater the chance that some of that information will be wrong.

Finally, you can reiterate the main point of the passage or paragraph, and think about which answer is most consistent with it. That answer will most likely be correct.

6) If you're still stuck, see whether there's a choice that looks like a right answer.

If you still can't figure out the answer, you need to switch from reading the passage to "reading" the test. Working this way will allow you to make an educated guess, even if you're not totally sure what's going on. Does one of the answers you're left with use extremely strong or limiting language (*no one, always, ever*)? There's a pretty good chance it's wrong. Does one of them refer to the topic in the plural, whereas the passage has a narrow focus? It's probably too broad.

In addition, ask yourself whether all of the answers you're left with actually make sense in context of both the test and the real world. For example, an answer stating that no scientific progress has been made in recent years is almost certain to be wrong. Yes, you should be very careful about relying on your outside knowledge of a subject, but it's okay to use common sense too.

7) If you're still stuck, skip it or guess.

You can always come back to it later if you have time. And if you're still stuck later on, you need to pick your favorite letter and fill it in. You should never leave anything blank.

Starting on the next page, we're going to look at some examples.

The sharing economy is a little like online
shopping, which started in America 15 years ago. At
first, people were worried about security. But having
made a successful purchase from, say, Amazon, they
5 felt safe buying elsewhere. Similarly, using Airbnb or
a car-hire service for the first time encourages people to
try other offerings. Next, consider eBay. Having started
out as a peer-to-peer marketplace, it is now dominated
by professional "power sellers" (many of whom started
10 out as ordinary eBay users). The same may happen with
the sharing economy, which also provides new
opportunities for enterprise. Some people have bought
cars solely to rent them out, for example. Incumbents
are getting involved too. Avis, a car-hire firm, has a share
15 in a sharing rival. So do GM and Daimler, two carmakers.
In the future, companies may develop hybrid models,
listing excess capacity (whether vehicles, equipment or
office space) on peer-to-peer rental sites. In the past,
new ways of doing things online have not displaced the
20 old ways entirely. But they have often changed them.
Just as internet shopping forced Walmart and Tesco to
adapt, so online sharing will shake up transport, tourism,
equipment-hire and more.
The main worry is regulatory uncertainty. Will
25 room-4-renters be subject to hotel taxes, for example?
In Amsterdam officials are using Airbnb listings to
track down unlicensed hotels. In some American cities,
peer-to-peer taxi services have been banned after
lobbying by traditional taxi firms. The danger is that
30 although some rules need to be updated to protect
consumers from harm, incumbents will try to destroy
competition. People who rent out rooms should pay tax,
of course, but they should not be regulated like a Ritz-
Carlton hotel. The lighter rules that typically govern
35 bed-and-breakfasts are more than adequate. The sharing
economy is the latest example of the internet's value to
consumers. This emerging model is now big and
disruptive enough for regulators and companies to have
woken up to it. That is a sign of its immense potential.
40 It is time to start caring about sharing.

1

The author suggests that the sharing economy
(line 11) could eventually

A) grow larger than the traditional economy.
B) be controlled by a particular group of sellers.
C) rely mostly on hybrid models.
D) depend exclusively on former eBay users.

The first thing to remember about a question like this is that the line reference is telling us
only that the phrase *sharing economy* – the key phrase – appears in line 11. The information we
need to answer the question is not necessarily in line 11. Let's start by reading the entire
sentence in which the phrase appears:

> **The same may happen with the sharing economy, which also provides new
> opportunities for enterprise.**

Unfortunately, we don't really get much information from this sentence. It tells us that *the
same may happen*, but we don't actually know what "the same" is.

In order to figure out what *the same* refers to, we need to back up some more and read the previous couple of sentences as well:

> **Next, consider eBay. Having started out as a peer-to-peer marketplace, it is now dominated by professional "power sellers" (many of whom started out as ordinary eBay users).**

Now we're getting someplace. The passage is telling us that the sharing economy as a whole could, like eBay, eventually become dominated (=controlled) by professional "power sellers" (=a particular group of sellers). So the answer is B).

Notice that the correct answer takes the wording of the passage and **rephrases it in more general terms**. The specific people mentioned in the passage (*power sellers*) become the much more general "particular group of sellers."

Notice also that if we had started reading at line 10 or 11 and kept going from there, we would never have found the answer in the passage. We might have eventually gotten to it by process of elimination, but the process would have been much less straightforward.

If the method described above seems like a reasonable – not to mention simpler – way to work, great. This book will provide you with numerous ways to help you figure things out on your own and reduce your reliance on the answer choices.

You might, however, be thinking something like, "Well *you* make it seem easy enough, but *I* would probably get confused if I tried to figure that out on my own." Or perhaps you're thinking something more along the lines of, "Ew… that seems like way too much *work*. Can't I just look at the answer choices?" So for you, here goes. One by one, we're going to consider the answer choices – very, very carefully.

A) grow larger than the traditional economy.

No, this answer is completely off-topic. It might sound reasonable, but there is no information about how the sharing economy compares to the traditional economy, either now or in the future. In fact, the phrase *traditional economy* never even appears. So A) is out.

B) be controlled by a particular group of sellers.

The "vague" answer. As a matter of fact, **the phrasing suggests that the answer is correct** – even in the absence of any other information. Again, if you started reading in line 10 or 11 and never backed up, you probably wouldn't find the information indicating that it was right. As discussed above, this answer rephrases the idea that a professional group of sellers (i.e., "a particular group") could eventually dominate the entire sharing economy, just as they now dominate eBay.

C) rely mostly on hybrid models.

Half-right, half-wrong. This answer takes a random word from the passage and uses it to create an answer that could sound either vaguely plausible or confusing (especially if you don't know what a hybrid is), but does not answer the question. The passage does indicate that some companies may develop hybrid models to list their inventory; it does not, however, suggest in any way that the sharing economy will come to rely *mostly* on hybrid models.

A hybrid, by the way, is something that is created by combining parts from two sources. For example, a hybrid car is a car that contains both a gasoline engine and an electric engine, either of which can be used to power it.

D) depend exclusively on former eBay users.

First off, the extreme word *exclusively* is a big warning sign that this answer is probably wrong, so you should be suspicious of it from the start. It's true that the author does *mention* eBay users right before the key phrase, but there's no direct relationship between the two things. The author is simply pointing out that many of the "power sellers" who eventually came to dominate eBay started out as regular users. We cannot in any way infer that the sharing economy as a whole will depend *only* on former eBay users ("power sellers" or otherwise). That is an interpretation that goes far beyond what the passage supports.

Besides, if you think about it logically, this answer doesn't really make sense. Even if you don't know anything about the sharing economy, the passage indicates that it involves a variety of companies in different fields (Amazon, Airbnb, GM). The idea that the sharing economy could depend only on former eBay users is completely at odds with that fact.

If you do know some basic things about the sharing economy, you can think of it this way: correct answers must always be supported by the passage, but they must also correspond to reality – many of the passages on the SAT are connected to current trends, debates, and controversies, and as a result, correct answers must reflect real-world facts.

To be clear: factually correct answers are not necessarily right, but factually incorrect answers are essentially guaranteed to be wrong.

General Tips for Reading Prep

And now, before we get started for real, some tidbits of test-prep wisdom:

If you're not in the habit of reading things written for educated adults, start. Now.

If you're unsure where to begin, check out Arts & Letters Daily (http://www.aldaily.com), which has links to dozens of publications written at SAT level and above. You cannot, however, read passively and expect your score to magically rise. Rather, you must **actively** and **consistently** practice the skills introduced in this book. Circle/underline the point, major transitions, and words that reveal tone; pay close attention to the introduction and conclusion for the topic and the author's opinion (see how quickly you can get the gist); notice when words are used in non-literal ways; and practice summarizing arguments briefly. The more you develop these skills independently, the easier it will become to apply them to the test.

Outside knowledge does matter.

One of the most frequently repeated truisms about the SAT is that you have to forget all of your outside knowledge and just worry about what's in the passage. That's mostly true... but not completely. First, just to be clear, an answer can be both factually correct and wrong if that particular fact is not discussed in the passage. That's what most people mean when they say to forget about outside knowledge. The reality, however, is that reading does not exist in a vacuum. It is always dependent upon ideas and debates that exist outside of the SAT. The more you know about the world, the more easily you'll be able to understand what you're reading. And if you see an answer you know is factually correct, it can't hurt to check it first.

Read exactly what's on the page, in order, from left to right.

This piece of advice may seem overwhelmingly obvious, but I cannot stress how important it is. When people feel pressured, they tend to start glomming onto random bits of information without fully considering the context. Although it is not necessary to read every word of a passage to get the gist of it, skipping around randomly is unlikely to help you either! Pay attention to what the author is telling you to pay attention to: when you see italics or words/phrases like *important* or *the point is*, you need to slow down and go word by word. **Put your finger on the page, and bracket or underline as you read; the physical connection between your eye and your hand will force you to focus in a way you wouldn't if you were just looking at the page. You're also far less likely to overlook key information.**

Be as literal as you possibly can.

While your English teacher might praise you for your imaginative interpretations, the College Board will not. Before you can understand the function of a piece of information or make a reasonable inference about it, you have to understand exactly what it's saying – otherwise, you'll have a faulty basis for your reasoning. When you sum things up, stick as closely as possible to the language of the passage. People often get themselves into trouble because they think that there's a particular way they're supposed to interpret passages that they just don't "get," when in reality they're not supposed to interpret anything. **In short, worry about what the author is actually saying, not what she or he might be trying to say.**

Answering SAT Reading questions is a process.

Working through Reading questions is sometimes a process of trial-and-error. You make an assumption based on how texts are usually put together and how the test is typically constructed, and much of the time it'll turn out to be right (it is a *standardized* test, after all). If you work from the understanding that main ideas are often stated in the conclusion, for example, you may sometimes be best served by looking at a set of lines at the end of the passage first. In other instances, it may make more sense to focus on a key word and start halfway through the passage.

When your initial assumption doesn't pan out, then your job is to reexamine your original assumption and work through the answers one-by-one, trying to figure out what you overlooked the first time around. If you're a strong reader willing to approach the exam with the attitude that you can reason your way systematically through each question, you'll eventually hit on the answer. Yes, this does take some time, but if you can get through most of the questions quickly, having to slow down occasionally won't make much of an impact. No, working this way is not easy to do when you're under pressure, but it does get results.

Draw a line through the entire answer, not just the letter.

Your goal is to deal with the smallest amount of information possible at any given time, and looking at answers you've already eliminated is an unnecessary distraction. If you get down to one option and it doesn't seem to work, you can always erase the lines, but only if you…

Always work in pencil.

It's a lot harder to reconsider answer choices when you've crossed them out in ink.

Flexibility is key.

To obtain a very high score, you need to be able to adapt your approach to the question at hand. People who insist on approaching every question the same way tend to fall short of their goals, while those who start out scoring in the stratosphere tend to adjust automatically (even if they think they're just reading the passage and answering the question every time). Sometimes you'll be able to answer a question based on your general understanding of the passage and won't need to reread anything. Sometimes you'll be able to go back to the passage, answer the question on your own, and then easily identify the correct answer when you look at the choices. Other times the answer will be far less straightforward and you'll have to go back and forth between the passage and the questions multiple times, eliminating answers as you go. Yet other times it might make more sense for you to begin by looking at the answer choices and eliminating those that are clearly wrong, then go back to the passage and seeing which remaining choice best fits. It's up to you to stay flexible and find the strategy that will get you to the answer most easily. For that reason, I have done my best, whenever possible, to offer multiple ways of approaching a given question.

The path to a perfect score is not linear.

Whereas math and writing scores can often be improved those last 100 or so points if you spend time internalizing just a few more key rules, the same cannot be said for reading. If you want a 750+ score, you *cannot skip steps* and start guessing or skimming through answers – you'll keep making just enough mistakes to hurt yourself. The SAT is a standardized test: if you keep approaching it the same way, you'll keep getting the same score. It's designed to work that way. If you want your score to change radically, you have to approach the test in a radically different way. Raising your score is also not just about how much practice you do: it does not matter how well you know the test if you do not fully understand what you are reading. Getting into the right mindset can take five minutes or five months, but until you've absorbed it, your score will probably stay more or less the same.

Don't rush.

I took the SAT twice in high school: the first time, I raced through the reading section, answering questions mostly on instinct, not thinking anything through, and finishing every section early. I was an incredibly strong reader and even recognized one of the passages from a book I'd read for pleasure, but I got a 710.

The second time I understood what I was up against: I broke down every single question, worked through it step-by-step, wrote out my reasoning process, and worked every question out as meticulously as if it were a math problem. It was one of the most exhausting things I'd ever done, and when I stumbled out of the exam room, I had absolutely no idea how I'd scored. I'd literally been focusing so hard I hadn't left myself the mental space to worry about how I was doing. Working that way was *hard*, but it got me an 800.

Summoning that level of focus is not easy. It's also terrifying because you don't have the "well, I maybe didn't try as hard as I could have" excuse. If you bomb, you have nowhere to put the blame. If you have excellent comprehension and can stand to do it, though, working that precisely is almost foolproof. It might take longer than you're used to in the beginning, but the more you go through the process, the more accurate you'll become and the less time you'll take. Skipping steps might save you time, but your score will suffer as a result.

Understand what the College Board wants.

Every SAT passage has two authors: the author of the individual passage, and the test-writers at the College Board. The highest scorers are often able to use a combination of close reading skills and knowledge about the test itself (themes, biases, types of answers likely to be correct), and they are able to employ both of those skills as needed in order to quickly identify the answer choices most likely to be correct and then check them out for real.

When I was in high school and uncertain about an answer, I trained myself to always ask, "What would the test writers consider correct?" It didn't matter that I couldn't put the patterns into words then. The point was that I was able to convince myself that what *I* personally thought was irrelevant. To score well, you have to think of the test in terms of what the College Board wants – not what you want. You have to abandon your ego completely and approach the test with the mindset that *the College Board is always right and what you think doesn't matter*. Then, once you've reached your goal, you can put the test out of your mind and never have to worry about it again (or at least until your own children take it).

The ability to do this is really important: occasionally the logic on certain questions will not be airtight. In those instances, you need to be able to consider the choices on their own and ask which one looks most like the sort of answer that is usually correct. It's not fair that the test writers can get away with being sloppy, but if it happens, you need to be prepared.

Be willing to consider that the test might break its own "rules."

For example, you can usually assume that answers containing extreme language such as *always, never, awe, incomprehensible, impossible*, etc. are incorrect and cross them off as soon as you see them. But you can't *always* assume that a particular pattern holds without carefully considering what the passage is actually saying. Correct answers will very occasionally contain this type of phrasing. If you're trying to score 800 or close to it, you need to stay open to the possibility that an answer containing one of those words could on occasion be correct.

General patterns are just that: general. That means you will sometimes encounter exceptions.

Fit the answer to the passage, not the passage to the answer.

If an answer could only *sort of kind of maybe possibly be true if you read the passage in a very specific way*, it's not right. Don't try to justify anything that isn't directly supported by specific wording in the passage.

Every word in the answer choice counts.

One incorrect word in an answer choice is enough to make the entire answer wrong. It doesn't matter how well the rest of the answer works; it doesn't matter how much you like the answer or think it should be right. If the author of the passage is clearly happy about a new scientific finding and an answer says *express skepticism about a recent finding*, that answer is wrong. The fact that the phrase *a recent finding* might have appeared in the passage is irrelevant. On the other hand…

Just because information is in a passage doesn't mean it's important.

One of the things the SAT tests is the ability to recognize important information and ignore irrelevant details. Reading SAT passages is not about absorbing every last detail but rather about understanding what you need to focus on and what you can let go. And that means…

Keep moving.

In my experience, students often encounter time problems because they either 1) get hung up on a section of the passage that they find confusing – a part that sometimes turns out to be irrelevant – and waste a lot of time rereading it; or 2) get stuck between two answer choices and sit there staring at them. To avoid falling into one of these traps, push yourself to keep moving. Go back to the passage and check out a specific aspect of one of the answers, circle things, write down what you know, or cross things out that clearly don't make sense. Doing something is better than doing nothing. Furthermore…

If something confuses you, ignore it and focus on what you do understand.

You have a limited amount of time to get through each section, and that means you need to be constantly figuring things out. **Skip around.** If you don't know how to work through a problem, you need to leave it and work on something you *can* answer. It doesn't matter if you have to leave a couple of the most time-consuming questions blank if doing so allows you to answer everything else correctly. Sometimes, there's no way to make certain questions (e.g., passage/graphic, support/undermine) go quickly. If they take too much time and you're not fixated on getting a perfect score, you can probably afford to skip a couple of them.

SAT Reading is not a guessing game.

This is just as true as it was before the quarter-point wrong-answer penalty was abolished. Yes, you might be able to jack up your score a bit by guessing strategically on a relatively small number of questions, but there is still no substitute for carefully thinking your way through each question. The chance of your reaching your score goal simply by being a lucky guesser on more than a few questions is very small indeed.

If you consistently get down to two choices and always pick the wrong one, that's a sign that you either don't really know how to answer the questions or that you're not reading carefully enough. I've had a lot of students tell me they always got down to two and then guessed wrong when in fact they were missing the entire point of the passage. That's not a test-taking problem; that's a comprehension problem.

If you are just not reading carefully enough, slow down, put your finger on the page, make sure you're getting every single word, and make a concerted effort to think things through before you pick an answer.

On the other hand, if you really aren't sure how to choose between answers, you need to figure out what particular skills you're missing and work on them. If you're misunderstanding the passage and/or answer choices because you don't know vocabulary, you need to keep a running list of unfamiliar words. Anything you see once is something you're likely to encounter again.

If you're getting thrown by complicated syntax, you need to spend more time reading SAT-level material. If you can't figure out what the author thinks, you need to focus on key phrases and places (e.g., last sentence of the first paragraph, end of the conclusion).

You also need to spend some time getting familiar with the kinds of answers that are usually correct and incorrect. If you know, for example, that options with extreme language such as *always, never,* or *most important* tend to be wrong, you'll be a lot less tempted to pick them – even if you think you *might* be able to argue for an interpretation that makes them work. **Remember: just because an answer is there doesn't mean it deserves serious consideration.** If you look for reasons to keep answers, you'll never get down to one.

But on the other hand…

Don't assume you'll always recognize the right answer when you see it.

Incorrect answers are written to sound plausible. You might get away with jumping to the answers on easy and medium questions, but you'll almost certainly fall down on at least some of the hard ones unless you do some legwork upfront. The test is designed that way. The fact that there are answer choices already there does not excuse you from having to think.

Moreover, **confusing does not equal wrong.** If there's any chance an answer could work, you have to leave it until you see something better. Sometimes the right answer just won't say what you're expecting it to say; in those cases, you need to keep an open enough mind to consider that you've been thinking in the wrong direction and be willing to go back and revise your original assumption.

There are no trick questions.

Reading questions may require you to apply very careful reasoning or make fine distinctions between ideas – but they're also set up so that you can figure them out. If you think your way carefully through a question and put the answer in your own words, then see an option choice that truly says the same thing, it's almost certainly correct.

Go back to the passage and read.

Even if you think you're certain of what the passage says in the lines cited, you probably need to go back and read it anyway (unless you can reason out the answer based on the main point). Stress makes memory unreliable, so don't assume you can trust yours. You could be absolutely certain that you remember the author mentioning a particular idea in line 15 when in fact it doesn't show up until five or ten lines later and refers to something that *someone else* thinks. Don't play games or be cocky. Just take the extra few seconds and check.

Don't ever read just half a sentence.

Context counts. If you read only the first or last half of a sentence, you might miss the fact that the author thinks exactly the *opposite* of what that half of the sentence says. You might also overlook the exact information you need to answer a question.

If the answer isn't in the lines you're given, it must be somewhere else.

If you read the line(s) referenced in the question and can't figure out the answer, chances are the information you need is located either before or after. Don't just assume you're missing something and read the same set of lines over and over again or, worse, guess. Again: be willing to revise your original assumption and start over. Yes, this will take time (although probably not as much as you think), but you're a lot more likely to get the question right.

When in doubt, reread the end of the conclusion.

The point of the passage is more likely to be located at the end of the conclusion, usually the last sentence or two, than it is just about anywhere else. If you get lost and start to panic, stop and reread it to focus yourself. It won't work all the time, but it will work often enough.

Writing things down is not a sign of weakness.

Most people don't have a huge problem writing down their work for math problems; the same, alas, cannot be said for reading. Unfortunately, one of the biggest differences between people scoring pretty well vs. exceptionally well is often their degree of willingness to write down each step of a problem. The very highest scorers tend to view writing each step down as a crucial part of the process necessary to get the right answer, whereas lower scorers often view writing as a drag on their time or a sign of weakness that they should be above. It's not either of those things. You can jot things down quickly, and the only person who has to read your handwriting is you. Writing also keeps you focused and takes pressure off of your working memory. If you're really certain what you're looking for, you probably don't need to spend the time. If you have any hesitation, though, it's worth your while. When you're under a lot of pressure, having even one less thing to worry about is a big deal. Besides, you probably wouldn't try to figure the hardest math problems out in your head, so why on earth would you work that way for reading?

The order in which you read the passage and do the questions doesn't really matter.

What truly matters is that you have the necessary close reading and reasoning skills to figure out or recognize the correct answers. **Strategy is not a substitute for skill**. Rather, it's a way of leveraging the skills you do have to work efficiently and with the least possible amount of second-guessing.

Don't fight the test.

It doesn't matter how much you want the answer to be C) instead of B). It never will be, and unless you want to file a complaint with the College Board, you're stuck. Instead of arguing about why your answer should have been right, try to understand why it was wrong. Chances are you misunderstood something or extrapolated a bit too far along the way. If you're serious about improving, your job is to adapt yourself to the mindset of the test because it certainly won't adapt itself to yours. Who knows, you might even learn something.

Vocabulary in Context

We're going to start by looking at vocabulary-in-context questions, which are among the most common types of questions to appear: there are usually eight or so per test (about 15% of the total), sometimes placed back-to-back. Compared to other types of Reading questions, vocabulary-in-context questions tend to be more straightforward and less dependent on the passage as a whole. That said, they can also be surprisingly subtle and tricky at times.

The prefix CON- means "with," so *context* literally means "with the text." Vocabulary-in-context questions thus require you to use clues in the text itself to determine the meanings of specific words and phrases. These questions come in two varieties: the vast majority test second definitions of common words (e.g., *poor, nature, clear*), but occasionally you may also be asked to identify the meanings of short phrases (e.g., *in its wake*).

The principle on which these questions are based can be summarized as follows:

Context determines meaning.

On the SAT, words can be used to mean whatever an author happens to want them to mean, regardless of their dictionary definitions. As long as you are able to 1) use information from the surrounding sentence(s) to determine the intended meaning of a word; and 2) match one of the choices to that meaning, you can find your way to the answer.

Sometimes, the word tested will be used in a way that's fairly similar to its most common meaning – but then again, sometimes it won't. With only a few exceptions, however, the words you are asked about will not be used in their most literal definition (e.g., *spill* to mean "knock over"). If they did, there would be no reason to test them in the first place! So as a general rule, if you see the usual definition of a word among the answer choices, you should assume that it is incorrect and only reconsider it if no other option fits.

It also means that when you see a question that says, *In line 14, "fine" most nearly means…*, you can think of the question as saying, *In line 14, _____ most nearly means*. The fact that *fine* rather than some other word happens to be used in the passage is irrelevant.

In some cases, a familiarity with common second meanings may be helpful. For example, *want* is often used to mean "lack," especially in old-fashioned writing. In other cases, though, words will be used in ways unlikely to appear on any vocabulary list. A common alternate meaning may even appear as an *incorrect* answer. So while you may find the list of second meanings on p. 51 helpful, you should be aware that it does not cover the full range of potential definitions.

Strategies:

1) Plug in your own word and find the answer choice that matches.

If you are able to use this strategy effectively, it is often the simplest and fastest way to answer vocabulary questions. The only potential difficulty is that sometimes, even if you provide a perfectly adequate synonym for the word in question, the correct answer will be a word that you find odd, or that you do not recognize as having the same meaning as the term you supplied. If you are a strong reader with a solid vocabulary, however, these issues should not normally pose a serious problem.

2) Plug each answer choice into the sentence.

Frequently, you'll be able to hear that a particular choice does not sound correct or have the right meaning within the context of a sentence. The only potential downside is that sometimes, as is true for #1, the correct word is not a word you would think to use. As a result, you might talk yourself out of choosing that answer because you think it sounds odd.

3) Play positive/negative, then plug in.

If you can determine from context whether the word is positive or negative, you can often eliminate at least one answer. You can then plug the remaining answers back into the sentence and see which one makes the most sense in context. In rare instances, you may even be able to use this technique to eliminate three answers, leaving you only one possibility.

Additional Points:

While some people feel most comfortable using a single approach for all vocabulary-in-context questions, it is also true that certain questions lend themselves better to certain approaches. On some straightforward questions you may find it easiest to plug in your own word, while on other, less clear-cut questions, a combination of positive/negative and process of elimination might provide the most effective strategy.

Second, you should pay particular attention to clues indicating that a word in question has a similar or opposite meaning to another word. For example, in the phrase *quiet and reserved*, the word *and* tells you that *reserved* must mean something similar to *quiet*; and in the phrase *delicate but sound*, the word *but* tells you that *sound* must mean roughly the opposite of *delicate*. On the other hand, if you cannot determine the meaning of a word from the sentence in which it appears, you must establish a slightly larger context. Read from the sentence above to the sentence below – one of those sentences will very likely include the information you need to answer the question.

Finally, don't get distracted by unfamiliar words in the answer choices. **It doesn't matter whether you know the definition of the wrong answers as long as you can identify the right answer.** The College Board is fond of using distractors whose definitions students are unlikely to know, while making correct answers relatively simple. As a result, you should never choose an answer like *egregious* just because it looks sophisticated. If anything, it's more likely to be wrong. **As a rule, always work from what you do know to what you don't know.** If you're not sure about a word, ignore it and deal with everything you know for sure first.

Starting on the next page, we're going to look at some examples.

Example #1

When Saburo joined the track and field team at Bukkyo High School, the sport was enjoying a popularity it had not known before the war. At the time, few schools could afford baseball bats or gymnastic
5 equipment. And there was something in the simplicity of the sport – the straight path to the goal, the dramatic finish line – that stirred the community to yells and often tears. On Sundays entire families came outdoors to cheer, Thermoses of cold wheat tea slung across their
10 chests. They sat on woven mats and munched on rice balls, roasted potatoes, hard-boiled eggs, and pickled shoots of fuki gathered up in the hills.

1

As used in line 7, "stirred" most nearly means

A) forced.

B) transformed.

C) inspired.

D) disturbed.

This is an excellent example of a question that lends itself well to playing positive/negative. The passage is clearly positive – track and field is enjoying a new *popularity,* and families *came outside to cheer* – so you can assume that the correct answer will be positive as well. Don't get thrown off by the reference to *yells and tears.*

Forced and *disturbed* are both negative, so A) and D) can be eliminated immediately. *Transformed* is positive, but it does not make any sense when it is plugged back into the sentence. B) can thus be eliminated as well. That leaves *inspired*, which logically refers to something that would cause great emotion.

Example #2

Every time a car drives through a major intersection, it becomes a data point. Magnetic coils of wire lie just beneath the pavement, registering each passing car. This starts a cascade of information: Computers tally the
5 number and speed of cars, shoot the data through underground cables to a command center and finally translate it into the colors red, yellow and green. On the seventh floor of Boston City Hall, the three colors splash like paint across a wall-sized map.

1

As used in line 3, "registering" most nearly means

A) preparing.

B) recording.

C) inscribing.

D) transmitting.

The passage is talking about *magnetic coils of wire* that notify computers of the cars' presence, beginning *a cascade of information.* Logically, the coils of wire must be *recording* each car.

Otherwise, you can play process of elimination. *Preparing* doesn't fit, so A) can be crossed out. If you don't know what *inscribing* (engraving) means, ignore C) for the moment and deal with the words you do know first.

Now, be very careful with D): the passage implies that the coils of wire transmit information about the cars to computers, but it is illogical to say that coils of wire *transmit each passing car.*

If you're stuck between B) and C), don't fall into the trap of assuming that the harder-looking word must be right. Instead, plug B) into the sentence: *Magnetic coils of wire lie just beneath the pavement, recording each passing car.* Yes, that makes sense. So the answer is B).

Example #3

Until the past few years, physicists agreed that the entire universe is generated from a few mathematical truths and principles of symmetry, perhaps throwing in a handful of parameters like the mass of an electron.

5 It seemed that we were closing in on a vision of our universe in which everything could be calculated, predicted, and understood. However, two theories, eternal inflation and string theory, now suggest that the same fundamental principles from which the laws of

10 nature derive may lead to many different self-consistent universes, with many different properties.

---

1 ▨▨▨▨▨▨▨▨▨▨▨▨▨▨▨▨▨▨▨▨▨▨

As used in line 5, "closing in on" most nearly means

A) experimenting.
B) approaching.
C) hypothesizing.
D) shutting down.

The beginning of the passage discusses the fact that physicists believed they were beginning to understand how to describe the universe mathematically. Given that context, *closing in on* must mean something like "getting close to." That is the definition of *approaching*, so B) is correct.

Playing process of elimination, A) can be eliminated because it does not make sense to say *It seemed that we were experimenting a vision of our universe...* Scientists could conduct experiments to gain a greater understanding of the universe, but it is not grammatically or logically possible to "experiment" a vision.

Be careful with C). It is true that a synonym for this word, *predicted*, does appear in the passage, but that meaning does not make sense in this context. The two sentences make it clear that physicists believed they were on the verge of possessing a thorough understanding of how the universe works. They were not <u>predicting</u> *a vision of [the] universe in which everything could be calculated, etc.* – that vision was already firmly in place.

To eliminate D), you can play positive/negative. The fact that scientists agreed that a major problem in physics was about to be solved tells you that all of the information before the word *however* in line 7 has a positive focus. As a result, you can assume that the correct answer will be positive as well. *Shutting down* is negative and thus can be eliminated.

That again leaves us with B) as the only possibility.

Now let's look at an example of a historical document. It's from an 1872 speech called "Self-Made Men," written and delivered by Frederick Douglass. The language here is somewhat more challenging, so we're going to spend more time breaking things down.

The various conditions of men and the different uses they make of their powers and opportunities in life, are full of puzzling contrasts and contradictions. Here, as elsewhere, it is easy to dogmatize, but it is not so easy
5 to define, explain and demonstrate. The natural laws for the government, well-being and progress of mankind, seem to be equal and are equal; but the subjects of these laws everywhere abound in inequalities, discords and contrasts. We cannot have fruit without flowers, but we
10 often have flowers without fruit. The promise of youth often breaks down in manhood, and real excellence often comes from unexpected quarters.
    The scene presented from this view is as a thousand arrows shot from the same point and aimed at the same
15 object. United in aim, they are divided in flight. Some fly too high, others too low. Some go to the right, others to the left. Some fly too far and others, not far enough, and only a few hit the mark. Such is life. United in the quiver, they are divided in the air.
20 Matched when dormant, they are unmatched in action.
    When we attempt to account for greatness we never get nearer to the truth than did the greatest of poets and philosophers when he classified the conditions of greatness: "Some are born great, some achieve
25 greatness and some have greatness thrust upon them..."
    Men of very ordinary faculties have, nevertheless, made a very respectable way in the world and have sometimes presented even brilliant examples of success. On the other hand, what is called genius is often found
30 by the wayside, a miserable wreck; the more deplorable and shocking because of the height from which it has fallen and the loss and ruin involved in the fall. There is, perhaps, a compensation in disappointment and in the contradiction of means to ends and promise
35 to performance. These imply a constant effort on the part of nature to hold the balance between all her children and to bring success within the reach of the humblest as well as of the most exalted.

1

As used in line 12, "quarters" most nearly means

A) divisions.
B) relations.
C) origins.
D) particles.

2

As used in line 20, "matched" most nearly means

A) parallel.
B) equal.
C) calm.
D) indistinguishable.

Question #1:

Let's start by considering the context. Essentially, Douglass is discussing the fact that some people are more successful in life than others (*The natural laws...seem to be equal, but the subjects of these laws everywhere abound in inequality*). He also mentions that some individuals start out with great promise but then fail to live up to their potential (*The promise of youth often breaks down in manhood*). The word *and* joins that idea to the second half of the sentence, where *quarters* appears, implying that the second half of the sentence must express a similar idea.

Logically, the second half of the sentence must indicate that "real excellence" comes from people who weren't originally expected to be excellent. In other words, this type of excellence often comes from unexpected *origins*. The answer is therefore C).

Alternately, you can try plugging each answer into the sentence.

A) ...the promise of youth often breaks down in manhood, and real excellence often comes from unexpected <u>divisions</u>.

That doesn't really make sense – excellence would be very unlikely to result from *divisions*. Even if you find the antiquated language difficult to decipher, that fact hasn't changed since the nineteenth century. So A) can be eliminated.

B) ...the promise of youth often breaks down in manhood, and real excellence often comes from unexpected <u>relations</u>.

Be careful with this answer. Yes, perhaps excellence can be the result of *relations*, but that meaning doesn't fit this particular context. The focus is on individuals who start out with a lot and achieve little vs. individuals who start out with little and achieve a lot.

C) ...the promise of youth often breaks down in manhood, and real excellence often comes from unexpected <u>origins</u>.

Yes, this fits with Douglass's discussion of people who achieve disproportionately to where they start out. Even if you don't understand every word of the passage, keeping that idea in mind can give you just enough information to get to the answer.

D) ...the promise of youth often breaks down in manhood, and real excellence often comes from unexpected <u>particles</u>.

No, this makes no sense whatsoever. **So the answer is C).**

Question #2:

This is a good example of a question in which it is helpful to keep the bigger picture in mind. If you can do so and avoid getting caught up in the particulars of Douglass's discussion about arrows, this question is a good deal more straightforward than the previous one.

What is the major focus on the passage? Inequality. More specifically, how people can start out from roughly the same conditions and yet end up in wildly different places. Given that context, *equal* is the most logical option. *Parallel* is too literal (the passage has nothing to do with math), and *calm* is off-topic, but be careful with *indistinguishable*. This word is too extreme: Douglass isn't referring to people who can't be told apart from one another, but rather ones who start out from roughly the same place in life.

The answer is therefore B).

Now try some additional questions on your own. Your goal in this exercise is to work through each question as far as you can before looking at the answers, so try to resist the temptation to jump ahead!

The various conditions of men and the different uses they make of their powers and opportunities in life, are full of puzzling contrasts and contradictions. Here, as elsewhere, it is easy to dogmatize, but it is not so easy
5 to define, explain and demonstrate. The natural laws for the government, well-being and progress of mankind, seem to be equal and are equal; but the subjects of these laws everywhere abound in inequalities, discords and contrasts. We cannot have fruit without flowers, but we
10 often have flowers without fruit. The promise of youth often breaks down in manhood, and real excellence often comes from unexpected quarters.

The scene presented from this view is as a thousand arrows shot from the same point and aimed at the same
15 object. United in aim, they are divided in flight. Some fly too high, others too low. Some go to the right, others to the left. Some fly too far and others, not far enough, and only a few hit the mark. Such is life. United in the quiver, they are divided in the air.
20 Matched when dormant, they are unmatched in action.

When we attempt to account for greatness we never get nearer to the truth than did the greatest of poets and philosophers when he classified the conditions of greatness: "Some are born great, some achieve
25 greatness and some have greatness thrust upon them…"

Men of very ordinary faculties have, nevertheless, made a very respectable way in the world and have sometimes presented even brilliant examples of success. On the other hand, what is called genius is often found
30 by the wayside, a miserable wreck; the more deplorable and shocking because of the height from which it has fallen and the loss and ruin involved in the fall. There is, perhaps, a compensation in disappointment and in the contradiction of means to ends and promise
35 to performance. These imply a constant effort on the part of nature to hold the balance between all her children and to bring success within the reach of the humblest as well as of the most exalted.

3

As used in line 26, "ordinary" most nearly means

1) Underline context clues

2) Your word OR positive/negative:

_____

A) accepted.
B) customary.
C) unremarkable.
D) habitual.

4

As used in line 36, "hold" most nearly means

1) Underline context clues

2) Your word OR positive/negative:

_____

A) grasp.
B) maintain.
C) purchase.
D) dominate.

Answers and explanations are at the end of this chapter (p. 61).

Second Meanings and Answer Choices

Vocabulary can also be tested in very indirect ways, even in questions that appear to test something else entirely. Whenever possible, you should pay close attention to answer choices that contain second meanings. If you have difficulty recognizing when words are being used in alternate meanings, or if having to think about answer choices this way seems too complicated given all the other things you have to worry about, this is probably not a good strategy for you. But if you are an **exceptionally strong reader** and want to have some fun with the test, this is a "game" you might play.

To be clear: you should never choose an answer only because it contains a second meaning. You can, however, give such answers special consideration and/or check them first.

Yogi Berra, the former Major League baseball catcher and coach, once remarked that you can't hit and think at the same time. Of course, since he also reportedly said, "I really didn't say everything I said,"
5   it is not clear we should take his statements at face value. Nonetheless, a widespread view — in both academic journals and the popular press — is that thinking about what you are doing, as you are doing it, interferes with performance. The idea is that once you
10 have developed the ability to play an arpeggio on the piano, putt a golf ball or parallel park, attention to what you are doing leads to inaccuracies, blunders and sometimes even utter paralysis. As the great choreographer George Balanchine would say to his
15 dancers, "Don't think, dear; just do."
    Perhaps you have experienced this destructive force yourself. Start thinking about just how to carry a full glass of water without spilling, and you'll end up drenched. How, exactly, do you initiate a telephone
20 conversation? Begin wondering, and before long, the recipient of your call will notice the heavy breathing and hang up. Our actions, the French philosopher Maurice Merleau-Ponty tells us, exhibit a "magical" efficacy, but when we focus on them, they degenerate
25 into the absurd. A 13-time winner on the Professional Golfers Association Tour, Dave Hill, put it like this: "You can't be thinking about the mechanics of the sport while you are performing."

1

The passage indicates that focusing on one's actions as they are performed

A) is an important component of improving a skill.
B) is more common among experts than it is among other people.
C) can result in a compromised performance.
D) leads to a superior level of performance.

This is a fairly straightforward question, but we're only interested in one word in one answer. Choice C) contains the word *compromised*. Now, *compromised* usually means "came to an agreement," but here it's being used in its second meaning: "put at risk." That single word suggests that C) deserves close attention. And in fact, C) is the correct answer.

The view discussed in the first paragraph can be summarized as "paying attention to an action while you do it makes you worse at it." But if you interpret *compromise* as meaning "come to an agreement," C) won't make sense. And that's precisely why the answer is written that way.

Common Second Meanings

Affect (v.) – to take on, assume; affected (adj.) – behaving in an artificial/pretentious way

Afford – to grant (e.g., to **afford** an opportunity)

Allow – to enable, permit

Appreciate – to take into account, recognize the merits of, OR to increase in value

Appropriate (app-row-pree-ATE) – to take from, steal

Arrest – to stop (not just put handcuffs on a criminal)

Assume – to take on responsibility for, acquire (e.g., to **assume** a new position)

Basic – fundamental, essential

Bent – liking or preference for

Capacity – ability

Chance (v.) – to attempt

Check – to control (e.g., the vaccine **checked** the spread of the disease)

Clear – obvious, evident

Common – widespread

Compromise (v.) – to endanger or make vulnerable (e.g., to **compromise** one's beliefs)

Constitution – build (e.g., a football player has a solid **constitution**)

Conviction – strong belief. Noun form of *convinced*.

Currency – acceptance, approval (of an idea)

Demonstrate – to establish (e.g., to **demonstrate** the validity of a hypothesis)

Economy – thrift (e.g., a writer who has an **economical** style is one who uses few words)

Element – component, aspect

Elevated – lofty, high-minded, idealistic

Establish – to prove, validate (e.g., to **establish** the accuracy of a theory)

Execute – to carry out (e.g., to **execute** an order)

Exercise – to put into use, carry out a function

Exploit – to make use of, take advantage of (does not carry a negative connotation)

Facility – the ability to do something easily (e.g., a **facility** for learning languages)

Faculty – ability or aptitude

Fancy (v.) – to take a liking to

Fine – (1) narrow, thin (e.g., fine lines); (2) delicate, elegant; (3) keen, highly attuned

Foil – to put a stop to (e.g., to **foil** a robbery)

Fundamental – basic, essential

Grave/Gravity – serious(ness)

Kicks – amusement (e.g., just for **kicks**)

Nature – character, personality

Observe – to follow (e.g., to **observe** a law)

Plastic/plasticity – able to be changed or shaped (e.g., brain **plasticity**)

Poor – inferior, substandard, ill

Provoke – to elicit (e.g., to **provoke** a reaction)

Qualify – to provide more information or detail about

Range – scope

Raw – unrefined, unfiltered

Realize – to achieve (a goal)

Reconcile – to bring together opposing or contradictory ideas

Relate/Relay - to pass on information, give an account of (a story)

Reservations – doubts, misgivings

Reserve – to hold off on (e.g., to **reserve** judgment)

Scale – level (e.g., the experiment was repeated on a larger **scale**)

Scrap (v.) – to eliminate

Sheer – utter, complete

Sound – firm, stable, reliable, valid (e.g., a **sound** argument)

Spare, Severe – plain, unadorned

Static – unchanging

Store (n.) – reserve, stock (e.g., to keep a **store** of food for emergencies)

Strength – significance

Sustain (v.) – to withstand

Temper – to moderate, make less harsh

Train – to fixate on (e.g., to **train** one's eyes on something)

Treat – to alter

Uniform (adj.) – constant, unvarying

Unqualified – absolute

Upset (v.) – to interfere with an expected outcome

Urge – to argue in favor of, advocate

Want (n.) – lack

Weight – seriousness, importance

Yield – to reveal (e.g., an experiment **yields** results)

Additional Words to Know

Arbitrary – done or decided randomly, without clear reason

Bolster – to provide support for (an argument)

Comprehensive – thorough, complete

Condone – to disregard or pardon an illegal or objectionable act

Deter – to discourage

Disparity – difference, gap

Diverge – to separate from

Doctrine – principle or set of teachings

Empirical – derived from experiment or observation

Endeavor – attempt

Esteem (v.) – to hold in high regard

Feasible – doable

Grievance – a wrong, grounds for complaint

Hypothesis – educated guess

Idealistic – cherishing noble or high-minded principles

Indifferent – not caring, utterly detached

Inevitable – unavoidable

Innate – inborn

Innovation – new invention or discovery

Legislation – laws

Lofty – high-minded, exalted

Moral – concerned with the rules of right and wrong

Paradox – apparent contradiction

Partisan – strong adherent to a party or idea

Phenomenon – occurrence

Pragmatic, Prudent – practical

Scrutinize – to examine closely

Skeptical – questioning, doubtful

Stagnation – failure to progress or grow

Stipulate – to specify a requirement

Subordinate – lower-ranking

Substantiate – to prove; unsubstantiated – unproven

Synthesize – to bring together, integrate

Undermine – to weaken, attack indirectly

Underscore – to emphasize

Vocabulary in Context Exercises

1. Math poses difficulties. There's little room for eyewitness testimony, seasoned judgment, a skeptical eye or transcendental rhetoric.

As used in line 2, "seasoned" "most nearly means

A) determined.
B) tasteful.
C) experienced.
D) objective.

2. Around the middle of the 20th century, science dispensed with the fantasy that we could easily colonize the other planets in our solar system. Science fiction writers absorbed the new reality: soon, moon and
5 asteroid settings replaced Mars and Venus.

As used in line 2 "dispensed with" most nearly means

A) distributed.
B) disposed of.
C) identified with.
D) renewed.

3. Conservationists have historically been at odds with the people who inhabit wildernesses. During the last half of the 20th century, millions of indigenous people were ousted from their homelands to establish
5 nature sanctuaries free of humans. Most succumbed to malnutrition, disease and exploitation. Such outcomes—coupled with the realization that indigenous groups usually help to stabilize ecosystems by, for instance, keeping fire at bay—have convinced major conservation
10 groups to take local human concerns into account. The World Wildlife Fund (WWF) now describes indigenous peoples as "natural allies," and the Nature Conservancy pledges to seek their "free, informed and prior" consent to projects impacting their territories.

As used in line 5, "free" most nearly means

A) liberated.
B) uncompensated.
C) devoid.
D) whole.

As used in line 7, "coupled" most nearly means

A) cooperated.
B) associated.
C) related.
D) combined.

As used in line 10, "account" most nearly means

A) contact.
B) consideration.
C) favor.
D) prominence.

4. Perhaps the most classic definition of a species is a group of organisms that can breed with each other to produce fertile offspring, an idea originally set forth in 1942 by evolutionary biologist Ernst Mayr. While
5 elegant in its simplicity, this concept has since come under fire by biologists, who argue that it didn't apply to many organisms, such as single-celled ones that reproduce asexually, or those that have been shown to breed with other distinct organisms to create hybrids.
10 Alternatives quickly arose. Some biologists championed an ecological definition that assigned species according to the environmental niches they fill (this animal recycles soil nutrients, this predator keeps insects in check). Others asserted that a species was a
15 set of organisms with physical characteristics that were distinct from others (the peacock's fanned tail, the beaks of Darwin's finches).
    The discovery of DNA's double helix prompted the creation of yet another definition, one in which scientists
20 could look for minute genetic differences and draw even finer lines denoting species. Based on a 1980 book by biologists Niles Eldredge and Joel Cracraft, under the definition of a phylogenetic species, animal species now can differ by just 2 percent of their DNA to be
25 considered separate.

1

As used in line 11, "championed" most nearly means

A) advocated.

B) denied.

C) counseled.

D) disrupted.

2

As used in line 18, "prompted" most nearly means

A) rejected.

B) elaborated.

C) spurred.

D) defended.

3

As used in line 21, "finer" most nearly means

A) narrower.

B) keener.

C) milder

D) daintier.

5. Citrus greening, the plague that could wipe out Florida's $9 billion orange industry, begins with the touch of a jumpy brown bug on a sun-kissed leaf. From there, the bacterial disease incubates in the
5 tree's roots, then moves back up the trunk in full force, causing nutrient flows to seize up. Leaves turn yellow, and the oranges, deprived of sugars from the leaves, remain green, sour, and hard. Many fall before harvest, brown necrotic flesh ringing failed stems.
10 For the past decade, Florida's oranges have been literally starving. Since it first appeared in 2005, citrus greening, also known by its Chinese name, huanglongbing, has swept across Florida's groves like a flood. With no hills to block it, the Asian citrus
15 psyllid—the invasive aphid relative that carries the disease—has infected nearly every orchard in the state. By one estimate, 80 percent of Florida's citrus trees are infected and declining.
    The disease has spread beyond Florida to nearly
20 every orange-growing region in the United States. Despite many generations of breeding by humanity, no citrus plant resists greening; it afflicts lemons, grapefruits, and other citrus species as well. Once a tree is infected, it will die. Yet in a few select
25 Floridian orchards, there are now trees that, thanks to innovative technology, can fight the greening tide.

1

As it is used in line 9, "ringing" most nearly means

A) nourishing.

B) implanting.

C) growing.

D) surrounding.

2

As it is used in line 24, "select" most nearly means

A) exclusive.

B) preferred.

C) particular.

D) conventional.

6. Chimps do it, birds do it, even you and I do it. Once you see someone yawn, you are compelled to do the same. Now it seems that wolves can be added to the list of animals known to spread yawns like a
5 contagion.

Among humans, even thinking about yawning can trigger the reflex, leading some to suspect that catching a yawn is linked to our ability to empathize with other humans. For instance, contagious yawning activates the
10 same parts of the brain that govern empathy and social know-how. And some studies have shown that humans with more fine-tuned social skills are more likely to catch a yawn.

1

As used in line 10, "govern" most nearly means

A) elect.
B) control.
C) charge.
D) require.

7. The following passage is adapted from Daniel Webster's speech to the Senate in support of the Compromise of 1850, the congressional effort to resolve the issues propelling the United States toward a civil war.

I wish to speak to-day, not as a Massachusetts man, nor as a Northern man, but as an American, and a member of the Senate of the United States. It is fortunate that there is a Senate of the United States; a
5 body not yet moved from its propriety, not lost to a just sense of its own dignity and its own high responsibilities, and a body to which the country looks, with confidence, for wise, moderate, patriotic, and healing counsels. It is not to be denied that we live in the midst of strong
10 agitations, and are surrounded by very considerable dangers to our institutions and government. The imprisoned winds are let loose. The East, the North, and the stormy South combine to throw the whole sea into commotion, to toss its billows to the skies, and
15 disclose its profoundest depths. I do not affect to regard myself, Mr. President, as holding, or as fit to hold, the helm in this combat with the political elements; but I have a duty to perform, and I mean to perform it with fidelity, not without a sense of existing dangers, but not
20 without hope. I have a part to act, not for my own security or safety, for I am looking out for no fragment upon which to float away from the wreck, if wreck there must be, but for the good of the whole, and the preservation of all; and there is that which will keep me
25 to my duty during this struggle, whether the sun and the stars shall appear, or shall not appear for many days. I speak to-day for the preservation of the Union.

1

As used in line 16, "fit" most nearly means

A) coordinated.
B) adjusted.
C) healthy.
D) suited.

2

As used in line 20, "part" most nearly means

A) aspect.
B) role.
C) section.
D) sliver.

8.   To understand what the new software—that is, analytics—can do that's different from more familiar software like spreadsheets, word processing, and graphics, consider the lowly photograph. Here the
5 relevant facts aren't how many bytes constitute a digital photograph, or a billion of them. That's about as instructive as counting the silver halide molecules used to form a single old-fashioned print photo. The important feature of a digital image's bytes is that, unlike
10 crystalline molecules, they are uniquely easy to store, transport, and manipulate with software. In the first era of digital images, people were fascinated by the convenience and malleability (think PhotoShop) of capturing, storing, and sharing pictures. Now, instead of
15 using software to manage photos, we can mine features of the bytes that make up the digital image. Facebook can, without privacy invasion, track where and when, for example, vacationing is trending, since digital images reveal at least that much. But more importantly, those
20 data can be cross-correlated, even in real time, with seemingly unrelated data such as local weather, interest rates, crime figures, and so on. Such correlations associated with just one photograph aren't revealing. But imagine looking at billions of photos over weeks,
25 months, years, then correlating them with dozens of directly related data sets (vacation bookings, air traffic), tangential information (weather, interest rates, unemployment), or orthogonal information (social or political trends). With essentially free super-computing,
30   we can mine and usefully associate massive, formerly unrelated data sets and unveil all manner of economic, cultural, and social realities.
      For science fiction aficionados, Isaac Asimov anticipated the idea of using massive data sets to predict
35 human behavior, coining it "psychohistory" in his 1951 Foundation trilogy. The bigger the data set, Asimov said then, the more predictable the future. With big-data analytics, one can finally see the forest, instead of just the capillaries in the tree leaves. Or to put it in more
40   accurate terms, one can see beyond the apparently random motion of a few thousand molecules of air inside a balloon; one can see the balloon itself, and beyond that, that it is inflating, that it is yellow, and that it is part of a bunch of balloons en route to a birthday party. The
45 data/software world has, until now, been largely about looking at the molecules inside one balloon.

1

As in line 15, "mine" most nearly means

A) exploit.
B) contain.
C) respond.
D) describe.

2

As used in line 31, "unveil" most nearly means

A) reveal.
B) analyze.
C) alter.
D) uphold.

3

As used in line 34, "anticipated" most nearly means

A) expected.
B) accumulated.
C) foresaw.
D) explained.

9. This passage is adapted from Sharon Tregaskis, "What Bees Tell Us About Global Climate Change," © 2010 by *Johns Hopkins Magazine.*

Standing in the apiary on the grounds of the U.S. Department of Agriculture's Bee Research Laboratory in Beltsville, Maryland, Wayne Esaias digs through the canvas shoulder bag leaning against his leg in search of

5 the cable he uses to download data. It's dusk as he runs the cord from his laptop—precariously perched on the beam of a cast-iron platform scale—to a small, battery-operated data logger attached to the spring inside the scale's steel column. In the 1800s, a scale like this

10 would have weighed sacks of grain or crates of apples, peaches, and melons. Since arriving at the USDA's bee lab in January 2007, this scale has been loaded with a single item: a colony of *Apis mellifera*, the fuzzy, black-and-yellow honey bee. An attached, 12-bit

15 recorder captures the hive's weight to within a 10th of a pound, along with a daily register of relative ambient humidity and temperature.

On this late January afternoon, during a comparatively balmy respite between the blizzards that

20 dumped several feet of snow on the Middle Atlantic states, the bees, their honey, and the wooden boxes in which they live weigh 94.5 pounds. In mid-July, as last year's unusually long nectar flow finally ebbed, the whole contraption topped out at 275 pounds, including

25 nearly 150 pounds of honey. "Right now, the colony is in a cluster about the size of a soccer ball," says Esaias, who's kept bees for nearly two decades and knows without lifting the lid what's going on inside this hive. "The center of the cluster is where the queen is, and

30 they're keeping her at 93 degrees—the rest are just hanging there, tensing their flight muscles to generate heat." Provided that they have enough calories to fuel their winter workout, a healthy colony can survive as far north as Anchorage, Alaska. "They slowly eat their

35 way up through the winter," he says. "It's a race: Will they eat all their honey before the nectar flows, or not?" To make sure their charges win that race, apiarists have long relied on scale hives for vital management clues. By tracking daily weight variations, a beekeeper can

40 discern when the colony needs a nutritional boost to carry it through lean times, whether to add extra combs for honey storage and even detect incursions by marauding robber bees—all without disturbing the colony. A graph of the hive's weight—which can

45 increase by as much as 35 pounds a day in some parts of the United States during peak nectar flow – reveals the date on which the bees' foraging was was most productive and provides a direct record of successful pollination. "Around here, the bees make

50 their living in the month of May," says Esaias, noting that his bees often achieve daily spikes of 25 pounds, the maximum in Maryland. "There's almost no nectar coming in for the rest of the year." A scientist by training and career oceanographer at NASA, Esaias

55 established the Mink Hollow Apiary in his Highland, Maryland, backyard in 1992 with a trio of hand-me-down hives and an antique platform scale much like the one at the Beltsville bee lab. Ever since, he's maintained a meticulous record of the bees' daily

60 weight, as well as weather patterns and such details as his efforts to keep them healthy. In late 2006, honey bees nationwide began disappearing in an ongoing syndrome dubbed colony collapse disorder (CCD). Entire hives went empty as bees inexplicably

65 abandoned their young and their honey. Commercial beekeepers reported losses up to 90 percent, and the large-scale farmers who rely on honey bees to ensure rich harvests of almonds, apples, and sunflowers became very, very nervous. Looking for clues, Esaias

70 turned to his own records. While the resulting graphs threw no light on the cause of CCD, a staggering trend emerged: In the span of just 15 seasons, the date on which his Mink Hollow bees brought home the most nectar had shifted by two weeks—from late May

75 to the middle of the month. "I was shocked when I plotted this up," he says. "It was right under my nose, going on the whole time." The epiphany would lead Esaias to launch a series of research collaborations, featuring honey bees and other pollinators, to

80 investigate the relationships among plants, pollinators, and weather patterns. Already, the work has begun to reveal insights into the often unintended consequences of human interventions in natural and agricultural ecosystems, and exposed significant

85 gaps in how we understand the effect climate change will have on everything from food production to terrestrial ecology.

1

As used in line 41, "lean" most nearly means

A) tilted.
B) scarce.
C) compact.
D) sunken.

2

As used in line 42, "incursions" most nearly means

A) intentions.
B) introductions.
C) intrusions.
D) initiatives.

3

As used in lines 49-50, "make their living" most nearly means

A) grow heavier.
B) accumulate funds.
C) behave aggressively.
D) are most productive.

4

As used in line 68, "rich" most nearly means

A) plentiful.
B) costly.
C) heavy.
D) fragrant.

10. The following passage is adapted from the novel *Summer* by Edith Wharton, initially published in 1917.

The hours of the Hatchard Memorial librarian were from three to five; and Charity Royall's sense of duty usually kept her at her desk until nearly half-past four. But she had never perceived that any practical
5 advantage thereby accrued either to North Dormer or to herself; and she had no scruple in decreeing, when it suited her, that the library should close an hour earlier. A few minutes after Mr. Harney's departure she formed this decision, put away her lace, fastened the shutters,
10 and turned the key in the door of the temple of knowledge. The street upon which she emerged was still empty: and after glancing up and down it she began to walk toward her house. But instead of entering she passed on, turned into a field-path and mounted to a
15 pasture on the hillside.

She let down the bars of the gate, followed a trail along the crumbling wall of the pasture, and walked on till she reached a knoll where a clump of larches shook out their fresh tassels to the wind. There she lay down
20 on the slope, tossed off her hat and hid her face in the grass. She was blind and insensible to many things, and dimly knew it; but to all that was light and air, perfume and color, every drop of blood in her responded. She loved the roughness of the dry mountain grass under
25 her palms, the smell of the thyme into which she crushed her face, the fingering of the wind in her hair and through her cotton blouse, and the creak of the larches as they swayed to it.

She often climbed up the hill and lay there alone for
30 the mere pleasure of feeling the wind and of rubbing her cheeks in the grass. Generally at such times she did not think of anything, but lay immersed in an inarticulate well-being. Today the sense of well-being was intensified by her joy at escaping from the library. She
35 liked well enough to have a friend drop in and talk to her when she was on duty, but she hated to be bothered about books. How could she remember where they were, when they were so seldom asked for? Orma Fry occasionally took out a novel, and her brother Ben was
40 fond of what he called "jography," and of books relating to trade and bookkeeping; but no one else asked for anything except, at intervals, "Uncle Tom's Cabin," or "Opening of a Chestnut Burr," or Longfellow. She had these under her hand, and could have found them
45 in the dark; but unexpected demands came so rarely that they exasperated her like an injustice....

She had liked the young man's looks, and his short-sighted eyes, and his odd way of speaking, that was abrupt yet soft, just as his hands were sun-burnt and sinewy, yet
50 with smooth nails like a woman's. His hair was sunburnt-looking too, or rather the colour of bracken after frost; eyes grey, with the appealing look of the shortsighted, his smile shy yet confident, as if he knew lots of things she had never dreamed of, and yet
55 wouldn't for the world have had her feel his superiority. But she did feel it, and liked the feeling; for it was new to her. Poor and ignorant as she was, and knew herself to be—humblest of the humble even in North Dormer, where to come from the Mountain was the worst
60 disgrace—yet in her narrow world she had always ruled. It was partly, of course, owing to the fact that lawyer Royall was "the biggest man in North Dormer"; so much too big for it, in fact, that outsiders, who didn't know, always wondered how it held him. In spite of
65 everything—and in spite even of Miss Hatchard— lawyer Royall ruled in North Dormer; and Charity ruled in lawyer Royall's house. She had never put it to herself in those terms; but she knew her power. Confusedly, the young man in the library had made her feel for the first
70 time what might be the sweetness of dependence. She sat up and looked down on the house where she held sway.

It stood just below her, cheerless and untended. Behind the house a bit of uneven ground with clothes-
75 lines strung across it stretched up to a dry wall, and beyond the wall a patch of corn and a few rows of potatoes strayed vaguely into the adjoining wilderness of rock and fern.

1

As used in line 21 "blind" most nearly means

A) weak.

B) unaware.

C) modest.

D) careless.

2

As used in line 72, "sway" most nearly means

A) motion.

B) influence.

C) relief.

D) interest.

Explanations: Vocabulary in Context Exercises

Additional Frederick Douglass Questions

3. C

This is a good example of a question in which the word you are asked about is used in one of its most common meanings — these do appear from time to time, and you should be careful not to overthink them. In this case, Douglass sets up a contrast between men with *ordinary faculties* (abilities, attributes) and *brilliant examples of success*. Logically, then, *ordinary* must mean the opposite of "brilliant," something along the lines of "dull" or "unexceptional." C) is the closest synonym for those words, making it the answer. The other options are all other common meanings of *ordinary*, but none fits the context here.

4. B

Douglass is essentially saying that nature evens things out by making some people with humble origins successful, and some people who started out with a lot of advantages less successful. To keep something even, or balanced, is to "maintain" it. B) is thus correct. If that seems like too much of a stretch, plug and in and play process of elimination. Nature cannot "purchase" anything, and it does not make sense to say that nature "grasps" the balance. "Dominate" does not fit either because something that is balanced is, by definition, evenly distributed.

End-of-Chapter Exercises

1.1 C

This is essentially a straightforward second meanings question since the passage gives very little context – a common second definition of *seasoned* is in fact "experienced," which is consistent with the meaning of the passage: judgment, even experienced judgment, plays no role in math because an answer is always right or wrong. "Determined" and "tasteful" do not fit logically, and "objective" is exactly the opposite of the correct idea.

2.1 B

The phrase *absorbed the new reality* indicates that an old reality no longer held true. What was that reality? That other planets in our solar system could easily be colonized. Logically, then, *dispensed* must mean something like "got rid of." B) is closest in meaning, so it is correct.

3.1 C

The phrase *millions of indigenous people were ousted* (removed) *from their homelands* implies that the nature sanctuaries did not contain people. *Free of humans* must therefore mean "devoid of (without) humans." You can also work by process of elimination. The answer must be negative, and "liberated" and "whole" are both positive. "Uncompensated" (unpaid) is negative but does not fit in context. That leaves C) as the only logical choice.

3.2 D

The sentence in which the word *coupled* appears provides a second reason why conservationists changed their approach towards the indigenous peoples whose habitats they were seeking to save. In that context, "combined" is most logical: the combination of understanding the terrible effects of displacement on indigenous peoples, and the recognition that indigenous peoples had a positive effect on ecosystems, persuaded the conservationists to alter their perspective.

3.3 B

The fact that conservationists groups altered their treatment of indigenous peoples indicates that conservationists were persuaded to "consider" – that is, to take into account – the impact of local human concerns.

4.1 A

The previous sentence states that *Alternative [explanations] quickly arose*, so logically, the sentence in which *championed* appears is describing one of those explanations. In addition, the phrase *Others asserted* in the following sentence indicates that the word in question must be positive and mean something similar to asserted. "Advocated" is the closest synonym, so A) is correct. Playing process of elimination, B) and D) are both negative and can be eliminated, and C) makes no sense in the context of a discussion about the definition of species.

4.2 C

The passage indicates that the discovery of DNA's double helix caused, or led to, another definition of the word *species*. Logically, then, the correct answer must be positive and convey the idea of causation. The closest synonym for those words is "spurred," so the answer is C). "Rejected" is negative, and neither "elaborated" nor "defended" fits the required definition.

4.3 A

The key phrase is *minute* (tiny) *genetic differences*, which indicates that *finer* must convey the idea of something very small. The answer that comes closest to the required meaning is "narrower" — such lines would indicate even more detailed criteria for distinguishing among species. "Keener"(more perceptive), "milder" (less harsh), and "daintier" (more delicate and charming) all do not fit.

5.1 D

The passage indicates that citrus greening is a disease that essentially takes over trees. In that context, "surrounding" is the only option that makes sense. In A), "nourishing" is exactly the opposite of what you're looking for, and B) and C) don't make sense when plugged in. The rotten part of the tree isn't "implanting" or "growing" the stems.

5.2 C

The word in question refers to the orchards that were "chosen" to receive the potential cure for citrus greening. Although this word is not an option, the correct answer must have a similar meaning. Be careful with A) and B). Both "exclusive" and "preferred" are positive and imply that the orchards chosen to receive the experimental technology were already special in some way, but the passage does not indicate that that was the case. "Conventional" does not fit either – things are usually described as "conventional" in order to set up a contrast with something new. Here, the cure is innovative, not the orchards themselves. That leaves "particular," which is neutral and captures the idea that a few specific orchards have been selected.

6.1 B

B) is a straightforward fit for a discussion of the brain - certain parts of that organ "control" particular social skills. They do not "elect," "charge," or "require" those skills.

7.1 D

The contradictor *but* in line 17 indicates that the statement before the semicolon forms a contrast to the idea that Webster *[has] a duty to perform, and [he] means to perform it*. Essentially, Webster is saying that he isn't particularly qualified to speak for the preservation of the Union, but he's going to do so anyway. In this context, qualified most nearly means "suited." If that definition seems like too much of a leap, play process of elimination. All of the other options are too literal, related to health and movement; none makes sense in a political context.

7.2 B

The key words *perform* (line 18) and *act* (line 20) indicate that Webster thinks of himself as playing a theatrical "role." The other options are all based on the most common meaning of *part* – that is, a portion – and do not make sense in context.

8.1 A

The sentence in which the word appears provides an important clue. The parallel structure of the phrase *instead of using software to manage photos, we can mine features* indicates that *mine* is being used as a synonym for *using*. In fact, "exploit" means "to make use of." That meaning is confirmed when the author describes all the information that bytes can be used to acquire.

8.2 A

If you plugged in your own word here, you might say something like "show" or "expose." "Reveal" is closest in meaning to those words, so A) is correct. Consider also the image suggested by the word *unveil* itself: a veil is a covering, and to pull off a veil is to reveal what is behind it.

8.3 C

The word *predict* in line 34 is an important clue, indicating that the correct answer must have a similar meaning. "Foresaw" (literally, "saw before") is closest in meaning, so it is correct.

9.1 B

The phrase *needs a nutritional boost* provides an important clue. Why would colonies need a nutritional boost? Because they aren't getting a lot of nutrients. In other words, nutrients are "scarce." Even though C) might sound strange to you when it is plugged in, it is the only answer that captures the correct meaning. "Tilted" and "sunken" can only be used to refer to the physical placement of objects, and "compact" (small) does not quite fit the context.

9.2 C

Don't get distracted by the word *marauder* (raiders) – it doesn't matter whether you know what it means. Focus on the phrase *robber bees*, which tells you the correct answer must be negative. Only "intrusions" is negative, so C) is correct.

9.3 D

Esaias is talking about when honey production *spikes*, so the correct word must be positive and consistent with the idea of a sharp increase. B) can be eliminated immediately because bees can't accumulate money. C) is negative and can be eliminated as well. Be careful with A): the amount of honey the bees produce is increasing, not the weight of the bees themselves. D) correctly indicates that the bees are most "productive," i.e., they produce the most honey.

9.4 A

The passage is talking about improved harvests, so if you plugged in your own word, you'd probably come up with something like "big" or "large." "Plentiful" is just a fancier synonym for those words, so it is correct. Be careful with B): "costly" means that the harvests themselves would cost more, not that they would bring in more money. C) doesn't quite fit because the focus is on harvest size, not weight. And D) is incorrect because "fragrant" (having a pleasant odor) is completely unrelated to harvest size.

10.1 B

The word in question is linked to *insensible* (unknowing) by the word *and*, so it must have a similar meaning. "Unaware" is the closest fit for that definition, so B) is correct.

If you're not sure what *insensible* means, consider the slightly larger context. The word *but* after the semicolon in line 22 indicates a contrast between the information before and after. *Blind* and *insensible* are opposed to the things Charity does respond to fully (light and air). You can therefore assume that the correct word must means something similar to "not knowing" or "not responding." If that doesn't get you to the answer, work by process of elimination. "Weak" does not make sense, so A) can be eliminated. C) does not fit either because the passage is focused on Charity's emotional state, not on her sense of humility or proper social conduct. D) also does not fit because there is nothing to suggest that Charity is sloppy or does not pay attention. Again, that leaves B) as the correct answer.

10.2 B

The key phrase is in lines 66-67, which indicate that Charity *ruled* in lawyer Royall's house. In that context, *sway* must mean something like "power." The closest match for that definition is "influence," so B) is correct.

Making the Leap:
From Concrete to Abstract

Before we look more closely at the various question types, we're going to examine a key element of comprehension – namely, the ability to move between specific wording and more abstract or general ideas. While you probably won't see many (if any) questions that directly test this skill, it is nevertheless crucial for navigating challenging passages.

One of the most common ways that both the authors of SAT Reading passages and the test-writers themselves move between specific phrasings and more general language is by using **pronouns** (*this*, *that*) and **abstract** or **compression nouns** (*notion, assertion, phenomenon*).

If you've already spent some time preparing for the multiple-choice Writing and Language portion of the SAT, you may be familiar with pronouns and antecedents (or referents), but even if you are, here's a refresher:

Pronoun = word that replaces a noun (e.g., *she, he, it, they, this, that*)

Antecedent/Referent = noun to which a pronoun refers

As a matter of fact, the testing of pronouns and antecedents is one of the places where the Reading and Writing Tests overlap. On the Writing and Language Test, the focus is primarily on identifying disagreement errors between pronouns and their antecedents.

For example:

Some **albino animals** have difficulty thriving in the wild because **1** <u>its</u> skin is insufficiently dark to absorb sunlight during harsh winters.

1

A) NO CHANGE
B) it's
C) their
D) they're

In the above sentence, the answer is C) because the singular pronoun *it* incorrectly refers to the plural noun *albino animals*. (Choice B) can be eliminated because *they're* = they are.)

Unfortunately, pronouns and antecedents tend to be less straightforward in Reading than in Writing. In the above sentence, for example, the antecedent is right there – *some albino animals* is the only noun to which *its* could logically refer.

Why Use Pronouns?

When it comes to Reading, determining which noun a particular pronoun refers to may sometimes require more effort than you are accustomed to making; however, the heavy use of pronouns is necessary in all but the simplest texts for reasons of style and clarity. It is important that you be able to connect pronouns back to their referents because without the ability to "track" an idea through a passage, you can easily lose track of the passage's focus and argument.

Compare the following two versions of this passage. First without pronouns:

> …Crowdsourcing is a wonderful tool, but **crowdsourcing** still fails in a very particular way, which is that any evaluation is swayed by the evaluations that have come before **that evaluation**. A barbershop with a one-star rating on Yelp as **that barbershop's** first review is subsequently more likely to accrue more negative reviews—and **that same barbershop**, were **that barbershop** to receive a four-star rating on Yelp as **that barbershop's** first review, would be more likely to accrue more subsequent positive reviews.

Notice how incredibly awkward and repetitive this version is. Now look at this version, which replaces the repeated nouns with pronouns:

> …Crowdsourcing is a wonderful tool, but **it** still fails in a very particular way, which is that any evaluation is swayed by the evaluations that have come before **it**. A barbershop with a one-star rating on Yelp as **its** first review is subsequently more likely to accrue more negative reviews—and that same barbershop, were **it** to receive a four-star rating on Yelp as **its** first review, would be more likely to accrue more subsequent positive reviews.

Notice how much smoother this version is. You don't get tangled up in the constant repetition of the same phrase, so it's much easier to read.

Pronouns won't always appear by themselves, though. Typically, a pronoun such as *this*, *that*, or *these* will appear in front of a noun, e.g., *this notion, these movements, such developments*. Sounds a lot more straightforward, right? Well…maybe yes, maybe no.

Sometime around third grade, you probably learned that a noun was a person, place, or thing. Pretty self-explanatory. When you learned that a noun was a "thing," however, you probably understood "thing" to mean an object like a bicycle or an apple or a house. That's certainly true. But words like *idea* or *assertion* or *concept* – words that don't refer to actual physical objects – are also nouns. These nouns are sometimes referred to as **abstract nouns** or **compression nouns** because they compress lots of information into a single word.

These types of words appear frequently in SAT passages, and understanding what they refer to is often crucial to comprehension. **In fact, the ability to recognize the relationship between abstract nouns and the ideas that they refer to is central to making sense out of many, if not most, passages.** If you can't draw the relationship between the noun, say, *phenomenon*, and the specific occurrence that it refers to, you probably can't answer a question that asks you to do exactly that. And you certainly can't answer a question that asks you what can be inferred about or what sort of information would support it.

What's more, these nouns, like pronouns, may appear **either before or after** the particular idea (argument, assertion, description, etc.) has been discussed, sometimes even in a different paragraph. If you encounter a question that requires you to identify what such a noun refers to, you must either continue reading to locate the necessary information, or more frequently, **back up and read from before the place where the noun appeared**.

Very often, when students are confused about this type of phase, they either reread the phrase in isolation and try to figure out what it's talking about (impossible) or start reading at the phrase and continue on for several lines, then become confused as to why they have no clearer an understanding of the phrase than they did when they started. As a result, they get caught in a loop of reading and rereading the wrong spot and, consequently, have no reliable means of determining the correct answer.

Let's look at an example. The phrase that includes the compression noun is in bold, and the information that it refers to is underlined.

The world is complex and interconnected, and the evolution of our communications system from a broadcast model to a networked one has added a new dimension to the mix. <u>The Internet has made us all less</u>
5 <u>dependent on professional journalists and editors for</u> <u>information about the wider world, allowing us to seek</u> <u>out information directly via online search or to receive</u> <u>it from friends through social media.</u> **But this enhanced convenience** comes with a considerable risk: that we
10 will be exposed to what we want to know at the expense of what we need to know. While we can find virtual communities that correspond to our every curiosity, there's little pushing us beyond our comfort zones to or into the unknown, even if the unknown may have
15 serious implications for our lives. There are things we should probably know more about—like political and religious conflicts in Russia or basic geography. But even if we knew more than we do, there's no guarantee that the knowledge gained would prompt us to act in a
20 particularly admirable fashion.

The phrase *this enhanced convenience* in lines 8-9 is a classic example of a compression noun. It refers not to a single thing but rather to an entire idea presented in the sentence before it:

> **The Internet has made us all less dependent on professional journalists and editors for information about the wider world, allowing us to seek out information directly via online search or to receive it from friends through social media.**

To make something convenient is to make it easier or less troublesome. The phrase *this enhanced* (improved) *convenience* refers to the fact that the Internet has made people's lives much easier because it allows them to obtain information on their own, eliminating their dependence on others. The author avoids repeating all of that information by condensing it into a mere three words.

If the author did not "compress" the information, the passage would read like this:

> **The Internet has made us all less dependent on professional journalists and editors for information about the wider world, allowing us to seek out information directly via online search or to receive it from friends through social media. But the fact that the Internet has made us less dependent on professional journalists and editors for information about the wider world, allowing us to seek out information directly via online search or to receive it from friends through social media, comes with a considerable risk...**

In this version, the second sentence repeats all of the information from the first sentence, creating an exceedingly long and awkward construction. In contrast, the phrase *enhanced convenience* allows the author to present his ideas in a much clearer, more concise manner.

Let's look at another example:

Yogi Berra, the former Major League baseball catcher and coach, once remarked that you can't hit and think at the same time. Of course, since he also reportedly said, "I really didn't say everything I said,"
5   it is not clear we should take his statements at face value. Nonetheless, a widespread view — in both academic journals and the popular press — is that thinking about what you are doing, as you are doing it, interferes with performance. <u>The idea is that once you</u>
10 <u>have developed the ability to play an arpeggio on the piano, putt a golf ball or parallel park, attention to what you are doing leads to inaccuracies, blunders and sometimes even utter paralysis.</u> As the great choreographer George Balanchine would say to his
15 dancers, "Don't think, dear; just do."
Perhaps you have experienced **this destructive force** yourself. Start thinking about just how to carry a full glass of water without spilling, and you'll end up drenched. How, exactly, do you initiate a telephone
20 conversation? Begin wondering, and before long, the recipient of your call will notice the heavy breathing and hang up. Our actions, the French philosopher Maurice Merleau-Ponty tells us, exhibit a "magical" efficacy, but when we focus on them, they degenerate
25 into the absurd. A 13-time winner on the Professional Golfers Association Tour, Dave Hill, put it like this: "You can't be thinking about the mechanics of the sport while you are performing."

Here, there's an additional twist. Not only does the phrase *this destructive force* refer to information before it, but that information is in a different paragraph. If you encountered a question that required you to understand what that phrase referred to and only read from line 16 on, you would likely become confused. You might eventually find your way to the answer, but you wouldn't really be sure. If, on the other hand, you simply backed up and read from the previous paragraph, things would be much more straightforward.

The Former and the Latter

One set of compression nouns that has a tendency to give people difficulty is "the former and the latter." Like other compression nouns, these nouns are used to refer back to words or ideas mentioned earlier in the same sentence or in a previous sentence. *The former* is used to refer back to the noun or phrase mentioned first, and *the latter* is used to refer back to the noun or phrase mentioned second.

Let's start with a straightforward example:

> **In the nineteenth century, both Thomas Edison and Nikola Tesla were well-known scientists, but <u>the former</u> is now considered one of the greatest American inventors, while <u>the latter</u> has fallen into obscurity.**

The beginning of the sentence refers to two individuals: Thomas Edison and Nikola Tesla. In the second half of the sentence, *the former* refers to Edison because his name occurs first, while *the latter* refers to Tesla because his name occurs second (*latter* is like *later*). That's easy enough to follow, but some passages may use these words in ways that you may have to work somewhat harder to follow.

For example:

> **All bodies in the solar system are heated by sunlight. They rid themselves of this heat in two ways: (1) by emitting infrared radiation and (2) by shedding matter. In long-lived bodies such as Earth, <u>the former process</u> prevails; for others, such as comets, <u>the latter</u> dominates.**

Let's look closely at what's going on in these sentences. (If this is an unfamiliar topic for you, that's all the better.) First, the author states that bodies in the solar system eliminate heat from the sun in two ways. Next, he lists those two ways. The first way is by emitting infrared radiation, and the second is by shedding matter. When he refers to those ways again in the following sentence, *the former* = emitting infrared radiation, and *the latter* = shedding matter.

Therefore, the final sentence means that old planets like Earth eliminate heat by emitting infrared radiation, but other objects like comets eliminate heat by shedding matter.

Note that occasionally, *the latter* may appear **before** *the former*. For example, the paragraph above could be written the following way:

> **All bodies in the solar system are heated by sunlight. They rid themselves of this heat in two ways: (1) by emitting infrared radiation and (2) by shedding matter. For some objects such as comets, <u>the latter</u> dominates; in long-lived bodies such as Earth, <u>the former process</u> prevails.**

Although the order of *the former* and *the latter* is switched, the last sentence has exactly the same meaning it had in the previous version.

Pronoun and Compression Noun Exercises

Directions: underline the word, phrase, or lines <u>in the passage</u> to which the compression noun in each sentence refers.

1.   What drives traffic on most "news" websites is not journalism but a combination of snark and celebrity clickbait. Much of it is churned out in soul-destroying content factories manned by inexperienced—and
5 therefore inexpensive—young people without the time or incentive to dig deeply into anything. This deficit is particularly acute where it matters most: in the kind of expensive, far-flung reporting that is either dangerous to the lives of those doing the work or harmful to the
10 bottom lines of the publications paying for it. The idea that readers will pay the actual cost of meaningful journalism has never been sustainable in the United States and has brought down nearly every entity that has tried to depend on it.

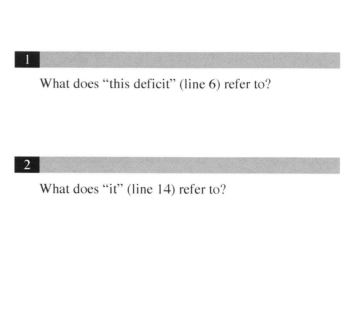

1

What does "this deficit" (line 6) refer to?

2

What does "it" (line 14) refer to?

2.   While humpback dolphins look quite similar to other dolphins, their genetics tells a different story. Researchers collected 235 tissue samples and 180 skulls throughout the animals' distribution, representing
5 the biggest dataset assembled to date for the animals. The team analyzed mitochondrial and nuclear DNA from the tissue, which revealed significant variations.
    Although the line between species, sub-species and populations is a blurry one, in this case, the researchers
10 are confident that the humpback dolphin is distinct enough to warrant the "species" title. The mitochondrial DNA turned up genetic signatures distinct enough to signal a separate species, and likewise, differences in the dolphins' skulls supported this divergence. Although
15 the nuclear DNA provided a slightly more confounding picture, it still clearly showed differences between the four species.

1

What does "this divergence" (line 14) refer to?

2

What does "it" (line 16) refer to?

3.   Soon after the Big Bang, there were tiny ripples: quantum fluctuations in the density of the seething ball of hot plasma. Billions of years later, those seeds have grown into galaxy clusters — sprawling groups of
5 hundreds or thousands of galaxies bound together by gravity. But there seems to be a mismatch. Results released last year suggest that as much as 40% of galaxy-cluster mass is missing when compared with the amount of clustering predicted by the ripples.
10 The findings have led theorists to propose physics beyond the standard model of cosmology to make up the difference.

1

What do "those seeds" (line 3) refer to?

2

What do "the findings" (line 10) refer to?

4. Conservationists have historically been at odds with the people who inhabit wildernesses. During the last half of the 20th century, millions of indigenous people were ousted from their homelands to establish nature sanctuaries free of humans. Most succumbed to
5 malnutrition, disease and exploitation. Such outcomes—coupled with the realization that indigenous groups usually help to stabilize ecosystems by, for instance, keeping fire at bay—have convinced major conservation groups to take local human concerns into account. The
10 World Wildlife Fund (WWF) now describes indigenous peoples as "natural allies," and the Nature Conservancy pledges to seek their "free, informed and prior" consent to projects impacting their territories.

1

What does "such outcomes" (line 5) refer to?

5. The starlings show up over Rome around dusk, heading for their roosts after a day of feeding in the countryside. In flocks of several hundred to several thousand, they form sinuous streams, whirling
5 cylinders, cones or ribbons spread across the sky like giant flags. Wheeling and dipping together, they reminded Andrea Cavagna, a physicist at the National Research Council of Italy, of atoms falling into place in a superfluid state of matter called a Bose-Einstein
10 condensate. Out of curiosity, Cavagna deployed a camera to record the flights. As a particle physicist, he says, "it was refreshing to work with something you can actually see." But keeping track of a thousand birds turned out to be much more complicated than a billion
15 billion atoms.
　　Cavagna was hardly the first scientist to be intrigued by these acrobatics—known, in a rare instance of technical language coinciding with poetry, as "murmurations." Other animals that travel in groups—
20 schooling fish, most obviously—show the same uncanny ability to move in apparent unison away from a predator or toward a food source.

1

What does "they" (line 4) refer to?

2

What do "these acrobatics" (line 17) refer to?

6.   I wish to speak to-day, not as a Massachusetts
man, nor as a Northern man, but as an American, and
a member of the Senate of the United States. It is
fortunate that there is a Senate of the United States;
5   a body not yet moved from its propriety, not lost to a just
sense of its own dignity and its own high responsibilities,
and a body to which the country looks, with confidence,
for wise, moderate, patriotic, and healing counsels.
It is not to be denied that we live in the midst of strong
10   agitations, and are surrounded by very considerable
dangers to our institutions and government. The
imprisoned winds are let loose. The East, the North,
and the stormy South combine to throw the whole sea
into commotion, to toss its billows to the skies, and
15   disclose its profoundest depths. I do not affect to regard
myself, Mr. President, as holding, or as fit to hold, the
helm in this combat with the political elements; but I
have a duty to perform, and I mean to perform it with
fidelity, not without a sense of existing dangers, but not
20   without hope. I have a part to act, not for my own
security or safety, for I am looking out for no fragment
upon which to float away from the wreck, if wreck there
must be, but for the good of the whole, and the
preservation of all; and there is that which will keep me
25   to my duty during this struggle, whether the sun and the
stars shall appear, or shall not appear for many days.
I speak to-day for the preservation of the Union.

1 What does "a body" (lines 5 and 7) refer to?

2 What does "its" (lines 14 and 15) refer to?

3 What does "it" (line 18) refer to?

7.   Chimps do it, birds do it, even you and I do it.
Once you see someone yawn, you are compelled to
do the same. Now it seems that wolves can be added
to the list of animals known to spread yawns like a
5   contagion.
   Among humans, even thinking about yawning can
trigger the reflex, leading some to suspect that catching
a yawn is linked to our ability to empathize with other
humans. For instance, contagious yawning activates the
10   same parts of the brain that govern empathy and social
know-how. And some studies have shown that humans
with more fine-tuned social skills are more likely to catch
a yawn.
   Similarly, chimpanzees, baboons and bonobos
15   often yawn when they see other members of their species
yawning. Chimps (Pan troglodytes) can catch yawns
from humans, even virtual ones. At least in primates,
contagious yawning seems to require an emotional
connection and may function as a demonstration of
20   empathy. Beyond primates, though, the trends are less
clear-cut. One study found evidence of contagious
yawning in birds but didn't connect it to empathy.

1 What do "the trends" (line 20) refer to?

2 What does "it" (line 22) refer to?

8.   It was one hundred and forty-four years ago that members of the Democratic Party first met in convention to select a Presidential candidate. A lot of years passed since 1832, and during that time it would

5 have been most unusual for any national political party to ask a Barbara Jordan to deliver a keynote address. But tonight, here I am. And I feel that notwithstanding the past that my presence here is one additional bit of evidence that the American Dream need not forever be

10 deferred.

Now that I have this grand distinction, what in the world am I supposed to say? I could list the problems which cause people to feel cynical, angry, frustrated: problems which include lack of integrity in government;

15 the feeling that the individual no longer counts; feeling that the grand American experiment is failing or has failed. I could recite these problems, and then I could sit down and offer no solutions. But I don't choose to do that either. The citizens of America expect more.

1

What does "this grand distinction" (line 11) refer to?

9.   The most ancient of all societies, and the only one that is natural, is the family: and even so the children remain attached to the father only so long as they need him for their preservation. As soon as this

5 need ceases, the natural bond is dissolved. The children, released from the obedience they owed to the father, and the father, released from the care he owed his children, return equally to independence. If they remain united, they continue so no longer naturally, but voluntarily; and

10 the family itself is then maintained only by convention.

This common liberty results from the nature of man. His first law is to provide for his own preservation, his first cares are those which he owes to himself; and, as soon as he reaches years of discretion, he is the sole

15 judge of the proper means of preserving himself, and consequently becomes his own master.

The family then may be called the first model of political societies: the ruler corresponds to the father, and the people to the children; and all, being born free

20 and equal, alienate their liberty only for their own advantage. The whole difference is that, in the family, the love of the father for his children repays him for the care he takes of them, while, in the State, the pleasure of commanding takes the place of the love which the chief

25 cannot have for the peoples under him.

1

What does "they" (line 9) refer to?

2

What does "this common liberty" (line 11) refer to?

10.   The sharing economy is a little like online
shopping, which started in America 15 years ago. At
first, people were worried about security. But having
made a successful purchase from, say, Amazon, they
5 felt safe buying elsewhere. Similarly, using Airbnb or
a car-hire service for the first time encourages people to
try other offerings. Next, consider eBay. Having started
out as a peer-to-peer marketplace, it is now dominated
by professional "power sellers" (many of whom started
10 out as ordinary eBay users). The same may happen with
the sharing economy, which also provides new
opportunities for enterprise. Some people have bought
cars solely to rent them out, for example. Incumbents
are getting involved too. Avis, a car-hire firm, has a share
15 in a sharing rival. So do GM and Daimler, two carmakers.
In the future, companies may develop hybrid models,
listing excess capacity (whether vehicles, equipment or
office space) on peer-to-peer rental sites. In the past,
new ways of doing things online have not displaced the
20 old ways entirely. But they have often changed them.
Just as internet shopping forced Walmart and Tesco to
adapt, so online sharing will shake up transport, tourism,
equipment-hire and more.
       The main worry is regulatory uncertainty. Will
25 room-4-renters be subject to hotel taxes, for example?
In Amsterdam officials are using Airbnb listings to track
down unlicensed hotels. In some American cities,
peer-to-peer taxi services have been banned after
lobbying by traditional taxi firms. The danger is that
30 although some rules need to be updated to protect
consumers from harm, incumbents will try to destroy
competition. People who rent out rooms should pay tax,
of course, but they should not be regulated like a Ritz-
Carlton hotel. The lighter rules that typically govern
35 bed-and-breakfasts are more than adequate. The sharing
economy is the latest example of the internet's value to
consumers. This emerging model is now big and
disruptive enough for regulators and companies to have
woken up to it. That is a sign of its immense potential. It
40 is time to start caring about sharing.

1

What does "it" (line 8) refer to?

2

What do "they" and "them" (line 20) refer to?

3

What does "this emerging model" (line 37)
refer to?

11. The following passage is adapted from "Scientists Discover Salty Aquifer, Previously Unknown Microbial Habitat Under Antarctica," © 2015 by Dartmouth College.

Using an airborne imaging system for the first time in Antarctica, scientists have discovered a vast network of unfrozen salty groundwater that may support previously unknown microbial life deep under the coldest, driest
5 desert on our planet. The findings shed new light on ancient climate change on Earth and provide strong evidence that a similar briny aquifer could support microscopic life on Mars. The scientists used SkyTEM, an airborne electromagnetic sensor, to detect and map
10 otherwise inaccessible subterranean features.

The system uses an antennae suspended beneath a helicopter to create a magnetic field that reveals the subsurface to a depth of about 1,000 feet. Because a helicopter was used, large areas of rugged terrain could
15 be surveyed. The SkyTEM team was funded by the National Science Foundation and led by researchers from the University of Tennessee, Knoxville (UTK), and Dartmouth College, which oversees the NSF's SkyTEM project.

20 "These unfrozen materials appear to be relics of past surface ecosystems and our findings provide compelling evidence that they now provide deep subsurface habitats for microbial life despite extreme environmental conditions," says lead author Jill Mikucki,
25 an assistant professor at UTK. "These new below-ground visualization technologies can also provide insight on glacial dynamics and how Antarctica responds to climate change."

Co-author Dartmouth Professor Ross Virginia is
30 SkyTEM's co-principal investigator and director of Dartmouth's Institute of Arctic Studies. "This project is studying the past and present climate to, in part, understand how climate change in the future will affect biodiversity and ecosystem processes," Virginia says.
35 "This fantastic new view beneath the surface will help us sort out competing ideas about how the McMurdo Dry Valleys have changed with time and how this history influences what we see today."

The researchers found that the unfrozen brines form
40 extensive, interconnected aquifers deep beneath glaciers and lakes and within permanently frozen soils. The brines extend from the coast to at least 7.5 miles inland in the McMurdo Dry Valleys, the largest ice-free region in Antarctica. The brines could be due to freezing and/or
45 deposits. The findings show for the first time that the Dry Valleys' lakes are interconnected rather than isolated; connectivity between lakes and aquifers is important in sustaining ecosystems through drastic climate change, such as lake dry-down events. The findings also challenge
50 the assumption that parts of the ice sheets below the pressure melting point are devoid of liquid water. In addition to providing answers about the biological adaptations of previously unknown ecosystems that persist in the extreme cold and dark of the Antarctic
55 winter, the new study could help scientists to understand whether similar conditions might exist elsewhere in the solar system, specifically beneath the surface of Mars, which has many similarities to the Dry Valleys. Overall, the Dry Valleys ecosystem –
60 cold, vegetation-free and home only to microscopic animal and plant life – resembles, during the Antarctic summer, conditions on the surface on Mars.

SkyTEM produced images of Taylor Valley along the Ross Sea that suggest briny sediments exist at
65 subsurface temperatures down to perhaps -68°F, which is considered suitable for microbial life. One of the studied areas was lower Taylor Glacier, where the data suggest ancient brine still exists beneath the glacier. That conclusion is supported by the presence
70 of Blood Falls, an iron-rich brine that seeps out of the glacier and hosts an active microbial ecosystem.

Scientists' understanding of Antarctica's underground environment is changing dramatically as research reveals that subglacial lakes are widespread
75 and that at least half of the areas covered by the ice sheet are akin to wetlands on other continents. But groundwater in the ice-free regions and along the coastal margins remains poorly understood.

1

What do "the findings" (line 5) refer to?

2

What does "this history" (line 37) refer to?

3

What does "that conclusion" (line 69) refer to?

12. This passage is adapted from Sharon Tregaskis, "What Bees Tell Us About Global Climate Change," © 2010 by *Johns Hopkins Magazine.*

Standing in the apiary on the grounds of the U.S. Department of Agriculture's Bee Research Laboratory in Beltsville, Maryland, Wayne Esaias digs through the canvas shoulder bag leaning against his leg in search of
5 the cable he uses to download data. It's dusk as he runs the cord from his laptop—precariously perched on the beam of a cast-iron platform scale—to a small, battery-operated data logger attached to the spring inside the scale's steel column. In the 1800s, a scale like this
10 would have weighed sacks of grain or crates of apples, peaches, and melons. Since arriving at the USDA's bee lab in January 2007, this scale has been loaded with a single item: a colony of *Apis mellifera*, the fuzzy, black-and-yellow honey bee. An attached, 12-bit
15 recorder captures the hive's weight to within a 10th of a pound, along with a daily register of relative ambient humidity and temperature.

On this late January afternoon, during a comparatively balmy respite between the blizzards that
20 dumped several feet of snow on the Middle Atlantic states, the bees, their honey, and the wooden boxes in which they live weigh 94.5 pounds. In mid-July, as last year's unusually long nectar flow finally ebbed, the whole contraption topped out at 275 pounds, including
25 nearly 150 pounds of honey. "Right now, the colony is in a cluster about the size of a soccer ball," says Esaias, who's kept bees for nearly two decades and knows without lifting the lid what's going on inside this hive. "The center of the cluster is where the queen is, and
30 they're keeping her at 93 degrees—the rest are just hanging there, tensing their flight muscles to generate heat." Provided that they have enough calories to fuel their winter workout, a healthy colony can survive as far north as Anchorage, Alaska. "They slowly eat their
35 way up through the winter," he says. "It's a race: Will they eat all their honey before the nectar flows, or not?" To make sure their charges win that race, apiarists have long relied on scale hives for vital management clues. By tracking daily weight variations, a beekeeper can
40 discern when the colony needs a nutritional boost to carry it through lean times, whether to add extra combs for honey storage and even detect incursions by marauding robber bees—all without disturbing the colony. A graph of the hive's weight—which can

45 increase by as much as 35 pounds a day in some parts of the United States during peak nectar flow – reveals the date on which the bees' foraging was was most productive and provides a direct record of successful pollination. "Around here, the bees make
50 their living in the month of May," says Esaias, noting that his bees often achieve daily spikes of 25 pounds, the maximum in Maryland. "There's almost no nectar coming in for the rest of the year." A scientist by training and career oceanographer at NASA, Esaias
55 established the Mink Hollow Apiary in his Highland, Maryland, backyard in 1992 with a trio of hand-me-down hives and an antique platform scale much like the one at the Beltsville bee lab. Ever since, he's maintained a meticulous record of the bees' daily
60 weight, as well as weather patterns and such details as his efforts to keep them healthy. In late 2006, honey bees nationwide began disappearing in an ongoing syndrome dubbed colony collapse disorder (CCD). Entire hives went empty as bees inexplicably
65 abandoned their young and their honey. Commercial beekeepers reported losses up to 90 percent, and the large-scale farmers who rely on honey bees to ensure rich harvests of almonds, apples, and sunflowers became very, very nervous. Looking for clues, Esaias
70 turned to his own records. While the resulting graphs threw no light on the cause of CCD, a staggering trend emerged: In the span of just 15 seasons, the date on which his Mink Hollow bees brought home the most nectar had shifted by two weeks—from late May
75 to the middle of the month. "I was shocked when I plotted this up," he says. "It was right under my nose, going on the whole time." The epiphany would lead Esaias to launch a series of research collaborations, featuring honey bees and other pollinators, to
80 investigate the relationships among plants, pollinators, and weather patterns. Already, the work has begun to reveal insights into the often unintended consequences of human interventions in natural and agricultural ecosystems, and exposed significant
85 gaps in how we understand the effect climate change will have on everything from food production to terrestrial ecology.

1

What does "the epiphany" (line 77) refer to?

2

What does "the work" (line 81) refer to?

76

Explanations: Pronoun and Compression Noun Exercises

1.1 This deficit = *news websites' combination of snark and celebrity clickbait...churned out...by young people without the time or incentive to dig deeply into anything* (lines 1-6).

1.2 It = *The idea that readers will pay the actual cost of meaningful journalism*

2.1 This divergence = the fact that humpback dolphins are a separate dolphin species, as indicated by the differences in mitochondrial DNA. (lines 8-13)

2.2 It = the nuclear DNA (line 15)

3.1 Those seeds = *tiny ripples: quantum fluctuations in the density of the seething ball of hot plasma.* (lines 1-3)

3.2 The findings = results indicating that *40% of galaxy-cluster mass is missing when compared with the amount of clustering predicted by the ripples.* (lines 6-9)

4.1 Such outcomes = *millions of indigenous people were ousted from their homelands to establish nature sanctuaries free of humans. Most succumbed to malnutrition, disease and exploitation.* (lines 2-5)

5.1 They = The starlings (line 1)

5.2 These acrobatics = The birds' movements: *sinuous streams, whirling cylinders, cones or ribbons spread across the sky like giant flags.* (lines 4-6)

6.1 A body = the Senate

6.2 Its = the whole sea's (line 13)

6.3 It = a duty (line 18)

7.1 The trends = *At least in primates, contagious yawning seems to require an emotional connection and may function as a demonstration of empathy.* (lines 17-20)

7.2 It = contagious yawning (lines 21-22)

8.1 This grand distinction = the selection of Barbara Jordan to deliver the Democratic keynote address (lines 3-7)

9.1 They = The father and the children (lines 6-7)

9.2 This common liberty = the fact that a father and children can *voluntarily* decide whether to maintain ties after the children are no longer dependent on the father for survival. (lines 8-10)

10.1 It = eBay (line 7)

10.2 They = the new ways; them = the old ways (lines 18-20)

10.3 This emerging model = the sharing economy (lines 35-36)

11.1 The findings = the discovery of *a vast network of unfrozen salty groundwater that may support previously unknown microbial life deep under the coldest, driest desert on our planet.* (lines 2-5)

11.2 This history = *how the McMurdo Dry Valleys have changed with time* (lines 36-37)

11.3 That conclusion = *ancient brine still exists beneath the glacier* (line 68)

12.1 The epiphany = Esaias's realization that *in the span of just 15 seasons, the date on which his Mink Hollow bees brought home the most nectar had shifted by two weeks — from late May to the middle of the month.* (lines 72-75)

12.2 The work = *a series of research collaborations, featuring honey bees and other pollinators, to investigate the relationships among plants, pollinators, and weather patterns* (lines 78-81)

The Big Picture

Every SAT will have a number of questions that test your understanding of the passage as a whole (or, in some cases, large sections of it). These question may ask you to identify which statement **best summarizes** a passage/section of a passage, or they may ask you to recognize an author's **point** or **central claim**. While these questions are worded in a straightforward manner, they can also be challenging because they require a leap from the concrete, specific details of a passage to an understanding of its broader themes.

It's no surprise, then, that I've had to spend a lot of time teaching people to stop looking so hard at the details. It's not that there's anything wrong with details – it's just that they're not always terribly relevant, or even relevant at all. Very often, smart, detail-oriented students have a tendency to worry about every single thing that sounds even remotely odd while missing something major staring them in the face. Frequently, they blame this on the fact that they've been taught in English class to read closely and pay attention to all the details.

Well, I have some news: when you're in college with a 500-page reading assignment that you have two days to get through, you won't have time to annotate every last detail – nor will your professors expect you to. Whether or not you're truly interested in what you're reading, your job will be to get the gist of the author's argument and then focus on a few key areas. And if you can't recognize those key areas, college reading will be, shall we say, a challenge. Unlike the books you are assigned in high school English class, most of what you read in college will not have easily-digestible summaries available courtesy of sparknotes.com.

But back to the SAT.

It's fairly common for people to simply grind to a halt when they encounter an unfamiliar turn of phrase. When they realize they haven't quite understood a line, they go back and read it again. If they still don't quite get it, they read it yet again. And before they know it, they've wasted two or three minutes just reading the same five lines over and over again. Then they start to run out of time and have to rush through the last few questions.

Almost inevitably, you will encounter some passages with bits that aren't completely clear – that's part of the test. The goal is to see whether you can figure out their meaning from the general context – you're not expected to get every word, especially not the first time around. If you get the gist, you can figure a lot of other things out, whereas if you focus on one little detail, you'll get . . . one little detail.

Identifying Topics

The topic is **the person, thing, or idea that is the primary subject or focus** of the passage. In most cases, **the topic is the word or phrase that appears most frequently throughout the passage, either by name or in rephrased form** (pronoun or compression noun). For example, a computer could also be referred to as "the machine," "the invention," or "the technology."

Normally, the topic will be introduced in the introduction – that, after all, is the purpose of an introduction. if you're not sure about the topic, the first sentence is usually a good place to start. If it isn't mentioned there, it will almost always be found in the next few sentences.

While this discussion might sound very basic, **the ability to identify topics is crucial because correct answer choices will refer to the topic**. In fact, the correct answer will sometimes be the *only* answer choice to mention the topic. Furthermore, many incorrect answers are wrong because they are off-topic, and you cannot recognize when a statement is off-topic unless you know what the topic *is*.

Let's look at an example of how that could play out in a passage.

Citrus greening, the **plague** that could wipe out Florida's $9 billion orange industry, begins with the touch of a jumpy brown bug on a sun-kissed leaf. From there, **the bacterial disease** incubates in the
5 tree's roots, then moves back up the trunk in full force, causing nutrient flows to seize up. Leaves turn yellow, and the oranges, deprived of sugars from the leaves, remain green, sour, and hard. Many fall before harvest, brown necrotic flesh ringing failed stems.
10 For the past decade, Florida's oranges have been literally starving. Since **it** first appeared in 2005, **citrus greening**, also known by its Chinese name, **huanglongbing**, has swept across Florida's groves like a flood. With no hills to block it, the Asian citrus
15 psyllid—the invasive aphid relative that carries **the disease**—has infected nearly every orchard in the state. By one estimate, 80 percent of Florida's citrus trees are infected and declining.
The disease has spread beyond Florida to nearly
20 every orange-growing region in the United States. Despite many generations of breeding by humanity, no citrus plant resists **greening**; **it** afflicts lemons, grapefruits, and other citrus species as well. Once a tree is infected, it will die. Yet in a few select Floridian
25 orchards, there are now trees that, thanks to innovative technology, can fight **the greening tide**.

In the passage above, the topic – citrus greening – is introduced in the very first sentence. In the entire remainder of the passage, it is only referred to by name one additional time (line 12). It is, however, referred to in many other ways: *the plague, the disease, the bacterial disease, hunaglongbing, the greening tide* and, of course, *it*.

If you have difficulty drawing the connection between the original term and its many variations, you can end up not fully understanding what the passage is about. You may also misunderstand the **scope** of the passage – that is, whether it's **general** or **specific**.

Often, when asked for the topic of a passage such as this, students say things like, "Ummm... I think it talks about oranges and stuff," or "it mentions Florida," or, a bit closer to the mark, "diseases."

Incidentally, I've witnessed this type of uncertainty even in high-scoring students. They know the test well enough to spot wrong answers to detail questions, but when asked to state something as straightforward as the topic in their own words, they're suddenly lost.

As a matter of fact, the topic is not in fact "diseases." It is actually one specific disease, namely **citrus greening**. That fact can become very important if you see a question like this:

Citrus greening, the plague that could wipe out Florida's $9 billion orange industry, begins with the touch of a jumpy brown bug on a sun-kissed leaf. From there, the bacterial disease incubates in the
5 tree's roots, then moves back up the trunk in full force, causing nutrient flows to seize up. Leaves turn yellow, and the oranges, deprived of sugars from the leaves, remain green, sour, and hard. Many fall before harvest, brown necrotic flesh ringing failed stems.

1

The references to yellow leaves and green, sour, and hard oranges in lines 6-9 primarily serve to

A) describe some effects of citrus greening.

B) point out the consequence of giving plants too many nutrients.

C) suggest that farmers often harvest their crops too early.

D) demonstrate the difficulty of growing crops in a humid climate.

The only answer that directly refers to the passage's topic is A), which is correct. Yes, this is a fairly straightforward question, but using the big picture lets you jump right to the answer.

To reiterate this for yourself, try an exercise: take a page from a book or piece of writing you're familiar with, one whose topic you know for sure. Now, as fast as you can, **count** how many times that topic – either the noun itself or a rephrased version of it – appears on the page. The number should be pretty high. Since you're already familiar with the subject, it should be easier for you to see the relationship between the topic and the various ways that it's referred to throughout the text. If you find it helpful, keep repeating this exercise until you can consistently identity topics quickly and accurately.

Important: when defining a topic, try to use no more than a couple of words (e.g., effects of social media, ant nests, women's equality) and avoid saying things like, "Well, so I think that basically the passage is like talking about xyz..." The former takes almost no time and gives you exactly the information you need; the latter is time-consuming, vague, and encourages you to view the topic as much more subjective than it actually is.

What's the Point?

The point of a passage is the **primary idea** that the author wants to convey. After the topic, the point should be the first thing you look for when you read a passage. Once you have identified it and underlined it or written it down, you can often skim through the rest of the passage – but before that, finding it needs to be your main goal.

I cannot state this strongly enough: If you keep the main point in mind, you can often eliminate answers simply because they do not make sense in context of it or, better yet, identify the correct answer because it is the only option that is consistent with it.

What's more, **focusing on finding the point means you don't have a chance to get distracted.** It reduces the chance that you'll spend five minutes trying to absorb three lines while losing sight of the big idea. And it stops you from wasting energy trying to convince yourself that the passage is interesting when you're actually bored out of your mind.

But let me begin by saying what a main point is **not**:

- It is not a **topic** such as "bears" or "the rise of social media."

- It is not a **theme** such as "oppression" or "overcoming."

A main point is an **argument** that answers the question "so what?" It tells us *why* the author thinks the topic is important, or what primary information about a topic he or she wants to convey to the reader.

You can use this "formula" to determine the point:

Topic + So What? = Main Point

Sometimes the author will directly state the main point in the passage itself, **most often in the introduction or beginning of the second paragraph, and then again for emphasis at the end of the conclusion.**

When you find the point, **you should underline it immediately**. If the author does not state the point directly, you should **write it yourself**.

It isn't terribly effective to discuss main points in the abstract, so on the next page, we're going to look at a passage.

Sometime near the end of the Pleistocene, a band
of people left northeastern Asia, crossed the Bering
land bridge when the sea level was low, entered
Alaska and became the first Americans. Since the
5   1930s, archaeologists have thought these people were
members of the Clovis culture. First discovered in
New Mexico in the 1930s, the Clovis culture is known
for its distinct stone tools, primarily fluted projectile
points. For decades, Clovis artifacts were the oldest
10 known in the New World, dating to 13,000 years ago.
But in recent years, researchers have found more and
more evidence that people were living in North and
South America before the Clovis.

The most recently confirmed evidence comes from
15 Washington. During a dig conducted from 1977 to 1979,
researchers uncovered a bone projectile point stuck in
a mastodon rib. Since then, the age of the find has been
debated, but recently anthropologist Michael Waters
and his colleagues announced a new radiocarbon date
20 for the rib: 13,800 years ago, making it 800 years older
than the oldest Clovis artifact. Other pre-Clovis
evidence comes from a variety of locations across the
New World.

In my experience, many students are not entirely clear on the difference between describing the content of a passage and summarizing its argument. Because the ability to summarize arguments quickly and accurately is one of the most crucial skills for success on SAT Reading, this confusion can become a major stumbling block.

> **Describing content** = recounting the information presented in the text, often in sequential "first x, then y, and finally z" form, without necessarily distinguishing between main points and supporting evidence.

> **Summarizing an argument** = identifying the essential point that the author wants to convey and eliminating any unnecessary detail. The goal is not to cover all of the information presented or to relate it in the sequence it appears in the passage, but rather to pinpoint the **overarching idea** that encapsulates the author's point.

Summarizing arguments requires you to make a leap from concrete to abstract because you must move beyond simply recounting the information presented to recognizing which parts are most important and relating them to other, more general ideas.

In order to make this leap, you must be able to separate the larger, more important ideas (which usually appear at the beginning and the end of a paragraph) from the details and supporting evidence (which usually appear in the middle of a paragraph). If you are able to identify main ideas, you will also find it much easier to identify information that supports them.

When students are asked to summarize the main point of a passage, however, they tend to respond in one of two ways:

1) They state the topic

The Clovis People

2) They describe the content

Uh… so the guy, he basically talks about how these people, I think they were called the Clovis people, right? They were like the first people who came across the Bering Strait to America… Oh no, wait, they weren't actually the first people to come across, it's just that they thought that those people were first. But so anyway those people settled in New Mexico, I think it said like 13,000 years ago? Only now he's saying that there were other people who were actually there before the Clovis, and then he says something about a mastodon rib and then something about radiocarbon dating (I remember 'cuz we learned about it in Chem this year). Oh yeah, and then he mentions the New World.

Notice how long, not to mention how vague, this version is. It doesn't really distinguish between important and unimportant information – everything gets mushed in together, and frankly it doesn't make a lot of sense. This summary gives us exactly zero help in terms of figuring out the main point. It also wastes *colossal* amounts of time.

This is not what you want to do.

Argument Summary:

New evidence shows the first inhabitants of the Americas were NOT Clovis people.

Notice how this version just hits the big idea and omits the details. All the details.

Argument Summary in super-condensed SAT terms:

New: CP ≠ 1st/ Ams.

Now notice how this version cuts out absolutely everything in order to focus on the absolute essentials. It doesn't even attempt to incorporate any sort of detail beyond the subject of the passage (Clovis People) and the "so what?" (they weren't the first people in the Americas).

So in just four words and a number, we've captured the essential information *without wasting any time.*

Point of a Paragraph

As mentioned earlier, the point of a paragraph is most likely to be located in two places: the **first (topic) sentence**, whose purpose is to state the point, or the **last sentence**, which often – but not always – serves to reiterate the point. While secondary points may be introduced in between, the body of a paragraph typically provides details or evidence to support the point.

For example, consider the following paragraph, which follows this pattern:

Sometimes it seems surprising that science functions at all. In 2005, medical science was shaken by a paper with the provocative title "Why most published research findings are false." Written by John
5 Ioannidis, a professor of medicine at Stanford University, it didn't actually show that any particular result was wrong. Instead, it showed that the statistics of reported positive findings were not consistent with how often one should *expect* to find them. **As Ioannidis concluded more**
10 **recently, "many published research findings are false or exaggerated, and an estimated 85 percent of research resources are wasted."**

The first sentence serves to introduce the main point, and the last sentence serves to reinforce it. The information in between expands on the original claim, explaining just what the author means by the assertion *Sometimes it seems surprising that science functions at all.*

Let's look at another example:

Conservationists have historically been at odds with the people who inhabit wildernesses. During the last half of the 20th century, millions of indigenous people were ousted from their homelands to establish
5 nature sanctuaries free of humans. Most succumbed to malnutrition, disease and exploitation. Such outcomes— coupled with the realization that indigenous groups usually help to stabilize ecosystems by, for instance, keeping fire at bay—have convinced major conservation
10 groups to take local human concerns into account. The World Wildlife Fund (WWF) now describes indigenous peoples as "natural allies," and the Nature Conservancy pledges to seek their "free, informed and prior" consent to projects impacting their territories.

Here, again, the topic sentence tells us what the paragraph will be about: the conflict between conservationists and the people who inhabit the lands those conservationist seek to protect. In this case, however, the last sentence does not merely reiterate the topic but rather moves it in a new direction, describing a possible solution to the conflict described in the paragraph.

On the next page, we're going to look at a full-length passage.

This passage is adapted from from Kristin Sainani, "What, Me Worry?" © 2014, *Stanford Magazine*.

According to a 2013 national survey by the American Psychological Association, the average stress level among adults is 5.1 on a scale of 10; that's one and a half points above what the
5 respondents judged to be healthy. Two-thirds of people say managing stress is important, and nearly that proportion had attempted to reduce their stress in the previous five years. Yet only a little over a third say they succeeded at doing so. More discouraging, teens
10 and young adults are experiencing higher levels of stress, and also are struggling to manage it.

"Stress has a very bad reputation. It's in pretty bad shape, PR-wise," acknowledges Firdaus Dhabhar, an associate professor of psychiatry and behavioral science
15 at Stanford. "And justifiably so," he adds.

Much of what we know about the physical and mental toll of chronic stress stems from seminal work by Robert Sapolsky beginning in the late 1970s. Sapolsky, a neuroendocrinologist, was among the first
20 to make the connection that the hormones released during the fight-or-flight response—the ones that helped our ancestors avoid becoming dinner—have deleterious effects when the stress is severe and sustained. Especially insidious, chronic exposure to
25 one of these hormones, cortisol, causes brain changes that make it increasingly difficult to shut the stress response down.

But take heart: Recent research paints a different portrait of stress, one in which it indeed has a positive
30 **side.** "There's good stress, there's tolerable stress, and there's toxic stress," says Bruce McEwen of Rockefeller University, an expert on stress and the brain who trained both Sapolsky and Dhabhar.

Situations we typically perceive as stressful—a
35 confrontation with a co-worker, the pressure to perform, a to-do list that's too long—are not the toxic type of stress that's been linked to serious health issues such as cardiovascular disease, autoimmune disorders, severe depression and cognitive impairment.
40 Short bouts of this sort of everyday stress can actually be a good thing: Just think of the exhilaration of the deadline met or the presentation crushed, the triumph of holding it all together. And, perhaps not surprisingly, it turns out that beating yourself up about
45 being stressed is counterproductive, as worrying about the negative consequences can in itself exacerbate any ill effects.

When Dhabhar was starting his graduate work in McEwen's lab in the early 1990s, "the absolutely
50 overwhelming dogma was that stress suppresses immunity." But this didn't make sense to him from an evolutionary perspective. If a lion is chasing you, he reasoned, your immune system should be ramping up, readying itself to heal torn flesh. It occurred to Dhabhar
55 that the effects of acute stress, which lasts minutes to hours, might differ from the effects of chronic stress, which lasts days to years.

Dhabhar likens the body's immune cells to soldiers. Because their levels in the blood plummet during acute
60 stress, "people used to say: 'See, stress is bad for you; your immune system's depressed,'" he says. "But most immune battles are not going to be fought in the blood." He suspected that the immune cells were instead traveling to the body's "battlefields"—sites most likely
65 to be wounded in an attack, like the skin, gut and lungs. In studies where rats were briefly confined (a short-term stressor), he showed that after an initial surge of immune cells into the bloodstream, they quickly exited the blood and took up positions precisely where he predicted they
70 would.

"His work was a pioneering demonstration of how important the difference is between acute and chronic stress," says Sapolsky, a professor of biology, neurology, and neurological sciences and neurosurgery.
75 "Overwhelmingly, the bad health effects of stress are those of chronic stress."

This strategic deployment of immune cells can speed wound healing, enhance vaccine effectiveness and potentially fight cancer. In 2009, Dhabhar's team
80 showed that knee surgery patients with robust immune redistribution following the stress of surgery recovered significantly faster and had better knee function a year later than those with a more sluggish mobilization. In other studies, volunteers who exercised or took a math
85 test (both acute stressors) immediately prior to being vaccinated had a heightened antibody response relative to volunteers who sat quietly. And in 2010, the researchers curbed the development of skin cancer in UV-exposed mice by stressing them before their
90 sunlamp sessions. **Dhabhar speculates that giving cancer patients low-dose injections of stress hormones might help prime their immune systems to fight the cancer. "It may not work out, but if it did, the benefits could be tremendous," he says.**

> Reiteration of
> Main Point

Although the author states the main point very clearly, you could simplify it further by writing something like "AS = GOOD!" ("acute stress is good"). Or, if you wanted to give more detail: "CS = bad, AS = good" ("chronic stress is bad, acute stress is good).

That information would come in handy if you encountered the following question:

1

What is the author's main point about stress?

A) It is more pervasive today than it was in earlier periods.
B) It can sometimes have beneficial effects.
C) It has been linked to a variety of ailments.
D) It can have a detrimental impact on personal relationships.

Acute stress GOOD = beneficial effects. All the correct answer does is take the very simple language of our main point and rephrase it in a moderately more sophisticated way.

So although you may have some difficulty "translating" the specific wording of the passage into the more abstract phrasing of the answer choices, your task will be far more difficult if you're not sure what idea you're looking for in the first place.

If, on the other hand, you simply understand the passage as a mass of details, you'll be much more likely to opt for an answer that mentions a word or phrase you remember from the passage but that doesn't actually capture the big picture.

Old Idea vs. New Idea

The "old idea" vs. "new idea" template is one of the most important concepts necessary for making sense out of SAT social science and science passages. It can essentially be summed up as "people used to believe *x*, but now they believe *y*." Authors using this model typically devote the first paragraph or two to discussing a traditionally accepted idea or theory, then shift to explaining why that theory is wrong and why a new theory – the theory that scientists or other researchers now believe – is actually correct.

Although authors will sometimes state flat-out that a particular idea is wrong, in other cases they will be less direct. They'll imply skepticism by putting particular words or phrases in quotation marks, or ask rhetorical questions such as *but is this really the case?* When the shift to the "new idea" occurs, you must pay close attention to that place because **the result or theory discussed will almost certainly be the point of the passage**. In some cases, opposing arguments or potential objections to the theory (counterarguments) will be discussed later in the passage, but in general, authors tend to stick to discussing "new ideas" once they've transitioned to them.

The following list provides some common phrases that signal when authors are discussing old vs. new ideas:

Old Idea

- Some/Many/Most people (scientists, researchers) believe...
- It is commonly thought that...
- Accepted/conventional wisdom holds that...
- In the past/For decades/Traditionally it was believed that...

New Idea

- However, But in fact, In reality...
- But is it really true/the case that...?
- It now seems (clear)/Researchers now think that...
- Recently, it has been found that...
- New research/evidence shows/suggests that...
- Another possibility is that...

As you read, it's up to you to keep track of what the old vs. new ideas are, and why they are false vs. true. **Don't rely on your memory: underline the information in the passage and mark it with a huge arrow or star, or summarize it yourself.** You may remember things up to a point, but if you don't make the key ideas clear for yourself, sooner or later you're likely to get confused and choose an answer that's exactly the opposite of the correct one.

Using the "Old Idea" to Predict Main Point and Attitude

One of the reasons that it is so crucial you be able to recognize the types of the phrases that signal "old ideas" is that those phrases often allow you to identify the point of the passage *before the author even states it.*

Think of it this way: if the introduction of a passage includes a sentence with the words *Many people think...*, that's an absolute giveaway that the idea that follows has been discredited (or at least strongly called into question), and that the scientists discussed in the passage will have a negative attitude toward that idea. Moreover, you can infer that the "new idea" – the one toward which scientists in the passage have a positive attitude – will be roughly the opposite. So from one sentence, it is possible to predict the main point AND the likely attitude in various parts of the passage.

Note: In earlier versions of *The Critical Reader*, I presented this framework in terms of the "They Say/I Say" model developed by Gerald Graff and Cathy Birkenstein in their book of the same name. I have chosen to eliminate that discussion in this edition because the passages used on the redesigned SAT are more straightforward and less nuanced, and thus less aligned with the type of reading Graff and Birkenstein discuss. I do, however, still strongly recommend their book as a superb aid for the transition to college-level reading and writing.

You should always keep reading just to make sure, but once you've confirmed that the author does in fact hold the view that the introduction suggests, you can often skim through much of the body of the passage. For example, consider a passage that begins this way:

> **Some scientists conclude** that music's influence may
> be a chance event, arising from its ability to hijack brain
> systems built for other purposes such as language, emotion
> and movement.

The phrase *some scientists conclude* is the equivalent of a flashing red signal indicating that the researchers discussed in the passage **disagree** with the idea that music's influence is a "chance event." We can very reasonably assume that these researchers believe music's influence is **not** a chance event, and that the remainder of the passage will explain why that is the case.

Some passages will also present the "old idea" a bit more subtly. For example:

> The Amazon Kindle—a "new and improved" version
> of which has just been released—comes on like a technology
> for our times: crisp, affordable, hugely capacious, capable of
> connecting to the Internet, and green. **How could one argue**
> 5 **with any of that?** Or with the idea that it will make the reading
> of texts once again seductive, using the same technology that
> has drawn people away from the page back to it.

Although this example is somewhat subtler than the previous, there are a couple of clues. First, the quotation marks in the first line imply **skepticism** (not everyone believes that the Kindle is actually new and improved). Second, the rhetorical question *How could one argue with any of that?* in lines 4-5 implies that author's answer is, *Well actually, some people* can *argue with that – and I'm going to tell you what they say.*

As a general rule, the presence of a contradictor such as *however* or *but* signals the transition from the old to the new idea. This shift typically occurs somewhere in the first or second paragraph, and usually no later than the beginning of the third paragraph. Whenever one of those words appears, you need to pay special attention to it. Not only will it provide important information about how the passage is structured, but it will also tell you where in the passage to focus because **the main idea will typically be stated after that transition**.

Look at the passage on the next page: it's a classic example of this kind of structure. We've looked at it before, but now we're going to look at it in a slightly different way.

If you simply scan the passage without really reading it, you should be able to spot the word *but* in line 11. That single word suggests that everything before it will have something to do with the old model (wrong), and that everything after it will have something to do with the new model (right). Sure enough, that's exactly how the passage works. Key phrases are underlined.

Sometime near the end of the Pleistocene, a band of people left northeastern Asia, crossed the Bering land bridge when the sea level was low, entered Alaska and became the first Americans. Since the
5 1930s, archaeologists have thought these people were members of the Clovis culture. First discovered in New Mexico in the 1930s, the Clovis culture is known for its distinct stone tools, primarily fluted projectile points. For decades, Clovis artifacts were the oldest
10 known in the New World, dating to 13,000 years ago. **But in recent years, researchers have found more and more evidence that people were living in North and South America before the Clovis.**

The most recently confirmed evidence comes from
15 **Washington. During a dig conducted from 1977 to 1979, researchers uncovered a bone projectile point stuck in a mastodon rib. Since then, the age of the find has been debated, but recently anthropologist Michael Waters and his colleagues announced a new**
20 **radiocarbon date for the rib: 13,800 years ago, making it 800 years older than the oldest Clovis artifact. Other pre-Clovis evidence comes from a variety of locations across the New World.**

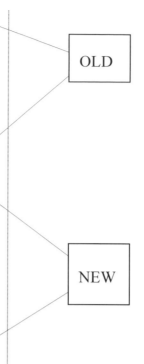

OLD

NEW

In order to avoid confusion, jot down for yourself the "old idea" and the "new idea." And by "jot down," I mean scribble in shorthand – you don't get points for neatness, and it should take you a few seconds at most.

O = CP 1st NA   (Clovis people first in North America)
N = Ppl in NA pre-CP   (People were in North America before Clovis)

If you are concerned that writing these things down will take too much time, just label them in the passage as is done above. But either way, **you must remember to look back at your notes!** I've witnessed many students underline the sentence where an answer was located but still get the question wrong because they forgot to look back at what they'd written.

Now let's look at a question:

1

The reference to the bone projectile point (line 16) serves primarily to

A) provide support for the claim that the Americas were inhabited before the Clovis arrived.

B) describe a tool used by prehistoric people in the Americas.

C) suggest that the Clovis people arrived in the Americas earlier than previously thought.

D) emphasize the difficulty of life during the Pleistocene era.

What's the author's point (i.e., claim)? That the Clovis People were NOT the first people to inhabit the Americas (OR: there were people in the Americas BEFORE the Clovis People).

We learn later in the passage the projectile point was dated at 13,800 years old but that the Clovis People arrived only 13,000 years ago. The author is therefore mentioning the projectile point as *evidence* that people inhabited the Americas before 13,000 years ago, i.e., before the Clovis People arrived. So the answer is A).

If you didn't have the main point straight, you could easily pick C), which is just a little bit off. It's not that the Clovis **themselves** arrived earlier than previously thought – it's that **another group** arrived before the Clovis.

Notice that the details of the line in question are borderline irrelevant: it doesn't matter if you know anything about projectile points and mastodons. All that counts is your ability to understand the importance of those details in context of the larger argument. If you understand the argument, you can see how the details fit; if you miss the argument, you'll have to start all over again with each new question.

In the passage on the following page, references to the "old idea" (conventional marketing wisdom) are underlined, and references to the "new idea" (what the author and his colleagues think) are in bold.

Notice that the author jumps back and forth between discussing these two viewpoints, using the transition *but* to signal that he is shifting from old to new. In longer passages, this type of switching is not unheard of. In such cases, you must read carefully in order to make sure you do not confuse the two.

This passage is adapted from Barry Schwartz, "More Isn't Always Better," © 2006 by *Harvard Business Review*.

Marketers assume that the more choices they offer, the more likely customers will be able to find just the right thing. They assume, for instance, that offering 50 styles of jeans instead of two increases the chances that
5 shoppers will find a pair they really like. **Nevertheless, research now shows that there can be too much choice; when there is, consumers are less likely to buy anything at all, and if they do buy, they are less satisfied with their selection.**

10 It all began with jam. In 2000, psychologists Sheena Iyengar and Mark Lepper published a remarkable study. On one day, shoppers at an upscale food market saw a display table with 24 varieties of gourmet jam. Those who sampled the spreads received a coupon for $1 off
15 any jam. On another day, shoppers saw a similar table, except that only six varieties of the jam were on display. The large display attracted more interest than the small one. **But when the time came to purchase, people who saw the large display were one-tenth as likely to buy as
20 people who saw the small display.**

**Other studies have confirmed this result that more choice is not always better. As the variety of snacks, soft drinks, and beers offered at convenience stores increases, for instance, sales volume and customer
25 satisfaction decrease. Moreover, as the number of retirement investment options available to employees increases, the chance that they will choose any decreases. These studies and others have shown not only that excessive choice can produce "choice
30 paralysis," but also that it can reduce people's satisfaction with their decisions, even if they made good ones. My colleagues and I have found that increased choice decreases satisfaction with matters as trivial as ice cream flavors and as significant as jobs.**

35 These results challenge what we think we know about human nature and the determinants of well-being. Both psychology and business have operated on the assumption that the relationship between choice and well-being is straightforward: The more choices people
40 have, the better off they are. In psychology, the benefits of choice have been tied to autonomy and control. In business, the benefits of choice have been tied to the benefits of free markets more generally. Added options make no one worse off, and they are bound to make
45 someone better off.

Choice *is* good for us, but its relationship to satisfaction appears to be more complicated than we had assumed. There is diminishing marginal utility in having alternatives; each new option subtracts a little

50 **from the feeling of well-being, until the marginal benefits of added choice level off. What's more, psychologists and business academics alike have largely ignored another outcome of choice: More of it requires increased time and effort and can lead to
55 anxiety, regret, excessively high expectations, and self-blame if the choices don't work out. When the number of available options is small, these costs are negligible, but the costs grow with the number of options. Eventually, each new option makes us feel
60 worse off than we did before.**

Without a doubt, having more options enables us, most of the time, to achieve better objective outcomes. Again, having 50 styles of jeans as opposed to two increases the likelihood that customers will find a pair
65 that fits. **But the subjective outcome may be that shoppers will feel overwhelmed and dissatisfied. This dissociation between objective and subjective results creates a significant challenge for retailers and marketers that look to choice as a way to enhance the
70 perceived value of their goods and services.**

**Choice can no longer be used to justify a marketing strategy in and of itself. More isn't always better, either for the customer or for the retailer. Discovering how much assortment is warranted is a
75 considerable empirical challenge. But companies that get the balance right will be amply rewarded.**

Fiction Passages: What if the Main Point Isn't Obvious?

Because fiction passages are not based on arguments but instead revolve around characters' actions/reactions and relationships, their "main points" can be more challenging. Furthermore, most passages are altered to fit into 85 or so lines, and the edits can sometimes be awkward. Add that to the lack of context, and it's no wonder that figuring out just what is happening can be a challenge.

Regardless of how faithful they are to the original, however, fiction passages typically focus on a specific situation, character trait, or relationship. **You can also think of the point as an extremely condensed (4-6 word) summary of the passage** – it answers the question "what is this passage about?" In fact, most fiction passages will be accompanied by a summary question, so if you've already summarized the passage for yourself, you'll have far less work to do and may be able to jump to the answer immediately.

As is true for all other types of passages, you should pay careful attention to major transitions, unusual punctuation, and strong language because they will virtually always appear at key places in the passage.

You should also pay particular attention to the places where important information is likely to appear: the introduction will present the character(s) and the general scenario, and the conclusion will reiterate the essential information that the author wants to convey about them.

If you are a very strong reader who is capable of getting the gist of a passage from a limited number of places, you may be able to skim through larger sections the same way you would in a natural or social science passage.

That said, fiction passages are often structured more unpredictably than non-fiction passages, and **you may need to read larger sections of fiction passages more closely**, trying to get a sense of who's involved and what they want (or don't want) while being careful not to waste too much time on unfamiliar or confusing language.

In addition, you should be careful to consider only the information provided by the author and not attempt to speculate about any larger meaning. What counts is your ability to understand the literal events of the passage and how they are conveyed by specific words and phrases. That's it. If you do go looking for some larger symbolism or start to make assumptions not explicitly supported by the passage, you can easily lose sight of the basics. In fact, most people have problems with passages like these not because there's a profound interpretation that can only be perceived through some mystical process, but rather because they aren't sufficiently *literal*.

On the next page, we're going to look at an example. The passage is divided into two sections. As you read, think about why the division occurs where it does.

The following passage is adapted from the novel
Summer by Edith Wharton, originally published in 1917.

   The hours of the Hatchard Memorial librarian were
from three to five; and Charity Royall's sense of duty
usually kept her at her desk until nearly half-past four.
But she had never perceived that any practical
5 advantage thereby accrued either to North Dormer or to
herself; and she had no scruple in decreeing, when it
suited her, that the library should close an hour earlier.
A few minutes after Mr. Harney's departure she formed
this decision, put away her lace, fastened the shutters,
10 and turned the key in the door of the temple of
knowledge. The street upon which she emerged was
still empty: and after glancing up and down it she began
to walk toward her house. But instead of entering she
passed on, turned into a field-path and mounted to a
15 pasture on the hillside.
   She let down the bars of the gate, followed a trail
along the crumbling wall of the pasture, and walked on
till she reached a knoll where a clump of larches shook
out their fresh tassels to the wind. There she lay down
20 on the slope, tossed off her hat and hid her face in the
grass. She was blind and insensible to many things, and
dimly knew it; but to all that was light and air, perfume
and color, every drop of blood in her responded. She
loved the roughness of the dry mountain grass under
25 her palms, the smell of the thyme into which she crushed
her face, the fingering of the wind in her hair and
through her cotton blouse, and the creak of the larches
as they swayed to it.
   She often climbed up the hill and lay there alone for
30 the mere pleasure of feeling the wind and of rubbing her
cheeks in the grass. Generally at such times she did not
think of anything, but lay immersed in an inarticulate
well-being. Today the sense of well-being was
intensified by her joy at escaping from the library. She
35 liked well enough to have a friend drop in and talk to
her when she was on duty, but she hated to be bothered
about books. How could she remember where they
were, when they were so seldom asked for? Orma Fry
occasionally took out a novel, and her brother Ben was
40 fond of what he called "jography," and of books
relating to trade and bookkeeping; but no one else asked
for anything except, at intervals, "Uncle Tom's Cabin,"
or "Opening of a Chestnut Burr," or Longfellow. She
had these under her hand, and could have found them
45 in the dark; but unexpected demands came so rarely
that they exasperated her like an injustice....

She had liked the young man's looks, and his short-
sighted eyes, and his odd way of speaking, that was abrupt
yet soft, just as his hands were sun-burnt and sinewy, yet

50 with smooth nails like a woman's. His hair was
sunburnt-looking too, or rather the colour of bracken
after frost; eyes grey, with the appealing look of the
shortsighted, his smile shy yet confident, as if he knew
lots of things she had never dreamed of, and yet
55 wouldn't for the world have had her feel his superiority.
But she did feel it, and liked the feeling; for it was new
to her. Poor and ignorant as she was, and knew herself
to be—humblest of the humble even in North Dormer,
where to come from the Mountain was the worst
60 disgrace—yet in her narrow world she had always ruled.
It was partly, of course, owing to the fact that lawyer
Royall was "the biggest man in North Dormer"; so
much too big for it, in fact, that outsiders, who didn't
know, always wondered how it held him. In spite of
65 everything—and in spite even of Miss Hatchard—
lawyer Royall ruled in North Dormer; and Charity ruled
in lawyer Royall's house. She had never put it to herself
in those terms; but she knew her power. Confusedly,
the young man in the library had made her feel for
70 the first time what might be the sweetness of
dependence. She sat up and looked down on the house
where she held sway.

If you're not sure how to determine the "point" of a fiction passage like this, don't worry. We're going to break it down.

Even if fiction passages do not contain arguments, they can often be divided into sections – usually no more than two or three. This passage can be divided into two basic parts:

1) Lines 1-46

In the first section, we are introduced to Charity Royall, the character on whom the passage focuses. We learn that she works as a librarian, that she dislikes her job, and that she's eager to escape from it. If we had to sum it up in a few words, we might say "Charity hates job." (If you're inclined to doodle, you could also write something like "Charity ☹ job.") This section contains a lot of description, so if you get the gist after a while, you can just skip down.

2) Lines 47-end

Sections change when new information is introduced or a shift in topic occurs. The introduction of a new character (the man) in line 47 indicates that a new section is beginning. This is where things start to get interesting. We learn that Charity is intrigued by the man and by the prospect of a different life that he represents, but we also learn that she "rules" in her house.

Taking both parts of the passage together, we thus have the central conflict: Charity is torn between her current life, part of which is unpleasant (she hates her job) and part of which is pleasant (she rules at home), and, the passage implies, the possibility of another life as the young man's wife. The first part of the passage thus serves to set up the second part – it explains why Charity would want her life to change.

The really, important part of the passage comes at the end. That's hardly a surprise because most **writing, even fiction, is usually structured so that the most important idea comes last**. What do we learn there? That Charity is *confused*. So a main point, we could put down something like: "Charity torn old/new life."

Note that this statement does not even try to cover all of the events. It simply states the **main conflict** the story is there to convey. It does not "interpret" anything – it simply condenses the information that is directly stated by the author. If we wanted to incorporate both parts of the passage into a main point, however, we could say:

C hates job BUT power at home, meets man → questions life

So to sum up: **if you find yourself confused, focus on the conclusion**, particularly the last few sentences. Don't waste time trying to figure out the relationship between the various parts of the passage if you're not sure upfront. If you understand the point of the conclusion, chances are that will be the point of the beginning as well. You can then use that information to answer various big-picture questions.

1

Which choice best summarizes the first two
paragraphs of the passage (lines 1-28)?

A) A woman who dislikes her job seeks solace
in nature.

B) A woman works hard at her job but is
persuaded to leave by a customer.

C) A woman feels overwhelmed by the demands
of her job and desires solitude in a library.

D) A woman spends a day in the wilderness to
avoid an unpleasant task.

2

Which choice provides the most accurate summary
of this passage?

A) A character is forced to make a momentous
decision after an unexpected meeting.

B) A character feels uncertain about her life
following a significant encounter.

C) A character holds great power at work
but feels powerless in her own home.

D) A character works hard at her job but is
persuaded to leave it by a man she meets.

Question #1:

The easiest way to answer this question is to use the main point. If you've written that
Charity hates her job, you can start by making an educated guess that A) is likely to be
correct. And in fact, A) describes precisely what happens in the first two paragraphs: Charity
dislikes her job and leaves it early one day to go sit on a grassy hill (=nature) and make
herself feel better (=seek solace).

If you haven't written the point, focus on the beginning of the first paragraph and the end of
the second. The first paragraph begins by describing Charity's decision to leave work, and
the second paragraph ends with her lying on a grassy hill. That sequence corresponds to A).

Question #2:

If you've written the main point, you've already gone most of the way toward the answer.
Basically, Charity is all torn up over the fact that she met this guy (=a significant encounter)
and now can't figure out what she wants (=feels uncertain). So the answer is B).

Be careful with A). Charity is thrown into confusion by her meeting with the young man, but
she isn't actually *forced* to make a "momentous decision." C) reverses the situation in the
passage: Charity is powerless at work, not at home. And D) is wrong because no one
persuades Charity to leave work.

Order of Events

You may also encounter questions that ask you to determine the sequence in which events discussed in a passage took place. Although having a solid big-picture understanding of the passage can help, that knowledge alone will not necessarily get you all the way to the answer.

The reason is that these questions are more likely to accompany passages that jump around in time – that is, passages that discuss events in an order different from the one in which they actually occurred. This is normally accomplished through the use of **flashback**, a technique in which an author describes an event or situation that occurred before the main action of the story.

For example, in the passage we've been looking at, the scene between Charity and the young man is introduced halfway through the passage; however, the event itself took place **before** the action of the passage itself, and Charity is simply remembering it during the passage.

Understanding that timeline would become very important if you encountered a question like this:

1

Which choice best describes the sequence of events described in this passage?

A) A woman dislikes her job and seeks solace in nature, where she reflects on a memorable encounter.

B) A woman works hard at her job but is persuaded to leave; she then returns home, where she interacts with another character.

C) A woman feels overwhelmed by the demands of her job and encounters a man with whom she spends the afternoon.

D) A woman has a significant encounter while at work, then leaves because she feels too conflicted to continue.

The most important thing to understand about a question like this is that it is not asking about the order in which events are discussed in the passage, but rather about the order in which the events actually took place.

If you're not clear about the fact that Charity's encounter with the man does **not** occur during the action of the passage, you might be tempted to choose either C) or D). A) is, however, the only answer that indicates that the encounter occurred before the time of the passage, so it is correct.

Supporting Examples: Working Backwards

Some questions will test your understanding of main points less directly. In fact, they will not explicitly ask about the main point at all. Rather, they'll test it "backwards," citing an example or list of examples and asking you to identify what point those items are used to support.

The correct answer will therefore restate either the point of a particular section or the point of the passage as a whole. Because **main points typically come <u>before</u> supporting examples, you should back up and read from at least a sentence before the line reference.** If you start at the line reference and keep going, you are likely to miss key information.

Let's look at an example:

Yogi Berra, the former Major League baseball catcher and coach, once remarked that you can't hit and think at the same time. Of course, since he also reportedly said, "I really didn't say everything I said,"
5 it is not clear we should take his statements at face value. Nonetheless, a widespread view — in both academic journals and the popular press — is that thinking about what you are doing, as you are doing it, interferes with performance. The idea is that once you
10 have developed the ability to play an arpeggio on the piano, putt a golf ball or parallel park, attention to what you are doing leads to inaccuracies, blunders and sometimes even utter paralysis. As the great choreographer George Balanchine would say to his
15 dancers, "Don't think, dear; just do."
   Perhaps you have experienced this destructive force yourself. Start thinking about just how to carry a full glass of water without spilling, and you'll end up drenched. How, exactly, do you initiate a telephone
20 conversation? Begin wondering, and before long, the recipient of your call will notice the heavy breathing and hang up. Our actions, the French philosopher Maurice Merleau-Ponty tells us, exhibit a "magical" efficacy, but when we focus on them, they degenerate
25 into the absurd. A 13-time winner on the Professional Golfers Association Tour, Dave Hill, put it like this: "You can't be thinking about the mechanics of the sport while you are performing."

1

The author mentions the "ability to play an arpeggio on the piano, putt a golf ball, or parallel park" (lines 10-12) as examples of actions that

A) require significant practice to master.
B) are best performed without conscious consideration.
C) can result in serious physical harm.
D) interfere with performance of more important tasks.

We're going to start with the sentence before the list – we know that it's important because it includes a set of dashes ("interesting" punctuation). What do we learn from that sentence? That according to a common viewpoint, *thinking about what you are doing, as you are doing it, interferes with performance.*

The examples that follow serve as examples of actions that become more difficult when they are performed with too much thought. In other words, they are actions that are performed better when undertaken "without conscious consideration." B) is thus correct.

Let's look at another example:

The following passage is adapted from Susan B. Anthony's Remarks to the Woman's Auxiliary Congress of the Public Press Congress, May 23, 1893.

Mrs. President and Sisters, I might almost say daughters—I cannot tell you how much joy has filled my heart as I have sat here listening to these papers and noting those characteristics that made each in its
5 own way beautiful and masterful. I would in no ways lessen the importance of these expressions by your various representatives, but I want to say that the words that specially voiced what I may call the up-gush of my soul were to be found in the paper read by Mrs. Swalm
10 on "The Newspaper as a Factor of Civilization." I have never been a pen artist and I have never succeeded with rhetorical flourishes unless it were by accident. But I have always admired supremely that which I could realize the least. The woman who can coin words and
15 ideas to suit me best would not be unlike Mrs. Swalm, and when I heard her I said: "That is worthy of Elizabeth Cady Stanton."

While I have been sitting here I have been thinking that we have made strides in journalism in the last forty
20 years. I recall the first time I ever wrote for a paper. The periodical was called the *Lily*. It was edited—and quite appropriately—by a Mrs. Bloomer. The next paper to which I contributed was the *Una*. These two journals were the only avenues women had through
20 which to face themselves in type to any extent worthy of note before the war. The press was as kind as it knew how to be. It meant well and did all for us it knew how to do. We couldn't ask it to do more than it knew how. But that was little enough and I tried an experiment
25 editing a newspaper myself. I started a paper and ran it for two years at a vast cost to every one concerned in it. I served seven years at lecturing to pay off the debt and interest on that paper and I considered myself fortunate to get off as easily as that.

1
The author uses the phrase "rhetorical flourishes" (line 12) as an example of

A) an accomplishment admired in women.
B) an outdated form of communication.
C) a skill at which she does not excel.
D) a task that she tried for many years to master.

The question asks what the phrase *rhetorical flourishes* is an **example** of, so it's telling us that the phrase is being used to support a **point**. Our job is to figure out what that point is.

The question refers to line 12, but we're going read the **entire sentence** in which the key phrase appears. The following sentence starts with an important transition, *but*, so we're going to read it as well.

What do we learn from those sentences? That rhetorical flourishes are something Anthony *never succeeded at unless it were by accident*. They're something she admires in other people, but that she has never been able to "realize" (that is, to achieve – note the second meaning!). In other words, she stinks at them, i.e., she does NOT excel. So the answer is C).

Main Point vs. Primary Purpose

Often, when students encounter questions asking about the primary purpose of a passage, they reiterate the main point, then become confused when an answer corresponding to it does not appear among the choices. Although the purpose and the point of the passage are related, sometimes directly and sometimes in ways that are less obvious, they are not precisely the same thing.

>**Main Point** – The primary **argument** the author is making. It is usually stated more or less directly in the passage, usually in the introduction and conclusion.

>**Primary Purpose** – The **rhetorical goal** of the passage as a whole (e.g., *explain, emphasize, question*). While the primary purpose is based on the overall passage, there is often a key sentence that will point to a particular answer.

For example, consider the following passage:

Chronic stress, it turns out, is extremely dangerous. While stress doesn't cause any single disease — in fact, the causal link between stress and ulcers has been largely disproved — it makes most diseases significantly worse.
5 The list of ailments connected to stress is staggeringly diverse and includes everything from the common cold and lower-back pain to Alzheimer's disease, major depressive disorder, and heart attack. Stress hollows out our bones and atrophies our muscles. It triggers adult-
10 onset diabetes and may also be connected to high blood pressure. In fact, numerous studies of human longevity in developed countries have found that psychosocial factors such as stress are the single most important variable in determining the length of a life. It's not that
15 genes and risk factors like smoking don't matter. It's that our levels of stress matter more.
   Furthermore, the effects of chronic stress directly counteract improvements in medical care and public health. Antibiotics, for instance, are far less effective
20 when our immune system is suppressed by stress; that fancy heart surgery will work only if the patient can learn to shed stress. As pioneering stress researcher Robert Sapolsky notes, "You can give a guy a drug-coated stent, but if you don't fix the stress problem, it
25 won't really matter. For so many conditions, stress is the major long-term risk factor. Everything else is a short-term fix."

1

The primary purpose of the passage is to

A) call attention to the harmful nature of a condition and describe some of its effects.

B) describe the results of a study and explain how its findings can be applied.

C) outline the history of an illness and point out its consequences for modern society.

D) discuss the results of Robert Sapolsky's research and its reception by the scientific community.

Main Point: Chronic stress = BAD. The very first sentence provides the point, and the rest of the passage serves to illustrate it with specific examples of the damage chronic stress can cause. That point corresponds exactly to A). We don't even need to check the other answers.

Now let's look back at the Wharton passage. We've already seen a question asking about the main point, but this time we're going to look at it in terms of overall purpose.

The following passage is adapted from the novel *Summer* by Edith Wharton, initially published in 1917.

The hours of the Hatchard Memorial librarian were from three to five; and Charity Royall's sense of duty usually kept her at her desk until nearly half-past four. But she had never perceived that any practical
5 advantage thereby accrued either to North Dormer or to herself; and she had no scruple in decreeing, when it suited her, that the library should close an hour earlier. A few minutes after Mr. Harney's departure she formed this decision, put away her lace, fastened the shutters,
10 and turned the key in the door of the temple of knowledge. The street upon which she emerged was still empty: and after glancing up and down it she began to walk toward her house. But instead of entering she passed on, turned into a field-path and mounted to a
15 pasture on the hillside.

She let down the bars of the gate, followed a trail along the crumbling wall of the pasture, and walked on till she reached a knoll where a clump of larches shook out their fresh tassels to the wind. There she lay down
20 on the slope, tossed off her hat and hid her face in the grass. She was blind and insensible to many things, and dimly knew it; but to all that was light and air, perfume and color, every drop of blood in her responded. She loved the roughness of the dry mountain grass under
25 her palms, the smell of the thyme into which she crushed her face, the fingering of the wind in her hair and through her cotton blouse, and the creak of the larches as they swayed to it.

She often climbed up the hill and lay there alone for
30 the mere pleasure of feeling the wind and of rubbing her cheeks in the grass. Generally at such times she did not think of anything, but lay immersed in an inarticulate well-being. Today the sense of well-being was intensified by her joy at escaping from the library. She
35 liked well enough to have a friend drop in and talk to her when she was on duty, but she hated to be bothered about books. How could she remember where they were, when they were so seldom asked for? Orma Fry occasionally took out a novel, and her brother Ben was
40 fond of what he called "jography," and of books relating to trade and bookkeeping; but no one else asked for anything except, at intervals, "Uncle Tom's Cabin," or "Opening of a Chestnut Burr," or Longfellow. She had these under her hand, and could have found them
45 in the dark; but unexpected demands came so rarely that they exasperated her like an injustice…

She had liked the young man's looks, and his short-sighted eyes, and his odd way of speaking, that was abrupt yet soft, just as his hands were sun-burnt and sinewy,
50 with smooth nails like a woman's. His hair was sunburnt-looking too, or rather the colour of bracken after frost; eyes grey, with the appealing look of the shortsighted, his smile shy yet confident, as if he knew lots of things she had never dreamed of, and yet
55 wouldn't for the world have had her feel his superiority. But she did feel it, and liked the feeling; for it was new to her. Poor and ignorant as she was, and knew herself to be—humblest of the humble even in North Dormer, where to come from the Mountain was the worst
60 disgrace—yet in her narrow world she had always ruled. It was partly, of course, owing to the fact that lawyer Royall was "the biggest man in North Dormer"; so much too big for it, in fact, that outsiders, who didn't know, always wondered how it held him. In spite of
65 everything—and in spite even of Miss Hatchard— lawyer Royall ruled in North Dormer; and Charity ruled in lawyer Royall's house. She had never put it to herself in those terms; but she knew her power. **Confusedly, the young man in the library had made her feel for**
70 **the first time what might be the sweetness of dependence. She sat up and looked down on the house where she held sway.**

1

The primary purpose of the passage is to

A) illustrate a family's daily life in a small town.

B) describe how a significant encounter causes a character to reevaluate her life.

C) call attention to the difference between a character's public and private behavior.

D) explain the influence of books on a main character's daily life.

If you encounter a "purpose of a passage" question right after you've finished reading the passage, your immediate thought might be, "Oh no, I was so focused on trying to get what was going on in the passage that I wasn't really thinking about the purpose. You mean now I have to go back and reread the whole thing so that I can figure it out?" Either that, or you might be inclined to leave that question for last, working through the detail-based questions first and using them to figure out the big picture.

Leaving a big-picture question for the end is certainly a fair strategy if you find it helpful (rereading an entire passage for the sake of a single question is a very bad idea), but if you get a good sense of the passage the first time you read it, you should be able to handle these questions upfront.

Even though this question asks about the purpose rather than the point, we need to start by reiterating the "point:"

C hates job BUT power at home, meets man → questions life (Charity hates her job even though she's powerful at home, but then she meets a guy and starts to question what she really wants.)

Or: **C unhappy but unsure/change**

Or: **What does C want?**

Or even just: **C = confused**

As discussed earlier, the most important part of the passage is the end of the conclusion, and it gives us pretty much all the information we need.

The correct answer is basically going to tell us that the purpose of the passage is to describe this girl who meets a guy and realizes that she doesn't know what the heck she wants. That's pretty much what B) says. It just phrases it from a slightly different angle and with more general wording. Charity's meeting with the man is "a significant encounter." We know it's significant because it causes her to start wondering what she really wants.

Otherwise, A) is wrong because the passage focuses on a single character, not a family; C) is wrong because the passage doesn't really tell us much about Charity's behavior at all – the focus is on her thoughts and feelings. Her interactions with other characters are mentioned, and she's certainly alone for a good portion of the passage, but Wharton does not go out of her way to call the reader's attention to any difference in how she *acts* in those two situations. D) is just plain wrong – the passage makes it clear that Charity can't stand her job at the library. There's also nothing to suggest that books themselves have influenced her daily life (for good or bad), only that she dislikes working with them.

The Big Picture Exercises

1.   To understand what the new software—that is, analytics—can do that's different from more familiar software like spreadsheets, word processing, and graphics, consider the lowly photograph. Here the
5 relevant facts aren't how many bytes constitute a digital photograph, or a billion of them. That's about as instructive as counting the silver halide molecules used to form a single old-fashioned print photo. The important feature of a digital image's bytes is that, unlike
10 crystalline molecules, they are uniquely easy to store, transport, and manipulate with software. In the first era of digital images, people were fascinated by the convenience and malleability (think PhotoShop) of capturing, storing, and sharing pictures. Now, instead of
15 using software to manage photos, we can mine features of the bytes that make up the digital image. Facebook can, without privacy invasion, track where and when, for example, vacationing is trending, since digital images reveal at least that much. But more importantly, those
20 data can be cross-correlated, even in real time, with seemingly unrelated data such as local weather, interest rates, crime figures, and so on. Such correlations associated with just one photograph aren't revealing. But imagine looking at billions of photos over weeks,
25 months, years, then correlating them with dozens of directly related data sets (vacation bookings, air traffic), tangential information (weather, interest rates, unemployment), or orthogonal information (social or political trends). With essentially free super-computing,
30 we can mine and usefully associate massive, formerly unrelated data sets and unveil all manner of economic, cultural, and social realities.
     For science fiction aficionados, Isaac Asimov anticipated the idea of using massive data sets to predict
35 human behavior, coining it "psychohistory" in his 1951 Foundation trilogy. The bigger the data set, Asimov said then, the more predictable the future. With big-data analytics, one can finally see the forest, instead of just the capillaries in the tree leaves. Or to put it in more
40 accurate terms, one can see beyond the apparently random motion of a few thousand molecules of air inside a balloon; one can see the balloon itself, and beyond that, that it is inflating, that it is yellow, and that it is part of a bunch of balloons en route to a birthday party. The
45 data/software world has, until now, been largely about looking at the molecules inside one balloon.

1

The main idea of the passage is that

A) Bytes have allowed people to capture and edit images in innovative ways.

B) New forms of technology allow users' activities to be tracked without violating privacy.

C) Recent developments in technology have transformed the way data is acquired and analyzed.

D) Modern technology was described in science fiction novels long before it was invented.

2

The author's central claim in the second paragraph is that

A) The predictions of science fiction writers tend to be more accurate than those of scientists.

B) All human behavior can be understood through the use of massive data sets.

C) Technological innovation is often inspired by the natural world.

D) Data sets will reveal unforeseen relationships between large-scale phenomena.

2. This passage is adapted from Jamaica Kincaid, *Annie John*, © 1985 Farrar, Straus and Giroux. The protagonist is a girl growing up in the Caribbean.

It was the first day of a new term, Miss Nelson said, so we would not be attending to any of our usual subjects; instead, we were to spend the morning in contemplation and reflection and writing something she
5 described as an "autobiographical essay." In the afternoon, we would read aloud to each other our auto-biographical essays. (I knew quite well about "autobiography" and "essay," but reflection and contemplation! A day at school spent in such a way!
10 Of course, in most books all the good people were always contemplating and reflecting before they did anything. Perhaps in her mind's eye she could see our future and, against all prediction, we turned out to be good people.) On hearing this, a huge sigh went up
15 from the girls.

Half the sighs were in happiness at the thought of sitting and gazing off into clear space, the other half in unhappiness at the misdeeds that would have to go unaccomplished. I joined the happy half, because I
20 knew it would please Miss Nelson, and, my own selfish interest aside, I liked so much the way she wore her ironed hair and her long-sleeved blouse and box-pleated skirt that I wanted to please her.

The morning was uneventful enough: a girl
25 spilled ink from her inkwell all over her uniform; a girl broke her pen nib and then made a big to-do about replacing it; girls twisted and turned in their seats and pinched each other's bottoms; girls passed notes to each other. All this Miss Nelson must have seen and
30 heard, but she didn't say anything—only kept reading her book: an elaborately illustrated edition of *The Tempest*, as later, passing by her desk, I saw. Midway in the morning, we were told to go out and stretch our legs and breathe some fresh air for a few minutes;
35 when we returned, we were given glasses of cold lemonade and a slice of bun to refresh us.

As soon as the sun stood in the middle of the sky, we were sent home for lunch. The earth may have grown an inch or two larger between the time I had
40 walked to school that morning and the time I went home to lunch, for some girls made a small space for me in their little band. But I couldn't pay much attention to them; my mind was on my new surroundings, my new teacher, what I had written in my nice new
45 notebook with its black-all-mixed-up-with-white cover and smooth lined pages (so glad was I to get rid of my old notebooks, which had on their covers a picture of a wrinkled-up woman wearing a crown on her head and a neckful and armfuls of diamonds and pearls—their
50 pages so coarse, as if they were made of cornmeal). I flew home. I must have eaten my food. By half past one, we were sitting under a flamboyant tree in a secluded part of our schoolyard, our auto-biographical essays in hand. We were about to read aloud what
55 we had written during our morning of contemplation and reflection. In response to Miss Nelson, each girl stood up and read her composition. One girl told of a much revered and loved aunt who now lived in England and of how much she looked forward to
60 one day moving to England to live with her aunt; one girl told of her brother studying medicine in Canada and the life she imagined he lived there (it seemed quite odd to me); one girl told of the fright she had when she dreamed she was dead, and of the matching
65 fright she had when she woke and found that she wasn't (everyone laughed at this, and Miss Nelson had to call us to order over and over); one girl told of how her oldest sister's best friend's cousin's best friend (it was a real rigmarole) had gone on a Girl Guide
70 jamboree held in Trinidad and met someone who millions of years ago had taken tea with Lady Baden-Powell; one girl told of an excursion she and her father had made to Redonda, and of how they had seen some booby birds tending their chicks. Things
75 went on in that way, all so playful, all so imaginative. I began to wonder about what I had written, for it was the opposite of playful and it was the opposite of imaginative. What I had written was heartfelt, and, except for the very end, it was all too true.

1

Which choice best summarizes the passage?

A) A character is apprehensive about attending new school but is reassured by her teacher.

B) A character is excited about attending a new school but struggles to make friends.

C) A character is eager to complete a school assignment but becomes anxious after observing her classmates' work.

D) A character admires her teacher but is disappointed by her teacher's reaction to her work.

The primary purpose of the passage is to

A) describe the interactions between a young girl and her peers.

B) recount a memorable episode in a young girl's life.

C) explain the influence of an important figure on a young girl's life.

D) explore the consequences of a young girl's decision.

3. The following passage is adapted from Olympe de Gouges, *Declaration of the Rights of Women*. It was initially published in 1791, during the French Revolution, and was written in response to the *Declaration of the Rights of Man* (1789).

Woman, wake up; the toxin of reason is being heard throughout the whole universe; discover your rights. The powerful empire of nature is no longer surrounded by prejudice, fanaticism, superstition, and
5 lies. The flame of truth has dispersed all the clouds of folly and usurpation. Enslaved man has multiplied his strength and needs recourse to yours to break his chains. Having become free, he has become unjust to his companion. Oh, women, women! When will you cease
10 to be blind? What advantage have you received from the Revolution? A more pronounced scorn, a more marked disdain. In the centuries of corruption you ruled only over the weakness of men. The reclamation of your patrimony, based on the wise decrees of nature –
15 what have you to dread from such a fine undertaking? Do you fear that our legislators, correctors of that morality, long ensnared by political practices now out of date, will only say again to you: women, what is there in common between you and us? Everything, you
20 will have to answer. If they persist in their weakness in putting this hypocrisy in contradiction to their principles, courageously oppose the force of reason to the empty pretensions of superiority; unite yourselves beneath the standards of philosophy; deploy all the
25 energy of your character. Regardless of what barriers confront you, it is in your power to free yourselves; you have only to want to. Let us pass not to the shocking tableau of what you have been in society; and since national education is in question at this moment, let us
30 see whether our wise legislators will think judiciously about the education of women.

Women have done more harm than good. Constraint and dissimulation have been their lot. What force has robbed them of, ruse returned to them; they had recourse
35 to all the resources of their charms, and the most irreproachable persons did not resist them. Poison and the sword were both subject to them; they commanded in crime as in fortune. The French government, especially, depended throughout the centuries on the nocturnal
40 administrations of women; the cabinet could keep no secrets as a result of their indiscretions; all have been subject to the cupidity and ambition of this sex, formerly contemptible and respected, and since the revolution, respectable and scorned.

45 In this sort of contradictory situation, what remarks could I not make! I have but a moment to make them, but this moment will fix the attention of the remotest posterity. Under the Old Regime, all was vicious, all was guilty; but could not the amelioration of
50 conditions be perceived even in the substance of vices? A woman only had to be beautiful or lovable; when she possessed these two advantages, she saw a hundred fortunes at her feet. If she did not profit from them, she had a bizarre character or a rare philosophy
55 which made her scorn wealth; then she was deemed to be like a crazy woman. A young, inexperienced woman, seduced by a man whom she loves, will abandon her parents to follow him; the ingrate will leave her after a few years, and the older she has
60 become with him, the more inhuman is his inconstancy; if she has children, he will likewise abandon them. If he is rich, he will consider himself excused from sharing his fortune with his noble victims. If some involvement binds him to his duties, he will
65 deny them, trusting that the laws will support him. If he is married, any other obligation loses its rights. Then what laws remain to extirpate vice all the way to its root? The law of dividing wealth and public administration between men and women. It can easily
70 be seen that one who is born into a rich family gains very much from such equal sharing. But the one born into a poor family with merit and virtue – what is her lot? Poverty and opprobrium. If she does not precisely excel in music or painting, she cannot be admitted to
75 any public function when she has all the capacity for it.

1

The central problem that the author describes in the second paragraph (lines 32-44) is that women

A) are encouraged by their husbands to secretly gather information.

B) have played a significant but unacknowledged role in political life.

C) have been responsible for undermining their own cause.

D) must play a more active role in civic life.

The author's main point in the passage is that

A) women and men must work together to improve conditions for women.

B) women must excel in the arts in order to gain approval from society.

C) women must unite to demand the rights that society has denied them.

D) women's lack of rights can be primarily attributed to government policies.

4. The following passage is adapted from Julian Jackson, "New Research Suggests Dinosaurs Were Warm-Blooded and Active" © 2011 by Julian Jackson.

New research from the University of Adelaide has added to the debate about whether dinosaurs were cold-blooded and sluggish or warm-blooded and active. Professor Roger Seymour from the University's School
5 of Earth & Environmental Sciences has applied the latest theories of human and animal anatomy and physiology to provide insight into the lives of dinosaurs.

Human thigh bones have tiny holes – known as the
10 "nutrient foramen" – on the shaft that supply blood to living bone cells inside. New research has shown that the size of those holes is related to the maximum rate that a person can be active during aerobic exercise. Professor Seymour has used this principle to evaluate
15 the activity levels of dinosaurs.

"Far from being lifeless, bone cells have a relatively high metabolic rate and they therefore require a large blood supply to deliver oxygen. On the inside of the bone, the blood supply comes usually from a single
20 artery and vein that pass through a hole on the shaft – the nutrient foramen," he says.

Professor Seymour wondered whether the size of the nutrient foramen might indicate how much blood was necessary to keep the bones in good repair. For
25 example, highly active animals might cause more bone 'microfractures,' requiring more frequent repairs by the bone cells and therefore a greater blood supply. "My aim was to see whether we could use fossil bones of dinosaurs to indicate the level of bone metabolic rate
30 and possibly extend it to the whole body's metabolic rate," he says. "One of the big controversies among paleobiologists is whether dinosaurs were cold-blooded and sluggish or warm-blooded and active. Could the size of the foramen be a possible gauge for dinosaur
35 metabolic rate?"

Comparisons were made with the sizes of the holes in living mammals and reptiles, and their metabolic rates. Measuring mammals ranging from mice to elephants, and reptiles from lizards to crocodiles, one
40 of Professor Seymour's Honors students, Sarah Smith, combed the collections of Australian museums, photographing and measuring hundreds of tiny holes in thigh bones.

"The results were unequivocal. The sizes of the holes
45 were related closely to the maximum metabolic rates during peak movement in mammals and reptiles," Professor Seymour says. "The holes found in mammals were about 10 times larger than those in reptiles."

These holes were compared to those of fossil
50 dinosaurs. Dr. Don Henderson, Curator of Dinosaurs from the Royal Tyrrell Museum in Alberta, Canada, and Daniela Schwarz-Wings from the Museum für Naturkunde Humboldt University Berlin, Germany measured the holes in 10 species of
55 dinosaurs from five different groups, including bipedal and quadrupedal carnivores and herbivores, weighing 50kg to 20,000kg.

"On a relative comparison to eliminate the differences in body size, all of the dinosaurs had
60 holes in their thigh bones larger than those of mammals," Professor Seymour says.

"The dinosaurs appeared to be even more active than the mammals. We certainly didn't expect to see that. These results provide additional weight to
65 theories that dinosaurs were warm-blooded and highly active creatures, rather than cold-blooded and sluggish."

Professor Seymour says following the results of this study, it's likely that a simple measurement of
70 foramen size could be used to evaluate maximum activity levels in other vertebrate animals.

1

The main purpose of the passage is to

A) Describe an experiment to resolve a scientific controversy and discuss its results.

B) Refute a commonly held belief about dinosaur behavior.

C) Compare the development of dinosaur bones to the development of mammal bones.

D) Explain how foramen size has been used to gauge activity levels in mammals.

Which of the following best summarizes the findings of Professor Seymour's study?

A) Foramen size can be used as a measure of growth rate in dinosaurs and other animals.

B) The density of dinosaurs' thigh bones conclusively proves that dinosaurs were warm-blooded.

C) The size of dinosaurs' foramens indicates that dinosaurs may have behaved more like mammals than like reptiles.

D) The size of the holes in the shafts of dinosaurs' thigh bones strongly suggests that dinosaurs were warm-blooded.

5. This passage is adapted from a 1950 speech by Dean Acheson, who served as Secretary of State from 1949 to 1953 and strongly influenced United States foreign policy during the Cold War.

However much we may sympathize with the Soviet citizens who for reasons bedded deep in history are obliged to live under it, we are not attempting to change the governmental or social structure of the Soviet
5 Union. The Soviet regime, however, has devoted a major portion of its energies and resources to the attempt to impose its system on other peoples. In this attempt it has shown itself prepared to resort to any method or stratagem, including subversion, threats, and even
10 military force.

Therefore, if the two systems are to coexist, some acceptable means must be found to free the world from the destructive tensions and anxieties of which it has been the victim in these past years and the continuance
15 of which can hardly be in the interests of any people.

I wish, therefore, to speak to you about those points of greatest difference which must be identified and sooner or later reconciled if the two systems are to live together, if not with mutual respect, at least in
20 reasonable security.

It is now nearly 5 years since the end of hostilities, and the victorious Allies have been unable to define the terms of peace with the defeated countries. This is a grave, a deeply disturbing fact. For our part, we do not
25 intend nor wish, in fact we do not know how, to create satellites. Nor can we accept a settlement which would make Germany, Japan, or liberated Austria satellites of the Soviet Union. The experience in Hungary, Rumania, and Bulgaria has been one of bitter disappointment and
30 shocking betrayal of the solemn pledges by the wartime Allies. The Soviet leaders joined in the pledge at Tehran that they looked forward "with confidence to the day when all peoples of the world may live free lives, untouched by tyranny, and according to their varying
35 desires and their own consciences." We can accept treaties of peace which would give reality to this pledge and to the interests of all in security.

With regard to the whole group of countries which we are accustomed to thinking of as the satellite area, the
40 Soviet leaders could withdraw their military and police force and refrain from using the shadow of that force to keep in power persons or regimes which do not command the confidence of the respective peoples, freely expressed through orderly representative processes.

45 In this connection, we do not insist that these governments have any particular political or social complexion. What concerns us is that they should be truly independent national regimes, with a will of their own and with a decent foundation in popular feeling.
50 The Soviet leaders could cooperate with us to the end that the official representatives of all countries are treated everywhere with decency and respect and that an atmosphere is created in which these representatives could function in a normal and helpful manner,
55 conforming to the accepted codes of diplomacy.

These are some of the things which we feel that Soviet leaders could do which would permit the rational and peaceful development of the coexistence of their system and ours. They are not things that go to
60 the depths of the moral conflict. They have been formulated by us, not as moralists but as servants of government, anxious to get on with the practical problems that lie before us and to get on with them in a manner consistent with mankind's deep longing for a
65 respite from fear and uncertainty.

Nor have they been formulated as a one-sided bargain. A will to achieve binding, peaceful settlements would be required of all participants. All would have to produce unmistakable evidence of their good faith.
70 All would have to accept agreements in the observance of which all nations could have real confidence.

The United States is ready, as it has been and always will be, to cooperate in genuine efforts to find peaceful settlements. Our attitude is not inflexible, our opinions
75 are not frozen, our positions are not and will not be obstacles to peace. But it takes more than one to cooperate. If the Soviet Union could join in doing these things I have outlined, we could all face the future with greater security. We could look forward to more than
80 the eventual reduction of some of the present tensions. We could anticipate a return to a more normal and relaxed diplomatic atmosphere and to progress in the transaction of some of the international business which needs so urgently to be done.

What is the main idea of the passage?

A) The Soviet Union's failure to adhere to international agreements poses an immediate threat to American security.

B) Relations between the Soviet Union and the United States will improve if the Soviet Union offers greater liberties to its citizens.

C) The Soviet Union will be unable to conduct normal relations with other countries until communism has been thoroughly destroyed.

D) The conduct of the United States toward the Soviet Union is a moral dilemma that cannot be easily resolved.

2

The primary purpose of the passage is to

A) Criticize the Soviet Union for its harsh treatment of peoples under its rule.

B) Suggest that the Soviet Union should model its diplomatic process on that of the United States.

C) Propose a course of action that would result in a reduction of tension between the Soviet Union and the United States.

D) Decry the use of a force as a tool for maintaining international order.

3

The main idea of the fourth paragraph (lines 21-37) is that

A) Leaders must act according to their conscience as well as their desires.

B) Control of Soviet satellites will be granted to the United States if the Soviet Union continues to behave unreliably.

C) Soviet control of Germany, Japan, and Austria would inevitably end in disaster.

D) The Soviet Union must abide by its promises in order for the United States to accept its treaties.

6. The following passage is adapted from George Orwell, "Keep the Aspidistra Flying," first published in 1936. Gordon, the protagonist, is a poet.

Gordon walked homeward against the rattling wind, which blew his hair backward and gave him more of a 'good' forehead than ever. His manner conveyed to the passers-by – at least, he hoped it did—that if he wore
5 no overcoat it was from pure caprice.

Willowbed Road, NW, was dingy and depressing, although it contrived to keep up a kind of mingy decency. There was even a dentist's brass plate on one of the houses. In quite two-thirds of them, amid the
10 lace curtains of the parlor window, there was a green card with 'Apartments' on it in silver lettering, above the peeping foliage of an aspidistra.*

Mrs. Wisbeach, Gordon's landlady, specialized in 'single gentlemen.' Bed-sitting-rooms, with gaslight laid
15 on and find your own heating, baths extra (there was a geyser), and meals in the tomb-dark dining-room with the phalanx of clotted sauce-bottles in the middle of the table. Gordon, who came home for his midday dinner, paid twenty-seven and six a week.
20 The gaslight shone yellow through the frosted transom above the door of Number 31. Gordon took out his key and fished about in the keyhole – in that kind of house the key never quite fits the lock. The darkish little hallway – in reality it was only a passage – smelt of
25 dishwater and cabbage. Gordon glanced at the japanned tray on the hall-stand. No letters, of course. He had told himself not to hope for a letter, and nevertheless had continued to hope. A stale feeling, not quite a pain, settled upon his breast. Rosemary might have written!
30 It was four days now since she had written. Moreover, he had sent out to magazines and had not yet had returned to him. The one thing that made the evening bearable was to find a letter waiting for him when he got home. But he received very few letters – four or five in a week
35 at the very most.

On the left of the hall was the never-used parlor, then came the staircase, and beyond that the passage ran down to the kitchen and to the unapproachable lair inhabited by Mrs. Wisbeach herself. As Gordon came in,
40 the door at the end of the passage opened a foot or so. Mrs. Wisbeach's face emerged, inspected him briefly but suspiciously, and disappeared again. It was quite impossible to get in or out of the house, at any time before eleven at night, without being scrutinized in this
45 manner. Just what Mrs. Wisbeach suspected you of it

was hard to say. She was one of those malignant respectable women who keep lodging-houses. Age about forty-five, stout but active, with a pink, fine-featured, horribly observant face, beautifully grey hair,
50 and a permanent grievance.

In the familiar darkness of his room, Gordon felt for the gas-jet and lighted it. The room was medium-sized, not big enough to be curtained into two, but too big to be sufficiently warmed by one defective oil lamp. It had
55 the sort of furniture you expect in a top floor back. White-quilted single-bed; brown lino floor-covering; wash-hand-stand with jug and basin of that cheap white ware which you can never see without thinking of chamberpots. On the window-sill there was a sickly
60 aspidistra in a green-glazed pot.

Up against this, under the window, there was a kitchen table with an inkstained green cloth. This was Gordon's 'writing' table. It was only after a bitter struggle that he had induced Mrs. Wisbeach to give him
65 a kitchen table instead of the bamboo 'occasional' table – a mere stand for the aspidistra – which she considered proper for a top floor back. And even now there was endless nagging because Gordon would never allow his table to be 'tidied up.' The table was in a
70 permanent mess. It was almost covered with a muddle of papers, perhaps two hundred sheets, grimy and dog-eared, and all written on and crossed out and written on again – a sort of sordid labyrinth of papers to which only Gordon possessed the key. There was a film of
75 dust over everything. Except for a few books on the mantelpiece, this table, with its mess of papers, was the sole mark Gordon's personality had left on the room.

*a bulbous plant with broad leaves, often used as a houseplant.

1

Which choice correctly states the order of events in the passage?

A) A character arrives home, is briefly observed by another character, and retires unhappily to his room.

B) A character arrives home, finds a letter that he has been expecting, and races to his room to read it.

C) A character sneaks into his house, then is stopped by another character with whom he has an unpleasant encounter.

D) A character who is waiting for a letter learns that it has not been sent; later, he narrowly avoids being seen by another character.

The primary purpose of the passage is to

A) describe the habits of a somewhat eccentric character.

B) illustrate the difficulties involved in being a writer.

C) foreshadow an ominous development in a character's life.

D) depict an unusual occurrence in a character's routine.

Explanations: The Big Picture Exercises

1.1 C

To find the answer to this question, focus on the end of the passage – the place where the author describes the true significance of all the technology he's described. The point is that big data allows people to see the big picture, and to identify relationships between seemingly unrelated phenomena. The correct answer must be related to that idea in some way. A) is very specific, referring only to "bytes." Likewise, D) focuses on science fiction, which is discussed in only a small part of the passage. Be careful with B) – it's supported by the passage (lines 16-19), but it's not a main idea. C) is much more general and consistent with the overall focus of the passage: the fact that new technology has changed the way data is acquired (through bytes) and analyzed (to reveal hidden relationships).

1.2 D

The key to answering this question is to understand that the author uses the "tree" and "balloon" metaphors. He's essentially saying that until now, people have only been able to examine various events in isolation, but that with massive data sets, we will be able to understand the big picture in a way that was impossible before. That corresponds to D), making it the correct answer.

2.1 C

To simplify this question, focus on the beginning and the end of the passage, using the answer choices to guide you. Each choice contains "attitude" words, so play positive/negative. The character's attitude at the beginning is positive, as indicated by the exclamation points in line 9 and the phrase *I joined the happy half.* A) can be eliminated because it begins with a negative word (*apprehensive*). Now consider the end. In line 76, the narrator states *I began to wonder at what I had written, for it was the opposite of playful,* indicating that she is questioning herself (negative). Unfortunately, B), C), and D) all end with negative attitude words. (Even though it does not help here, this step is still important because you may be able to use it to identify the correct answer to other questions.) So think about the context: the narrator isn't "struggling to make friends," so eliminate B). Nor is she "disappointed by her teacher's reaction to her work" – in fact, we have no information about how her teacher reacted. That leaves C), which correctly corresponds to the fact that the narrator becomes nervous after listening to her classmates read their work.

2.2. B

If you were to answer this question very quickly in your own words, you might say something along the lines of "describe some stuff that happened to this girl at school." That might not get you to the answer, but it would get you thinking in the right direction. A) doesn't quite fit: the passage only briefly alludes to the narrator's interaction with her peers. You might not be sure about B), so leave it. C) might seem attractive, but think carefully: although the narrator is very clear that she admires her teacher, we don't get any information about Miss Nelson's specific influence on the narrator's life. D) is incorrect because the only decision the narrator makes in the passage is to write her "auto-biographical" essay about a topic important to her, and the passage does not really describe the consequences of that decision beyond indicating that the narrator was nervous about reading her work. So that leaves B), which is the only answer general enough to encompass the entire passage.

3.1 C

Don't be fooled by the long line reference. You only need the first sentence to answer the question. De Gouges' assertion that *Women have done more harm than good* directly corresponds to the idea that women have undermined their own cause. The answer is therefore C).

3.2 C

If you've written the main point (women must demand rights/stop hurting each other), you can probably jump right to C). Otherwise, focus on the beginning of the passage, where de Gouges makes her most impassioned pleas. Throughout the whole first section, she begs women to stand up and reclaim their rights. In line 23, toward the end of the introduction, she directly calls upon women to *unite*. Playing process of elimination, A) is incorrect because de Gouges asserts that women must take their rights on their own, without waiting for men to help them. (In lines 16-23, she implies that men will resist women's attempts at claiming their rights.) Although de Gouges does mention that women can gain a position in society only by excelling in music or painting, B) is incorrect because that is a secondary point (mentioned in one place) compared to her insistence that women must demand their rights. D) is incorrect because de Gouges implies that society as a whole, including women themselves, is responsible for women's inferior position.

4.1 A

Lines 31-35 provide the exact information you need to answer this question. The passage describes Professor Seymour's experiment, which was designed to resolve the "big controversy" of whether dinosaurs were warm-blooded or cold-blooded.

4.2 D

Although it might seem tempting to start by looking at the answers, it is worthwhile to take a moment and state the answer in your own words before looking at the choices. If you're not sure, look at the end of the passage – a good part of the answer is right there in lines 64-68. What were Professor Seymour's findings? Basically, that the large size of the holes in the dinosaurs' thigh bones strongly suggests that dinosaurs were warm-blooded and active. That makes D) the answer. A) is incorrect because Professor Seymour used foramen size as an indicator of metabolic rate, not growth rate. The use of foramen size was also a starting point of his experiment, not a finding. B) is incorrect because the focus was on the size of the holes in dinosaurs' thigh bones, not the density. Furthermore, the study "proved" nothing; it simply added weight to the theory that dinosaurs were warm-blooded. C) is incorrect because the passage says nothing about the relationship between foramen size and behavior.

5.1 B

Focus on the end of the passage. What does Acheson indicate? That the United States wants to find a way to peacefully coexist with the Soviet Union. So the answer must be relatively positive. A), C), and D) are all negative, leaving B) as the only option.

5.2 C

This is essentially the same question as 5.1, just phrased a little differently. What is Acheson's point? That the United States wants to find a way to peacefully coexist with the Soviet Union. In other words, he wants the tension between those countries to be reduced, making C) the answer. Be careful with A). Although Acheson does criticize the Soviets' treatment of people living under its regime, that is not his main point. There is no information to support B), and D) goes far beyond the passage. The focus is specifically on US-Soviet relations, not international order in general.

5.3 D

The fact that you have a 17-line reference indicates that you do *not* need to read the whole thing. Focus on the beginning and the end. In this case, the beginning doesn't provide much information relevant to the question. The end, however, gives you more to work with. The statement that *We can accept treaties of peace that would give reality to this pledge and to the interests of all in security* indicates that the United States would be willing to work with the Soviet Union if the latter would keep its promises. That idea corresponds directly to D).

6.1 A

Start by focusing on the beginning of the passage and matching it to the beginning of one of the answer choices. What does the very beginning of the passage indicate? That Gordon is on his way home. That corresponds most directly to A) and B), so eliminate C) and D). If you have a pretty good grasp of the passage, there's a good chance you remember that Gordon did *not* receive a letter, eliminating B). Otherwise, focus on the end of the passage. It's a description of Gordon's room, and there's nothing about a letter, again pointing to A).

6.2 A

The passage basically recounts an episode from Gordon's life: he comes home, he tries unsuccessfully to avoid his nosy landlady, and then he goes to his extremely messy room. There's absolutely nothing to suggest that something bad is going to happen to him, nor is there any information that would suggest that the events of the passage are anything unusual in Gordon's life. That eliminates C) and D). B) might seem tempting to you, but the passage doesn't really focus on the fact that Gordon is a writer, or the difficulties of that career. The descriptions are more intended to illustrate that Gordon is a somewhat odd person (=somewhat eccentric), a purpose that corresponds to A).

4 Supporting Evidence

Before we go any further, it would strongly behoove us to take a look at one of the key features of the redesigned SAT: paired "supporting evidence" questions.

If you look through an SAT Reading Test, you'll undoubtedly notice a number of questions that look like this:

2

Which choice provides the best evidence for the answer to the previous question?

A) Lines 5-7 ("This...declaration")
B) Lines 24-25 ("It...answers")
C) Lines 44-46 ("Between...past")
D) Lines 46-48 ("Still...issued")

The first time most people look at this type of question, their reaction is something along the lines of, "Whoa, that looks *really* complicated."

While these questions are not necessarily easy (although some of them can be surprisingly straightforward), they are generally not nearly as complicated as they appear – provided that you're prepared and willing to work through them very systematically.

But first, the basics. Supporting evidence questions are primarily paired with two other question types: **literal comprehension** (questions that ask what the passage states or indicates), and **inference** (questions that ask what the passage suggests or implies). As we'll see in Chapters 5 and 6, these two question types are actually very similar. In some cases, they are nearly interchangeable. While not every single literal comprehension and inference question will be followed by a supporting evidence question, the vast majority will follow this pattern.

Next, **the most important thing to understand is that paired questions are not really two questions at all but rather a single question asked two different ways. In fact, the information needed to answer the first question will always be contained among the answer choices to the second question.** The answer to the first question is essentially a rephrased version of the correct lines cited in the second question. True supporting evidence questions – ones that ask you to identify the lines that support an idea discussed in the passage – are much less common, appearing no more than a few times per test.

Third, supporting evidence pairs come in two types. In the vast majority of cases, the first question will not contain a line reference. From time to time, however, it will contain a line reference. Unless you are an extraordinarily strong reader who can simply read and answer every question in order, the two types of questions can require different approaches.

As mentioned earlier, you should take a few moments upfront, before you answer any of the questions, **and mark the supporting evidence question pairs. Furthermore, when a literal comprehension or inference question appears at the bottom of a page, you MUST remember to check the following page for a supporting evidence question.**

If you don't know any better, a likely reaction to these types of questions is as follows: you read the first question and, realizing that there's no line reference, return to the passage and begin to hunt for the answer. You have a general idea of where it might be, but when you check that spot and don't see it, you start to get a little nervous.

You start skimming faster and faster, your eyes racing over the page, until finally you see something that seems to fit. You're not totally sure, but you've already spent a few minutes looking and can't afford to waste any more time, so you bubble the answer in.

When you see that the next question is a supporting evidence question, your stomach sinks. You think that the right answer should be somewhere around the spot where you found the answer to the previous question, but none of quotes are located there.

One by one, you plug in each of the answers. You get rid of two choices that are clearly wrong, but the remaining answers both seem possible. You sit and stare at them, not sure how to choose. You still have half a section left, though, so you need to move on. Finally, you pick the one that feels a little more right and hope for the best.

This scenario is one you want to avoid at all costs. If it occurs multiple times, you'll get tired very quickly – and you'll still have two Math sections to go.

The key to answering paired questions is to plug the answer choices from the second question into the first question, then use that information to answer both questions simultaneously.

The line references in the second question tell you that the answer to the first question is located either in or very close to one of the four sections of the passage cited. Instead of randomly scanning the passage for the answer to the first question and wasting untold amounts of time and energy in the process, using the answers to the second question allows you to focus on four specific places – one of which **must** provide the correct answer

That is why marking question pairs is so important: if you don't know a supporting evidence question is coming, you can't use the second question to help you.

So, for example, a set of questions that looks like this...

1

The author indicates which of the following about mixed-use developments?

A) They are a recent development.
B) They reduce architectural variety.
C) They create healthier neighborhoods.
D) They increase dependence on automobiles.

2

Which choice provides the best evidence for the answer to the previous question?

A) Lines 5-7 ("This...complicated")
B) Lines 24-25 ("It...recognized")
C) Lines 44-46 ("Between...past")
D) Lines 46-48 ("Still...issued")

...can be rewritten to look like this:

1

The author indicates which of the following about mixed-use developments?

A) Lines 5-7 ("This...complicated")
B) Lines 24-25 ("It...recognized")
C) Lines 44-46 ("Between...past")
D) Lines 46-48 ("Still...issued")

Then, one by one, read each line reference and determine whether it provides the answer to Question #1. When you find the correct set of lines, you have the answers to both questions.

Remember that you do not necessarily need to check the line references in order. If you remember that the topic of Question #1 was discussed in a particular part of the passage and see a line reference corresponding to that section, you might want to start with it.

Important: In some instances, it may be necessary to read before and/or after a line reference for context. If you read the lines in question and are unsure whether they answer the question, do not – I repeat, do not – eliminate the answer simply because you are confused. Read a sentence or two before to a sentence or two after to see where the lines fit within the argument.

Supporting and Contradicting Claims

At this point, we're going to consider another type of question whose answers involve sets of line references. Although these questions and answers may look similar to the examples we've just looked at, there are some important differences.

First, these questions are not **part of paired sets but rather appear alone**. Second, their **answers consist solely of lines references**; you must identify the lines that **support** an idea discussed within the passage. In some cases, you may also be asked to identify the lines that **contradict** an idea or claim described in the question.

Note: As mentioned earlier, these questions appear much less frequently than supporting evidence pairs, typically no more than a couple of times per test. That said, more of them are included on the administered exams in the *Official Guide* (Tests 5-8) than on the earlier, non-administered tests, so it appears that they are becoming a fixture of the exam.

If you approach these questions methodically, they can become quite straightforward. *But you can't get impatient, and you can't skip steps, no matter how much you want to just get the answer.* If you're not really certain what a question is asking, OR you don't feel that you can focus properly, you are better off simply skipping it and returning to it if you have time.

The process for answering single supporting evidence questions can be broken into three main steps:

1) Identify the claim, and rephrase it if necessary.

If the claim is stated simply in the question, underline it. If it's worded more complexly, rephrase it more simply and write it down. You can't determine whether a set of lines would support an idea unless you know what that idea is.

2) Determine what sort of information would support the claim.

You should at least attempt to do this on your own and not assume you'll be able to recognize the information from the answer choices.

3) Check the answers.

Remember that in some cases, you may need to read above/below the lines referenced for context. Remember also not to eliminate any answers just because you find them confusing.

On the next page, we're going to look at an example.

This passage is adapted from Barry Schwartz, "More Isn't Always Better," © 2006 by *Harvard Business Review*.

Marketers assume that the more choices they offer, the more likely customers will be able to find just the right thing. They assume, for instance, that offering 50 styles of jeans instead of two increases the chances that
5 shoppers will find a pair they really like. Nevertheless, research now shows that there can be too much choice; when there is, consumers are less likely to buy anything at all, and if they do buy, they are less satisfied with their selection.
10 It all began with jam. In 2000, psychologists Sheena Iyengar and Mark Lepper published a remarkable study. On one day, shoppers at an upscale food market saw a display table with 24 varieties of gourmet jam. Those who sampled the spreads received a coupon for $1 off
15 any jam. On another day, shoppers saw a similar table, except that only six varieties of the jam were on display. The large display attracted more interest than the small one. But when the time came to purchase, people who saw the large display were one-tenth as likely to buy as
20 people who saw the small display.

Other studies have confirmed this result that more choice is not always better. As the variety of snacks, soft drinks, and beers offered at convenience stores increases, for instance, sales volume and customer
25 satisfaction decrease. Moreover, as the number of retirement investment options available to employees increases, the chance that they will choose any decreases. These studies and others have shown not only that excessive choice can produce "choice
30 paralysis," but also that it can reduce people's satisfaction with their decisions, even if they made good ones. My colleagues and I have found that increased choice decreases satisfaction with matters as trivial as ice cream flavors and as significant as jobs.
35 These results challenge what we think we know about human nature and the determinants of well-being. Both psychology and business have operated on the assumption that the relationship between choice and well-being is straightforward: The more choices people
40 have, the better off they are. In psychology, the benefits of choice have been tied to autonomy and control. In business, the benefits of choice have been tied to the benefits of free markets more generally. Added options make no one worse off, and they are bound to make
45 someone better off.

Choice *is* good for us, but its relationship to satisfaction appears to be more complicated than we had assumed. There is diminishing marginal utility in having alternatives; each new option subtracts a little
50 from the feeling of well-being, until the marginal benefits of added choice level off. What's more, psychologists and business academics alike have largely ignored another outcome of choice: More of it requires increased time and effort and can lead to
55 anxiety, regret, excessively high expectations, and self-blame if the choices don't work out. When the number of available options is small, these costs are negligible, but the costs grow with the number of options. Eventually, each new option makes us feel
60 worse off than we did before.

Without a doubt, having more options enables us, most of the time, to achieve better objective outcomes. Again, having 50 styles of jeans as opposed to two increases the likelihood that customers will find a pair
65 that fits. But the subjective outcome may be that shoppers will feel overwhelmed and dissatisfied. This dissociation between objective and subjective results creates a significant challenge for retailers and marketers that look to choice as a way to enhance the
70 perceived value of their goods and services.

Choice can no longer be used to justify a marketing strategy in and of itself. More isn't always better, either for the customer or for the retailer. Discovering how much assortment is warranted is a
75 considerable empirical challenge. But companies that get the balance right will be amply rewarded.

1

Which choice best supports the author's claim that an excess of choice can lead consumers to become overwhelmed?

A) Lines 3-5 ("They...like")
B) Lines 18-20 ("people...display")
C) Lines 46-48 ("Choice...assumed")
D) Lines 73-75 ("Discovering...challenge")

Although this question asks about the relationship between ideas in the passage, it is unnecessary to find the original claim in the passage. Even if you hadn't read a word of the passage, the question would still tell you exactly what idea you needed to find supporting evidence for – namely, that an excess of choice can overwhelm consumers.

That's a pretty straightforward argument, but if you wanted to restate it more simply to keep yourself focused, you could write something like, "Too much choice = BAD." Now all you have to do is find the lines that most directly support that idea. That's the main point of the passage, so the answer could be pretty much anywhere. As a result, we can simply check the answers in order.

A) They assume, for instance, that offering 50 styles of jeans instead of two increases the chances that shoppers will find a pair they really like.

No. We're looking for an option that discusses choice leading to *dissatisfaction*. These lines discuss exactly the opposite idea.

B) People who saw the large display were one-tenth as likely to buy as people who saw the small display.

Yes, this fits. Consider the context: the author is describing the outcome of Iyengar and Lepper's study, which found that people who are given too many options are often unable to decide at all. If you're clear about that, you can stop right here. If you're not sure, however, keep going.

C) Choice is good for us, but its relationship to satisfaction appears to be more complicated than we had assumed.

Be careful here. The lines indicate that the relationship between choice and satisfaction is problematic, but they don't directly support the idea that people are overwhelmed by too many choices.

D) Discovering how much assortment is warranted is a considerable empirical challenge.

This is the "confusing" answer, filled with unusual phrasing and abstract, challenging phrasing (*warranted, considerable empirical challenge*). In context, these lines simply indicate that it isn't yet clear when choice stops being a good thing and starts being a bad one. So no, this answer is off-topic.

The answer is therefore B).

This question could also be asked the other way around, as a "contradict" question:

A marketer claims that more choices are always beneficial. Which of the following statements in the passage contradicts the marketer's claim?

A) Lines 3-5 ("They...like")
B) Lines 18-20 ("people...display")
C) Lines 46-48 ("Choice...assumed")
D) Lines 73-75 ("Discovering...challenge")

First of all, note that although this question is phrased from the opposite perspective, it is actually the exact same question we just worked through.

Because the phrasing of the question is more complicated and thus potentially more confusing, it is definitely worth your while to take a moment and simplify/rewrite the question before looking at the answer choices.

The question is asking us to identify what idea in the passage contradicts the marketer's claim, so the correct answer must state the **opposite** of the marketer's claim. To find the idea you're looking for, simply stick the word NOT into the original claim.

> **Original claim:** more choice = beneficial

> **Negated:** more choice = NOT beneficial

Therefore, the correct answer must support the idea that more choice is NOT beneficial.

With this information, you can work through the answer choices the same way as in the previous question, checking each option against the idea that more choice is NOT better. Again, B) is the only choice that fits.

Important: Even if you are a very strong reader with an excellent memory, it is very important that you write down each step of questions like this. Although you may not have any difficulty answering them, it is all too easy to forget and accidentally look for an idea that is exactly the opposite of the one you should be looking for. Sooner or later, there's a good chance you'll slip up and lose what should have been relatively easy points. **This is not about your ability to get questions right, but rather to ensure that you don't get questions wrong.** Memories do strange things under pressure, and you're better off not taking the risk.

Supporting and Contradicting Claims Exercises

1.   The sharing economy is a little like online shopping, which started in America 15 years ago. At first, people were worried about security. But having made a successful purchase from, say, Amazon, they
5 felt safe buying elsewhere. Similarly, using Airbnb or a car-hire service for the first time encourages people to try other offerings. Next, consider eBay. Having started out as a peer-to-peer marketplace, it is now dominated by professional "power sellers" (many of whom started
10 out as ordinary eBay users). The same may happen with the sharing economy, which also provides new opportunities for enterprise. Some people have bought cars solely to rent them out, for example. Incumbents are getting involved too. Avis, a car-hire firm, has a share
15 in a sharing rival. So do GM and Daimler, two carmakers. In the future, companies may develop hybrid models, listing excess capacity (whether vehicles, equipment or office space) on peer-to-peer rental sites. In the past, new ways of doing things online have not displaced the
20 old ways entirely. But they have often changed them. Just as internet shopping forced Walmart and Tesco to adapt, so online sharing will shake up transport, tourism, equipment-hire and more.
     The main worry is regulatory uncertainty. Will
25 room-4-renters be subject to hotel taxes, for example? In Amsterdam officials are using Airbnb listings to track down unlicensed hotels. In some American cities, peer-to-peer taxi services have been banned after lobbying by traditional taxi firms. The danger is that
30 although some rules need to be updated to protect consumers from harm, incumbents will try to destroy competition. People who rent out rooms should pay tax, of course, but they should not be regulated like a Ritz-Carlton hotel. The lighter rules that typically govern
35 bed-and-breakfasts are more than adequate. The sharing economy is the latest example of the internet's value to consumers. This emerging model is now big and disruptive enough for regulators and companies to have woken up to it. That is a sign of its immense potential. It
40 is time to start caring about sharing.

1

Which choice provides the best evidence for the author's claim that sharing-based companies may face serious challenges from established companies?

A) Lines 5-7 ("Similarly...offerings")

B) Lines 14-15 ("Avis...rival")

C) Lines 27-29 ("In...firms")

D) Lines 32-34 ("People...hotel")

2. This passage is adapted from Abraham Lincoln's First Inaugural Address, delivered in 1861.

I hold that in contemplation of universal law and of the Constitution the Union of these States is perpetual...

If the United States be not a government proper, but
5 an association of States in the nature of contract merely, can it, as a contract, be peaceably unmade by less than all the parties who made it? One party to a contract may violate it—break it, so to speak—but does it not require all to lawfully rescind it?

10 Descending from these general principles, we find the proposition that in legal contemplation the Union is perpetual confirmed by the history of the Union itself. The Union is much older than the Constitution. It was formed, in fact, by the Articles of Association in 1774.
15 It was matured and continued by the Declaration of Independence in 1776. It was further matured, and the faith of all the then thirteen States expressly plighted and engaged that it should be perpetual, by the Articles of Confederation in 1778. And finally, in 1787, one of
20 the declared objects for ordaining and establishing the Constitution was "to form a more perfect Union."

But if destruction of the Union by one or by a part only of the States be lawfully possible, the Union is less perfect than before the Constitution, having lost the
25 vital element of perpetuity.

It follows from these views that no State upon its own mere motion can lawfully get out of the Union; that resolves and ordinances to that effect are legally void, and that acts of violence within any State or
30 States against the authority of the United States are insurrectionary or revolutionary, according to circumstances.

I therefore consider that in view of the Constitution and the laws the Union is unbroken, and to the extent of
35 my ability, I shall take care, as the Constitution itself expressly enjoins upon me, that the laws of the Union be faithfully executed in all the States...

In doing this there needs to be no bloodshed or violence, and there shall be none unless it be forced
40 upon the national authority. The power confided to me will be used to hold, occupy, and possess the property and places belonging to the Government and to collect the duties and imposts; but beyond what may be necessary for these objects, there will be no invasion, no
45 using of force against or among the people anywhere. Where hostility to the United States in any interior locality shall be so great and universal as to prevent competent resident citizens from holding the Federal offices, there will be no attempt to force obnoxious
50 strangers among the people for that object. While the strict legal right may exist in the Government to enforce the exercise of these offices, the attempt to do so would be so irritating and so nearly impracticable withal that I deem it better to forego for the time the uses of such
55 offices.

1

Which choice provides the best support for Lincoln's claim that the Union must be preserved as a whole?

A) Lines 29-31 ("acts...revolutionary")
B) Lines 35-37 ("I shall...States")
C) Lines 40-42 ("The power...Government")
D) Lines 46-50 ("Where...object")

3. The following passage is adapted from Olympe de Gouges, *Declaration of the Rights of Women*. It was initially published in 1791, during the French Revolution, and was written in response to the *Declaration of the Rights of Man* (1789).

Woman, wake up; the toxin of reason is being heard throughout the whole universe; discover your rights. The powerful empire of nature is no longer surrounded by prejudice, fanaticism, superstition, and
5 lies. The flame of truth has dispersed all the clouds of folly and usurpation. Enslaved man has multiplied his strength and needs recourse to yours to break his chains. Having become free, he has become unjust to his companion. Oh, women, women! When will you cease
10 to be blind? What advantage have you received from the Revolution? A more pronounced scorn, a more marked disdain. In the centuries of corruption you ruled only over the weakness of men. The reclamation of your patrimony, based on the wise decrees of nature –
15 what have you to dread from such a fine undertaking? Do you fear that our legislators, correctors of that morality, long ensnared by political practices now out of date, will only say again to you: women, what is there in common between you and us? Everything, you
20 will have to answer. If they persist in their weakness in putting this hypocrisy in contradiction to their principles, courageously oppose the force of reason to the empty pretensions of superiority; unite yourselves beneath the standards of philosophy; deploy all the
25 energy of your character. Regardless of what barriers confront you, it is in your power to free yourselves; you have only to want to. Let us pass not to the shocking tableau of what you have been in society; and since national education is in question at this moment, let us
30 see whether our wise legislators will think judiciously about the education of women.
    Women have done more harm than good. Constraint and dissimulation have been their lot. What force has robbed them of, ruse returned to them; they had recourse
35 to all the resources of their charms, and the most irreproachable persons did not resist them. Poison and the sword were both subject to them; they commanded in crime as in fortune. The French government, especially, depended throughout the centuries on the nocturnal
40 administrations of women; the cabinet could keep no secrets as a result of their indiscretions; all have been subject to the cupidity and ambition of this sex, formerly contemptible and respected, and since the revolution, respectable and scorned.

45 In this sort of contradictory situation, what remarks could I not make! I have but a moment to make them, but this moment will fix the attention of the remotest posterity. Under the Old Regime, all was vicious, all was guilty; but could not the amelioration of
50 conditions be perceived even in the substance of vices? A woman only had to be beautiful or amiable; when she possessed these two advantages, she saw a hundred fortunes at her feet. If she did not profit from them, she had a bizarre character or a rare philosophy
55 which made her scorn wealth; then she was deemed to be like a crazy woman. A young, inexperienced woman, seduced by a man whom she loves, will abandon her parents to follow him; the ingrate will leave her after a few years, and the older she has
60 become with him, the more inhuman is his inconstancy; if she has children, he will likewise abandon them. If he is rich, he will consider himself excused from sharing his fortune with his noble victims. If some involvement binds him to his duties, he will
65 deny them, trusting that the laws will support him. If he is married, any other obligation loses its rights. Then what laws remain to extirpate vice all the way to its root? The law of dividing wealth and public administration between men and women. It can easily
70 be seen that one who is born into a rich family gains very much from such equal sharing. But the one born into a poor family with merit and virtue – what is her lot? Poverty and opprobrium. If she does not precisely excel in music or painting, she cannot be admitted to
75 any public function when she has all the capacity for it.

1

Which choice most effectively supports the author's claim that women have undermined their own cause?

A) Lines 40-41 ("the cabinet…indiscretions")
B) Lines 53-55 ("If…wealth")
C) Lines 59-61 ("the older…inconstancy")
D) Lines 73-75 ("If…for it")

4. The following passage is adapted from "Makerspaces, Hackerspaces, and Community Scale Production in Detroit and Beyond," © 2013 by Sean Ansanelli.

During the mid-1980s, spaces began to emerge across Europe where computer hackers could convene for mutual support and camaraderie. In the past few years, the idea of fostering such shared, physical spaces
5 has been rapidly adapted by the diverse and growing community of "makers," who seek to apply the idea of "hacking" to physical objects, processes, or anything else that can be deciphered and improved upon.

A hackerspace is described by hackerspaces.org as
10 a "community-operated physical space where people with common interests, often in computers, technology, science, digital art or electronic art, can meet, socialize, and/or collaborate." Such spaces can vary in size, available technology, and membership structure (some
15 being completely open), but generally share community-oriented characteristics. Indeed, while the term "hacker" can sometimes have negative connotations, modern hackerspaces thrive off of community, openness, and assimilating diverse viewpoints – these
20 often being the only guiding principles in otherwise informal organizational structures.

In recent years, the city of Detroit has emerged as a hotbed for hackerspaces and other DIY ("Do-It-Yourself") experiments. Several hackerspaces
25 can already be found throughout the city and several more are currently in formation. Of course, Detroit's attractiveness for such projects can be partially attributed to cheap real estate, which allows aspiring hackers to acquire ample space for experimentation.
30 Some observers have also described this kind of making and tinkering as embedded in the DNA of Detroit's residents, who are able to harness substantial intergenerational knowledge and attract like-minded individuals.
35 Hackerspaces (or "makerspaces") can be found in more commercial forms, but the vast majority of spaces are self-organized and not-for-profit. For example, the OmniCorp hackerspace operates off member fees to cover rent and new equipment, from laser cutters to
40 welding tools. OmniCorp also hosts an "open hack night" every Thursday in which the space is open to the general public. Potential members are required to attend at least one open hack night prior to a consensus vote by the existing members for admittance; no
45 prospective members have yet been denied.

A visit to one of OmniCorp's open hack nights reveals the vast variety of activity and energy existing in the space. In the main common room alone, activities range from experimenting with sound installations and

50 learning to program Arduino boards to building speculative "oloid" shapes – all just for the sake of it. With a general atmosphere of mutual support, participants in the space are continually encouraged to help others.
55 One of the most active community-focused initiatives in the city is the Mt. Elliot Makerspace. Jeff Sturges, former MIT Media Lab Fellow and Co-Founder of OmniCorp, started the Mt. Elliot project with the aim of replicating MIT's Fab Lab model on a smaller, cheaper
60 scale in Detroit. "Fab Labs" are production facilities that consist of a small collection of flexible computer-controlled tools that cover several different scales and various materials, with the aim to make "almost anything" (including other machines). The Mt. Elliot
65 Makerspace now offers youth-based skill development programs in eight areas: Transportation, Electronics, Digital Tools, Wearables, Design and Fabrication, Food, Music, and Arts. The range of activities is meant to provide not only something for everyone, but a well-
70 rounded base knowledge of making to all participants.

While the center receives some foundational support, the space also derives significant support from the local community. Makerspaces throughout the city connect the space's youth-based programming directly to
75 school curriculums.

The growing interest in and development of hacker/makerspaces has been explained, in part, as a result of the growing maker movement. Through the combination of cultural norms and communication
80 channels from open source production as well as increasingly available technologies for physical production, amateur maker communities have developed in virtual and physical spaces.

1

Which choice best supports the author's claim that hackerspaces are generally welcoming and tolerant organizations?

A) Lines 24-26 ("Several...formation")
B) Lines 44-45 ("no...denied")
C) Lines 48-51 ("In...shapes")
D) Lines 71-73 ("While...community")

5. The following passage is adapted from "The Origin of the Ocean Floor" by Peter Keleman, © 2009 by The National Geographic Society.

At the dark bottom of our cool oceans, 85 percent of the earth's volcanic eruptions proceed virtually unnoticed. Though unseen, they are hardly insignificant. Submarine volcanoes generate the solid
5 underpinnings of all the world's oceans massive slabs of rock seven kilometers thick.

Geophysicists first began to appreciate the smoldering origins of the land under the sea, known formally as ocean crust, in the early 1960s. Sonar
10 surveys revealed that volcanoes form nearly continuous ridges that wind around the globe like seams on a baseball. Later, the same scientists strove to explain what fuels these erupting mountain ranges, called mid-ocean ridges. Basic theories suggest that because ocean
15 crust pulls apart along the ridges, hot material deep within the earth's rocky interior must rise to fill the gap. But details of exactly where the lava originates and how it travels to the surface long remained a mystery.

In recent years mathematical models of the
20 interaction between molten and solid rock have provided some answers, as have examinations of blocks of old seafloor now exposed on the continents. These insights made it possible to develop a detailed theory describing the birth of ocean crust. The process
25 turns out to be quite different from the typical layperson's idea, in which fiery magma fills an enormous chamber underneath a volcano, then rages upward along a jagged crack. Instead the process begins dozens of kilometers under the seafloor, where
30 tiny droplets of melted rock ooze through microscopic pores at a rate of about 10 centimeters a year, about as fast as fingernails grow.

Closer to the surface, the process speeds up, culminating with massive streams of lava pouring
35 over the seafloor with the velocity of a speeding truck. Deciphering how liquid moves through solid rock deep underground not only explains how ocean crust emerges but also may elucidate the behavior of other fluid-transport networks, including the river systems
40 that dissect the planet's surface.

Far below the mid-ocean ridge volcanoes and their countless layers of crust-forming lava is the mantle, a 3,200-kilometer-thick layer of scorching hot rock that forms the earth's midsection and surrounds its
45 metallic core. At the planet's cool surface, upthrusted mantle rocks are dark green, but if you could see them in their rightful home, they would be glowing red- or even white-hot. The top of the mantle is about 1,300 degrees Celsius, and it gets about one degree
50 hotter with each kilometer of depth. The weight of overlying rock means the pressure also increases with depth about 1,000 atmospheres for every three kilometers.

Knowledge of the intense heat and pressure in
55 the mantle led researchers to hypothesize in the late 1960s that ocean crust originates as tiny amounts of liquid rock known as melt almost as though the solid rocks were "sweating." Even a minuscule release of pressure (because of material rising from
60 its original position) causes melt to form in microscopic pores deep within the mantle rock.

Explaining how the rock sweat gets to the surface was more difficult. Melt is less dense than the mantle rocks in which it forms, so it will
65 constantly try to migrate upward, toward regions of lower pressure. But what laboratory experiments revealed about the chemical composition of melt did not seem to match up with the composition of rock samples collected from the mid-ocean ridges,
70 where erupted melt hardens.

Using specialized equipment to heat and squeeze crystals from mantle rocks in the laboratory, investigators learned that the chemical composition of melt in the mantle varies depending on the depth
75 at which it forms; the composition is controlled by an exchange of atoms between the melt and the minerals that make up the solid rock it passes through. The experiments revealed that as melt rises, it dissolves one kind of mineral, orthopyroxene, and
80 precipitates, or leaves behind, another mineral, olivine. Researchers could thus infer that the higher in the mantle melt formed, the more orthopyroxene it would dissolve, and the more olivine it would leave behind. Comparing these experimental findings
85 with lava samples from the mid-ocean ridges revealed that almost all of them have the composition of melts that formed at depths greater than 45 kilometers.

1

A student states that the ocean crust is formed by explosive volcanic eruptions. Is the student correct or incorrect, and which lines provide the best support?

A) Correct, lines 14-16 ("Basic…gap")
B) Correct, lines 26-28 ("fiery…crack")
C) Incorrect, lines 30-33 ("tiny…grow")
D) Incorrect, lines 45-48 ("At…white-hot")

Explanations: Supporting and Contradicting Claims Exercises

1.1 C

Since the question does not provide a line reference and is sufficiently detail-based that you are unlikely to remember the answer, start by plugging in the line reference. You're looking for a section that discusses challenges to "sharing-based" companies. A) is incorrect because although lines 5-7 discuss examples of sharing-based companies, they focus on the likelihood that people will continue to use them after a single experience; challenges from traditional companies are not mentioned. Be careful with B). The word *rival* might suggest competition to you, but in fact this section is discussing the opposite: Avis is an example of a traditional company that is getting involved in the sharing economy, not opposing it. C) is correct because lines 27-29 provide a clear example of an instance in which existing taxi companies successfully opposed "peer-to-peer" ride-share companies. D) is incorrect because lines 32-34 have nothing to do with challenges by traditional companies; the author simply voices his opinion regarding regulation.

2.1 A

The question essentially asks you to find support for the point of the passage, so it isn't immediately clear where in the passage the answer is most likely to be located. If you work in order, though, you'll hit on the answer right away – provided that you back up and get the full context. The key to identifying A) as the answer is to look at the beginning of the paragraph: *It follows from these views that no State upon its own mere motion can lawfully get out of the Union.* Lines 29-31 are used to support this idea. In fact, they are part of the same sentence. A) is thus correct.

3.1 A

If you don't happen to remember where de Gouges discusses how women have undermined their own cause, the easiest way to find the answer is to skim topic sentences. The information is presented so clearly that this approach is actually a more efficient strategy for finding the answer than is plugging in each choice. In line 32, de Gouges clearly states that *Women have done more harm than good*, suggesting that the correct set of lines is most likely located nearby. A) contains the only line reference in that paragraph, so check it first because it will almost certainly be used to support that idea. Indeed, lines 40-41 provide a clear example of how women have hurt themselves, indicating that *the cabinet* (that is, the French government) *could keep no secrets as a result of their indiscretions.*

4.1 B

The correct answer must support the idea that hackerspaces "are generally welcoming and tolerant organizations," so plug in each set of lines and see whether it fits. A) is incorrect because lines 24-26 only indicate that hackerspaces can be found throughout Detroit; there's no information about whether they're welcoming or not, and you can't infer that information from those lines. B) is correct because the statement that *no prospective members have yet been denied* directly implies that makerspaces are pretty relaxed about whom they allow to join. C) is incorrect because lines 48-51 provide no information about makerspaces' atmosphere; they only indicate what people actually do at makerspaces. D) is incorrect because lines 71-73 only indicate that makerspaces are supported by the community. Again, there is no information about whether makerspaces are welcoming.

5.1 C

The key to answering this question is to be aware of the "old idea/new idea" structure, because that is exactly what this question targets. The third paragraph indicates that *the typical layperson's idea* of how ocean crust forms revolves around a massive underwater explosion. That's the <u>wrong</u> idea. In line 28, the word *Instead* signals the transition to the correct explanation: tiny droplets of melted rock ooze up at an incredibly slow rate. That information indicates that the student's statement is incorrect, so the answer is C).

If you haven't clued into that information while reading the passage and plug in the answers individually, you run a serious risk of falling into the trap in B). That answer cites the lines describing what people typically believe, but the phrase *the typical layperson's idea* isn't included in the line reference. If you miss that information, you could easily think that the information in B) describes what actually occurs rather than a mistaken understanding of the phenomenon. A) is incorrect because lines 14-16 only state that hot material within the earth rises to the surface, but they do not explain *how* that occurs. D) is incorrect because lines 45-48 only describe the rocks before they rise to the surface – they say nothing about how that change takes place.

5 Literal Comprehension: Same Idea, Different Words

Literal comprehension questions ask you to identify what a passage **states** or **indicates**.

They can be phrased in the following ways:

- The author's discussion of antibiotics indicates that...

- The author states that which of the following is a longstanding tradition?

- According to the passage, Wang's experiment produced what result?

These most straightforward and common Reading questions essentially require you to understand ideas well enough to recognize accurate **summaries** of them. When you read my example of the typical, long-winded response many students give when asked to summarize the main point of a passage (p. 84), you might have laughed, but the truth is that the ability to pick out the most important ideas in a piece of writing and condense them into a concise, direct statement is a crucial skill both for the SAT and school.

Because this is the SAT, however, those summaries will rarely use the exact same wording as that found in the passage. That would just be too easy. **The test is whether you understand the ideas well enough to recognize when they're stated using different, often more general, language.** Correct answers thus require you to recognize **paraphrased** versions of ideas, ones that contain **synonyms for key words in the passage.** If you understand the idea, you'll probably be fine; if you're too focused on the details, you might miss it completely.

Most literal comprehension questions will be followed by supporting evidence questions, and will not contain line references. In general, you should use the line references in the supporting evidence question to narrow down the location of the answer to the preceding, literal comprehension question.

Although these questions are asked in a very straightforward way, they can also be challenging. In addition to having to check multiple locations in the passage for the answer, you must sometimes navigate very challenging syntax and vocabulary. Furthermore, you must connect the specific words of the correct set of lines to the more abstract language of the answers.

We're going to start by looking at some examples of literal comprehension questions. The first one is quite a bit shorter than what you'll encounter on the SAT, but it's useful to illustrate a point.

Experimental scientists occupy themselves with observing and measuring the cosmos, finding out what stuff exists, no matter how strange that stuff may be. Theoretical physicists, on the other hand, are
5 not satisfied with observing the universe. They want to know why. They want to explain all the properties of the universe in terms of a few fundamental principles and parameters. These fundamental principles, in turn, lead to the "laws of nature," which govern the behavior
10 of all matter and energy.

1

This passage indicates that theoretical physicists' primary goal is to

A) identify all of the objects that exist in the universe.

B) learn to control the laws of nature.

C) understand the universe at its most basic level.

D) observe the cosmos in great detail.

The first thing that you probably notice when you look at the answer choices is that pretty much all of them contain bits and pieces of ideas mentioned in the passage. The question, however, is asking you not to identify words or phrases from the passage but rather to make a small leap from the **specific words** used in the passage to the **rephrased idea**.

In this case, the author begins to discuss theoretical physicists in line 4. What do we learn about these people? That *they want to know why. They want to explain all the properties of the universe in terms of a few _fundamental_ principles and parameters.* The key here is to understand that *fundamental* means something like "basic" or "essential." The sentence is saying that theoretical physicists want to explain how the universe works at its deepest underlying level.

And that is exactly what C) says. **Same idea, different words.**

Let's look at another example. It's from a speech by Daniel Webster, delivered shortly before the Civil War.

I wish to speak to-day, not as a Massachusetts man, nor as a Northern man, but as an American, and a member of the Senate of the United States. It is fortunate that there is a Senate of the United States; a
5 body not yet moved from its propriety, not lost to a just sense of its own dignity and its own high responsibilities, and a body to which the country looks, with confidence, for wise, moderate, patriotic, and healing counsels. It is not to be denied that we live in the midst of strong
10 agitations, and are surrounded by very considerable dangers to our institutions and government.

1

According to Webster, which statement about the Senate is true?

A) Its role has begun to shift in recent years.

B) It may not survive the threat to its existence.

C) It remains fully aware of of its obligations.

D) It underestimates the challenges faced by the United States.

In this case, the key phrase is found in lines 5-6, where Webster describes the Senate as a *body* (organization) *not yet moved from its propriety, not lost to a just sense of its own dignity and its own high responsibilities.* In other words, despite all of the conflicts swirling around, the Senate retains a full understanding of its position and duties, i.e., *it remains fully aware of its obligations.* C) is thus correct.

On the next page, we're going look at a literal comprehension question paired with a supporting evidence question. We'll start with a set in which the first question contains a line reference since that setup is a bit more straightforward.

This passage is adapted from from Kristin Sainani, "What, Me Worry?" © 2014, *Stanford Magazine*.

According to a 2013 national survey by the American Psychological Association, the average stress level among adults is 5.1 on a scale of 10; that's one and a half points above what the
5 respondents judged to be healthy. Two-thirds of people say managing stress is important, and nearly that proportion had attempted to reduce their stress in the previous five years. Yet only a little over a third say they succeeded at doing so. More discouraging, teens
10 and young adults are experiencing higher levels of stress, and also are struggling to manage it.

"Stress has a very bad reputation. It's in pretty bad shape, PR-wise," acknowledges Firdaus Dhabhar, an associate professor of psychiatry and behavioral science
15 at Stanford. "And justifiably so," he adds.

Much of what we know about the physical and mental toll of chronic stress stems from seminal work by Robert Sapolsky beginning in the late 1970s. Sapolsky, a neuroendocrinologist, was among the first
20 to make the connection that the hormones released during the fight-or-flight response—the ones that helped our ancestors avoid becoming dinner—have deleterious effects when the stress is severe and sustained. Especially insidious, chronic exposure to
25 one of these hormones, cortisol, causes brain changes that make it increasingly difficult to shut the stress response down.

But take heart: Recent research paints a different portrait of stress, one in which it indeed has a positive
30 side. "There's good stress, there's tolerable stress, and there's toxic stress," says Bruce McEwen of Rockefeller University, an expert on stress and the brain who trained both Sapolsky and Dhabhar.

Situations we typically perceive as stressful—a
35 confrontation with a co-worker, the pressure to perform, a to-do list that's too long—are not the toxic type of stress that's been linked to serious health issues such as cardiovascular disease, autoimmune disorders, severe depression and cognitive impairment.
40 Short bouts of this sort of everyday stress can actually be a good thing: Just think of the exhilaration of the deadline met or the presentation crushed, the triumph of holding it all together. And, perhaps not surprisingly, it turns out that beating yourself up about
45 being stressed is counterproductive, as worrying about the negative consequences can in itself exacerbate any ill effects.

When Dhabhar was starting his graduate work in McEwen's lab in the early 1990s, "the absolutely
50 overwhelming dogma was that stress suppresses immunity." But this didn't make sense to him from an evolutionary perspective. If a lion is chasing you, he reasoned, your immune system should be ramping up, readying itself to heal torn flesh. It occurred to Dhabhar
55 that the effects of acute stress, which lasts minutes to hours, might differ from the effects of chronic stress, which lasts days to years.

Dhabhar likens the body's immune cells to soldiers. Because their levels in the blood plummet during acute
60 stress, "people used to say: 'See, stress is bad for you; your immune system's depressed,'" he says. "But most immune battles are not going to be fought in the blood." He suspected that the immune cells were instead traveling to the body's "battlefields"—sites most likely
65 to be wounded in an attack, like the skin, gut and lungs. In studies where rats were briefly confined (a short-term stressor), he showed that after an initial surge of immune cells into the bloodstream, they quickly exited the blood and took up positions precisely where he predicted they
70 would.

"His work was a pioneering demonstration of how important the difference is between acute and chronic stress," says Sapolsky, a professor of biology, neurology, and neurological sciences and neurosurgery.
75 "Overwhelmingly, the bad health effects of stress are those of chronic stress."

This strategic deployment of immune cells can speed wound healing, enhance vaccine effectiveness and potentially fight cancer. In 2009, Dhabhar's team
80 showed that knee surgery patients with robust immune redistribution following the stress of surgery recovered significantly faster and had better knee function a year later than those with a more sluggish mobilization. In other studies, volunteers who exercised or took a math
85 test (both acute stressors) immediately prior to being vaccinated had a heightened antibody response relative to volunteers who sat quietly. And in 2010, the researchers curbed the development of skin cancer in UV-exposed mice by stressing them before their
90 sunlamp sessions. Dhabhar speculates that giving cancer patients low-dose injections of stress hormones might help prime their immune systems to fight the cancer. "It may not work out, but if it did, the benefits could be tremendous," he says.

1

Based on the passage, research indicates that long-term stress (line 17)

A) inhibits the production of cortisol.
B) can create a sense of excitement.
C) becomes progressively harder to reduce.
D) produces a heightened antibody response.

2

Which choice provides the best evidence for the answer to the previous question?

A) Lines 9-11 ("teens…manage it")
B) Lines 24-27 ("Especially…down")
C) Lines 41-42 ("Just…crushed")
D) Lines 52-53 ("If…ramping up")

We're going to start by thinking about what the passage tells us about chronic stress. Before we even reread anything, we can make some assumptions.

First, we know that the passage is about the benefits of *acute* stress ("new idea"), and that the author's attitude toward that phenomenon is positive.

We also know that long-term stress (i.e., chronic stress, on which "old ideas" about stress are based) is the opposite of acute stress, and that the author's attitude toward long-term stress is therefore negative. As a result, we can assume that the correct answer to Question #1 will be negative as well.

B) is clearly positive: creating a "sense of excitement" is something that *acute* stress can do, not chronic stress. Don't get fooled by this choice.

If you know something about biology, you might also be able to eliminate D). The body produces antibodies to help it fight infection – that's a good thing. So D) doesn't make sense either. This is a good example of an instance in which outside knowledge is helpful.

Now, having narrowed the possible answers to A) and C), we're going to shift gears a bit and approach this pair of questions from a slightly different angle. Let's start by thinking about where in the passage the correct lines are most likely located. The reference to line 17 in Question #1 suggests that the answer to that question is probably found relatively close to the beginning of the passage. In addition, chronic stress = old idea, and "old ideas" are typically discussed first. Because the lines referenced in A) and B) of Question #2 are closest to the beginning, they're our top contenders for the right answer.

With that in mind, we're going to check each set of line references in Question #2, paying particular attention to those cited in A) and B), and keeping in mind that the correct answer must support the idea that chronic stress = bad.

134

Lines referenced in Question #2:

A) teens and young adults are experiencing higher levels of stress, and also are struggling to manage it. (lines 9-11)

No. This answer is negative, but it is completely unrelated to either A) or C) in Question #1.

B) Especially insidious, chronic exposure to one of these hormones, cortisol, causes brain changes that make it increasingly difficult to shut the stress response down. (lines 24-27)

Yes, this makes sense. *Chronic* is a synonym for *long-term*, and if you need confirmation, the beginning of the paragraph uses the phrase *chronic stress*. This, however, is where you need to be careful. If you spot the word *cortisol* and jump to pick A) in Question #1, you'll get in trouble. The lines above indicate that chronic stress leads to the production of cortisol (*cortisol causes brain changes*), whereas A) in Question #1 states that chronic stress *inhibits* (shuts down) cortisol production. Right hormone, wrong idea.

That leaves C) in Question #1. Why is that answer correct? The passage states that cortisol *make[s] it increasingly difficult* (=progressively harder) to stop the body from responding to stress. In other words, the more chronically stressed you are, the more cortisol you produce, which in turn makes it even harder for your body to calm down, i.e., to reduce stress.

If you want to stop there, you can, but if you feel compelled to check the other answers, you can do so as well. Just don't spend too much time on them.

C) Just think of the exhilaration of the deadline met or the presentation crushed. (lines 41-42)

The "trick" answer. If you hadn't thought through the question upfront and determined that the correct answer had to be negative, you could easily – and incorrectly – assume that these lines supported B) in Question #1.

D) If a lion is chasing you…your immune system should be ramping up. (lines 52-53)

Again, careful. These lines refer to acute stress, not chronic stress. If you didn't make that distinction, however, you could potentially try to stretch this answer into a justification for B) in Question #1 as well.

So that leaves us with B), the correct answer to Question #2.

Important: If you're a very strong reader able to keep track of things easily, you can start with the answers closest to the original line reference, but otherwise you should work in order. If, however, the lines that you used to determine the answer to the first question appear as an answer to the second question, you can simply select that answer and move on. If you answer the first question as you read, you should also mark the lines you used to answer it so that you don't have to spend time finding them again.

At this point, we're going to use the same passage and look at a question pair without a line reference in the first question.

1 ▨▨▨▨▨▨▨▨▨▨▨▨▨▨▨▨▨▨▨▨▨▨

Based on information in the passage, acute stress
has which physical effect?

A) It stimulates an immune response in vulnerable
   areas of the body.
B) It forces cortisol to collect in the bloodstream.
C) It produces an antibody response more powerful
   than that produced by exercise.
D) It cause the body's natural defenses to weaken.

2 ▨▨▨▨▨▨▨▨▨▨▨▨▨▨▨▨▨▨▨▨▨▨

Which choice provides the best evidence for the
answer to the previous question?

A) Lines 24-27 ("chronic...down")
B) Lines 45-47 ("worrying...effects")
C) Lines 63-65 ("immune...lungs")
D) Lines 84-87 ("volunteers...quietly")

The first thing we're going to do is plug the second set of answer choices into the first
question so that we get this:

1 ▨▨▨▨▨▨▨▨▨▨▨▨▨▨▨▨▨▨▨▨▨▨

Based on information in the passage, acute stress
has which physical effect?

A) Lines 24-27 ("chronic...down")
B) Lines 45-47 ("worrying...effects")
C) Lines 63-65 ("immune...lungs")
D) Lines 84-87 ("volunteers...quietly")

Now we have something concrete to work with. Instead of just randomly skimming the
passage looking for bits that seem as if they might be relevant, we've narrowed our focus to
four specific places to look for the answer.

The next step is to check each answer. The key phrase in the question is "acute stress," so the
correct answer must be related to that phenomenon.

If you find that doing so helps you, you can bracket off each line reference in the text, either
before you start working through the answers or as you come to each one. Just remember
that you may need to skim the surrounding lines for context.

A) chronic exposure to one of these hormones, cortisol, causes brain changes that make it increasingly difficult to shut the stress response down.

Be very, very careful here. This statement might seem to support B) in Question #1, but the end of the previous statement indicates that cortisol is a result of stress that is *sustained*, i.e., chronic, whereas the question asks about *acute* stress. So these lines are actually off-topic.

B) worrying about the negative consequences can in itself exacerbate any ill effects.

These lines are essentially saying that worrying about stress can make people more stressed out. This answer is also off-topic because the lines don't specifically discuss acute stress.

C) immune cells were instead traveling to the body's "battlefields" – sites most likely to be wounded in an attack, like the skin, gut, and lungs.

In order to determine whether this statement answers the question, you need to back up and obtain some context. In some cases you will only need to back up a sentence or two, but here you need to go all the way back to the end of the previous paragraph. Lines 54-57 indicate that Dhabhar made this hypothesis in the context of a study designed to determine whether acute stress could have positive effects. So this section is talking about the right type of stress. In addition, lines 66-70 indicate that Dhabhar's experiment confirmed his hypothesis, so the statement in question does in fact describe an effect of acute stress.

D) volunteers who exercised or took a math test (both acute stressors) immediately prior to being vaccinated had a heightened antibody response relative to volunteers who sat quietly.

Clearly, this answer discusses the effects of acute stress as well, so it's also a contender.

Now we're going to backtrack and see which of the statements in the previous question is directly supported by either C) or D).

1

Based on information in the passage, acute stress has which physical effect?

A) It stimulates an immune response in vulnerable areas of the body.
B) It forces cortisol to collect in the bloodstream.
C) It produces an antibody response more powerful than that produced by exercise.
D) It cause the body's natural defenses to weaken.

C) in Question #2 is consistent with A) in Question #1 above): sites *most likely to be wounded in at attack* = vulnerable areas of the body. A) also rephrases the passage – a good sign.

D) in Question #2 is a little trickier. Although lines 84-87 do indicate that acute stress produced *a heightened antibody response,* they do not indicate that the response was "more powerful" than it was after exercise. It could be true, but we don't have enough information.

A) is thus the correct answer to Question #1, and C) is the correct answer to Question #2.

Other Approaches

If you're a strong reader and/or excel at playing process of elimination, you'll probably find that you don't always need – or want – to look back at the passage for the first question in a supporting evidence pair.

You might also find the strategy discussed above too complicated, preferring to look back at the passage and then answer the questions in order. I do not generally advocate this strategy since line references constitute such an important source of information. But that said, it may make sense to approach certain individual questions this way. You should, however, be aware that a major pitfall of ignoring line references initially is that the information you need to answer the first question might not appear until close to the end of a (long) passage. If you begin to panic halfway through because you haven't found the answer yet, you can easily fall into a loop of skimming randomly and guessing.

Otherwise, when you either remember the answer to the first question or are able to figure it out logically by using the main point or eliminating answers, you may also find yourself a bit irritated by the supporting evidence question. You understand the gist of the passage and just *know* what the right answer is. Why should you have to go and find support for something that seems so obvious?

As far as problems go, this is a pretty good one to have. If you're a strong enough reader to figure out the point on your own and identify the correct answer based on it, you're probably a strong enough reader to figure out what sort of information is consistent with it. All you have to do is look through the line references and pick out the one that fits.

In other cases, however, working by process of elimination might allow you to eliminate an option or two but not identify the correct answer with certainty. For instance, let's reconsider the question we just looked at on the previous page. If you work from the understanding that acute stress = good, you might be able to cross out D) because that answer is clearly negative. And if you happen to remember that cortisol is associated with chronic rather than acute stress, you might also be able to eliminate B). But then you're left with A) and C). What do you do?

At that point, you want to think logically about where the necessary information is most likely to be located. Benefits of acute stress = new idea. "New ideas" tend to be discussed after "old ideas", so you can make an educated guess that the correct lines will appear somewhere in the second half of the passage. As a result, you can check C) and D) in Question #2 first. If you read carefully and establish the context for those lines, you shouldn't have too much trouble connecting C) in Question #2 to A) in Question #1. Even if you're uncertain about A), you can still play process of elimination: lines 84-87 do not indicate that the antibody response produced by acute stress is more powerful than that produced by exercise.

Starting on the next page, we're going to look at some additional examples.

Citrus greening, the plague that could wipe out Florida's $9 billion orange industry, begins with the touch of a jumpy brown bug on a sun-kissed leaf. From there, the bacterial disease incubates in the
5 tree's roots, then moves back up the trunk in full force, causing nutrient flows to seize up. Leaves turn yellow, and the oranges, deprived of sugars from the leaves, remain green, sour, and hard. Many fall before harvest, brown necrotic flesh ringing failed stems.
10 For the past decade, Florida's oranges have been literally starving. Since it first appeared in 2005, citrus greening, also known by its Chinese name, *huanglongbing*, has swept across Florida's groves like a flood. With no hills to block it, the Asian citrus
15 psyllid—the invasive aphid relative that carries the disease—has infected nearly every orchard in the state. By one estimate, 80 percent of Florida's citrus trees are infected and declining.
The disease has spread beyond Florida to nearly
20 every orange-growing region in the United States. Despite many generations of breeding by humanity, no citrus plant resists greening; it afflicts lemons, grapefruits, and other citrus species as well. Once a tree is infected, it will die. Yet in a few select Floridian
25 orchards, there are now trees that, thanks to innovative technology, can fight the greening tide.
The pressure to find solutions keeps growing. Even without disease, the orange industry is under stress. It's losing land to housing developments; it's losing
30 customers to the spreading notion that orange juice is a sugary, not healthy, drink.

The citrus industry, slow to prevent the greening disease, has partially redirected its advertising budget and invested heavily in research—reportedly $90
35 million so far. Southern Gardens Citrus, one of the largest growers, supports Mirkov's work. The federal government, too, has contributed, with this year's farm bill directing $125 million toward the fight against citrus greening.

1

The passage indicates that citrus greening affects trees by

A) flooding them with particles of virus.
B) depriving them of key nutrients.
C) destroying the groves where they are planted.
D) altering their genetic structure.

2

Which choice provides the best evidence for the answer to the previous question?

A) Lines 6-9 ("Leaves...planet")
B) Lines 14-17 ("With...state")
C) Lines 21-22 ("Despite...greening")
D) Lines 29-31 ("It's losing...drink")

When you work this way, you should start by identifying/underlining the key word or phrase that indicates the specific focus of the question. Here, the key phrase is *affects trees*.

Then, go back to the passage to skim for that idea, **remembering to pull your index finger down the page as you skim and to pay close attention to the introduction, the conclusion, and the first and last sentences of paragraphs.** Even in shorter passages, key information is most likely to be located in those places.

To reiterate: if you decide to skim the passage for the key information and do not have a clear idea of where that information is, it is crucial that you cover the entire passage. One very common mistake students make is to assume that the necessary information must be buried somewhere in the middle of the passage. Consequently, they skip the beginning and start searching from the second or third paragraph, with the result that they never find what they're looking for – and that's a shame since the answer is often quite straightforward.

That is precisely the case here: the information you need is located in the introduction. The phrase *begins with the touch of a jumpy brown bug on a sun-kissed leaf* indicates that the author is about to launch into a description of citrus greening's effects on trees. The statement that *[citrus greening causes] nutrient flows to seize up* points you directly to B) in Question #1.

Notice, however, that that phrase does not appear in any of the sets of line references in Question #2. Instead, the correct answer to Question #2, A), cites lines that support or expand on the point by describing how leaves dry up when they are deprived of sugar. In this case, that is not a major issue because A) includes the only set of lines to appear in the introduction – a placement that immediately suggests that it is the answer.

In general, though, **if you choose to answer paired supporting evidence questions in order, it is a good idea to bracket off the lines you used to determine the answer to the first question.** If they happen to be cited in one of the answers to the second question, you have the answers to both questions. And even if the exact lines on which you based your answer aren't cited, there's a good chance that the correct set of lines will appear right nearby.

The answer to the questions we just looked at were based on an easily overlooked detail. Without a truly exceptional memory, most readers would have to return to the passage to answer them. In other cases, however, you may be able to use a big-picture understanding of the passage to answer the first question quickly. You can then check each set of lines against the idea you know it must contain.

Let's look at an example based on the same passage:

1

According to the author's description, citrus greening could best be described as

A) mysterious.
B) benign.
C) ancient.
D) devastating.

2

Which choice provides the best evidence for the answer to the previous question?

A) Lines 17-18 ("By...declining")
B) Lines 24-26 ("Yet...tide")
C) Lines 29-31 ("It's...drink")
D) Lines 32-35 ("The citrus...far")

Question #1 could actually be considered a vocabulary question in reverse. Instead of identifying the meaning of a specific word in the passage, you must use the wording of the passage to identify the correct definition from among the answer choices.

Although the question does not provide a line reference, there is no need to go searching through the passage for the answer. If you're gotten the gist of the passage, you can pretty much answer it on your own. What's the point? CG = AWFUL (citrus greening is awful). Assuming you know the definition of *devastating*, you can jump to D) right away. Note that it's irrelevant whether you know the definitions of the incorrect answers (especially *benign*) as long as you know the definition of the correct answer.

Note that it's irrelevant whether you know the definitions of the other words (especially *benign*) as long as you do know what *devastating* means.

Now all you have to do is find the lines that say as much. Since a good part of the passage is devoted to making the point that citrus greening is devastating, you probably shouldn't try to figure out the lines on your own. There are just too many places where they could be located. Even so, it shouldn't be too hard to work from the answers provided.

A) By one estimate, 80 percent of Florida's citrus trees are infected and declining.

Yes, this is consistent with the idea that citrus greening is devastating. 80 percent is an enormous loss. Because this answer fits, you can stop reading right there. If you really wanted to make sure, you could check the remaining answers, but especially in this case, it's not really necessary.

Why? Think about how the passage is organized. Everything up until line 24 is basically focused on emphasizing how awful the effects of citrus greening are. After line 24, the focus switches to stopping the disease. Logically, the correct set of lines must appear before line 24. A) contains the only set of lines to meet that criterion, so it must be correct.

Using Line References to Make Educated Guesses

If you want to get really ambitious, you can occasionally use a word in a line reference to identify the likely answer to Question #2. This strategy does require close attention to detail as well as some very logical thinking, but it can also get you to the answer much more quickly. For example, take another look at this question:

1

The passage indicates that citrus greening affects trees by

A) Lines 7-9 ("Leaves...planet")
B) Lines 14-17 ("With...state")
C) Lines 21-22 ("Despite...greening")
D) Lines 29-31 ("It's losing...drink")

Notice that Question #1 asks about the effect on *trees*. If you start with that information and very, very carefully consider the words at the beginnings and ends of line references in Question #2, you can make an educated guess.

Which answer includes a word related to the trees? Choice A), which contains the word *leaves*. That one, tiny clue is enough to suggest that C) is worth checking first. And when you plug it in, you can see that it does in fact answer the question.

But to reiterate: you should **never** choose an answer this way without going back to the passage and getting the full context. This strategy is only useful insofar as it can occasionally get you to the correct answer *faster*. Leaping to conclusions can get you into a lot of trouble on the SAT – it's much safer not to risk it.

Literal Comprehension Exercises

1. The world is complex and interconnected, and the evolution of our communications system from a broadcast model to a networked one has added a new dimension to the mix. The Internet has made us all less
5 dependent on professional journalists and editors for information about the wider world, allowing us to seek out information directly via online search or to receive it from friends through social media. But this enhanced convenience comes with a considerable risk: that we
10 will be exposed to what we want to know at the expense of what we need to know. While we can find virtual communities that correspond to our every curiosity, there's little pushing us beyond our comfort zones to or into the unknown, even if the unknown may have
15 serious implications for our lives. There are things we should probably know more about—like political and religious conflicts in Russia or basic geography. But even if we knew more than we do, there's no guarantee that the knowledge gained would prompt us to act in a
20 particularly admirable fashion.

1

The passage indicates that internet users tend to seek information in a manner that is

A) impulsive.

B) unadventurous.

C) creative.

D) reckless.

2

Which choice provides the best evidence for the answer to the previous question?

A) Lines 1-4 ("The world…mix")

B) Lines 4-6 ("The Internet…world")

C) Line 13 ("there's…zones")

D) Lines 17-20 ("But…fashion")

2. Chimps do it, birds do it, even you and I do it. Once you see someone yawn, you are compelled to do the same. Now it seems that wolves can be added to the list of animals known to spread yawns like a
5 contagion.
  Among humans, even thinking about yawning can trigger the reflex, leading some to suspect that catching a yawn is linked to our ability to empathize with other humans. For instance, contagious yawning activates the
10 same parts of the brain that govern empathy and social know-how. And some studies have shown that humans with more fine-tuned social skills are more likely to catch a yawn.
  Similarly, chimpanzees, baboons and bonobos
15 often yawn when they see other members of their species yawning. Chimps (Pan troglodytes) can catch yawns from humans, even virtual ones. At least in primates, contagious yawning seems to require an emotional connection and may function as a demonstration of
20 empathy. Beyond primates, though, the trends are less clear-cut. One study found evidence of contagious yawning in birds but didn't connect it to empathy. A 2008 study showed that dogs (Canis lupus familiaris) could catch yawns from humans, and another showed
25 that dogs were more likely to catch the yawn of a familiar human rather than a stranger. But efforts to see if dogs catch yawns from each other and to replicate the results have so far had no luck.

1

The passage indicates that the people most likely to catch yawns are

A) detail oriented.

B) easily persuaded.

C) attuned to others.

D) chronically fatigued.

2

Which choice provides the best evidence for the answer to the previous question?

A) Lines 3-5 ("Now…contagion")

B) Lines 9-11 ("For…know-how")

C) Lines 21-22 ("One…empathy")

D) Lines 26-28 ("But…luck")

3

The passage indicates that the connection between empathy and yawning in birds and dogs, in comparison to humans, is

A) more uncertain.
B) less uncertain.
C) impossible to establish.
D) a controversial topic.

4

Which choice provides the best evidence for the answer to the previous question?

A) Lines 3-4 ("Now...yawns")
B) Lines 14-16 ("Similarly...yawning")
C) Lines 20-21 ("Beyond...clear-cut")
D) Lines 23-26 ("A 2008...stranger")

3. The following passage is adapted from George Orwell, "Keep the Aspidistra Flying," first published in 1936. Gordon, the protagonist, is a poet.

Gordon walked homeward against the rattling wind, which blew his hair backward and gave him more of a 'good' forehead than ever. His manner conveyed to the passers-by – at least, he hoped it did—that if he wore
5 no overcoat it was from pure caprice.

Willowbed Road, NW, was dingy and depressing, although it contrived to keep up a kind of mingy decency. There was even a dentist's brass plate on one of the houses. In quite two-thirds of them, amid the
10 lace curtains of the parlor window, there was a green card with 'Apartments' on it in silver lettering, above the peeping foliage of an aspidistra.*

Mrs. Wisbeach, Gordon's landlady, specialized in 'single gentlemen.' Bed-sitting-rooms, with gaslight laid
15 on and find your own heating, baths extra (there was a geyser), and meals in the tomb-dark dining-room with the phalanx of clotted sauce-bottles in the middle of the table. Gordon, who came home for his midday dinner, paid twenty-seven and six a week.

20 The gaslight shone yellow through the frosted transom above the door of Number 31. Gordon took out his key and fished about in the keyhole – in that kind of house the key never quite fits the lock. The darkish little hallway – in reality it was only a passage – smelt of
25 dishwater and cabbage. Gordon glanced at the japanned tray on the hall-stand. No letters, of course. He had told himself not to hope for a letter, and nevertheless had continued to hope. A stale feeling, not quite a pain, settled upon his breast. Rosemary might have written!
30 It was four days now since she had written. Moreover, he had sent out to magazines and had not yet had returned to him. The one thing that made the evening bearable was to find a letter waiting for him when he got home. But he received very few letters – four or five in a week
35 at the very most.

On the left of the hall was the never-used parlor, then came the staircase, and beyond that the passage ran down to the kitchen and to the unapproachable lair inhabited by Mrs. Wisbeach herself. As Gordon came in,
40 the door at the end of the passage opened a foot or so. Mrs. Wisbeach's face emerged, inspected him briefly but suspiciously, and disappeared again. It was quite impossible to get in or out of the house, at any time before eleven at night, without being scrutinized in this
45 manner. Just what Mrs. Wisbeach suspected you of it

was hard to say. She was one of those malignant respectable women who keep lodging-houses. Age about forty-five, stout but active, with a pink, fine-featured, horribly observant face, beautifully grey hair,
50 and a permanent grievance.

In the familiar darkness of his room, Gordon felt for the gas-jet and lighted it. The room was medium-sized, not big enough to be curtained into two, but too big to be sufficiently warmed by one defective oil lamp. It had
55 the sort of furniture you expect in a top floor back. White-quilted single-bed; brown lino floor-covering; wash-hand-stand with jug and basin of that cheap white ware which you can never see without thinking of chamberpots. On the window-sill there was a sickly
60 aspidistra in a green-glazed pot.

Up against this, under the window, there was a kitchen table with an inkstained green cloth. This was Gordon's 'writing' table. It was only after a bitter struggle that he had induced Mrs. Wisbeach to give him
65 a kitchen table instead of the bamboo 'occasional' table – a mere stand for the aspidistra – which she considered proper for a top floor back. And even now there was endless nagging because Gordon would never allow his table to be 'tidied up.' The table was in a
70 permanent mess. It was almost covered with a muddle of papers, perhaps two hundred sheets, grimy and dog-eared, and all written on and crossed out and written on again – a sort of sordid labyrinth of papers to which only Gordon possessed the key. There was a film of
75 dust over everything. Except for a few books on the mantelpiece, this table, with its mess of papers, was the sole mark Gordon's personality had left on the room.

*a bulbous plant with broad leaves, often used as a houseplant.

1

Based on the passage, "that kind of house" (line 22) is one that is

A) large and rambling.

B) gloomy and rundown.

C) tidy and cheerful.

D) utterly neglected.

2

Which choice provides the best evidence for the answer to the previous question?

A) Lines 6-8 ("Willowbed...decency")

B) Lines 9-12 ("In...apidastra")

C) Lines 18-19 ("Gordon...week")

D) Lines 26-28 ("He...hope")

3

The passage indicates that the encounter between Gordon and Mrs. Wisbeach was

A) inevitable.

B) drawn out.

C) cordial.

D) unexpected.

4

Which choice provides the best evidence for the answer to the previous question?

A) Lines 32-33 ("The one...home")

B) Lines 36-39 ("On...herself")

C) Lines 42-45 ("It was...manner")

D) Lines 46-50 ("She...grievance")

5

The narrator indicates that the papers in Gordon's room were

A) an unrecognized masterpiece.

B) hidden from view.

C) a source of embarrassment.

D) comprehensible to Gordon alone.

6

Which choice provides the best evidence for the answer to the previous question?

A) Lines 52-55 ("The room...back")

B) Lines 63-65 ("It was...table")

C) Lines 73-74 ("a sort...key")

D) Lines 75-77 ("Except...room")

4. The following passage is adapted from Wiebke Brauer, "The Miracle of Space," © 2014 by *Smart Magazine.*

Imagine a world where you share the available space with others: without signs, sidewalks, or bicycle lanes. A vision otherwise known as shared space –
and one that becomes more and more relevant with
5 the crowding of our cities. While this might sound like urban science fiction or, possibly, impending chaos mixed with survival of the fittest, this particular concept is the declared dream of many traffic planners.
Shared space means streets freed of signs and
10 signals; streets solely governed by right of way, leaving road users to their own devices. In order to restructure public space, it removes all superfluous interventions and contradictory guidelines. Many countries are currently in the process of installing – or at least
15 discussing – such 'lawless' areas: Germany and the Netherlands, Denmark and the UK, Switzerland and the USA, but also Australia and New Zealand.
One could argue that shared spaces have been around for a long time, simply under different terms
20 and titles. Back in the 1970s, for example, residents enjoyed mixed traffic areas, traffic calming, and play streets. And yet, these were not quite the same: Shared space involves a new and radical push for equal rights of all road users, pedestrian and otherwise. And
25 while it was British urban designer Ben Hamilton-Baillie who coined the actual term, the concept itself was developed in the mid-1990s under former Dutch traffic manager Hans Monderman. Shortly before his death in 2006, Monderman explained the basic tenets
30 of shared space as such: "The problem with traffic engineers is that when there's a problem with a road, they always try to add something. To my mind, it's much better to remove things."
Indeed, studies have shown that in many places –
35 where signs and traffic lights have been removed and where each and every one is responsible for their own actions in ungoverned space – the rate of accidents goes down. The reason: the traditional strict separation between cars, cyclists, and pedestrians encourages
40 clashes at crossings. And although shared space requires cars to lower their speed, it also cuts down on journey times since it encourages a continuous flow of traffic instead of bringing it to a halt through traffic signals.
45 Monderman was utterly convinced that shared space would work anywhere in the world because, underneath it all, people are basically the same, despite any cultural differences. In an interview, he stated that "emotions and issues are the same everywhere. You should be able

50 to read a street like a book. If you insist on constantly guiding people and treating them like idiots, you shouldn't be surprised if they act like idiots after a while."
At the same time, the threat of looming idiocy
55 is not the most pressing reason for a future traffic management rethink. Recent city planning, for example, has evolved along the same lines around the world: think highways and flyovers dissecting the city's natural fabric, dedicated pedestrian zones, and
60 large shopping malls. Clear-cut boundaries between driving, work, life, and shopping are emphasized by a thicket of signs. The result: ultimate, well-ordered bleakness. At night, you might find yourself in an empty, soulless pedestrian zone. A lot of the time,
65 urbanization simply translates as uniformity.
In recent years, however, city and traffic planners have decided to tackle this issue with "road space attractiveness" measures to breathe new spirit into lifeless satellite towns. Their goal: a new definition
70 of space and mobility against the background that the notion of "might is right" – and only if those in power stick to the rules – is more than outdated. The unregulated and unorthodox approach of shared space makes it obvious to each and every individual
75 that this concept requires cooperation, that sharing is the new having.
Critics of Monderman and Hamilton-Baillie have voiced that no rules implies the inevitable return of "might is right." Yet who says that chaos
80 reigns in the absence of order? That's a questionable statement. Shared space certainly requires a new mindset and we can't expect a swift shift away from traditional traffic planning – bigger, further, faster.
But the vision of no more set traffic cycles, fewer
85 linear and predefined patterns, of freely flowing and intermingling participants in an open and boundless space, is equally unfettered and fascinating. A vision in the spirit of Pericles who wrote around 450 BC that "you need freedom for happiness and courage
90 for freedom."

1

The passage indicates that in areas where traffic signals are removed, traveling becomes

A) safer and less time consuming.

B) safer and more time consuming.

C) more dangerous and less time consuming.

D) more dangerous and more time consuming.

2

According to the author, recent city planning has primarily resulted in

A) isolated neighborhoods.

B) a lack of variety.

C) stylistic incoherence.

D) urban revitalization.

3

Which choice provides the best evidence for the answer to the previous question?

A) Lines 13-15 ("Many…areas")

B) Lines 30-32 ("The problem…things")

C) Lines 48-49 ("emotions …everywhere")

D) Lines 64-65 ("A…uniformity")

5. This passage is adapted from a 1950 speech by Dean Acheson, who served as Secretary of State from 1949 to 1953 and strongly influenced United States foreign policy during the Cold War.

However much we may sympathize with the Soviet citizens who for reasons bedded deep in history are obliged to live under it, we are not attempting to change the governmental or social structure of the Soviet
5 Union. The Soviet regime, however, has devoted a major portion of its energies and resources to the attempt to impose its system on other peoples. In this attempt it has shown itself prepared to resort to any method or stratagem, including subversion, threats, and even
10 military force.

Therefore, if the two systems are to coexist, some acceptable means must be found to free the world from the destructive tensions and anxieties of which it has been the victim in these past years and the continuance
15 of which can hardly be in the interests of any people.

I wish, therefore, to speak to you about those points of greatest difference which must be identified and sooner or later reconciled if the two systems are to live together, if not with mutual respect, at least in
20 reasonable security.

It is now nearly five years since the end of hostilities, and the victorious Allies have been unable to define the terms of peace with the defeated countries. This is a grave, a deeply disturbing fact. For our part, we do not
25 intend nor wish, in fact we do not know how, to create satellites. Nor can we accept a settlement which would make Germany, Japan, or liberated Austria satellites of the Soviet Union. The experience in Hungary, Rumania, and Bulgaria has been one of bitter disappointment and
30 shocking betrayal of the solemn pledges by the wartime Allies. The Soviet leaders joined in the pledge at Tehran that they looked forward "with confidence to the day when all peoples of the world may live free lives, untouched by tyranny, and according to their varying
35 desires and their own consciences." We can accept treaties of peace which would give reality to this pledge and to the interests of all in security.

With regard to the whole group of countries which we are accustomed to thinking of as the satellite area, the
40 Soviet leaders could withdraw their military and police force and refrain from using the shadow of that force to keep in power persons or regimes which do not command the confidence of the respective peoples, freely expressed through orderly representative processes.

45 In this connection, we do not insist that these governments have any particular political or social complexion. What concerns us is that they should be truly independent national regimes, with a will of their own and with a decent foundation in popular feeling.
50 The Soviet leaders could cooperate with us to the end that the official representatives of all countries are treated everywhere with decency and respect and that an atmosphere is created in which these representatives could function in a normal and helpful manner,
55 conforming to the accepted codes of diplomacy.

These are some of the things which we feel that Soviet leaders could do which would permit the rational and peaceful development of the coexistence of their system and ours. They are not things that go to
60 the depths of the moral conflict. They have been formulated by us, not as moralists but as servants of government, anxious to get on with the practical problems that lie before us and to get on with them in a manner consistent with mankind's deep longing for a
65 respite from fear and uncertainty.

Nor have they been formulated as a one-sided bargain. A will to achieve binding, peaceful settlements would be required of all participants. All would have to produce unmistakable evidence of their good faith.
70 All would have to accept agreements in the observance of which all nations could have real confidence.

The United States is ready, as it has been and always will be, to cooperate in genuine efforts to find peaceful settlements. Our attitude is not inflexible, our opinions
75 are not frozen, our positions are not and will not be obstacles to peace. But it takes more than one to cooperate. If the Soviet Union could join in doing these things I have outlined, we could all face the future with greater security. We could look forward to more than
80 the eventual reduction of some of the present tensions. We could anticipate a return to a more normal and relaxed diplomatic atmosphere and to progress in the transaction of some of the international business which needs so urgently to be done.

1

What is the author's main point about regimes in the satellite area?

A) Their leaders are susceptible to outside influences because they lack confidence.

B) The United States would not dictate their policies as long as they were elected freely.

C) They should model themselves directly on successful democracies.

D) They should refrain from behaving aggressively toward neighboring countries.

2

Which choice provides the best evidence for the answer to the previous question?

A) Lines 38-41 ("With...force")

B) Lines 45-48 ("In...regimes")

C) Lines 50-52 ("The Soviet...respect")

D) Lines 67-68 ("A will...participants")

3

The author uses Hungary, Rumania, and Bulgaria (lines 28-29) as examples of

A) Soviet leaders' betrayal of their pledge at Tehran.

B) newly liberated satellites of the Soviet Union.

C) countries that the United States want to transform into satellites.

D) nations that have expressed the desire to accept peace treaties.

4

The author describes the Soviet Union as a regime characterized by

A) flexibility.

B) corruption.

C) ruthlessness.

D) loyalty.

5

Which choice provides the best evidence for the answer to the previous question?

A) Lines 7-10 ("In...force")

B) Lines 16-19 ("I...together")

C) Lines 21-23 ("It is...countries")

D) Lines 31-34 ("The Soviet...tyranny")

6. The following passage is adapted from "Scientists Discover Salty Aquifer, Previously Unknown Microbial Habitat Under Antarctica," © 2015 by Dartmouth College.

Using an airborne imaging system for the first time in Antarctica, scientists have discovered a vast network of unfrozen salty groundwater that may support previously unknown microbial life deep under the coldest, driest
5 desert on our planet. The findings shed new light on ancient climate change on Earth and provide strong evidence that a similar briny aquifer could support microscopic life on Mars. The scientists used SkyTEM, an airborne electromagnetic sensor, to detect and map
10 otherwise inaccessible subterranean features.

The system uses an antennae suspended beneath a helicopter to create a magnetic field that reveals the subsurface to a depth of about 1,000 feet. Because a helicopter was used, large areas of rugged terrain could
15 be surveyed. The SkyTEM team was funded by the National Science Foundation and led by researchers from the University of Tennessee, Knoxville (UTK), and Dartmouth College, which oversees the NSF's SkyTEM project.
20 "These unfrozen materials appear to be relics of past surface ecosystems and our findings provide compelling evidence that they now provide deep subsurface habitats for microbial life despite extreme environmental conditions," says lead author Jill Mikucki,
25 an assistant professor at UTK. "These new below-ground visualization technologies can also provide insight on glacial dynamics and how Antarctica responds to responds to climate change."

Co-author Dartmouth Professor Ross Virginia is
30 SkyTEM's co-principal investigator and director of Dartmouth's Institute of Arctic Studies. "This project is studying the past and present climate to, in part, understand how climate change in the future will affect biodiversity and ecosystem processes," Virginia says.
35 "This fantastic new view beneath the surface will help us sort out competing ideas about how the McMurdo Dry Valleys have changed with time and how this history influences what we see today."

The researchers found that the unfrozen brines form
40 extensive, interconnected aquifers deep beneath glaciers and lakes and within permanently frozen soils. The brines extend from the coast to at least 7.5 miles inland in the McMurdo Dry Valleys, the largest ice-free region in Antarctica. The brines could be due to freezing and/or
45 deposits. The findings show for the first time that the Dry Valleys' lakes are interconnected rather than isolated; connectivity between lakes and aquifers is important in sustaining ecosystems through drastic climate change, such as lake dry-down events. The findings also challenge

50 the assumption that parts of the ice sheets below the pressure melting point are devoid of liquid water.

In addition to providing answers about the biological adaptations of previously unknown ecosystems that persist in the extreme cold and dark of the Antarctic
55 winter, the new study could help scientists to understand whether similar conditions might exist elsewhere in the solar system, specifically beneath the surface of Mars, which has many similarities to the Dry Valleys. Overall, the Dry Valleys ecosystem – cold,
60 vegetation-free and home only to microscopic animal and plant life – resembles, during the Antarctic summer, conditions on the surface on Mars.

SkyTEM produced images of Taylor Valley along the Ross Sea that suggest briny sediments exist at
65 subsurface temperatures down to perhaps -68°F, which is considered suitable for microbial life. One of the studied areas was lower Taylor Glacier, where the data suggest ancient brine still exists beneath the glacier. That conclusion is supported by the presence of Blood
70 Falls, an iron-rich brine that seeps out of the glacier and hosts an active microbial ecosystem.

Scientists' understanding of Antarctica's underground environment is changing dramatically as research reveals that subglacial lakes are widespread
75 and that at least half of the areas covered by the ice sheet are akin to wetlands on other continents. But groundwater in the ice-free regions and along the coastal margins remains poorly understood.

1

The passage indicates that the "unfrozen salty groundwater" (line 3) was once

A) contained in isolated lakes.
B) locked in glaciers.
C) devoid of any life.
D) found at the earth's surface.

2

Which choice provides the best evidence for the answer to the previous question?

A) Lines 5-6 ("The findings...Earth")
B) Lines 20-21 ("These...ecosystems")
C) Lines 31-34 ("This...processes")
D) Lines 47-48 ("connectivity...change")

3 ▮▮▮▮▮▮▮▮▮▮▮▮▮▮▮▮▮▮▮▮▮▮▮▮▮▮

Based on the passage, a novel finding of the
SkyTEM project was that

A) shifting plates below the Antarctic surface can
create major earthquakes.

B) certain regions of Antarctica bear a similarity
to the surface of Mars.

C) interconnected lakes and aquifers create hardy
ecosystems.

D) biodiversity in Antarctica is decreasing rapidly
as a result of climate change.

4 ▮▮▮▮▮▮▮▮▮▮▮▮▮▮▮▮▮▮▮▮▮▮▮▮▮▮

Which choice provides the best evidence for the
answer to the previous question?

A) Lines 8-10 ("The scientists...features")

B) Lines 25-28 ("These...change")

C) Lines 45-49 ("The findings...events")

D) Lines 75-76 ("at least...continents")

7. The following passage is adapted from Jane Austen, *Northanger Abbey*, originally published in 1817.

No one who had ever seen Catherine Morland in her infancy would have supposed her born to be an heroine. Her situation in life, the character of her father and mother, her own person and disposition, were all
5 equally against her. Her father was a clergyman, without being neglected, or poor, and a very respectable man, though his name was Richard—and he had never been handsome. He had a considerable independence besides two good livings—and he was not in the least addicted
10 to locking up his daughters. Her mother was a woman of useful plain sense, with a good temper, and, what is more remarkable, with a good constitution. She had three sons before Catherine was born; and instead of dying in bringing the latter into the world, as anybody
15 might expect, she still lived on—lived to have six children more—to see them growing up around her, and to enjoy excellent health herself. A family of ten children will be always called a fine family, where there are heads and arms and legs enough for the number;
20 but the Morlands had little other right to the word, for they were in general very plain, and Catherine, for many years of her life, as plain as any. She had a thin awkward figure, a sallow skin without colour, dark lank hair, and strong features—so much for her person; and
25 not less unpropitious for heroism seemed her mind. She was fond of all boy's plays, and greatly preferred cricket not merely to dolls, but to the more heroic enjoyments of infancy, nursing a dormouse, feeding a canary-bird, or watering a rose-bush. Indeed she had
30 no taste for a garden; and if she gathered flowers at all, it was chiefly for the pleasure of mischief—at least so it was conjectured from her always preferring those which she was forbidden to take. Such were her propensities—her abilities were quite as extraordinary.
35 She never could learn or understand anything before she was taught; and sometimes not even then, for she was often inattentive, and occasionally stupid. Her mother was three months in teaching her only to repeat the "Beggar's Petition"; and after all, her
40 next sister, Sally, could say it better than she did. Not that Catherine was always stupid—by no means; she learnt the fable of "The Hare and Many Friends" as quickly as any girl in England. Her mother wished her to learn music; and Catherine was sure she should like it,
45 for she was very fond of tinkling the keys of the old forlorn spinner; so, at eight years old she began. She learnt a year, and could not bear it; and Mrs. Morland, who did not insist on her daughters being accomplished in spite of incapacity or distaste, allowed her to leave
50 off. The day which dismissed the music-master was one of the happiest of Catherine's life. Her taste for drawing was not superior; though whenever she could obtain the outside of a letter from her mother or seize upon any other odd piece of paper, she did what she
55 could in that way, by drawing houses and trees, hens and chickens, all very much like one another. Writing and accounts she was taught by her father; French by her mother: her proficiency in either was not remarkable, and she shirked her lessons in both
60 whenever she could. What a strange, unaccountable character!—for with all these symptoms of profligacy at ten years old, she had neither a bad heart nor a bad temper, was seldom stubborn, scarcely ever quarrelsome, and very kind to the little ones, with
65 few interruptions of tyranny; she was moreover noisy and wild, hated confinement and cleanliness, and loved nothing so well in the world as rolling down the green slope at the back of the house.

1

The narrator indicates that on the whole, the Morlands' appearance was

A) unremarkable.

B) intimidating.

C) uncommonly attractive.

D) somewhat peculiar.

2

Which choice provides the best evidence for the answer to the previous question?

A) Lines 5-8 ("Her…handsome")

B) Lines 10-12 ("Her…constitution")

C) Lines 17-18 ("A family…family")

D) Lines 20-21 ("but…plain")

3

As presented in the passage, Catherine could best be described as

A) charming.
B) heroic.
C) rambunctious.
D) gifted.

4

Which choice provides the best evidence for the answer to the previous question?

A) Lines 30-31 ("and...mischief")
B) Lines 33-34 ("Such...extraordinary")
C) Line 41 ("Not...means")
D) Lines 65-66 ("she...cleanliness")

5

The narrator indicates that Mrs. Morland was

A) weak and sickly.
B) sturdy and practical.
C) short-tempered and irritable.
D) creative and enthusiastic.

6

The passage indicates that Catherine responded to her parents' lessons by

A) participating eagerly.
B) turning them into games.
C) avoiding them if possible.
D) refusing to pay attention.

Explanations: Literal Comprehension Exercises

1.1-2 B, C

If you use the main point of the passage (people stick to familiar w/Internet), you can identify B) as the correct answer to 1.1 right away. When you go to plug in line references, you already know that the correct set of lines must be related to the idea that the Internet does not encourage people to learn about unfamiliar topics. Only C) contains lines that explicitly address that idea (*there's little pushing us beyond our comfort zones*), so it is the answer to 1.2.

If you don't remember the answer from the passage, the easiest way to approach this pair of questions is to plug in the line references from 1.2. The lines cited in A) and B) provide no information about how Internet users behave online, and D) does not discuss how Internet users actually behave – it only speculates about what *might* happen if they found new information. Again, only C) explicitly describes how users behave: they stick to their comfort zones, i.e., are unadventurous.

2.1-2 C, B

The easiest way to answer this question is to use the main point and answer the questions in order. Main point: yawns = empathy in primates, BUT animals? (Yawns are associated with empathy in primates, but the association isn't clear in other animals.) Empathy = attuned to others, making C) the answer to 2.1. The correct answer to 2.2 must support the association between empathy and yawning. That answer is B) because lines 9-11 state that yawning is governed by the same parts of the brain that govern empathy.

2.3-4 A, C

The easiest way to approach this question is to use the main point: yawning = empathy in primates, BUT not clear for animals. Not clear = more *un*certain. For 2.4, the correct lines must indicate it isn't clear whether empathy is related to yawning in non-primate animals. Now consider how the passage is organized: the author first discusses primates, including humans, then switches to non-primates toward the end. You can thus focus on the later line references, narrowing your choices to C) and D). C) is correct because lines 20-21 state that the relationship between yawning and empathy in non-primates is *less clear-cut* (=more uncertain).

3.1-2 B, A

The first question provides a line reference, so start by using it. What information do we get about *that kind of house* in and around line 22? That it's *darkish* and smells of *dishwater and cabbage* (lines 23-25). In other words, it's not a very pleasant place. In 3.1, C) can be eliminated because it's clearly positive. D) is a bit too extreme, so you can assume it's wrong as well. If you're still not sure about B), check the line references in 3.2, and see whether they provide any additional direction. A) provides that direction. Lines 6-8 indicate that the neighborhood is *dingy and depressing*. That is consistent with B) in 3.1, and A) is the answer to 3.2.

3.3-4 A, C

Because there's no line reference in 3.3, plug in the line references from 3.4 in order. You can eliminate A) quickly because lines 32-33 are about Rosemary's letters, not Mrs. Wisbeach. Lines 36-39 mention Mrs. Wisbeach but provide no information about Gordon's actual encounter with her, so B) can be eliminated as well. C) is correct because lines 42-45 state that *It was quite impossible to get in or out of the house…without being scrutinized.* That means Mrs. Wisbeach caught Gordon every single time. In other words, their encounter was "inevitable." That makes A) the answer to 3.3 and C) the answer to 3.4.

3.5-6 D, C

Because there's no line reference in 3.5, plug in the line references from 3.6. You can eliminate A) and B) quickly because lines 52-55 and 63-65 have nothing to do with Gordon's papers. C) is correct because lines 73-74 indicate that only Gordon possessed the "key" to his *labyrinth of papers.* In other words, he was the only person to whom the papers were comprehensible. That makes D) the answer to 3.5 and C) the answer to 3.6.

4.1 A

If you know the main point (eliminating traffic signals improves traffic), you can make an educated guess that either A) or B) is the answer to 4.1 because those are the most positive answers. Then, when you go back to the passage, you only have to determine whether driving without traffic signals takes more or less time. To search for this information efficiently, look for the key word "time." If you scan from the beginning, you'll find the answer in lines 41-42, where the author states that *[removing traffic signals] also <u>cuts down</u> on journey times* – that is, removing traffic signals makes trips less time-consuming. A) is thus correct.

4.2-3 B, D

Because there's no line reference in 4.2, plug in the line references in 4.3 in order. A) can be eliminated because lines 13-15 only indicate that many countries are creating areas without traffic signals, and B) can be eliminated because lines 30-32 only discuss Monderman's problem with traffic engineering – neither answer provides any information about urban planning. C) is incorrect because the quote only reveals Monderman's belief that removing traffic signals can work anywhere. Like A) and B), this answer says nothing about urban planning. D) is correct because in line 65, the phrase *urbanization simply translates as uniformity* is used to support the idea that *Recent city planning… has evolved along the same lines around the world.* In other words, it's the same everywhere, i.e., uniform. That makes B) the answer to 4.2 and D) the answer to 4.3.

5.1-2 B, B

Although this is a main point question, it focuses on only a small part of the passage. Unless you remember the answer, you should plug in the line references from 5.2 and work through them in order. Remember, though, that main points are most likely to be found in topic sentences, so you want to pay particular attention to line references involving them. Be very careful with A). Lines 38-41 do discuss satellite areas, and if you're not working carefully, the reference to *withdrawing force* might seem to support D) in 5.1. The problem is that lines 38-41 focus on the Soviets' behavior toward satellite regimes, not on the satellite regimes' behavior toward other countries. So A) doesn't work. For B), the fact that lines 45-48 include a topic sentence should immediately alert you to their potential importance. What do we learn from those lines? That the United States is **not** primarily concerned that *these [satellite] governments have any particular social or political complexion.* In other words, the United States doesn't care what the people living under Soviet control choose, as long as they are given the opportunity to choose freely. That idea corresponds to B) in 5.1 and makes B) the correct answer to 5.2 as well.

5.3 A

The question asks what Hungary, Rumania, and Bulgaria are examples of, so your job is to figure out what point those countries are cited to support. Remember that the reference to lines 28-29 does not indicate that the answer will be in those lines; it simply gives you a starting point. Because lines 28-29 are right in the middle of the paragraph, you need to read from a few lines above to a few lines below for context. The sentence in which the key words from the passage appear indicates that the Soviets have broken their promises *(pledges)*, and the next sentence indicates that they pledged their belief in freedom at Tehran. Logically, Hungary, Romania, and Bulgaria are examples of the Soviets' broken Tehran pledge, so A) is the answer. B) is incorrect because those countries have not been liberated – the passage implies just the opposite. C) is incorrect because Acheson clearly states that United States does not want satellites. D) is incorrect because the passage provides no information about these countries' desire to accept peace treaties.

5.4-5 C, A

If you know that the Soviet Regime was the United States' enemy during the Cold War, you can probably narrow down the answers to B) and C) since those are the only negative options. But even if you don't know anything about Soviet-American Cold War relations, this is a fairly straightforward question: plugging in line references will allow you to identify the answer almost immediately. Lines 7-10 state that the Soviet Union *has shown itself prepared to resort to any method or stratagem, including subversion, threats, and even military force.* That is the definition of "ruthless," making C) the answer to 5.4 and A) the answer to 5.5.

6.1-2 D, B

Although you're given a line reference, it provides little information other than the fact that the unfrozen groundwater *may support previously unknown microbial life.* The question asks what this water "once" was, so plug in the line references and see which one provides information about frozen groundwater in the <u>past</u>. Lines 5-6 only indicate a possible use for the findings about groundwater. They say nothing about the groundwater in the past, so A) can be eliminated. The key to recognizing B) as the correct answer to 6.2 is to recognize that the phrase *these unfrozen materials* refers to unfrozen groundwater – if you overlook the fact the author is referring to the same thing two different ways, you'll overlook the answer. Lines 20-21 state that the groundwater was part of past *surface* ecosystems, indicating that D) is the correct answer to 6.1. Otherwise, C) and D) can be eliminated in 6.2 because lines 31-34 focus on the future, not the past, and lines 47-48 only discuss an advantage of interconnected lakes.

6.3-4 C, C

If you remember reading about how the SkyTEM project's findings could help scientists better understand life on Mars, you might be tempted to pick B) and then look for a set of lines in 6.4 to support that answer. Unfortunately, there isn't one. So plug in the answers in order, looking for information about the findings from the project. A) in 6.4 is incorrect because 8-10 just describe SkyTEM itself; they say nothing about its findings, novel or otherwise. B) in 6.4 is incorrect because lines 25-28 only indicate what the project *could* find, not what it has actually found. C) in 6.4 is correct because the phrase *findings show <u>for the first time</u>* indicates a "novel" (new) finding, namely that connectivity between bodies of water can help ecosystems handle difficult periods (=create hardier ecosystems). That makes C) the answer to 6.3 as well. D) in 6.4 is incorrect because lines 75-76 do not describe a novel finding specific to the SkyTEM project.

7.1-2 A, D

Unless you happen to remember the discussion of the Morlands' appearances (unlikely, since it comprises a very small section of the passage), the easiest way to work through this question is to plug each line reference from 7.2 into 7.1. A) is incorrect because lines 5-8 only provide information about Mr. Morland, not the family as a whole. B) is incorrect because lines 10-12 focus on Mrs. Morland's personality, not on her appearance; they also say nothing about the rest of the family. C) is incorrect because lines 17-18 refer to the size of the Morland family, not to the appearance of its members. D) is correct because lines 20-21 indicate that the Morlands' appearance was *plain*, i.e., unremarkable. A) is thus the correct answer to 7.1.

7.3-4 C, D

If you've gotten the gist of the passage, you should be able to eliminate B) and D). The narrator's whole point is that Catherine isn't particularly heroic or gifted. If you're stuck between A) and C), check the answers in 7.4 in order. There is nothing in lines 30-31 to suggest that Catherine was charming, so eliminate A). Likewise, neither lines 33-34 nor line 41 provides any information about those qualities. D) is the answer to 7.4 because the description of Catherine as *noisy and wild* in lines 65-66 directly supports the idea of rambunctiousness. That makes C) the answer to 7.3.

7.5 B

Since the question itself does not provide a line reference and there is no supporting evidence question to narrow down the location of answer, the fastest way to answer 7.5 is to start from the beginning of the passage and skim for references to Mrs. Morland, pulling your finger down the page as you read. Working this way, you'll find the answer very quickly. Lines 10-12 state that Catherine's mother *was a woman of useful plain sense* (=practical)*, with a good temper, and, what is more remarkable, with a good constitution* (=sturdy). That makes B) correct.

7.6 C

If you get the gist of the passage, you should be able to eliminate both A) and B) right away. The narrator is pretty clear that Catherine isn't a particularly enthusiastic student. To decide between the remaining answers, you'll most likely need to locate the correct section of the passage; unfortunately, there's no supporting evidence question to guide you. The key phrase in the question is "parents' lessons," so skim from the beginning of the passage, searching for those words or related phrases. The answer appears in lines 56-60, which indicate that Catherine's mother taught her French and her father accounting, and that *she shirked her lessons in both whenever she could.* In other words, she avoided her lessons if possible, making C) the answer. Be very careful with D): not paying attention is not the same thing as shirking, which means "evading" or, more colloquially, "blowing off." Although not paying attention would certainly be consistent with Catherine's general behavior, the specific wording in this section of the passage points to C).

6 Reasonable Inferences

Inference questions test what a particular section of a passage **suggests** or **implies**. They are less common than literal comprehension questions but are often accompanied by supporting evidence questions as well. They are usually phrased in the following ways:

- In lines x-y, King implies that freedom...

- The author of the passage suggests that physicists may eventually...

- It can be most reasonably inferred from the passage that long-distance runners...

The most important thing to understand about inference questions is that they are essentially literal comprehension questions with a twist. Correct answers simply make explicit what the passage implies. All of the necessary information is there; you just have to put the pieces together.

It is also essential to understand that inferences on the SAT are much smaller than the kinds of inferences you may be accustomed to making in English class. For example, if you read a novel in which a character becomes angry, you might think that the author is suggesting that the character is a bad person or warning the reader not to behave in the same way. On the SAT, the only thing that you can infer is that the character is not happy and, if it is suggested in the passage, the reason the character experiences that emotion.

It is true that some inference questions will require you to make slightly larger leaps than others, but only *slightly* larger. **Although answers to inference questions will not be stated word-for-word in the passage, the passage will always contain specific wording that clearly corresponds to a particular idea, event, or relationship in the correct answer.**

As a result, the presence of supporting evidence questions can actually make inference questions easier. Instead of having to consider the entire passage AND make the correct inference, the supporting evidence question will at least provide specific locations for the information you need to make a valid inference.

Because inference questions ask you to go a step beyond what the author is literally saying, you should be prepared to work very carefully and avoid leaping to conclusions. That is true everywhere, but it is especially true here. If you don't feel ready to handle an inference question when you first encounter it, skip it and come back to it after you have answered the more straightforward questions.

Fallacies and Incorrect Answers

Statements that go outside the bounds of what can be determined logically from a given assertion are known as **fallacies**; incorrect answer choices to inference questions are fallacies, and they involve various types of faulty reasoning. On the SAT, fallacies can be difficult to identify because you are required to sift through so much information, some of which is relevant and some of which is not.

The key to dealing with inference questions is to make sure that you are absolutely clear about the literal meaning of the lines in question. Ideally, you should take a couple of seconds, make sure you understand them, **jot down a short (3-4 word) summary**, and look for the answer closest in overall meaning to that statement. That answer should be correct.

Because the right answer might be phrased in a way you're not expecting, it is crucial that you not eliminate any answer without making sure you really understand what it's saying and how it relates to the lines in question. Knowing how to recognize a couple of common fallacies can also help you identify incorrect answers more easily.

One very common type of fallacy involves **speculation**: that is, an answer *could* be true based on the information in the passage, but there isn't enough information to judge whether it is *actually* true. Some of these answers are quite obviously wrong because they are so far outside the bounds of what is discussed in the passage that they are patently absurd, while others sound so plausible that it seems that they should be true. In fact, **some of them may be true – they just won't be supported by the passage**.

Another common type of fallacy involves the reasoning, "if *x* is true in one case, then *x* is true in all cases/has always been true," or "if *x* is true for one member of a group, then it is true for all members of that group." In reality, the only thing that *x* being true in one particular case suggests is that *x* is true in that one particular case. It does not automatically mean that *x* will be true in any other case or for any other person.

Such fallacies are characterized by **extreme words** such as *always*, *never*, *all*, and *only*. You should be suspicious of any answer choice that contains this type of wording. To be sure, there are cases in which a given statement will imply that a particular fact applies to all (or no) situations/people, but they are comparatively rare.

Important: Make sure that you pay close attention to answer choices that are phrased negatively (ones that contain the word *not*) or that contain double negatives (e.g., *not impossible* = possible). Unless you carefully work out what this type of wording actually means, it is very easy to become confused by it.

This is very important because one of the easiest ways to create a valid inference is to rewrite the original statement from a different angle. For example, if a passage states that a particular star is much older than the Earth, a valid inference is that the star is **not** younger than the Earth.

Let's look at some examples of reasonable and unreasonable inferences. Consider the following sentences:

Every time a car drives through a major intersection, it becomes a data point. Magnetic coils of wire lie just beneath the pavement, registering each passing car.

Because the author refers to *magnetic coils of wire* immediately after he states that a car becomes a data point every time it drives through a major intersection, we can infer that the magnetic coils of wire play a role in turning cars into data points. Although the author does not directly state that one is a result of the other, he strongly implies it by placing those two pieces of information next to one another. Given how texts are normally structured, there is essentially no other reason to mention the magnetic coils in that particular place.

Because the author states that the magnetic coils of wire record the cars from below the pavement, we can infer that coils of wire do not need to be above ground to do their job.

We cannot, however, infer that magnetic coils are the **best** way of tracking cars' movement; these sentences give us nothing to compare the cars to.

Likewise, we cannot infer that magnetic coils are **only** – or even **mostly** – used below the pavement, or that their **only/primary** use is to track cars. Those things might very well be true, but we do not have enough information to determine whether they are actually true.

Let's look at another example. It's excerpted from a passage we've seen before, but we're just going to look at a small part of it.

10   For the past decade, Florida's oranges have been
literally starving. Since it first appeared in 2005,
citrus greening, also known by its Chinese name,
huanglongbing, has swept across Florida's groves
like a flood. With no hills to block it, the Asian citrus
15 psyllid—the invasive aphid relative that carries the
disease—has infected nearly every orchard in the
state. By one estimate, 80 percent of Florida's citrus
trees are infected and declining.

We're going to focus on lines 11-17 – the second and third sentences, particularly the third sentence. We can make several inferences from those lines. First, from the statement *With no hills to block it, the Asian citrus psyllid…has infected nearly every orchard in the state*, we can reasonably infer that the Asian citrus psyllid **can** be stopped by hills. We can also infer that not every orchard in the state has been infected, i.e., **some** orchards in the state have **not** been infected.

If we back up to the second sentence, we can also infer that Florida's citrus groves do **not** have hills – if they did, the Asian citrus psyllid would be unable to spread *like a flood*.

Let's look at some more examples.

This passage is from Barbara Jordan's keynote address at the 1976 Democratic National Convention. A Texas native, Jordan was the first African-American woman to represent the Deep South in Congress.

It was one hundred and forty-four years ago that members of the Democratic Party first met in convention to select a Presidential candidate. A lot of years passed since 1832, and during that time it would
5 have been most unusual for any national political party to ask a Barbara Jordan to deliver a keynote address. But tonight, here I am. And I feel that notwithstanding the past that my presence here is one additional bit of evidence that the American Dream need not forever be
10 deferred.

Now that I have this grand distinction, what in the world am I supposed to say? I could list the problems which cause people to feel cynical, angry, frustrated: problems which include lack of integrity in government;
15 the feeling that the individual no longer counts; feeling that the grand American experiment is failing or has failed. I could recite these problems, and then I could sit down and offer no solutions. But I don't choose to do that either. The citizens of America expect more.

20 We are a people in search of a national community. We are a people trying not only to solve the problems of the present, unemployment, inflation, but we are attempting on a larger scale to fulfill the promise of America. We are attempting to fulfill our national purpose,
25 to create and sustain a society in which all of us are equal.

And now we must look to the future. Let us heed the voice of the people and recognize their common sense. If we do not, we not only blaspheme our political heritage, we ignore the common ties that bind all
30 Americans. Many fear the future. Many are distrustful of their leaders, and believe that their voices are never heard. Many seek only to satisfy their private interests. But this is the great danger America faces – that we will cease to be one nation and become instead a collection
35 of interest groups: city against suburb, region against region, individual against individual; each seeking to satisfy private wants. If that happens, who then will speak for America? Who then will speak for the common good? This is the question which must be answered in 1976:
40 Are we to be one people bound together by common spirit, sharing in a common endeavor; or will we become a divided nation? For all of its uncertainty, we cannot flee the future. We must address and master the future together. It can be done if we restore the belief that we
45 share a sense of national community, that we share a common national endeavor.

There is no executive order; there is no law that can require the American people to form a national community. This we must do as individuals, and if we
50 do it as individuals, there is no President of the United States who can veto that decision.

As a first step, we must restore our belief in ourselves. We are a generous people, so why can't we be generous with each other?
55 And now, what are those of us who are elected public officials supposed to do? We call ourselves "public servants" but I'll tell you this: We as public servants must set an example for the rest of the nation. It is hypocritical for the public official to admonish and
60 exhort the people to uphold the common good if we are derelict in upholding the common good. More is required of public officials than slogans and handshakes and press releases.

If we promise as public officials, we must deliver.
65 If we as public officials propose, we must produce. If we say to the American people, "It is time for you to be sacrificial" – sacrifice. And again, if we make mistakes, we must be willing to admit them. What we have to do is strike a balance between the idea that
70 government should do everything and the idea that government ought to do nothing.

Let there be no illusions about the difficulty of forming this kind of a national community. It's tough, difficult, not easy. But a spirit of harmony will survive
75 in America only if each of us remembers, when self-interest and bitterness seem to prevail, that we share a common destiny.

We cannot improve on the system of government handed down to us by the founders of the Republic.
80 There is no way to improve upon that. But what we can do is to find new ways to implement that system and realize our destiny.

1

The author most strongly suggests which of the following about the "common endeavor" (line 41)

A) It represents an impossible ideal.
B) It has the potential to be destroyed by uncertainty.
C) It cannot be realized through legislation.
D) It represents a combination of public and private interests.

Which choice provides the best evidence for the answer to the previous question?

A) Lines 33-35 ("But…groups")
B) Lines 42-43 ("For…future")
C) Lines 47-49 ("There is…community")
D) Lines 56-58 ("We…nation")

There are a few ways to go about answering this question.

Option 1: The Shortcut

Remember that little trick we talked about way back in Chapter 1, the one about second meanings often signaling correct answers?

Well, there's an answer here that includes a common word used in its second meaning: *realized*, in choice C). *Realized* normally means "became aware of," but here it's used to mean "achieved." That usage signals that C) is likely correct, but you still need to check.

The line references in Question #2 tell you that the answers to both questions are located somewhere between lines 33 and 58. If you're a strong reader and skim through that section with a clear idea of what you're looking for, you'll find the answer in lines 47-49.

No executive order; no law = cannot be realized (accomplished) through legislation.

Option 2: Answer the Question Yourself

The fact that you're given a line reference means that you have a pretty good chance of being able to answer the question on your own without having to plug in every line reference.

The only potential downside is that the lines you come up with to support your answer might not be the same lines provided in the second question, so you might have to do a bit more reading around than you'd like.

The first thing to do is to define the key phrase *common endeavor*.

Let's consider the context of the passage. Jordan's main concern is that the United States is becoming fragmented into *a collection of interest groups: city against suburb, region against region, individual against individual; each seeking to satisfy private wants.* In fact, if we were to write a main point, we might say something like "America must UNITE f/future."

Coming back to the key phrase, Jordan essentially answers the question a couple of lines down when she states that *We (all Americans)* <u>must</u> *address and master the future together.* So the correct answer must be consistent with that idea.

The author most strongly suggests which of the following about the "common endeavor" (line 41)

A) It represents an impossible ideal.
B) It has the potential to be destroyed by uncertainty.
C) It cannot be realized through legislation.
D) It represents a combination of public and private interests.

When you look at the answer choices, there's unfortunately no option that *directly* rephrases the idea that Americans must come together. You can, however, play process of elimination pretty effectively.

A) can be eliminated because Jordan states in line 44 that *it can be done*. The extreme word *impossible* also suggests that the answer is wrong.

B) takes a word (*uncertainty*) from the passage and presents it in a different context. The passage only states that the future is unavoidable despite the fact that it is uncertain (The phrase *for all* means "despite"). As a result, this answer is off-topic.

C) is an answer you might overlook initially. You must be careful not to eliminate it simply because you don't remember anything about it. If you have a very strong sense of logic, you may be able to figure out that if the "endeavor" depends on the American people's uniting, then by definition, it cannot be accomplished by legislation. But if you're not sure, just leave this option alone for the time being.

D) might seem tempting because Jordan does refer to private interests in line 32; however, she cites them as a *danger* to the common good, something that distracts people from focusing on what they have in common. So this answer indicates exactly the opposite of what the passage says.

That leaves you with C). Now, you must check each line reference to see whether it supports the idea of something that cannot be accomplished through legislation. Although the process may be somewhat tedious, the good news is that you at least have a general idea of what information the correct lines must convey.

Again, you can use the information in Question #2 to tell you that the answer to Question #1 is located somewhere between lines 33 and 58. Because that is only 26 lines, you may find it easiest to simply reread that section of the passage until you hit on the necessary information. In line 47, the phrases *no executive order* and *no law* are directly consistent with the idea of legislation, making C) the answer to Question #2 as well as Question #1.

A), B), and D) can be eliminated as possible answers to Question #2 because the lines they cite are all off-topic.

Option 3: Plug in Line References

When you're given a line reference in the first question, this method usually isn't ideal because it can end up being unnecessarily confusing and time consuming. But that said, we're going to try it anyway, just to see how it works.

Even though we're going to rely more heavily on the passage from the start than we did for the other methods, we still need to do some work upfront.

Again, we're going to define the key phrase *common endeavor* in context of the main point (Americans must UNITE f/future) so that we know what we're looking for when we go back to the passage.

Next, we can check each set of lines to see whether it matches the idea in the key phrase. Remember, though, that because this is an inference question, the correct answer may be stated from a somewhat different angle.

A) **But this is the great danger America faces – that we will cease to be one nation and become instead a collection of interest groups.**

These lines are related to the same general idea as the key phrase, but they tell us only about the *danger*. The endeavor itself is to unite, and these lines discuss the opposite.

B) **For all of its uncertainty, we cannot flee the future.**

No, this has nothing to do with people uniting. It's off-topic.

C) **There is no executive order; there is no law that can require the American people to form a national community.**

Even if you're not sure about this one, the phrase *national community* should make you pay closer attention because it's directly related to the idea of people uniting.

D) **We call ourselves "public servants" but I'll tell you this: We as public servants must set an example for the rest of the nation.**

This has nothing to do with the American people uniting.

The only answer that seems generally consistent with the question is C). Now you can work backwards, looking at the answers to the first question. Lines 47-49 clearly support the idea that the "endeavor" cannot be accomplished through legislation, giving you C) as the answer to Question #1.

At this point, we're going to look at some inference questions without line references. Although these questions may seem more difficult than ones with line references, it is sometimes possible to use the big picture, as well as an understanding of how texts are structured, to identify correct answers without too much fuss.

Every time a car drives through a major intersection, it becomes a data point. Magnetic coils of wire lie just beneath the pavement, registering each passing car. This starts a cascade of information: Computers tally the
5 number and speed of cars, shoot the data through underground cables to a command center and finally translate it into the colors red, yellow and green. On the seventh floor of Boston City Hall, the three colors splash like paint across a wall-sized map.
10 To drivers, the color red means stop, but on the map it tells traffic engineers to leap into action. Traffic control centers like this one—a room cluttered with computer terminals and live video feeds of urban intersections— represent the brain of a traffic system. The city's network
15 of sensors, cables and signals are the nerves connected to the rest of the body. "Most people don't think there are eyes and ears keeping track of all this stuff," says John DeBenedictis, the center's engineering director. But in reality, engineers literally watch our every move,
20 making subtle changes that relieve and redirect traffic.
The tactics and aims of traffic management are modest but powerful. Most intersections rely on a combination of pre-set timing and computer adaptation. For example, where a busy main road intersects with a quiet residential
25 street, the traffic signal might give 70 percent of "green time" to the main road, and 30 percent to the residential road. (Green lights last between a few seconds and a couple minutes, and tend to shorten at rush hour to help the traffic move continuously.) But when traffic
30 overwhelms the pre-set timing, engineers override the system and make changes.

1 ▨▨▨▨▨▨▨▨▨▨▨▨▨▨▨▨▨

It is reasonable to infer that improvements in traffic flow

A) are more difficult to achieve at certain hours of the day.

B) occur near traffic control centers.

C) can be attributed to pre-set systems.

D) are the result of intervention by traffic engineers.

2 ▨▨▨▨▨▨▨▨▨▨▨▨▨▨▨▨▨

Which choice provides the best evidence for the answer to the previous question?

A) Lines 4-7 ("computers…green")

B) Lines 11-14 ("Traffic…system")

C) Lines 18-20 ("But…traffic")

D) Lines 22-23 ("Most…adaptation")

Because this passage isn't too long, it's reasonable to try answering Question #1 without using any of the line references in Question #2.

If you work from the main point (which ideally you should have underlined), you can actually answer this question very, very quickly. What's the point? That traffic engineers see everything. Where is it located? In lines 18-20 (*But…traffic*). In Question #1, D) essentially rephrases the main point, and C) in Question #2 cites those exact lines.

If you're not sure you can reliably use this type of shortcut, you can of course plug in.

1 ▨▨▨▨▨▨▨▨▨▨▨▨▨▨▨▨▨

It is reasonable to infer that improvements in traffic flow

A) Lines 4-7 ("computers…green")

B) Lines 11-14 ("Traffic…system")

C) Lines 18-20 ("But…traffic")

D) Lines 22-23 ("Most…adaptation")

A) **Computers tally the number and speed of cars, shoot the data through underground cables to a command center and finally translate it into the colors red, yellow and green.**

No. This tells us nothing about traffic flow, only about how the movements of individual cars are recorded.

B) **Traffic control centers like this one—a room cluttered with computer terminals and live video feeds of urban intersections— represent the brain of a traffic system.**

This line extends the metaphor between a traffic control center and the human body. It doesn't actually talk about traffic itself.

C) **But in reality, engineers literally watch our every move, making subtle changes that relieve and redirect traffic.**

Here we finally do have some information about traffic. What do engineers do? They make changes that *relieve* traffic (that is, make it less jammed). In other words, they improve its flow. So this answer works. Note also the second meaning of *relieve*.

D) **Most intersections rely on a combination of pre-set timing and computer adaptation.**

This choice only talks about intersections (specific), not traffic (general).

So the answer is C). Now we can work backwards. If engineers are constantly watching people, making changes to *relieve and redirect traffic*, then improved traffic flow must be the result of their intervention. So the answer to Question #1 is D).

Let's try a longer passage.

The following passage is adapted from Willa Cather, *My Antonia*, originally published in 1918. The narrator recounts his life on the Nebraska plains as a boy.

On the afternoon of that Sunday I took my first long ride on my pony, under Otto's direction. After that Dude and I went twice a week to the post-office, six miles east of us, and I saved the men a good
5 deal of time by riding on errands to our neighbors. When we had to borrow anything, I was always the messenger.

All the years that have passed have not dimmed my memory of that first glorious autumn. The new country
10 lay open before me: there were no fences in those days, and I could choose my own way over the grass uplands, trusting the pony to get me home again. Sometimes I followed the sunflower-bordered roads.

I used to love to drift along the pale-yellow cornfields,
15 looking for the damp spots one sometimes found at their edges, where the smartweed soon turned a rich copper color and the narrow brown leaves hung curled like cocoons about the swollen joints of the stem. Sometimes I went south to visit our German neighbors and to
20 admire their catalpa grove, or to see the big elm tree that grew up out of a deep crack in the earth and had a hawk's nest in its branches. Trees were so rare in that country, and they had to make such a hard fight to grow, that we used to feel anxious about them, and visit them
25 as if they were persons. It must have been the scarcity of detail in that tawny landscape that made detail so precious.

Sometimes I rode north to the big prairie-dog town to watch the brown earth-owls fly home in the late afternoon
30 and go down to their nests underground with the dogs. Antonia Shimerda liked to go with me, and we used to wonder a great deal about these birds of subterranean habit. We had to be on our guard there, for rattlesnakes were always lurking about. They came to pick up an easy
35 living among the dogs and owls, which were quite defenseless against them; took possession of their comfortable houses and ate the eggs and puppies. We felt sorry for the owls. It was always mournful to see them come flying home at sunset and disappear under
40 the earth.

But, after all, we felt, winged things who would live like that must be rather degraded creatures. The dog-town was a long way from any pond or creek. Otto Fuchs said he had seen populous dog-towns in the desert where
45 there was no surface water for fifty miles; he insisted that some of the holes must go down to water—nearly two hundred feet, hereabouts. Antonia said she didn't believe it; that the dogs probably lapped up the dew in the early morning, like the rabbits.

50 Antonia had opinions about everything, and she was soon able to make them known. Almost every day she came running across the prairie to have her reading lesson with me. Mrs. Shimerda grumbled, but realized it was important that one member of the family should
55 learn English. When the lesson was over, we used to go up to the watermelon patch behind the garden. I split the melons with an old corn-knife, and we lifted out the hearts and ate them with the juice trickling through our fingers. The white melons we did not touch, but we
60 watched them with curiosity. They were to be picked later, when the hard frosts had set in, and put away for winter use. After weeks on the ocean, the Shimerdas were famished for fruit. The two girls would wander for miles along the edge of the cornfields, hunting for
65 ground-cherries.

Antonia loved to help grandmother in the kitchen and to learn about cooking and housekeeping. She would stand beside her, watching her every movement. We were willing to believe that Mrs. Shimerda was a
70 good housewife in her own country, but she managed poorly under new conditions. I remember how horrified we were at the sour, ashy-grey bread she gave her family to eat. She mixed her dough, we discovered, in an old tin peck-measure that had been used about the
75 barn. When she took the paste out to bake it, she left smears of dough sticking to the sides of the measure, put the measure on the shelf behind the stove, and let this residue ferment. The next time she made bread, she scraped this sour stuff down into the fresh dough to
80 serve as yeast.

1

It is most reasonable to infer that access to the land during the narrator's youth was

A) reserved for a small group of settlers.
B) less restricted than it later became.
C) prohibited by the narrator's neighbors.
D) controlled by Antonia Shimerda's family.

2

Which choice provides the best evidence for the answer to the previous question?

A) Lines 9-12 ("The new...again")
B) Lines 18-22 ("Sometimes...branches")
C) Lines 33-34 ("We...about")
D) Lines 62-65 ("After...cherries")

167

This question might look complicated, but it's actually much simpler than it appears. Although it appears to ask you to wade through a huge amount of information, it can actually be solved relatively quickly – if, that is, you think carefully about what the correct lines are saying.

This time, we're going to start by combining the two questions into one:

1

It is most reasonable to infer that access to the land during the narrator's youth was

A) Lines 9-12 ("The new...again")
B) Lines 18-22 ("Sometimes...branches")
C) Lines 33-34 ("We...about")
D) Lines 62-65 ("After...cherries")

If we start by checking out the line references in order, we'll hit on the answer immediately:

A) **The new country lay open before me: there were no fences in those days, and I could choose my own way over the grass uplands, trusting the pony to get me home again.**

The first thing to notice is that these lines contain a colon, and colons are important because they signal explanations. You always want to pay close attention to the information after a colon, and this is no exception.

What do we learn after the colon? That *there were no fences in those days, and I could choose my own way over the grass uplands*. In other words, the narrator had pretty much unrestricted access to the land. The phrase *in those days* suggests that this is no longer the case – in other words, access to the land was "less restricted" than it became later on.

A) is thus the answer to Question #2, and B) is the answer to Question #1.

That was a lot easier than it looked, right?

You could, of course, try to work through the two questions in order, but in this case that approach could end up being both confusing and extremely time-consuming. Not only does the passage not provide a line reference, but the aspect of the passage that it asks about is so general that it is hard to pinpoint even a general area where the necessary information would most likely appear. And because the information is hidden in the middle of a paragraph close to the beginning, you are unlikely to remember specific details from that paragraph. Even if you circled the colon in line 10 as you read through the passage, the chance of your remembering to focus on that particular spot while answering this question would be extremely slim.

One more. We're going to try a science passage, this time without a supporting evidence question after it.

The following passage is adapted from "The Origin of the Ocean Floor" by Peter Keleman, © 2009 by The National Geographic Society.

At the dark bottom of our cool oceans, 85 percent of the earth's volcanic eruptions proceed virtually unnoticed. Though unseen, they are hardly insignificant. Submarine volcanoes generate the solid underpinnings
5 of all the world's oceans massive slabs of rock seven kilometers thick.

Geophysicists first began to appreciate the smoldering origins of the land under the sea, known formally as ocean crust, in the early 1960s. Sonar
10 surveys revealed that volcanoes form nearly continuous ridges that wind around the globe like seams on a baseball. Later, the same scientists strove to explain what fuels these erupting mountain ranges, called mid-ocean ridges. Basic theories suggest that because ocean
15 crust pulls apart along the ridges, hot material deep within the earth's rocky interior must rise to fill the gap. But details of exactly where the lava originates and how it travels to the surface long remained a mystery.

In recent years mathematical models of the
20 interaction between molten and solid rock have provided some answers, as have examinations of blocks of old seafloor now exposed on the continents. These insights made it possible to develop a detailed theory describing the birth of ocean crust. The process
25 turns out to be quite different from the typical layperson's idea, in which fiery magma fills an enormous chamber underneath a volcano, then rages upward along a jagged crack. Instead the process begins dozens of kilometers under the seafloor, where
30 tiny droplets of melted rock ooze through microscopic pores at a rate of about 10 centimeters a year, about as fast as fingernails grow.

Closer to the surface, the process speeds up, culminating with massive streams of lava pouring
35 over the seafloor with the velocity of a speeding truck. Deciphering how liquid moves through solid rock deep underground not only explains how ocean crust emerges but also may elucidate the behavior of other fluid-transport networks, including the river systems
40 that dissect the planet's surface.

Far below the mid-ocean ridge volcanoes and their countless layers of crust-forming lava is the mantle, a 3,200-kilometer-thick layer of scorching hot rock that forms the earth's midsection and surrounds its
45 metallic core. At the planet's cool surface, upthrusted mantle rocks are dark green, but if you could see them in their rightful home, they would be glowing red- or even white-hot. The top of the mantle is about 1,300 degrees Celsius, and it gets about one degree
50 hotter with each kilometer of depth. The weight of overlying rock means the pressure also increases with depth about 1,000 atmospheres for every three kilometers.

Knowledge of the intense heat and pressure in
55 the mantle led researchers to hypothesize in the late 1960s that ocean crust originates as tiny amounts of liquid rock known as melt almost as though the solid rocks were "sweating." Even a minuscule release of pressure (because of material rising from
60 its original position) causes melt to form in microscopic pores deep within the mantle rock.

Explaining how the rock sweat gets to the surface was more difficult. Melt is less dense than the mantle rocks in which it forms, so it will
65 constantly try to migrate upward, toward regions of lower pressure. But what laboratory experiments revealed about the chemical composition of melt did not seem to match up with the composition of rock samples collected from the mid-ocean ridges,
70 where erupted melt hardens.

Using specialized equipment to heat and squeeze crystals from mantle rocks in the laboratory, investigators learned that the chemical composition of melt in the mantle varies depending on the depth
75 at which it forms; the composition is controlled by an exchange of atoms between the melt and the minerals that make up the solid rock it passes through. The experiments revealed that as melt rises, it dissolves one kind of mineral, orthopyroxene, and
80 precipitates, or leaves behind, another mineral, olivine. Researchers could thus infer that the higher in the mantle melt formed, the more orthopyroxene it would dissolve, and the more olivine it would leave behind. Comparing these experimental findings
85 with lava samples from the mid-ocean ridges revealed that almost all of them have the composition of melts that formed at depths greater than 45 kilometers.

1

The author's discussion of mid-ocean ridges suggests that these ridges

A) are composed of orthopyrexene and olivine.
B) are maintained by the exchange of atoms.
C) are subject to less pressure than mantle rock is.
D) produce a wide range of minerals.

Start by identifying the key phrase (*mid-ocean ridges*) and locating it in the passage. It is very important that you look for the entire phrase because it appears in only a few places. If you look for a more general term, for example *ocean*, you won't know where to focus.

The key phrase appears in lines 13-14 and again in line 41, but be careful. Mid-ocean ridges are only mentioned; the author doesn't discuss them in-depth. If you focus too intently on those places, you're likely to get caught in a loop of reading and rereading, trying to figure out why you can't seem to find an answer that fits.

Remember: if you can't find the answer in the place you're looking, it has to be somewhere else. (Provided, of course, that you understand the passage.)

So move on. If you keep scanning, focusing on the first and last sentence of each paragraph, you'll hit the third appearance of the key phrase in line 69. At this point, you must remember to **back up** and read for context (as opposed to starting at line 69 and reading from there). The purpose of a final sentence is to reiterate a point or draw a conclusion from the preceding information. In addition, this sentence starts with *but*, and you can't know what idea it's contradicting until you back up.

What do we learn from that paragraph? Basically, that "melt" migrates from the mantle upward to areas of lower pressure, ultimately hardening at the mid-ocean ridge. We can therefore assume that the mid-ocean ridge must be under less pressure than the mantle – which is exactly what C) says.

If that seems like an awfully large jump to make on your own, let's play process of elimination.

A) doesn't work because the passage only states that orthopyrexene and olivine are present in melt. It says nothing about those minerals in relationship to mid-ocean ridges.

B) is an answer you need to be careful with. The phrase *exchange of atoms* does appear, but only in regard to the chemical composition of melt in the mantle. Again, there is nothing about mid-ocean ridges.

See above for C). If you're not sure, leave it.

D) is vague and might therefore seem plausible, but unfortunately there's nothing in the passage to support the statement that mid-ocean ridges "produce a wide range of minerals." Don't waste too much time looking. If it's not there, it's not there.

Unstated Assumptions

Another type of inference question asks you to recognize an **unstated assumption** that can be determined from the passage. When unstated-assumption questions accompany natural science passages, they may ask you to identify the **underlying question** or **hypothesis** that was tested in an experiment. Or, they may ask you to identify a statement with which the author or an individual discussed in the passage would agree or disagree.

Answers to these questions follow the same basic rules as answers to other inference questions do. They may take information from the passage and restate it in a somewhat more general manner. They may also "fill in the blanks" by explicitly spelling out the underlying logic on which a particular belief or conclusion is based.

Incorrect answers, on the other hand, will go beyond the bounds of what can reasonably be inferred from the passage. They may include information that is factually true but irrelevant to the lines in question. They may also use some of the same wording that is found in the passage and alter it just enough so that it means something different from what it means in the passage.

That said, we're still going to look at some examples – just in case.

After the one-way front door, the first supermarket feature you inevitably encounter is the produce department. There's a good reason for this: the sensory impact of all those scents, textures, and colors (think
5 fat tomatoes, glossy eggplants, luscious strawberries) makes us feel both upbeat and hungry. Similarly the store bakery is usually near the entrance, with its scrumptious and pervasive smell of fresh-baked bread; as is the flower shop, with its buckets of tulips, bouquets
10 of roses, and banks of greenery. The message we get right off the bat is that the store is a welcoming place, fresh, natural, fragrant, and healthy, with comforting shades of grandma's kitchen.
The cruel truth is that the produce department is less
15 garden and kitchen than stage set. Lighting is chosen to make fruits and veggies appear at their brightest and best; and – according to Martin Lindstrom, author of *Brandwashed: Tricks Companies Use to Manipulate Our Minds and Persuade Us to Buy*—the periodic sprays of
20 fresh water that douse the produce bins are all for show. Though used to give fresh foods a deceptive dewy and fresh-picked look, the water actually has no practical purpose. In fact, it makes vegetables spoil faster than they otherwise would.

1

An unstated assumption made by the author about vegetables is that their

A) appearance is not a reliable indicator of their freshness.

B) nutritional qualities are often exaggerated.

C) fragrance is off-putting to some customers.

D) location within a supermarket depends on their popularity.

Because there's no line reference, the first thing you need to do is **identify the key word and find it in the passage**. To reiterate: the key word tells us the specific focus (topic) of the question. Here, the key word is "vegetables", so that's what we're going to look for.

This is where you need to be careful. The beginning of the passage provides some specific examples of vegetables (tomatoes, eggplant), but the key word itself does not appear. To find it, you need to go to the second paragraph. We get *veggies* in line 16, and *vegetables* in line 23.

While your first instinct might be to check these references in order, you're actually better off checking the second one first. Why? Because it's in the last sentence, and the last sentence is always important. That sentence also begins with the transition *In fact*, whose purpose is to emphasize the preceding idea. So it's doubly important.

What do we learn from that section? That vegetables get sprayed with water so that they'll look fresh, *even though* spraying them makes them spoil faster. In other words, they might look nice, but they might not be all that fresh. That makes the answer A).

Notice that if you'd gotten stuck on the first paragraph, you could have easily fallen into a loop of reading and rereading, and never figured how to get to the answer. B), C), and D) are never addressed in the passage, but all of them sound plausible enough to seem like reasonable guesses if you don't really know what you're doing.

Next, consider this excerpt from the "ocean floor" passage:

Knowledge of the intense heat and pressure in
55 the mantle led researchers to hypothesize in the late
1960s that ocean crust originates as tiny amounts
of liquid rock known as melt almost as though the
solid rocks were "sweating." Even a minuscule
release of pressure (because of material rising from
60 its original position) causes melt to form in
microscopic pores deep within the mantle rock.
     Explaining how the rock sweat gets to the
surface was more difficult. Melt is less dense than
the mantle rocks in which it forms, so it will
65 constantly try to migrate upward, toward regions of
lower pressure. But what laboratory experiments
revealed about the chemical composition of melt
did not seem to match up with the composition of
rock samples collected from the mid-ocean ridges,
70 where erupted melt hardens.

1

In line 66, the author refers to "laboratory experiments." Which of the following was an assumption researchers made during those experiments?

OR:

In line 66, the author refers to "laboratory experiments." Based on the passage, which of the following is a hypothesis the author suggests was tested in those experiments?

A) Melted rock contains lower levels of orthopyrexene than of olivine.

B) Melt is composed exclusively of olivine and orthopyrexene.

C) Orthopyrexene only dissolves at depths greater than 45 kilometers.

D) Rock sweat and hardened erupted melt have similar chemical compositions.

Although the word *assumption* only appears in the first version, both questions are in fact testing the same thing. In the second version, the word *suggests* indicates that this is an inference question, meaning that the correct answer will not be stated word-for-word in the passage. You are, however, given a line reference, so there is a clear starting point.

The key to answering questions like this is to remember that the correct answer only requires you to make a very **small** leap from the passage. If you try to juggle too many pieces of information at once, you'll get confused and end up staring at the answers without any idea of how to decide between them.

We're going to start by reading the sentence that includes the line reference:

> **But what laboratory experiments revealed about the chemical composition of melt did not seem to match up with the composition of rock samples collected from the mid-ocean ridges, where erupted melt hardens.**

The phrase *did not seem to match up* tells us that researchers found something different from what they were expecting. What did they find? That the chemical composition of the melt from the mantle ("rock sweat") didn't match the melt from the mid-ocean ridge.

Logically, then, what was their starting assumption? That the chemical composition of the two types of melt would match. That makes D) the correct answer.

One more:

Sometimes it seems surprising that science functions at all. In 2005, medical science was shaken by a paper with the provocative title "Why most published research findings are false." Written by John
5 Ioannidis, a professor of medicine at Stanford University, it didn't actually show that any particular result was wrong. Instead, it showed that the statistics of reported positive findings was not consistent with how often one should *expect* to find them. As Ioannidis concluded more
10 recently, "many published research findings are false or exaggerated, and an estimated 85 percent of research resources are wasted."
   It's likely that some researchers are consciously cherry-picking data to get their work published.
15 And some of the problems surely lie with journal publication policies. But the problems of false findings often begin with researchers unwittingly fooling themselves: they fall prey to cognitive biases, common modes of thinking that lure us toward wrong but
20 convenient or attractive conclusions. "Seeing the reproducibility rates in psychology and other empirical science, we can safely say that something is not working out the way it should," says Susann Fiedler, a behavioral economist at the Max Planck Institute for Research on
25 Collective Goods in Bonn, Germany. "Cognitive biases might be one reason for that."
   Psychologist Brian Nosek of the University of Virginia says that the most common and problematic bias in science is "motivated reasoning": We interpret
30 observations to fit a particular idea. Psychologists have

shown that "most of our reasoning is in fact rationalization," he says. In other words, we have already made the decision about what to do or to think, and our "explanation" of our reasoning is really a justification for
35 doing what we wanted to do—or to believe—anyway. Science is of course meant to be more objective and skeptical than everyday thought—but how much is it, really?

1

Based on the passage, Nosek would be most likely to agree with which of the following statements?

A) The empirical sciences are less vulnerable to bias than are other scientific fields.

B) Scientists should attempt to become aware of their preconceptions.

C) The majority of false findings are the result of deliberate distortion.

D) Science is a fundamentally irrational pursuit.

Despite the phrasing of the question, it's only a very small step from the wording of the passage to the correct answer.

Start by reiterating what Nosek thinks: *the most common and problematic bias in science is "motivated reasoning": We interpret observations to fit a particular idea. Psychologists have shown that "most of our reasoning is in fact rationalization," he says.* (lines 28-32)

Essentially, he's saying that that scientists draw false conclusions because they are focusing on or overemphasizing the data that confirms their biases. The author of the passage also states in lines 17-18 that most researchers who fall into this trap are *unwittingly fooling themselves* – that is, the researchers are themselves unaware of their skewed perception. We can therefore assume that Nosek's comments are intended to apply to researchers in that situation.

Given that context, it is reasonable to assume that Nosek would believe in the importance of researchers becoming aware of their own biases. After all, scientists who are unaware of their biases (= preconceptions) obviously cannot take them into account when performing research, whereas scientists who are attuned to their biases can at least take steps to correct for them. B) is thus correct.

Playing process of elimination, A) is incorrect because the passage only discusses the problem of bias in scientific fields – there is no comparison made to other fields.

C) is incorrect because the passage indicates that *the problem [of false findings] often begins with researchers unwittingly fooling themselves* (lines 16-17). In other words, the researchers are unaware that they are distorting the data – the exact opposite of distorting it deliberately.

Note the extreme language in D): *fundamentally irrational pursuit*. In fact, this assertion is much too strong: the passage discusses the fact that many individual researchers are prone to unconscious bias. It does not, however, go so far as to suggest that science itself is essentially irrational.

Inference Exercises

1.   Conservationists have historically been at odds
with the people who inhabit wildernesses. During the
last half of the 20th century, millions of indigenous
people were ousted from their homelands to establish
nature sanctuaries free of humans. Most succumbed to
5 malnutrition, disease and exploitation. Such outcomes—
coupled with the realization that indigenous groups
usually help to stabilize ecosystems by, for instance,
keeping fire at bay—have convinced major conservation
groups to take local human concerns into account. The
10 World Wildlife Fund (WWF) now describes indigenous
peoples as "natural allies," and the Nature Conservancy
pledges to seek their "free, informed and prior" consent
to projects impacting their territories.

1

It can be reasonably inferred from the passage that
conservation groups

A) were initially unaware that indigenous groups
helped maintain ecosystems.

B) have helped millions of indigenous people
remain in their homelands.

C) have gradually become more radical in their
demands.

D) have reduced outbreaks of disease among
indigenous peoples.

2.   Chronic stress, it turns out, is extremely dangerous.
While stress doesn't cause any single disease — in fact,
the causal link between stress and ulcers has been largely
disproved — it makes most diseases significantly worse.
5 The list of ailments connected to stress is staggeringly
diverse and includes everything from the common cold
and lower-back pain to Alzheimer's disease, major
depressive disorder, and heart attack. Stress hollows out
our bones and atrophies our muscles. It triggers adult-
10 onset diabetes and may also be connected to high blood
pressure. In fact, numerous studies of human longevity
in developed countries have found that psychosocial
factors such as stress are the single most important
variable in determining the length of a life. It's not that
15 genes and risk factors like smoking don't matter. It's
that our levels of stress matter more.
      Furthermore, the effects of chronic stress directly
counteract improvements in medical care and public
health. Antibiotics, for instance, are far less effective
20 when our immune system is suppressed by stress; that
fancy heart surgery will work only if the patient can
learn to shed stress. As pioneering stress researcher
Robert Sapolsky notes, "You can give a guy a drug-
coated stent, but if you don't fix the stress problem, it
25 won't really matter. For so many conditions, stress is
the major long-term risk factor. Everything else is a
short-term fix."

1

The passage suggests that the effects of genes on
human longevity

A) are not yet fully understood.

B) can be altered by certain medications.

C) are less significant than the effects of stress.

D) are entirely irrelevant when compared to the
effects of stress.

2

Which choice provides the best evidence for the
answer to the previous question?

A) Lines 5-6 ("The list...diverse")

B) Lines 8-9 ("Stress...muscles")

C) Lines 14-16 ("It's not...more")

D) Lines 19-20 ("Antibiotics...stress")

3. The following passage is adapted from Jane Austen, *Northanger Abbey*, originally published in 1817.

No one who had ever seen Catherine Morland in her infancy would have supposed her born to be an heroine. Her situation in life, the character of her father and mother, her own person and disposition, were all
5 equally against her. Her father was a clergyman, without being neglected, or poor, and a very respectable man, though his name was Richard—and he had never been handsome. He had a considerable independence besides two good livings—and he was not in the least addicted
10 to locking up his daughters. Her mother was a woman of useful plain sense, with a good temper, and, what is more remarkable, with a good constitution. She had three sons before Catherine was born; and instead of dying in bringing the latter into the world, as anybody
15 might expect, she still lived on—lived to have six children more—to see them growing up around her, and to enjoy excellent health herself. A family of ten children will be always called a fine family, where there are heads and arms and legs enough for the number;
20 but the Morlands had little other right to the word, for they were in general very plain, and Catherine, for many years of her life, as plain as any. She had a thin awkward figure, a sallow skin without colour, dark lank hair, and strong features—so much for her person; and
25 not less unpropitious for heroism seemed her mind. She was fond of all boy's plays, and greatly preferred cricket not merely to dolls, but to the more heroic enjoyments of infancy, nursing a dormouse, feeding a canary-bird, or watering a rose-bush. Indeed she had
30 no taste for a garden; and if she gathered flowers at all, it was chiefly for the pleasure of mischief—at least so it was conjectured from her always preferring those which she was forbidden to take. Such were her propensities—her abilities were quite as extraordinary.
35 She never could learn or understand anything before she was taught; and sometimes not even then, for she was often inattentive, and occasionally stupid. Her mother was three months in teaching her only to repeat the "Beggar's Petition"; and after all, her
40 next sister, Sally, could say it better than she did. Not that Catherine was always stupid—by no means; she learnt the fable of "The Hare and Many Friends" as quickly as any girl in England. Her mother wished her to learn music; and Catherine was sure she should like it,
45 for she was very fond of tinkling the keys of the old forlorn spinner; so, at eight years old she began. She learnt a year, and could not bear it; and Mrs. Morland, who did not insist on her daughters being accomplished in spite of incapacity or distaste, allowed her to leave
50 off. The day which dismissed the music-master was one of the happiest of Catherine's life. Her taste for drawing was not superior; though whenever she could obtain the outside of a letter from her mother or seize upon any other odd piece of paper, she did what she
55 could in that way, by drawing houses and trees, hens and chickens, all very much like one another. Writing and accounts she was taught by her father; French by her mother: her proficiency in either was not remarkable, and she shirked her lessons in both
60 whenever she could. What a strange, unaccountable character!—for with all these symptoms of profligacy at ten years old, she had neither a bad heart nor a bad temper, was seldom stubborn, scarcely ever quarrelsome, and very kind to the little ones, with
65 few interruptions of tyranny; she was moreover noisy and wild, hated confinement and cleanliness, and loved nothing so well in the world as rolling down the green slope at the back of the house.

1

An unstated assumption in the narrator's description of Catherine is that a heroine is typically

A) bold and daring.

B) brilliant and beautiful.

C) wild and rebellious.

D) independent and carefree.

2

The narrator suggests that Catherine's mother responded to her daughter's behavior with

A) frequent irritation.

B) general indifference.

C) easy indulgence.

D) utter perplexity.

3

Which choice provides the best evidence for the answer to the previous question?

A) Lines 13-15 ("and...on")

B) Lines 20-21 ("for...plain")

C) Lines 38-40 ("Her...did")

D) Lines 47-50 ("and...off")

4

The narrator implies that Catherine was strongly motivated to do things that

A) were unusually difficult.

B) were taught by her parents.

C) were not permitted.

D) her siblings were unable to accomplish.

5

Which choice provides the best evidence for the answer to the previous question?

A) Lines 26-27 ("She...dolls")

B) Lines 30-33 ("and...take")

C) Lines 43-44 ("Her...music")

D) Lines 54-56 ("she...another")

6

The narrator's references to a dormouse, canary-bird, and rose bush (lines 28-29) most strongly suggest that Catherine

A) could behave in a cruel manner.

B) preferred to play alone than with other children.

C) rejected a range of conventionally feminine activities.

D) was aware of her exceptional behavior.

4. The following passage is adapted from Wiebke Brauer, "The Miracle of Space," © 2014 by *Smart Magazine*.

Imagine a world where you share the available space with others: without signs, sidewalks, or bicycle lanes. A vision otherwise known as shared space – and one that becomes more and more relevant with
5 the crowding of our cities. While this might sound like urban science fiction or, possibly, impending chaos mixed with survival of the fittest, this particular concept is the declared dream of many traffic planners.
Shared space means streets freed of signs and
10 signals; streets solely governed by right of way, leaving road users to their own devices. In order to restructure public space, it removes all superfluous interventions and contradictory guidelines. Many countries are currently in the process of installing – or at least
15 discussing – such 'lawless' areas: Germany and the Netherlands, Denmark and the UK, Switzerland and the USA, but also Australia and New Zealand.
One could argue that shared spaces have been around for a long time, simply under different terms
20 and titles. Back in the 1970s, for example, residents enjoyed mixed traffic areas, traffic calming, and play streets. And yet, these were not quite the same: Shared space involves a new and radical push for equal rights of all road users, pedestrian and otherwise. And
25 while it was British urban designer Ben Hamilton-Baillie who coined the actual term, the concept itself was developed in the mid-1990s under former Dutch traffic manager Hans Monderman. Shortly before his death in 2006, Monderman explained the basic tenets
30 of shared space as such: "The problem with traffic engineers is that when there's a problem with a road, they always try to add something. To my mind, it's much better to remove things."
Indeed, studies have shown that in many places –
35 where signs and traffic lights have been removed and where each and every one is responsible for their own actions in ungoverned space – the rate of accidents goes down. The reason: the traditional strict separation between cars, cyclists, and pedestrians encourages
40 clashes at crossings. And although shared space requires cars to lower their speed, it also cuts down on journey times since it encourages a continuous flow of traffic instead of bringing it to a halt through traffic signals.
45   Monderman was utterly convinced that shared space would work anywhere in the world because, underneath it all, people are basically the same, despite any cultural differences. In an interview, he stated that "emotions and issues are the same everywhere. You should be able

50 to read a street like a book. If you insist on constantly guiding people and treating them like idiots, you shouldn't be surprised if they act like idiots after a while."
At the same time, the threat of looming idiocy
55 is not the most pressing reason for a future traffic management rethink. Recent city planning, for example, has evolved along the same lines around the world: think highways and flyovers dissecting the city's natural fabric, dedicated pedestrian zones, and
60 large shopping malls. Clear-cut boundaries between driving, work, life, and shopping are emphasized by a thicket of signs. The result: ultimate, well-ordered bleakness. At night, you might find yourself in an empty, soulless pedestrian zone. A lot of the time,
65 urbanization simply translates as uniformity.
In recent years, however, city and traffic planners have decided to tackle this issue with "road space attractiveness" measures to breathe new spirit into lifeless satellite towns. Their goal: a new definition
70 of space and mobility against the background that the notion of "might is right" – and only if those in power stick to the rules – is more than outdated. The unregulated and unorthodox approach of shared space makes it obvious to each and every individual
75 that this concept requires cooperation, that sharing is the new having.
Critics of Monderman and Hamilton-Baillie have voiced that no rules implies the inevitable return of "might is right." Yet who says that chaos
80 reigns in the absence of order? That's a questionable statement. Shared space certainly requires a new mindset and we can't expect a swift shift away from traditional traffic planning – bigger, further, faster.
But the vision of no more set traffic cycles, fewer
85 linear and predefined patterns, of freely flowing and intermingling participants in an open and boundless space, is equally unfettered and fascinating. A vision in the spirit of Pericles who wrote around 450 BC that "you need freedom for happiness and courage
90 for freedom."

1

The passage suggests that the most pressing reason for overhauling the way traffic is managed is that

A) the removal of traffic signal results in more varied and vibrant urban spaces.

B) drivers are unlikely to take responsibility for their actions when they are left alone.

C) overreliance on traffic signals makes drivers hesitant and indecisive.

D) accidents are more likely to occur when traffic signals are present.

2

Based on the passage, it is reasonable to infer that those in charge of planning traffic

A) are strongly opposed to Hans Monderman's proposal.

B) believe that drivers' behavior does not vary across cultures.

C) believe that abolishing traffic signals would lead to chaos.

D) are frequently opposed to the use of traffic signals.

3

Which choice provides the best evidence for the answer to the previous question?

A) Lines 7-8 ("this…planners")

B) Lines 20-22 ("Back…streets")

C) Lines 50-53 ("If…while")

D) Lines 56-58 ("Recent…world")

5. This passage is from Samuel Gompers, "What Does the Working Man Want?" 1890. Gompers, a Scottish Immigrant, was the founder of the American Federation of Labor and helped workers to organize and fight for fairer working conditions.

My friends, we have met here today to celebrate the idea that has prompted thousands of working-people of Louisville and New Albany to parade the streets; that prompts the toilers of Chicago to turn out by their
5 fifty or hundred thousand of men; that prompts the vast army of wage-workers in New York to demonstrate their enthusiasm and appreciation of the importance of this idea; that prompts the toilers of England, Ireland, Germany, France, Italy, Spain, and Austria to defy the
10 manifestos of the autocrats of the world and say that on May the first, 1890, the wage-workers of the world will lay down their tools in sympathy with the wage-workers of America, to establish a principle of limitations of hours of labor to eight hours for sleep,
15 eight hours for work, and eight hours for what we will.
It has been charged time and again that were we to have more hours of leisure we would merely devote it to the cultivation of vicious habits. They tell us that the eight-hour movement can not be enforced, for the
20 reason that it must check industrial and commercial progress. I say that the history of this shows the reverse. I say that is the plane on which this question ought to be discussed—that is the social question. As long as they make this question an economic one, I am willing to
25 discuss it with them. I would retrace every step I have taken to advance this movement did it mean industrial and commercial stagnation. But it does not mean that. It means greater prosperity; it means a greater degree of progress for the whole people.
30 They say they can't afford it. Is that true? Let us see for one moment. If a reduction in the hours of labor causes industrial and commercial ruination, it would naturally follow increased hours of labor would increase the prosperity, commercial and industrial.
35 If that were true, England and America ought to be at the tail end, and China at the head of civilization.
Why, when you reduce the hours of labor, just think what it means. Suppose men who work ten hours a day had the time lessened to nine, or men who
40 work nine hours a day have it reduced to eight; what does it mean? It means millions of golden hours and opportunities for thought. Some men might say you will go to sleep. Well, the ordinary man might try to sleep sixteen hours a day, but he would soon find he could
45 not do it long. He would probably become interested in some study and the hours that have been taken from manual labor are devoted to mental labor, and the mental labor of one hour produce for him more wealth than the physical labor of a dozen hours.
50 I maintain that this is a true proposition—that men under the short-hour system not only have opportunity to improve themselves, but to make a greater degree of prosperity for their employers. Why, my friends, how is it in China, how is it in
55 Spain, how is it in India and Russia, how is it in Italy? Cast your eye throughout the universe and observe the industry that forces nature to yield up its fruits to man's necessities, and you will find that where the hours of labor are the shortest the progress of invention in
60 machinery and the prosperity of the people are the greatest. It has only been under the great influence of our great republic, were our people have exhibited their great senses, that we can move forward, upward and onward, and are watched with interest in our
65 movements of progress and reform.

1

Based on the passage, Gompers implies that in comparison to workers in the United States, workers in China (line 36)

A) enjoy greater prosperity.
B) are more industrious.
C) spend more hours at work.
D) are less fairly compensated.

2

Gompers suggests that one of the main consequences of long working hours in the United States is that

A) civic participation is reduced.
B) important discoveries go unmade.
C) workers are too exhausted to perform their jobs.
D) the quality of work declines.

3

Which choice provides the best evidence for the answer to the previous question?

A) Lines 16-18 ("It...habits")
B) Lines 22-23 ("I...question")
C) Lines 31-34 ("If...industrial")
D) Lines 46-49 ("the hours...hours")

6. The following passage is adapted from Michael Anft, "Solving the Mystery of Death Valley's Walking Rocks," © 2011 by *Johns Hopkins Magazine*.

For six decades, observers have been confounded by the movement of large rocks across a dry lake bed in California's Death Valley National Park. Leaving flat trails behind them, rocks that weigh up to 100
5　pounds seemingly do Michael Jackson's moonwalk across the valley's sere, cracked surface, sometimes traveling more than 100 yards. Without a body of water to pick them up and move them, the rocks at Racetrack Playa, a flat space between the valley's high cliffs,
10　have been the subject of much speculation, including whether they have been relocated by human pranksters or space aliens. The rocks have become the desert equivalent of Midwestern crop circles. "They really are a curiosity," says Ralph Lorenz, a planetary scientist at
15　the Applied Physics Laboratory. "Some [people] have mentioned UFOs. But I've always believed that this is something science could solve."

It has tried. One theory holds that the rocks are blown along by powerful winds. Another posits that
20　the wind pushes thin sheets of ice, created when the desert's temperatures dip low enough to freeze water from a rare rainstorm, and the rocks go along for the ride. But neither theory is rock solid. Winds at the playa aren't strong enough—some scientists believe that
25　they'd have to be 100 miles per hour or more—to blow the rocks across the valley. And rocks subject to the "ice sailing theory" wouldn't create trails as they moved.

Lorenz and a team of investigators believe that a
30　combination of forces may work to rearrange Racetrack Playa's rocks. "We saw that it would take a lot of wind to move these rocks, which are larger than you'd expect wind to move," Lorenz explains. "That led us to this idea that ice might be picking up the
35　rocks and floating them." As they explained in the January issue of *The American Journal of Physics*, instead of moving along with wind-driven sheets of ice, the rocks may instead be lifted by the ice, making them more subject to the wind's force. The key, Lorenz
40　says, is that the lifting by an "ice collar" reduces friction with the ground, to the point that the wind now has enough force to move the rock. The rock moves, the ice doesn't, and because part of the rock juts through the ice, it marks the territory it has covered.
45　Lorenz's team came to its conclusion through a combination of intuition, lab work, and observation— not that the last part was easy. Watching the rocks travel is a bit like witnessing the rusting of a hubcap. Instances of movement are rare and last for only a few

50　seconds. Lorenz's team placed low-resolution cameras on the cliffs (which are about 30 miles from the nearest paved road) to take pictures once per hour. For the past three winters, the researchers have weathered extreme temperatures and several flat tires to measure how
55　often the thermometer dips below freezing, how often the playa gets rain and floods, and the strength of the winds. "The measurements seem to back up our hypothesis," he says. "Any of the theories may be true at any one time, but ice rafting may be the best explan-
60　ation for the trails we've been seeing. We've seen trails like this documented in Arctic coastal areas, and the mechanism is somewhat similar. A belt of ice sur- rounds a boulder during high tide, picks it up, and then drops it elsewhere." His "ice raft theory" was also
65　borne out by an experiment that used the ingenuity of a high school science fair. Lorenz placed a basalt pebble in a Tupperware container with water so that the pebble projected just above the surface. He then turned the container upside down in a baking tray filled with a
70　layer of coarse sand at its base, and put the whole thing in his home freezer. The rock's "keel" (its protruding part) projected downward into the sand, which simu- lated the cracked surface of the playa (which scientists call "Special K" because of its resemblance to cereal
75　flakes). A gentle push or slight puff of air caused the Tupperware container to move, just as an ice raft would under the right conditions. The pebble made a trail in the soft sand. "It was primitive but effective," Lorenz says of the experiment. Lorenz has spent the
80　last 20 years studying Titan, a moon of Saturn. He says that Racetrack Playa's surface mirrors that of a dried lakebed on Titan. Observations and experiments on Earth may yield clues to that moon's geology. "We also may get some idea of how climate affects
85　geology—particularly as the climate changes here on Earth," Lorenz says. "When we study other planets and their moons, we're forced to use Occam's razor— sometimes the simplest answer is best, which means you look to Earth for some answers. Once you get out
90　there on Earth, you realize how strange so much of its surface is. So, you have to figure there's weird stuff to be found on Titan as well." Whether that's true or not will take much more investigation. He adds: "One day, we'll figure all this out. For the moment, the moving
95　rock present a wonderful problem to study in a beautiful place."

1

It is reasonable to conclude that one of the scientists' goals in studying Racetrack Playa was to

A) investigate how life could be supported on Titan.
B) understand the effects of climate change.
C) understand the geology of a range of planets.
D) discover the limitations of wind power.

2

Which choice provides the best evidence for the answer to the previous question?

A) Lines 23-26 ("Winds...valley")
B) Lines 52-57 ("For...winds")
C) Lines 75-77 ("A gentle...conditions")
D) Lines 83-86 ("We...Earth")

3

The passage implies that scientists rejected the theory that the rocks were carried on sheets of ice pushed by the wind because

A) the winds were too weak to move the rocks.
B) the rocks left a trace of their movement.
C) rock is too dense to be moved by wind.
D) the rocks had too much friction with the ground.

4

Which choice provides the best evidence for the answer to the previous question?

A) Lines 26-28 ("And...moved")
B) Lines 37-39 ("instead...force")
C) Lines 49-50 ("Instances...seconds")
D) Lines 62-64 ("A belt...elsewhere")

7. The following passage is adapted from "Makerspaces, Hackerspaces, and Community Scale Production in Detroit and Beyond," © 2013 by Sean Ansanelli.

During the mid-1980s, spaces began to emerge across Europe where computer hackers could convene for mutual support and camaraderie. In the past few years, the idea of fostering such shared, physical spaces
5 has been rapidly adapted by the diverse and growing community of "makers," who seek to apply the idea of "hacking" to physical objects, processes, or anything else that can be deciphered and improved upon.

A hackerspace is described by hackerspaces.org as
10 a "community-operated physical space where people with common interests, often in computers, technology, science, digital art or electronic art, can meet, socialize, and/or collaborate." Such spaces can vary in size, available technology, and membership structure (some
15 being completely open), but generally share community-oriented characteristics. Indeed, while the term "hacker" can sometimes have negative connotations, modern hackerspaces thrive off of community, openness, and assimilating diverse viewpoints – these
20 often being the only guiding principles in otherwise informal organizational structures.

In recent years, the city of Detroit has emerged as a hotbed for hackerspaces and other DIY ("Do-It-Yourself") experiments. Several hackerspaces
25 can already be found throughout the city and several more are currently in formation. Of course, Detroit's attractiveness for such projects can be partially attributed to cheap real estate, which allows aspiring hackers to acquire ample space for experimentation.
30 Some observers have also described this kind of making and tinkering as embedded in the DNA of Detroit's residents, who are able to harness substantial intergenerational knowledge and attract like-minded individuals.

35 Hackerspaces (or "makerspaces") can be found in more commercial forms, but the vast majority of spaces are self-organized and not-for-profit. For example, the OmniCorp hackerspace operates off member fees to cover rent and new equipment, from laser cutters to
40 welding tools. OmniCorp also hosts an "open hack night" every Thursday in which the space is open to the general public. Potential members are required to attend at least one open hack night prior to a consensus vote by the existing members for admittance; no
45 prospective members have yet been denied.

A visit to one of OmniCorp's open hack nights reveals the vast variety of activity and energy existing in the space. In the main common room alone, activities range from experimenting with sound installations and
50 learning to program Arduino boards to building speculative "oloid" shapes – all just for the sake of it. With a general atmosphere of mutual support, participants in the space are continually encouraged to help others.

55 One of the most active community-focused initiatives in the city is the Mt. Elliot Makerspace. Jeff Sturges, former MIT Media Lab Fellow and Co-Founder of OmniCorp, started the Mt. Elliot project with the aim of replicating MIT's Fab Lab model on a smaller, cheaper
60 scale in Detroit. "Fab Labs" are production facilities that consist of a small collection of flexible computer-controlled tools that cover several different scales and various materials, with the aim to make "almost anything" (including other machines). The Mt. Elliot
65 Makerspace now offers youth-based skill development programs in eight areas: Transportation, Electronics, Digital Tools, Wearables, Design and Fabrication, Food, Music, and Arts. The range of activities is meant to provide not only something for everyone, but a well-
70 rounded base knowledge of making to all participants.

While the center receives some foundational support, the space also derives significant support from the local community. Makerspaces throughout the city connect the space's youth-based programming directly to
75 school curriculums.

The growing interest in and development of hacker/makerspaces has been explained, in part, as a result of the growing maker movement. Through the combination of cultural norms and communication
80 channels from open source production as well as increasingly available technologies for physical production, amateur maker communities have developed in virtual and physical spaces.

Publications such as *Wired* are noticing the
85 transformative potential of this emerging movement and have sought to devote significant attention to its development. Chief editor Chris Anderson recently published a book entitled *Makers*, in which he proclaims that the movement will become the next Industrial
90 Revolution. Anderson argues such developments will allow for a new wave of business opportunities by providing mass-customization rather than mass-production.

The transformative potential of these trends goes
95 beyond new business opportunities or competitive advantages for economic growth. Rather, these trends demonstrate the potential to actually transform economic development models entirely.

Based on the passage, it can be reasonably inferred that hackerspaces are organized in a manner that is

A) strictly regulated.

B) wild and chaotic.

C) informal and accommodating.

D) rigid and hierarchical.

Which choice provides the best evidence for the answer to the previous question?

A) Lines 3-6 ("In…makers")

B) Lines 18-21 ("modern…structures")

C) Lines 35-37 ("Hackerspaces…profit")

D) Lines 46-48 ("A visit…space")

The author implies that one potential challenge for new hackerspaces involves

A) zoning restrictions.

B) lack of publicity.

C) local protests.

D) property costs.

Which choice provides the best evidence for the answer to the previous question?

A) Lines 16-17 ("Indeed…connotations")

B) Lines 26-29 ("Of…experimentation")

C) Lines 37-40 ("For…tools")

D) Lines 71-73 ("While…community")

8. The following passage is adapted from Julian Jackson, "New Research Suggests Dinosaurs Were Warm-Blooded and Active" © 2011 by Julian Jackson.

New research from the University of Adelaide has added to the debate about whether dinosaurs were cold-blooded and sluggish or warm-blooded and active. Professor Roger Seymour from the University's School
5 of Earth & Environmental Sciences has applied the latest theories of human and animal anatomy and physiology to provide insight into the lives of dinosaurs.

Human thigh bones have tiny holes – known as the
10 "nutrient foramen" – on the shaft that supply blood to living bone cells inside. New research has shown that the size of those holes is related to the maximum rate that a person can be active during aerobic exercise. Professor Seymour has used this principle to evaluate
15 the activity levels of dinosaurs.

"Far from being lifeless, bone cells have a relatively high metabolic rate and they therefore require a large blood supply to deliver oxygen. On the inside of the bone, the blood supply comes usually from a single
20 artery and vein that pass through a hole on the shaft – the nutrient foramen," he says.

Professor Seymour wondered whether the size of the nutrient foramen might indicate how much blood was necessary to keep the bones in good repair. For
25 example, highly active animals might cause more bone 'microfractures,' requiring more frequent repairs by the bone cells and therefore a greater blood supply. "My aim was to see whether we could use fossil bones of dinosaurs to indicate the level of bone metabolic rate
30 and possibly extend it to the whole body's metabolic rate," he says. "One of the big controversies among paleobiologists is whether dinosaurs were cold-blooded and sluggish or warm-blooded and active. Could the size of the foramen be a possible gauge for dinosaur
35 metabolic rate?"

Comparisons were made with the sizes of the holes in living mammals and reptiles, and their metabolic rates. Measuring mammals ranging from mice to elephants, and reptiles from lizards to crocodiles, one
40 of Professor Seymour's Honors students, Sarah Smith, combed the collections of Australian museums, photographing and measuring hundreds of tiny holes in thigh bones.

"The results were unequivocal. The sizes of the holes
45 were related closely to the maximum metabolic rates during peak movement in mammals and reptiles," Professor Seymour says. "The holes found in mammals were about 10 times larger than those in reptiles."

These holes were compared to those of fossil
50 dinosaurs. Dr. Don Henderson, Curator of Dinosaurs from the Royal Tyrrell Museum in Alberta, Canada, and Daniela Schwarz-Wings from the Museum für Naturkunde Humboldt University Berlin, Germany measured the holes in 10 species of
55 dinosaurs from five different groups, including bipedal and quadrupedal carnivores and herbivores, weighing 50kg to 20,000kg.

"On a relative comparison to eliminate the differences in body size, all of the dinosaurs had
60 holes in their thigh bones larger than those of mammals," Professor Seymour says.

"The dinosaurs appeared to be even more active than the mammals. We certainly didn't expect to see that. These results provide additional weight to
65 theories that dinosaurs were warm-blooded and highly active creatures, rather than cold-blooded and sluggish."

Professor Seymour says following the results of this study, it's likely that a simple measurement of
70 foramen size could be used to evaluate maximum activity levels in other vertebrate animals.

---

1 ▨▨▨▨▨▨▨▨▨▨▨▨▨▨▨▨▨▨▨▨▨▨▨▨▨▨▨▨

Based on the passage, it can be reasonably inferred that a creature with a small foramen would most likely be

A) cold-blooded.

B) warm-blooded.

C) smaller than average.

D) larger than average.

---

2 ▨▨▨▨▨▨▨▨▨▨▨▨▨▨▨▨▨▨▨▨▨▨▨▨▨▨▨▨

An unstated assumption in the passage is that

A) warm- or cold-bloodedness cannot be determined by an animal's activity level.

B) some prehistoric creatures were physiologically similar to modern ones.

C) foramen size can be an unreliable indicator of activity level.

D) mammal bones are significantly larger than reptile bones.

Explanations: Inference Exercises

1.1 A

This question does not provide a line reference, but the passage gives you a subtle clue of where to look. The most "interesting" punctuation it contains is a set of dashes (lines 5-8), and the information between them provides you with the information necessary to answer the question. The statement that conservation groups came to the *realization that indigenous groups usually help to stabilize ecosystems* implies that the groups were not always aware of that fact — in other words, they were unaware of indigenous groups' ability to stabilize (= maintain) ecosystems. B) and D) are incorrect because the passage indicates exactly the opposite: *millions of indigenous people were ousted* (forced) *from their homelands* because of conservationists' efforts to create human-free zones, and many of them *succumbed to disease.* C) is entirely unsupported by the passage.

2.1-2 C, C

The passage focuses on stress, so it is logical to assume that the correct answer to 2.1 will be related to that topic. That makes C) and D) the likeliest answers. In D), however, the extreme phrase "<u>entirely</u> irrelevant" suggests that this answer is wrong. When you go through the line references for 2.2, your key word is "genes." Lines 5-6, 8-9, and 19-20 all mention stress, but only 14-16 mention genes. What do those lines tell us? That *levels of stress matter more [than genes and risk factors like smoking].* In other words, genes and risky behaviors matter *less.* C) is thus correct.

3.1 B

Throughout the passage, the narrator describes the various ways in which Catherine is unsuited to being a heroine, so it can be inferred that a heroine should be all of the things that Catherine is <u>not</u>. One of the major points of the passage is that Catherine is a less-than-brilliant student who prefers to blow off her lessons. It can thus be inferred that a heroine should be very intelligent and/or studious. Likewise, lines 22-24 indicate that Catherine is *plain*, whereas heroines are typically beautiful. The other answers refer to attributes that could be associated with Catherine.

3.2-3 C, D

If you know that Mrs. Morland is generally good-natured, you can identify C) as the correct answer to 3.2 because it is the only positive option. Otherwise, start by plugging in the line references, looking for information that suggests how Mrs. Morland responded to Catherine's antics. Lines 13-15 are unrelated to that topic, so A) can be eliminated. Lines 20-21 focus on the Morlands' physical appearance, and lines 38-40 say nothing about Mrs. Morland's reaction to the length of time it took Catherine to learn the "Beggar's Petition," so B) and C) can also be eliminated. D) is the answer to 3.3 because lines 47-50 indicate that Mrs. Morland allowed Catherine to stop music lessons, suggesting that she responded to her daughter's lack of brilliance/perseverance without a fuss. That corresponds most directly to C) in 3.2.

3.4-5 C, B

If you understand the passage well enough to know that Catherine is somewhat naughty, you can reasonably assume that the answer to 3.4 is C). Then, you can plug in the line references to 3.5, looking for statements to support that idea. Otherwise, the question is broad enough that you are best off plugging in the line references, looking for information about what most motivates Catherine. Lines 26-27 indicate she preferred boys' games, but no answer in 3.4 corresponds to that idea. Lines 30-33 correctly suggest Catherine's propensity for doing things that were forbidden, i.e., not allowed, making C) the answer to 3.4. Lines 43-44 and 54-56 do not provide information that supports an answer in 3.4.

3.6 C

The point of the sentence in which the references to a dormouse, canary-bird, and rose bush appear (lines 28-29) is that Catherine preferred boys' games. That is just another way of saying that she "rejected conventionally feminine activities."

4.1 A

Using the big picture, you might be able to eliminate B) in 4.1 upfront; the passage indicates that drivers are *more* likely to take responsibility for their behavior in the absence of traffic signals. The other answers in 4.1 are all ideas included in the passage – the question is which one the author considers "most pressing." That is your key phrase, and it appears in line 55. A) is correct because lines 54-56 state that *At the same time, the threat of looming idiocy is* not *the most pressing reason for a future traffic management rethink.* The implication is that the information that follows will indicate the most pressing reason for a traffic management rethink. What information follows? A description of bland, soulless urban spaces that could be revitalized by the elimination of traffic divisions. That corresponds to A).

4.2-3 D, A

The question in 4.2 provides very little direction, so start by plugging in line references – you'll find the answer almost immediately. Lines 7-8 state that *this concept is the declared dream of many traffic planners.* What does "this concept" refer to? A world *without signs, sidewalks, or bicycle lanes.* In other words, most traffic planners agree with Monderman that traffic signals should be abolished. The answer to 4.2 is therefore D), and the answer to 4.3 is A).

5.1 C

The sentence in which the word *China* appears states that *If that were true, England and America ought to be at the tail end, and China at the head of civilization.* To figure out what *that* refers to, you must back up and read the beginning of the paragraph. That section states that if fewer working hours caused a decline in national prosperity, then more hours would increase prosperity. The statement that *China [would be] at the head of civilization* if national prosperity resulted from long working hours implies that Chinese workers put in very long hours. C) is thus correct.

5.2-3 B, D

This is a general enough question that you are best off plugging in the line references in 5.3, unless you happen to remember the answer to 5.2. In lines 16-18, *It has been charged* indicates that Gompers is citing the conventional wisdom – that is, what he does not believe. Eliminate A). B) and C) are incorrect because lines 22-23 and 31-34 do not discuss the *consequences* of long working hours. D) is correct because lines 46-49 suggest that workers could make important discoveries if they were given more free time (*the mental labor of one hour produces for him more wealth than the physical labor of a dozen hours*). The answer to 5.2 is therefore B), and the answer to 5.3 is D).

6.1-2 B, D

If you remember the discussion of Titan from the passage, you might be tempted to pick A) – but be careful! None of the lines provided in 6.2 supports the idea that the scientists were attempting to understand how Titan could support life. In fact, the passage only directly indicates that scientists wanted to understand Titan's *geology* (lines 82-83). So plug in the line references from 6.2. The only set of lines to directly support an answer in 6.1 is D): in lines 83-86, Lorenz states that *We may also may get some idea of how climate affects geology – particularly as the climate changes here on Earth.* It can thus be inferred that one of his goals in conducting research on Racetrack Playa is to understand the potential effects of climate change.

6.3-4 B, A

6.3 is phrased in a somewhat complicated manner, so start by rephrasing the question to make sure you're clear on what it's asking. You might say something like, "Why did scientists reject the theory that the rocks were carried on ice?" It's unlikely you'll remember the answer, so start by plugging in. Lines 26-28 give you the answer immediately – the only challenge is to recognize that they give you the answer. These lines refer to the "ice-sailing theory," and in order to recognize that this theory posits that the rocks were carried on ice (lines 19-23), you must back up and read the full paragraph. What does the passage indicate about the weakness in that theory? The passage states that rocks moved by ice *wouldn't create trails as they moved.* Logically, then, scientists rejected the ice-sailing theory because the Racetrack Playa rocks *did* leave trails. That is what B) says, so it is the answer to 6.3, and A) is the answer to 6.4.

7.1-2 C, B

One of the major points that the author makes about makerspaces/hackerspaces is that they're flexible and open/non-exclusive. If you have that big-picture understanding, you can immediately identify C) as the most likely answer to 7.1 and then check the line references in 7.2 to confirm. Otherwise, start by plugging in the line references. A) is incorrect because lines 3-6 only describe the community of "makers" themselves (diverse and growing) – they do not describe how makerspaces are organized. B) is the answer to 7.2 because lines 18-21 indicate that *community, openness, and assimilating diverse viewpoints* are often these spaces' *only* guiding principles. In other words, the organizations are loosely structured. In 7.1, B) is too extreme: having a loose structure is not the same thing as being "wild and chaotic." D) is exactly the opposite of what the passage describes – makerspaces are informal and egalitarian, not "rigid" or "hierarchical" (having a strict chain of command). C) is thus the best fit for 7.1.

7.3-4 D, B

This is a real detail-based question, so it's unlikely you'll remember the answer to 7.3. Work by plugging in from 7.4. A) is incorrect because lines 16-17 only state that the term "hacking" can have negative connotations; they don't indicate any particular challenge to hackerspaces consistent with an answer in 7.3. B) is subtle but correct. Lines 26-29 indicate that Detroit is particularly well-suited to fostering hackerspaces because of *cheap real estate*, implying that (higher) real estate costs could pose an obstacle to hackerspace growth elsewhere. The answer to 7.3 is thus D). Nothing in either lines 37-40 or 71-73 directly supports any of the answers in 7.3.

8.1 A

Consider the passage and Seymour's experiment as a whole: the primary hypothesis was that because warm-bloodedness is associated with large holes in the bone (high metabolic rate), the presence of large bone holes in dinosaurs would indicate warm-bloodedness. Logically, the opposite would hold true as well: small holes in the bone would indicate cold-bloodedness. That is what A) says, so it is correct.

8.2 B

The premise of Seymour's study was that foramen size could be studied as an indicator of metabolic level in dinosaurs (prehistoric creatures) because foramen size could be studied as an accurate indicator of metabolic level in reptiles and mammals (present-day creatures). In order for the findings to be meaningful, the bodies of prehistoric creatures must have functioned in a way that was similar to the bodies of modern-day creatures. That is essentially what B) says, so it is correct.

Extended Reasoning and Analogies

The vast majority of inference questions that appear on the SAT are similar to the ones we looked at in the previous chapter – that is, their correct answers either rephrase the information in the passage from a different angle, or directly state information that the passage implies but does not explicitly convey.

In a small number of cases, however, you may be asked to make larger inferences, ones that require you to extend your reasoning beyond the passage itself.

These questions take two major forms:

The first type asks you to use the information from the passage to determine how a figure discussed in the passage would mostly likely respond to a **hypothetical situation** – that is, one not discussed in the passage. These are essentially assumption questions taken one step further: you must be able to identify the underlying logic in order to apply it to a new situation. You can expect to encounter one, perhaps two, of these questions per test.

The second type consists of **analogy** questions, which ask you to identify the answer containing a scenario that is "most analogous to," "most similar to," or "most like," the scenario described in a short section of the passage. Analogy questions **do not appear on every exam** and should therefore not be a major concern; however, you should have a general idea of how to work through them in case you encounter one.

On the next page, we're going to start by looking at the first type.

Sometimes it seems surprising that science functions at all. In 2005, medical science was shaken by a paper with the provocative title "Why most published research findings are false." Written by John

5   Ioannidis, a professor of medicine at Stanford University, it didn't actually show that any particular result was wrong. Instead, it showed that the statistics of reported positive findings was not consistent with how often one should *expect* to find them. As Ioannidis concluded more

10 recently, "many published research findings are false or exaggerated, and an estimated 85 percent of research resources are wasted."

It's likely that some researchers are consciously cherry-picking data to get their work published.

15 And some of the problems surely lie with journal publication policies. But the problems of false findings often begin with researchers unwittingly fooling themselves: they fall prey to cognitive biases, common modes of thinking that lure us toward wrong but

20 convenient or attractive conclusions. "Seeing the reproducibility rates in psychology and other empirical science, we can safely say that something is not working out the way it should," says Susann Fiedler, a behavioral economist at the Max Planck Institute for Research on

25 Collective Goods in Bonn, Germany. "Cognitive biases might be one reason for that."

Psychologist Brian Nosek of the University of Virginia says that the most common and problematic bias in science is "motivated reasoning": We interpret

30 observations to fit a particular idea. Psychologists have shown that "most of our reasoning is in fact rationalization," he says. In other words, we have already made the decision about what to do or to think, and our "explanation" of our reasoning is really a justification for

35 doing what we wanted to do—or to believe—anyway. Science is of course meant to be more objective and skeptical than everyday thought—but how much is it, really?

Based on the passage, to which of the following situations would Nosek most likely object?

A) A team of researchers knowingly publishes misleading information in an attempt to obtain funding.

B) A team of researchers publishes a study based on statistics that were not independently verified.

C) A researcher deliberately publishes a study whose results conflict with those obtained by experts in the field.

D) A researcher who is known to believe in paranormal activity publishes a study that supports its existence.

Which choice provides the best evidence for the answer to the previous question?

A) Lines 7-9 ("Instead…them")
B) Lines 13-14 ("It's likely…published")
C) Lines 29-30 ("We…idea")
D) Lines 36-37 ("Science…thought")

This question is phrased in a somewhat roundabout manner, so the first thing to do is simplify it. Basically, it's asking what type of situation Nosek would think was bad.

The easiest way to proceed after this is to use the main point, which appears in the second and third paragraphs: Cognitive biases → bad research. Or, more thoroughly, scientists may unconsciously project their assumptions onto their research and, consequently, interpret results in such a way that confirms their existing beliefs.

If you approach the question with that idea in mind, you've already established the criteria for the answer to Question #1. The only option consistent with the idea of a researcher obtaining results that clearly supported a pre-existing belief is D) – all the others are off-topic. (Incidentally, that answer is based on an actual case in which a Cornell psychology professor published a study in a major journal claiming that he had found proof of ESP.)

For Question #2, you simply need to find the lines consistent with the point. We could just plug in each of the line references in order, but in this case there's a trick: if you look at the passage, you'll notice that Nosek's name does not actually appear until the last paragraph. As a result, you can assume that the correct set of lines must begin after line 27, eliminating A) and B). C) is consistent with the point – scientists interpret data to fit their existing biases – and is therefore correct. It is unnecessary to even check D).

Analogy questions also involve situations and individuals completely unconnected to the passage itself. You are responsible for drawing the connection between the specific wording in the passage and the more general situation it describes, and for recognizing which of the answers describes the same essential scenario. Analogy questions do not typically have shortcuts but instead require multiple steps of logic. If you follow the steps below, however, they can become fairly straightforward.

1) Go back to the passage and read the exact lines provided in the question.

Analogy questions are not context-based questions. Provided you understand the general section of the passage well enough for those lines to make sense, you should be able to answer the question based only on the lines given. Reading more than a few words before/after for necessary context will most likely confuse you.

2) Quickly rephrase the scenario presented.

Take a moment and reiterate for yourself exactly what's going on in those lines. Who are the people in question, what are they doing, and what is the outcome?

3) Sum up the scenario in general terms. Write it down.

This is the crucial step. You have to understand what's going on in more abstract terms in order to draw the analogy. What you write can be very short and simple, but if you don't have something to look at to keep you focused, you'll usually find it more difficult to identify the correct answer.

4) Check the answers one at a time, in order.

As you read each answer, think about whether it matches the general "template" for the scenario you've established in Step 3. If it clearly doesn't match, cross it out; if there's any chance it could work, leave it. If you're left with more than one answer, determine which one matches the template more closely – that will be the correct answer.

To reiterate: going through these steps need not be time-consuming. In fact, it is possible to complete them very, very quickly. But you should do your best to avoid skipping steps. If you don't define the relationships precisely upfront, it's very easy to get confused and lose track of just what you're looking for.

Let's look at an example:

For science fiction aficionados, Isaac Asimov anticipated the idea of using massive data sets to predict human behavior, coining it "psychohistory" in his 1951 Foundation trilogy. The bigger the data set, Asimov said
5 then, the more predictable the future. With big-data analytics, one can finally see the forest, instead of just the capillaries in the tree leaves. Or to put it in more accurate terms, one can see beyond the apparently random motion of a few thousand molecules of air inside
10 a balloon; one can see the balloon itself, and beyond that, that it is inflating, that it is yellow, and that it is part of a bunch of balloons en route to a birthday party. The data/software world has, until now, been largely about looking at the molecules inside one balloon.

1

Which of the following is most analogous to the situation described in lines 5-10 ("With…balloon")?

A) A scientist makes a groundbreaking discovery and receives an award.

B) A classical musician successfully releases an album of contemporary songs.

C) A tourist is able to observe an entire city and the surrounding region from a skyscraper.

D) A private company partners with a local government to build a new shopping district.

We're going to apply the process described on the previous page to determine the answer:

1) Reread only the lines in question.

Lines 5-10 state:

With big-data analytics, one can finally see the forest, instead of just the capillaries in the tree leaves. Or to put it in more accurate terms, one can see beyond the apparently random motion of a few thousand molecules of air inside a balloon; one can see the balloon itself, and beyond that, that it is inflating, that it is yellow, and that it is part of a bunch of balloons en route to a birthday party. The data/software world has, until now, been largely about looking at the molecules inside one balloon.

2) Reiterate lines in your own words.

Before big data, could only see details; now see everything

You can scribble something down if you find it helpful, but if you think writing will take too much time or doesn't seem necessary, you can skip this step.

3) Rephrase #2 in a more general way and <u>write it down</u>.

Small pic. → big pic.

Notice the shorthand here. This is similar to a "main point" exercise – the goal is to capture the general idea as simply and quickly as possible, and to have something to look at when you check the answers so that you don't get distracted.

4) Find the answer that matches the summary in #3

One-by-one, we're going to check the answers in order.

A) A scientist makes a groundbreaking discovery and receives an award.

No. This has nothing to do with seeing the big picture. Careful not to get caught up in associative thinking here. The fact that the passage has scientific *topic* does not mean that the *situation* in the passage is the same as the one in the answer choice.

B) A classical musician successfully releases an album of contemporary songs.

Successfully switching from one genre of music to another is not at all the same thing as moving from the small picture to the big one. So B) is out.

C) A tourist is able to observe an entire city and the surrounding region from a skyscraper.

Maybe. It doesn't explicitly discuss moving from the small picture to the big picture, but it does capture the idea of being able to see beyond one's immediate surroundings from a high-up vantage point. That is similar to *see[ing] beyond the apparently random motion of a few thousand molecules of air inside a balloon; one can see the balloon itself, and beyond that, that it is inflating.*

So we keep C).

D) A private company partners with a local government to build a new shopping district.

No, the collaboration between public and private has nothing to do with moving from the small picture to the big picture. This answer is completely off-topic.

So the answer is C). It might not match exactly, but out of all the choices, it comes closest.

You could also be asked to identify an analogy within the passage itself. For example:

Every time a car drives through a major intersection, it becomes a data point. Magnetic coils of wire lie just beneath the pavement, registering each passing car. This starts a cascade of information: Computers tally the
5 number and speed of cars, shoot the data through underground cables to a command center and finally translate it into the colors red, yellow and green. On the seventh floor of Boston City Hall, the three colors splash like paint across a wall-sized map.
10 To drivers, the color red means stop, but on the map it tells traffic engineers to leap into action. Traffic control centers like this one—a room cluttered with computer terminals and live video feeds of urban intersections—represent the brain of a traffic system. The city's network
15 of sensors, cables and signals are the nerves connected to the rest of the body. "Most people don't think there are eyes and ears keeping track of all this stuff," says John DeBenedictis, the center's engineering director. But in reality, engineers literally watch our every move,
20 making subtle changes that relieve and redirect traffic.
The tactics and aims of traffic management are modest but powerful. Most intersections rely on a combination of pre-set timing and computer adaptation. For example, where a busy main road intersects with a quiet residential
25 street, the traffic signal might give 70 percent of "green time" to the main road, and 30 percent to the residential road. (Green lights last between a few seconds and a couple minutes, and tend to shorten at rush hour to help the traffic move continuously.) But when traffic
30 overwhelms the pre-set timing, engineers override the system and make changes.

1

Which of the following is most like the "sensors, cables, and signals?"

A) "Magnetic coils of wire" (line 2)

B) "the colors red, yellow, and green" (line 7)

C) "the brain of a traffic system" (line 14)

D) "a combination of pre-set timing and computer adaptation" (lines 22-23)

Sensors, cables, and signals refer to the specific instruments that traffic engineers use to channel information from the streets into traffic control centers, so we're essentially looking for an **example** of one of those things. There's no shortcut; we need to check each answer.

That said, we'll find the answer pretty quickly. For A), the passage tells us that the magnetic coils of wire register the number/speed of cars and transmit that information through underground cables to traffic control centers, so this is exactly what we're looking for.

Otherwise, B) is wrong because the colors listed are a result of the information transmitted, not the tools for transmitting the information. C) is wrong because *the brain of a traffic system* is the actual traffic control center, and we're looking for the tools the control center uses. And D) is wrong because *a combination of pre-set timing and computer adaptation* is mentioned as an example of the tactics/aims of traffic management. It's a way of managing traffic at intersections, not a tool for relaying information back to traffic engineers.

Extended Reasoning and Analogy Exercises

1.   Around the middle of the 20th century, science dispensed with the fantasy that we could easily colonize the other planets in our solar system. Science fiction writers absorbed the new reality: soon, moon and
5   asteroid settings replaced Mars and Venus.

1

Which of the following is most analogous to the situation described in the passage?

A)   A writer realizes that he is unlikely to become a successful novelist and accepts a job at a magazine instead.

B)   A musician continues to perform despite receiving unfavorable reviews from critics.

C)   A pilot is forced to make an emergency landing after encountering bad weather during a flight.

D)   A politician retires from office after becoming involved in a scandal.

2.   Why is the connection between smells and memories so strong? The reason for these associations is that the brain's olfactory bulb is connected to both the amygdala (an emotion center) and to the
5   hippocampus, which is involved in memory. And, because smells serve a survival function (odors can keep us from eating spoiled or poisonous foods), some of these associations are made very quickly, and may even involve a one-time association.

1

As described in the passage, the connection between smells and memories is most like which of the following?

A)   a driver has an accident at an intersection and refuses to drive past it again.

B)   a child insists on wearing clothes of a particular color every day.

C)   a young woman inexplicably develops an allergy to a common household item.

D)   a food manufacturer develops a technology to prevent its products from spoiling.

3.   Experimental scientists occupy themselves with observing and measuring the cosmos, finding out what stuff exists, no matter how strange that stuff may be. Theoretical physicists, on the other hand, are not
5   satisfied with observing the universe. They want to know why. They want to explain all the properties of the universe in terms of a few fundamental principles and parameters. These fundamental principles, in turn, lead to the "laws of nature," which govern the
10 behavior of all matter and energy.

1

Theoretical physicists' goal, as indicated in the passage, is most similar to which of the following?

A)   A biologist observing changes in a specimen over an extended period of time.

B)   Members of a community rebuilding a house destroyed in a storm.

C)   An astronaut undergoes years of training to prepare for a journey into space.

D)   A linguist seeking to discover the underlying features common to distantly related languages.

4.   The sharing economy is a little like online shopping, which started in America 15 years ago. At first, people were worried about security. But having made a successful purchase from, say, Amazon, they
5 felt safe buying elsewhere. Similarly, using Airbnb or a car-hire service for the first time encourages people to try other offerings. Next, consider eBay. Having started out as a peer-to-peer marketplace, it is now dominated by professional "power sellers" (many of whom started
10 out as ordinary eBay users). The same may happen with the sharing economy, which also provides new opportunities for enterprise. Some people have bought cars solely to rent them out, for example. Incumbents are getting involved too. Avis, a car-hire firm, has a share
15 in a sharing rival. So do GM and Daimler, two carmakers. In the future, companies may develop hybrid models, listing excess capacity (whether vehicles, equipment or office space) on peer-to-peer rental sites. In the past, new ways of doing things online have not displaced the
20 old ways entirely. But they have often changed them. Just as internet shopping forced Walmart and Tesco to adapt, so online sharing will shake up transport, tourism, equipment-hire and more.
    The main worry is regulatory uncertainty. Will
25 room-4-renters be subject to hotel taxes, for example? In Amsterdam officials are using Airbnb listings to track down unlicensed hotels. In some American cities, peer-to-peer taxi services have been banned after lobbying by traditional taxi firms. The danger is that
30 although some rules need to be updated to protect consumers from harm, incumbents will try to destroy competition. People who rent out rooms should pay tax, of course, but they should not be regulated like a Ritz-Carlton hotel. The lighter rules that typically govern
35 bed-and-breakfasts are more than adequate. The sharing economy is the latest example of the internet's value to consumers. This emerging model is now big and disruptive enough for regulators and companies to have woken up to it. That is a sign of its immense potential. It
40 is time to start caring about sharing.

1

Which action would best address a concern about the sharing economy discussed in the passage?

A) Prohibiting established businesses from competing with casual sellers.

B) Imposing stricter regulations on individual room rentals.

C) Establishing clear tax guidelines for services in the sharing economy.

D) Informing buyers more thoroughly about their consumer rights.

5.   Every day you wake up with a slightly less connected brain than the night before. New research in mice reveals that during sleep the connections between brain cells, which hold information learned throughout the
5   day, undergo massive shrinkage. The process makes room for learning new memories while shedding weak ones. As author Marie Kondo would put it, this is the brain's very own "life-changing magic of tidying up."

"When we are awake, learning and adapting to the
10   environment, synapses—or the connections between neurons—get strengthened and grow," says neuroscientist Chiara Cirelli of the University of Wisconsin–Madison. "But you can't keep growing the synapses. At some point, you will saturate them."
15   After more than a decade of study, Cirelli and her colleagues have finally found direct evidence that synapses reset at night. They reported their findings in *Science*. Using electron microscopy to look at thousands of ultrathin brain slices taken from awake and sleeping
20   mice, they found that after sleep, the size of most synapses—specifically, the surface area where two neurons touch each other—shrank by about 18 percent.

Although the findings were in mice, Cirelli suspects this synaptic resetting also occurs in people. Indirect
25   evidence, for example, from electrophysiological recordings of the human brain before and after sleep, is consistent with this idea, she says.

This shrinkage appears to spare important memories. About 20 percent of synapses, which were the largest
30   and may hold well-established memories, did not shrink. Less important memories may not get entirely axed but merely pared down—although each synapse shrinks, the overall pattern of connections that constitute a memory remains.

1

Which of the following hypothetical findings would support the hypothesis that synaptic resettling occurs in humans?

A) An increase in the space where neurons meet in the evening.
B) A reduction in the space where neurons meet in the evening.
C) An increase in the space where neurons meet early in the morning.
D) A reduction in the space where neurons meet early in the morning.

2

Which choice provides the best evidence for the answer to the previous question?

A) Lines 9-11 ("When we…grow")
B) Lines 20 22 ("they found…percent")
C) Lines 29-30 ("About…shrink")
D) Lines 32-34 ("although…remains")

6.   The public has been worried about the safety of
genetically modified (GM) foods since scientists at the
University of Washington developed the first
genetically modified tobacco plants in the 1970s. In the
5 mid-1990s, when the first GM crops reached the
market, Greenpeace, the Sierra Club, Ralph Nader,
Prince Charles and a number of celebrity chefs took
highly visible stands against them. Consumers in
Europe became particularly alarmed: a survey
10 conducted in 1997, for example, found that 69 percent
of the Austrian public saw serious risks in GM foods,
compared with only 14 percent of Americans.
    But as medical researchers know, nothing can really
be "proved safe." One can only fail to turn up
15 significant risk after trying hard to find it—as is the
case with GM crops.
    Although it might seem creepy to add virus DNA to
a plant, doing so is, in fact, no big deal, proponents say.
Viruses have been inserting their DNA into the
20 genomes of crops, as well as humans and all other
organisms, for millions of years. They often deliver the
genes of other species while they are at it, which is why
our own genome is loaded with genetic sequences that
originated in viruses and nonhuman species.
25   Could eating plants with altered genes allow new
DNA to work its way into our own? It is theoretically
possible but hugely improbable. Scientists have never
found genetic material that could survive a trip through
the human gut and make it into cells. Besides, we are
30 routinely exposed to—we even consume—the viruses
and bacteria whose genes end up in GM foods. The
bacterium B. thuringiensis, for example, which
produces proteins fatal to insects, is sometimes enlisted
as a natural pesticide in organic farming.
35   In any case, people have consumed as many as
trillions of meals containing genetically modified
ingredients over the past few decades. Not a single
verified case of illness has ever been attributed to the
genetic alterations.
40   Critics often disparage U.S. research on the safety
of genetically modified foods, which is often funded
or even conducted by GM companies, such as Monsanto.
But much research on the subject comes from the
European Commission, the administrative body of the
45 E.U., which cannot be so easily dismissed as an industry
tool. The European Commission has funded 130 research
projects, carried out by more than 500 independent teams,
on the safety of GM crops. None of those studies found
any special risks from GM crops.

1

Based on the passage, a study of GM food safety
conducted by which of the following would be most
likely to reassure critics?

A) A group of researchers who are not affiliated
with the agricultural industry.

B) A private institute whose clients also include
producers of GM foods.

C) A food corporation that wants to expand its
distribution of GM foods.

D) A pharmaceutical company that produces
medications derived from GM plants.

2

Which choice provides the best evidence for the
answer to the previous question?

A) Lines 9-11 ("a survey…foods")

B) Lines 19-21 ("Viruses…years")

C) Lines 35-39 ("In any…alterations")

D) Lines 46-48 ("The European…crops")

7. This passage is adapted from Sharon Tregaskis, "What Bees Tell Us About Global Climate Change," © 2010 by *Johns Hopkins Magazine*.

Standing in the apiary on the grounds of the U.S. Department of Agriculture's Bee Research Laboratory in Beltsville, Maryland, Wayne Esaias digs through the canvas shoulder bag leaning against his leg in search of
5 the cable he uses to download data. It's dusk as he runs the cord from his laptop—precariously perched on the beam of a cast-iron platform scale—to a small, battery-operated data logger attached to the spring inside the scale's steel column. In the 1800s, a scale like this
10 would have weighed sacks of grain or crates of apples, peaches, and melons. Since arriving at the USDA's bee lab in January 2007, this scale has been loaded with a single item: a colony of *Apis mellifera*, the fuzzy, black-and-yellow honey bee. An attached, 12-bit
15 recorder captures the hive's weight to within a 10th of a pound, along with a daily register of relative ambient humidity and temperature.

On this late January afternoon, during a comparatively balmy respite between the blizzards that
20 dumped several feet of snow on the Middle Atlantic states, the bees, their honey, and the wooden boxes in which they live weigh 94.5 pounds. In mid-July, as last year's unusually long nectar flow finally ebbed, the whole contraption topped out at 275 pounds, including
25 nearly 150 pounds of honey. "Right now, the colony is in a cluster about the size of a soccer ball," says Esaias, who's kept bees for nearly two decades and knows without lifting the lid what's going on inside this hive. "The center of the cluster is where the queen is, and
30 they're keeping her at 93 degrees—the rest are just hanging there, tensing their flight muscles to generate heat." Provided that they have enough calories to fuel their winter workout, a healthy colony can survive as far north as Anchorage, Alaska. "They slowly eat their
35 way up through the winter," he says. "It's a race: Will they eat all their honey before the nectar flows, or not?" To make sure their charges win that race, apiarists have long relied on scale hives for vital management clues. By tracking daily weight variations, a beekeeper can
40 discern when the colony needs a nutritional boost to carry it through lean times, whether to add extra combs for honey storage and even detect incursions by marauding robber bees—all without disturbing the colony. A graph of the hive's weight—which can

45 increase by as much as 35 pounds a day in some parts of the United States during peak nectar flow – reveals the date on which the bees' foraging was was most productive and provides a direct record of successful pollination. "Around here, the bees make
50 their living in the month of May," says Esaias, noting that his bees often achieve daily spikes of 25 pounds, the maximum in Maryland. "There's almost no nectar coming in for the rest of the year." A scientist by training and career oceanographer at NASA, Esaias
55 established the Mink Hollow Apiary in his Highland, Maryland, backyard in 1992 with a trio of hand-me-down hives and an antique platform scale much like the one at the Beltsville bee lab. Ever since, he's maintained a meticulous record of the bees' daily
60 weight, as well as weather patterns and such details as his efforts to keep them healthy. In late 2006, honey bees nationwide began disappearing in an ongoing syndrome dubbed colony collapse disorder (CCD). Entire hives went empty as bees inexplicably
65 abandoned their young and their honey. Commercial beekeepers reported losses up to 90 percent, and the large-scale farmers who rely on honey bees to ensure rich harvests of almonds, apples, and sunflowers became very, very nervous. Looking for clues, Esaias
70 turned to his own records. While the resulting graphs threw no light on the cause of CCD, a staggering trend emerged: In the span of just 15 seasons, the date on which his Mink Hollow bees brought home the most nectar had shifted by two weeks—from late May
75 to the middle of the month. "I was shocked when I plotted this up," he says. "It was right under my nose, going on the whole time." The epiphany would lead Esaias to launch a series of research collaborations, featuring honey bees and other pollinators, to
80 investigate the relationships among plants, pollinators, and weather patterns. Already, the work has begun to reveal insights into the often unintended consequences of human interventions in natural and agricultural ecosystems, and exposed significant
85 gaps in how we understand the effect climate change will have on everything from food production to terrestrial ecology.

1

Based on the passage, to which of the following hypothetical outcomes would research into the bees' disappearance most likely lead?

A) The cultivation of hybrid fruits and vegetables.
B) Larger-scale production of the most profitable crops.
C) More sophisticated tools for studying insect behavior.
D) A heightened awareness of how shifts in the climate impact crop growth.

2

Which choice provides the best evidence for the answer to the previous question?

A) Lines 58-61 ("Ever...healthy")
B) Lines 65-69 ("Commercial...nervous")
C) Lines 72-74 ("In...weeks")
D) Lines 81-87 ("Already...ecology")

Explanations: Extended Reasoning and Analogy Exercises

1.1 A

What is the scenario described in the passage? Science fiction writers realized that it was not realistic for humans to easily colonize other planets, so they changed their works to incorporate that new reality by focusing on asteroids and the moon.

General scenario: realize *x* is unrealistic, adjust expectations to do *y*.

The key word in (A) is *instead*. The answer describes a person who realizes that a goal is unrealistic and changes plans accordingly (takes a job at a magazine).

B) describes the opposite of the required scenario because the musician *continues* to perform when faced with discouragement. In C), the pilot is *forced* to land, whereas the science fiction writers make a choice to focus on something new. And in D), the politician does not leave his or her career because it is unrealistic but rather because he or she is involved in some type of wrongdoing.

2.1 A

What characterizes the relationship between smells and memories? It's very strong because it serves a survival function: things that smell bad are more likely to be harmful, and thus people learn to avoid things associated with those types of things.

General scenario: learn that *x* is potentially harmful after a brief exposure, so avoid *x*.

A) is correct because it describes a situation in which a person was exposed to a negative situation once and, as a result, goes out of the way not to experience that situation again. B) is incorrect because the child's preference is clearly positive. Although the scenario in C) is negative, it does not describe someone who went out of his or her way to *avoid* a negative situation after a previous exposure. D) plays on associative interference by using the word *food*, which appears in the passage; however, keeping food from spoiling is a positive thing, so this answer cannot be correct.

3.1 D

What is theoretical physicists' goal? *They want to know why. They want to explain all the properties of the universe in terms of a few fundamental principles and parameters.* (lines 6-8)

General scenario: want to know the general rules governing a particular phenomenon.

D) is correct because the linguist wants to "discover the underlying features" that distantly related languages have in common. The underlying assumption is that all languages must have similarities, or that there is a set of rules governing how language works. A) describes what a biologist (an experimental scientist) does, *not* a theoretical physicist. B) and C) are entirely unrelated to the passage. The scenario in B) involves people collaborating to achieve a goal, and the one in C) involves a person who spends a lot of time preparing for a difficult undertaking.

4.1 C

The key word in the question is *concern*, so start by scanning the passage for that idea. You'll find a synonym for it in the topic sentence of the second paragraph (line 24): *The main worry is regulatory uncertainty.* The question in the following sentence – *Will room-4-renters be subject to hotel taxes* – and the reference to taxes again at the end of line 32 indicate that the lack of clarity regarding taxation is a problem the sharing economy needs to tackle. That makes the answer C). Be careful with A and B), though. For A), the passage only mentions that the peer-to-peer marketplace gradually came to be dominated by professional sellers. It does not, however, indicate that this shift was a bad thing. If anything, the phrase *new opportunities for enterprise* implies just the opposite. If you focus initially on the word *regulatory*, you might jump to connect it to "regulations" in B). But in fact, the passage is saying the opposite of what B) says, namely that individuals who rent out rooms on a casual basis should be subject only to *loose* regulations (*The lighter rules that typically govern bed-and-breakfasts are more than adequate*). D) can be eliminated because it is entirely unsupported by the passage.

5.1-2 D, B

Although 5.1 may seem to depend on a very small detail, you can answer it most easily by using the big picture. The discussion in the second half of the passage (line 15 to the end) revolves around the fact that scientist believe synapses – the space where neurons come into contact with one another – shrink during sleep. Logically, then, an early-morning reduction in people's synapse size would be consistent with that fact. That makes D) the answer to 5.1. That answer is directly supported by lines 20-22, which indicate that mouse synapses shrank during sleep. B) is thus the answer to 5.2.

6.1-2 A, D

The answer to this question is located in the last paragraph, so if you read the entire passage and look at the question right afterward, you might be able to respond based on memory. Otherwise, you can scan for the key word *critics*, which appears in the topic sentence of the last paragraph (lines 40-42). The key statement here is that research on GM foods sponsored by the European Commission *cannot be dismissed as an industry tool* – that is, it is not under pressure to report findings that would present GM crops in a positive light – because it is carried out by *independent* teams. The key phrase *not affiliated with the agricultural industry* indicates that the researchers in A) are independent. All of the other answers describe researchers who could be biased toward GM foods in some way. Because this topic is discussed in the last paragraph, the correct answer to 6.2 must appear there as well. That makes D), whose lines include a reference to *independent teams*, the only option.

7.1-2 D, D

The question is asking about a possible result of research into the bees' disappearance. Discussions of what research could lead to in the future tend to come after discussions of the research itself, so it's reasonable to assume that the correct lines must appear at the end. As a result, it makes the most sense to start by plugging in D) of Question #2. What do we learn in in lines 81-87? That the research on bees *has exposed significant gaps in how we understand the effect climate change will have on everything from food production to terrestrial ecology.* Climate change = shifts in the climate. We can reasonably infer that this research may eventually close some of those gaps, i.e., lead to a "heightened awareness" of the effects of climate change on crops. D) is thus the correct answer to both questions.

Reading for Function

If you've already spent some time studying for the SAT, you've most likely had the following experience: you see a question that asks you the primary purpose of a few lines or a paragraph. You go back, read the lines, and feel pretty confident that you understand what they're saying. When you look at the answers, however, they don't seem to have anything to do with what you've just read.

You go back to the passage, frantically rereading, trying to figure out what you've missed, then look back at the answers. Clear as mud. You get rid of a couple that are obviously wrong but find yourself stuck between B) and C), which both seem equally plausible. You remember hearing that C) is the most common answer, so you decide to just pick it and hope for the best.

This scenario typically stems from the fact that most people don't truly understand that function questions are not asking *what* the lines say but rather *why* they say it. In short, you cannot understand function without understanding content, but understanding content alone is not enough to understand function.

One of the things that people often find very foreign is the fact that the SAT not only tests the ability to comprehend *what* is written in a passage but also *how* it's written. Unlike literal comprehension questions, which require you to identify a paraphrased version of an idea contained in the passage, **function questions ask you to move beyond understanding the literal meaning of specific content in the passage to understanding the more abstract role of that content within the larger context of the passage or paragraph.**

In other words, these questions ask you to identify **the point that the information in question supports.** In this sense, function questions are very similar to "example" questions: both ask you to work backwards from the supporting evidence to the larger idea.

While answers to function questions are based on the specific wording in the passage, you should keep in mind that **the answers themselves are not stated word-for-word in the passage.** In fact, the answer choices will sometimes be phrased in much more general or abstract language than what appears in the passage; you are responsible for drawing the connection between the two.

That said, you should **always keep in mind the topic of the passage because the correct answer may refer to it**, either directly or in rephrased form.

Types of Function Questions

Function questions can ask about either a small section of a passage – punctuation, words, phrases or sentences, paragraphs – or the passage as a whole. (Note: questions that ask about the purpose of a passage are discussed with other big-picture questions in Chapter 3.)

They are typically phrased in the following ways:

- The primary purpose of the passage is to...

- The main purpose of the second paragraph (lines x-y) is to...

- The quotation/phrase, etc. in lines x-y primarily serves to...

And their answers fall into two categories:

1) Those that can **only** be answered by looking at the specific wording in the lines provided in the question. In such cases, the lines will typically contain phrasing, punctuation, or a key transition that points to a particular answer.

2) Those that **cannot** be obtained by looking at the lines provided in the question but that instead depend on contextual information.

For the second type of question especially, line references simply tell you where the information in question is located – they do <u>not</u> tell you its relationship to anything else in the passage. **The information necessary to obtain the answer will often be located either before the line(s) referenced in the question or, less frequently, after.**

Unfortunately, there is no way to tell upfront which category a particular question will fall into. As a result, **you should generally be prepared to read a sentence or two before and after the lines provided, then focus on the appropriate section as necessary.**

Important: If the lines given in the question are relatively close to the beginning of a paragraph, you should back up and begin reading from there. Topic sentences will nearly always give you the point of a paragraph, making it much easier for you to understand the role of a particular word or sentence within it. If the lines are in the middle of a paragraph, especially a long paragraph, you probably do not need to go all the way back to the beginning but can instead back up a sentence or two as necessary.

Because SAT Reading focuses heavily on relationships between ideas, it follows that questions are frequently based on the places in a passage where ideas come into contact with one another – that is, where new information is introduced, or where there is a change in focus, point of view, or tone.

The relationships between these ideas are sometimes indicated through the use of specific words, phrases, and types of punctuation, which correlate with particular function words. The chart on the next page lists some of the most common examples, along with their functions.

Functions of Key Words and Punctuation

Continuers		Contradictors

Continuers

Continue

Additionally
Also
And
As well as
Finally
First
Furthermore
In addition
Moreover
Next
Then

Illustrate, Support

For example
For instance
One reason/another reason

Explain

Because
Explanation
That is
The answer is
The reason is

Colon
Dash

Define

That is (to say)
Properly speaking

Colon
Dash
Parentheses

Compare

As
Just as
Like(wise)
Much as
Similarly

Speculate

Could
If
It is possible
May
Maybe
Might
Perhaps

Call attention to
Underscore, Highlight
Emphasize

Indeed
In fact
Let me be clear

Capital letters
Exclamation point
Italics
Repetition (of a word, phrase)

Indicate Importance

Central
Crucial
Essential
Fundamental
Important
Key
Significant
The point/goal is

Draw a conclusion

As a result
Consequently
Hence
So
Thereby
Therefore
Thus

Qualify

Dashes
Parentheses

Contradictors

Contrast

(Al)though
But
Despite
However
In contrast
In spite of
Instead
Meanwhile
Nevertheless
On the contrary
On the other hand
Otherwise
Rather
Still
Whereas
While
Yet

Question,
Imply skepticism

But is it really true…?

Question mark
Quotation marks

Let's look at some examples:

Every time a car drives through a major intersection, it becomes a data point. Magnetic coils of wire lie just beneath the pavement, registering each passing car. This starts a cascade of information: Computers tally the
5   number and speed of cars, shoot the data through underground cables to a command center and finally translate it into the colors red, yellow and green. On the seventh floor of Boston City Hall, the three colors splash like paint across a wall-sized map.
10 To drivers, the color red means stop, but on the map it tells traffic engineers to leap into action. Traffic control centers like this one—a room cluttered with computer terminals and live video feeds of urban intersections—represent the brain of a traffic system. The city's network
15 of sensors, cables and signals are the nerves connected to the rest of the body. "Most people don't think there are eyes and ears keeping track of all this stuff," says John DeBenedictis, the center's engineering director. But in reality, engineers literally watch our every move,
20 making subtle changes that relieve and redirect traffic.
The tactics and aims of traffic management are modest but powerful. Most intersections rely on a combination of pre-set timing and computer adaptation. For example, where a busy main road intersects with a quiet residential
25 street, the traffic signal might give 70 percent of "green time" to the main road, and 30 percent to the residential road. (Green lights last between a few seconds and a couple minutes, and tend to shorten at rush hour to help the traffic move continuously.) But when traffic
30 overwhelms the pre-set timing, engineers override the system and make change.

1

The reference to "the color red" (line 10) serves mainly to

A) emphasize the importance of obeying traffic signals.
B) indicate that drivers and traffic engineers can react to information in different ways.
C) explain why traffic engineers are more active than other workers.
D) point out a striking feature of the map in Boston City Hall.

If we're going to try to answer the question on our own, the first thing we must do is make sure that we understand what it's asking. The phrase *serves mainly to* indicates that it's a purpose or function question. We could therefore rephrase the question as, "Why does the author use the phrase *the color red* in that spot?" or "What point does the author use the phrase *the color red* to support?"

Although you might be rolling your eyes and saying, "Duh, yeah, that's *obviously* what it's asking," rephrasing the question is crucial because it forces you to clarify just what sort of information you're looking for. If you skipped this step, you might simply start by summarizing what the lines say – which is not what you're being asked to do.

Because this is a function question, we must establish **context**. Line 10 is part of the first sentence of the paragraph, i.e., the topic sentence. That sentence normally serves to introduce a topic, so we probably don't need to back up. We do, however, need to read the entire sentence carefully.

Let's examine the full sentence:

> **To drivers, the color red means stop, <u>but</u> on the map it tells traffic engineers to leap into action.**

Notice that the sentence is divided into two parts separated by a comma, and that the key phrase appears in the second part. Very often, when students encounter a sentence that contains multiple parts like this, they read only one part and overlook the information they need to answer the question.

That is exactly what could happen in this case. The second half of the sentence begins with the transition *but*, which signals the introduction of new, contradictory information. When *but* (or a synonym such as *however* or *yet*) appears, you should always pay close attention to what follows. If you stop before the transition, you'll miss key information.

Here, the full sentence indicates that red means **different things** to drivers (stop) vs. traffic engineers (leap into action). That is what B) says, so it is correct. **Same idea, different words.**

Alternately, we can play process of elimination:

A) emphasize the importance of obeying traffic signals.

This answer might seem reasonable, especially if you don't look back at the passage. After all, everyone knows that red = stop. In context, however, that association is way **off-topic**. The rest of the paragraph focuses on the ways in which traffic engineers are able to keep track of what happens in a city's streets. Traffic safety never even enters into the discussion.

B) indicate that drivers and traffic engineers can react to information in different ways.

If you take the time to read lines 10-11 carefully, this probably won't be overly difficult to identify as the right answer. Again, the word *but* provides a shortcut: by definition, a sentence with that word in it is discussing two contradictory, i.e., different, ideas.

C) explain why traffic engineers are more active than other workers.

In general, you need to be careful with comparisons because they are often beyond the scope of a passage. In this case, the comparison is between traffic engineers and drivers; other workers are not mentioned. Don't get distracted by the word *active*. If you don't read carefully, you might see the phrase *leap up* and assume that C) is right because someone who leaps up is being active.

D) point out a striking feature of the map in Boston City Hall.

Again, this answer seems vaguely plausible. If you read from the previous sentence, you would see that the map in Boston City Hall is indeed mentioned. Because red is a striking color, you might also assume that the reference is intended to emphasize that quality. Sure, there's nothing in the passage to *explicitly* support that interpretation, but hey, nothing really suggests it's wrong either. The problem is that this reasoning is based on **associative thinking** – connecting things that are only loosely related because you personally associate them – and it almost always spells trouble on the SAT. The fact that two ideas are discussed close to one another does not necessarily mean that there is a relationship between them.

Let's look at another question:

Every time a car drives through a major intersection, it becomes a data point. Magnetic coils of wire lie just beneath the pavement, registering each passing car. This starts a cascade of information: Computers tally the
5 number and speed of cars, shoot the data through underground cables to a command center and finally translate it into the colors red, yellow and green. On the seventh floor of Boston City Hall, the three colors splash like paint across a wall-sized map.
10 To drivers, the color red means stop, but on the map it tells traffic engineers to leap into action. Traffic control centers like this one—a room cluttered with computer terminals and live video feeds of urban intersections— represent the brain of a traffic system. The city's network
15 of sensors, cables and signals are the nerves connected to the rest of the body. "Most people don't think there are eyes and ears keeping track of all this stuff," says John DeBenedictis, the center's engineering director. But in reality, engineers literally watch our every move,
20 making subtle changes that relieve and redirect traffic.
The tactics and aims of traffic management are modest but powerful. Most intersections rely on a combination of pre-set timing and computer adaptation. For example, where a busy main road intersects with a quiet residential
25 street, the traffic signal might give 70 percent of "green time" to the main road, and 30 percent to the residential road. (Green lights last between a few seconds and a couple minutes, and tend to shorten at rush hour to help the traffic move continuously.) But when traffic
30 overwhelms the pre-set timing, engineers override the system and make change.

1

The author mentions "sensors, cables, and signals" (line 15) in order to

A) describe a problem commonly faced by traffic engineers.

B) point out some important differences between traffic control centers and the brain.

C) list some items typically found in traffic control centers.

D) provide examples of ways drivers' actions can be monitored remotely.

If we wanted to simplify this question, we could say something like, "Why does the passage mention *sensors, cables, and signals*?" Or, "What point is the reference to *sensors, cables, and signals* used to support?"

The line reference is smack in the middle of the paragraph, where supporting evidence usually appears. To figure out what point it supports, we must focus on the beginning and the end of the paragraph, where main points are typically stated.

The beginning of the paragraph introduces the comparison between a traffic control center and the brain. Logically, the sentence that includes the key phrase (*The city's network of sensors, cables and signals...*) must serve to further develop that comparison.

The problem here is that no answer is consistent with that idea. As a result, we must read the rest of the paragraph, paying close attention to the last sentence. The presence of the word *but* suggests that it will be very important.

What idea is presented in the last sentence? Traffic engineers are able to watch people's every move. Why? Because of the sensors, cables, and signals that relay information from the streets back to them. So the phrase in question is there to explain how traffic engineers can monitor drivers' behavior from a distance, i.e., remotely. That makes the correct answer D).

Granted, this question isn't easy; figuring it out without consulting the answers is a challenge. At the same time, however, you cannot assume that you will automatically recognize the correct answer when you see it. Sometimes you will have to do a bit more work upfront than you'd prefer, in order to avoid confusion.

A) describe a problem commonly faced by traffic engineers.

The paragraph doesn't discuss a problem at all. It's completely off-topic.

B) point out some important differences between traffic control centers and the brain.

Remember that every word in an answer choice counts – it takes only one wrong word to make the whole thing incorrect. That's the case here. The author draws a comparison between traffic control centers and the brain, but this answer just mentions "differences," which aren't discussed at all. This answer describes exactly the opposite of what's going on in the passage.

C) list some items typically found in traffic control centers.

Be careful here. The passage does mention traffic control centers and sensors, cables, and signals in very close proximity to one another. The problem is that the passage only states that computer terminals and live video feeds are items found in traffic control centers (lines 12-13). In the next sentence, the author indicates that sensors, cables, and signals are the *nerves* present throughout the city – not in traffic control centers. So C) is out.

D) provide examples of ways drivers' actions can be monitored remotely.

If you work by process of elimination and conclusively eliminate the other choices for the reasons discussed above, you can safely choose D). If, however, you simply read the answers without checking each one, you can easily eliminate this type of answer – either because you don't remember the information, or because you don't think it sounds right.

If you're stuck between D) and another answer, you can follow the same steps described earlier and read to the end of the paragraph. When you get to the last sentence, you can see that the statement *engineers literally watch our every move* (line 19) directly corresponds to the idea of monitoring drivers' actions remotely. Again, that makes D) correct.

On the next page, we're going to look at a full-length passage.

This passage is adapted from Kristin Sainani, "What, Me Worry?" © 2014, *Stanford* magazine.

According to a 2013 national survey by the American Psychological Association, the average stress level among adults is 5.1 on a scale of 10; that's one and a half points above what the
5 respondents judged to be healthy. Two-thirds of people say managing stress is important, and nearly that proportion had attempted to reduce their stress in the previous five years. Yet only a little over a third say they succeeded at doing so. More discouraging, teens
10 and young adults are experiencing higher levels of stress, and also are struggling to manage it.

"Stress has a very bad reputation. It's in pretty bad shape, PR-wise," acknowledges Firdaus Dhabhar, an associate professor of psychiatry and behavioral science
15 at Stanford. "And justifiably so," he adds.

Much of what we know about the physical and mental toll of chronic stress stems from seminal work by Robert Sapolsky beginning in the late 1970s. Sapolsky, a neuroendocrinologist, was among the first
20 to make the connection that the hormones released during the fight-or-flight response—the ones that helped our ancestors avoid becoming dinner—have deleterious effects when the stress is severe and sustained. Especially insidious, chronic exposure to
25 one of these hormones, cortisol, causes brain changes that make it increasingly difficult to shut the stress response down.

But take heart: Recent research paints a different portrait of stress, one in which it indeed has a positive
30 side. "There's good stress, there's tolerable stress, and there's toxic stress," says Bruce McEwen of Rockefeller University, an expert on stress and the brain who trained both Sapolsky and Dhabhar.

Situations we typically perceive as stressful—a
35 confrontation with a co-worker, the pressure to perform, a to-do list that's too long—are not the toxic type of stress that's been linked to serious health issues such as cardiovascular disease, autoimmune disorders, severe depression and cognitive impairment.
40 Short bouts of this sort of everyday stress can actually be a good thing: Just think of the exhilaration of the deadline met or the presentation crushed, the triumph of holding it all together. And, perhaps not surprisingly, it turns out that beating yourself up about
45 being stressed is counterproductive, as worrying about the negative consequences can in itself exacerbate any ill effects.

When Dhabhar was starting his graduate work in McEwen's lab in the early 1990s, "the absolutely
50 overwhelming dogma was that stress suppresses immunity." But this didn't make sense to him from an evolutionary perspective. If a lion is chasing you, he reasoned, your immune system should be ramping up, readying itself to heal torn flesh. It occurred to Dhabhar
55 that the effects of acute stress, which lasts minutes to hours, might differ from the effects of chronic stress, which lasts days to years.

Dhabhar likens the body's immune cells to soldiers. Because their levels in the blood plummet during acute
60 stress, "people used to say: 'See, stress is bad for you; your immune system's depressed,'" he says. "But most immune battles are not going to be fought in the blood." He suspected that the immune cells were instead traveling to the body's "battlefields"—sites most likely
65 to be wounded in an attack, like the skin, gut and lungs. In studies where rats were briefly confined (a short-term stressor), he showed that after an initial surge of immune cells into the bloodstream, they quickly exited the blood and took up positions precisely where he predicted they
70 would.

"His work was a pioneering demonstration of how important the difference is between acute and chronic stress," says Sapolsky, a professor of biology, neurology, and neurological sciences and neurosurgery.
75 "Overwhelmingly, the bad health effects of stress are those of chronic stress."

This strategic deployment of immune cells can speed wound healing, enhance vaccine effectiveness and potentially fight cancer. In 2009, Dhabhar's team
80 showed that knee surgery patients with robust immune redistribution following the stress of surgery recovered significantly faster and had better knee function a year later than those with a more sluggish mobilization. In other studies, volunteers who exercised or took a math
85 test (both acute stressors) immediately prior to being vaccinated had a heightened antibody response relative to volunteers who sat quietly. And in 2010, the researchers curbed the development of skin cancer in UV-exposed mice by stressing them before their
90 sunlamp sessions. Dhabhar speculates that giving cancer patients low-dose injections of stress hormones might help prime their immune systems to fight the cancer. "It may not work out, but if it did, the benefits could be tremendous," he says.

The discussion of knee surgery patients in lines 79-83 primarily serves to

A) emphasize the connection between physical activity and health.
B) compare the effects of acute and chronic stress on the healing process.
C) explain how stress can hinder recovery from illness and injury.
D) illustrate the body's ability to repair itself by sending certain cells to injured areas.

What function does the fifth paragraph (lines 34-47) serve in the passage as a whole?

A) It describes the destructive toll of stress on the human body.
B) It provides examples that undermine conventional perceptions of stress.
C) It calls attention to the dangers of a range of maladies.
D) It highlights the prominence of stress in daily life.

Question #1: This question is nice enough to provide you with a line reference, so start by reading it: *In 2009, Dhabhar's team showed that knee surgery patients with robust immune redistribution following the stress of surgery recovered significantly faster and had better knee function a year later than those with a more sluggish mobilization.*

Essentially, these lines tell us that patients with a stronger immune response (*immune redistribution*) did better after surgery than patients with weaker immune responses.

Now, take the remaining answers in order. A) doesn't fit because the focus is on patients' response at a cellular level. Physical activity is not mentioned. B) might seem tempting; however, this answer misses the mark in a very important way. The lines in question do make a comparison, but it's between patients with strong vs. weak immune responses, not acute vs. chronic stress. In addition, this section of the passage focuses pretty much exclusively on acute stress. C) is incorrect because the passage indicates that a strong immune response, which is prompted by acute stress, helps people heal. *Hindering* (getting in the way of) *recovery* is exactly the opposite.

That leaves D), which you might initially have trouble connecting back to the passage. The key is to recognize that in the second half of the passage, the author uses different words to describe the same phenomenon. In the lines referenced, the author refers to *robust immune redistribution*. That phrase actually refers back to the phenomenon described in lines 63-65, namely that acute stress causes immune cells (=certain cells) to migrate to parts of the body that are under attack. Same idea, different words.

Question #2: "Purpose of a paragraph" questions appear frequently, so you should make sure that you are comfortable working through them. In most cases, you should start by focusing on the **end of the previous paragraph and the beginning of the paragraph in question** – if not the topic sentence alone, then the first couple of sentences. If you can't figure out the answer from those places, then you should check the last sentence. In this case, though, the first sentence gives you everything you need. Even better, it contains some very interesting punctuation, namely a set of dashes. What is between those dashes? A list of examples. Examples of what? Of ways in which stress can be good.

Now, consider that information in context. The beginning of the passage makes it clear that stress has *traditionally* been viewed as harmful (=conventional perceptions). Given that, the discussion of stress as something that helps people thrive and conquer difficult situations serves to contradict (=undermine) that perception. The answer is therefore B).

"Vague" Answers

So far, we've looked at answer choices that spelled things out pretty clearly. Occasionally, though, you might see a set of answers that is a lot more abstract. For instance:

A) justify an approach.
B) offer an explanation.
C) promote a theory.
D) refute a claim.

When confronted with this kind of phrasing, a lot of people are understandably confused. The key is to understand that these types of answers move from concrete to abstract in two different ways: first, through a function word such as *explain* or *refute*; and second, by rephrasing the content of the passage in a more general way.

Although making the connection between the answers and the passage can take some getting used to, the process for answering these questions is the same: read from a sentence or two before the line reference to a sentence or two after, paying attention to strong language and "unusual" punctuation. You should find the information you need.

Note that a long line reference often does not indicate a lot of important information. In general, the longer the line reference, the smaller the amount of relevant text.

Let's look at some examples:

Most people have so-called flashbulb memories of where they were and what they were doing when something momentous happened. (Unfortunately, staggeringly terrible news seems to come out of the
5   blue more often than staggeringly good news.) But as clear and detailed as these memories feel, psychologists have discovered they are surprisingly inaccurate.

1

The function of the last sentence (lines 5-7) is to

A) acknowledge a point.
B) highlight a misconception.
C) criticize a tradition.
D) propose an alternative.

What information does the last sentence convey? That flashbulb memories are *inaccurate*. Inaccurate = a misconception. That makes the answer B). Easy, right?

The correct answer could also be phrased this way:

Most people have so-called flashbulb memories of where they were and what they were doing when something momentous happened. (Unfortunately, staggeringly terrible news seems to come out of the
5   blue more often than staggeringly good news.) But as clear and detailed as these memories feel, psychologists have discovered they are surprisingly inaccurate.

1

The function of the last sentence (lines 5-7) is to

A) acknowledge a point.
B) indicate an unexpected discovery.
C) criticize a tradition.
D) propose an alternative.

In this case, the key word is *surprising*. Surprising = unexpected, hence B) again.

One more:

Sometime near the end of the Pleistocene, a band of people left northeastern Asia, crossed the Bering land bridge when the sea level was low, entered Alaska and became the first Americans. Since the
5 1930s, archaeologists have thought these people were members of the Clovis culture. First discovered in New Mexico in the 1930s, the Clovis culture is known for its distinct stone tools, primarily fluted projectile points. For decades, Clovis artifacts were the oldest
10 known in the New World, dating to 13,000 years ago. But in recent years, researchers have found more and more evidence that people were living in North and South America before the Clovis.
   The most recently confirmed evidence comes from
15 Washington. During a dig conducted from 1977 to 1979, researchers uncovered a bone projectile point stuck in a mastodon rib. Since then, the age of the find has been debated, but recently anthropologist Michael Waters and his colleagues announced a new radiocarbon date
20 for the rib: 13,800 years ago, making it 800 years older than the oldest Clovis artifact. Other pre-Clovis evidence comes from a variety of locations across the New World.

1 ▓▓▓▓▓▓▓▓▓▓▓▓▓▓▓▓▓▓▓▓▓▓▓▓▓▓▓

In context of the passage as a whole, the primary purpose of the second paragraph (lines 14-23) is to

A) concede a point.
B) support a claim.
C) criticize a tradition.
D) celebrate a discovery.

Before we look at how to answer the question for real, let's look at a common mistake: considering the paragraph only from the standpoint of its content.

If you summarized the **content** of the second paragraph, you might say that it talks about some very old discoveries that researchers have made in the New World.

When looking at the answer choices, you might seize on the statement ...*During a dig conducted from 1977 to 1979, researchers uncovered a bone projectile point stuck in a mastodon rib* and conclude that since that's consistent with the idea of "a finding," then D) would make sense. You might not be sure about the "celebrate" part, but discoveries are exciting, particularly ones involving almost 14,000-year-old objects, so obviously that's something people would want to celebrate, right? (Wrong.)

As discussed earlier, the problem with this approach is that it relies on a fundamental misconception of what the question is asking. The question is <u>not</u> asking what the second paragraph says. Rather, it is asking about the second paragraph's **function** within the passage, and its relationship to the first paragraph.

To figure out the second paragraph's function, you must back up and figure out its relationship to the first paragraph. There are only two paragraphs here, so it is unnecessary to take anything else into consideration.

If you read the last sentence of the first paragraph, you can see that it begins with the very important contradictor *but*. The use of this transition signals a shift to the "new idea" – in this case, the idea that people were living in the Americas before the Clovis.

Now, look at the first sentence of the second paragraph: *The most recently confirmed <u>evidence</u> comes from Washington*. This sentence is essentially telling us that paragraph's function is to provide evidence for (=support), the idea (=a claim) that the Clovis were not the first people to inhabit the Americas. The answer is therefore B).

Playing Positive and Negative with Function Questions

One of the simplest ways to approach function questions and eliminate answer choices quickly is to play positive/negative. Positive passages or portions of passages typically have positive answers, while negative passages and portions of passages typically have negative ones.

Although answer choices often contain function verbs that are more neutral than the language of the passage itself, the information in the rest of the answer may be distinctly positive or negative. Even if this strategy alone does not get you all the way to the correct answer, it can allow you to quickly eliminate one or two choices upfront, giving you more time to focus on smaller distinctions between the remaining answers.

The chart on p. 216 provides some examples of common positive, negative, and neutral function words that are likely to appear in answer choices.

Let's look at an example:

These are stimulating times for anyone interested in questions of animal consciousness. On what seems like a monthly basis, scientific teams announce the results of new experiments, adding to a preponderance
5 of evidence that we've been underestimating animal minds, even those of us who have rated them fairly highly. New animal behaviors and capacities are observed in the wild, often involving tool use—or at least object manipulation—the very kinds of activity
10 that led the distinguished zoologist Donald R. Griffin to found the field of cognitive ethology (animal thinking) in 1978: octopuses piling stones in front of their hideyholes, to name one recent example; or dolphins fitting marine sponges to their beaks in order to dig for
15 food on the seabed; or wasps using small stones to smooth the sand around their egg chambers, concealing them from predators. At the same time neurobiologists have been finding that the physical structures in our own brains most commonly held responsible for
20 consciousness are not as rare in the animal kingdom as had been assumed. Indeed they are common. All of this work and discovery appeared to reach a kind of crescendo last summer, when an international group of prominent neuroscientists meeting at the University of
25 Cambridge issued "The Cambridge Declaration on Consciousness in Non-Human Animals," a document stating that "humans are not unique in possessing the neurological substrates that generate consciousness." It goes further to conclude that numerous documented
30 animal behaviors must be considered "consistent with experienced feeling states."

1

The reference to hideyholes, marine sponges, and small stones in lines 13-15 serves mainly to

A) describe ways that animals hide themselves from predators.

B) point out that tools produced by animals are less complex than human tools.

C) provide instances of novel animal behavior in the wild.

D) indicate the limits of animal consciousness.

This is a science passage, so its tone is relatively neutral. If we look more closely, however, we can see that the author's attitude is actually pretty positive. Again, this is hardly a surprise. Authors of science passages almost always regard new discoveries as good things – that is why they're writing about them in the first place.

In this case, the first sentence of the passage, *These are <u>stimulating</u> times for anyone interested in questions of animal consciousness*, tells us that the author has a positive attitude toward his subject. Even if you find the phrasing somewhat confusing, the presence of the word *stimulating* is a big clue, suggesting that the correct answer will be either positive or neutral. Any negative option can be eliminated.

When we look at the answer choices, we can notice that B) and D) contain negative phrases (*less complex* and *limits*). Both answers can thus be eliminated immediately.

That leaves us with only two possibilities, but we still have to be careful. Remember that answers to function questions are often found **before** the lines referenced, and A) refers to something that is mentioned **after**. The answer is constructed that way precisely because so many students will begin reading at line 13 and not consider any information before it. The problem is that small stones are discussed only in relation to wasps; they have nothing to do with the other animals/examples mentioned.

The point is actually found all the way back in lines 7-8: *New animal behaviors and capacities are observed in the wild, often involving tool use*. In addition to the word *new*, the dashes in that sentence indicate that it is important. C) rephrases that sentence, so it is correct.

Shortcut: C) uses the word *novel* in its second meaning ("new"). Even in the absence of any other information, that usage suggests that C) has an above-average chance of being correct.

Very important: as is true for answers to Reading questions in general, function answers that contain **extreme language**, either positive or negative (e.g., *condemn, attack, prove*), are usually **incorrect**.

A note about proving and disproving: One common point of confusion concerns the terms *prove* and *disprove*. Many high school students are accustomed to hearing teachers repeatedly tell them to "prove their thesis," and so it seems logical that SAT authors would do the same. This, alas, is one of the major differences between high school and college: while high school assignments tend to be framed in terms of black-and-white, the reality is that authors who write for adult readers are far more **nuanced** – that is, that they discuss *theories* that can be supported, illustrated, challenged, etc., but that cannot be definitively proved or disproved. As a result, answers that contain these words are typically far outside the bounds of what any author could accomplish in 85 lines or so.

Common Function Words and Phrases

Positive	Negative	Neutral
Support	**Refute**	**Describe**
Advance (a claim)	Attack*	Characterize
Affirm	Challenge	Convey
Bolster	Condemn*	Depict
Claim	Contradict	Discuss
Defend	Criticize	Dramatize
Exemplify	Debate	Evoke
Illustrate	Decry	Portray
Prove*	Deny	Present
Provide (evidence)	Discredit*	Represent
Offer (an example)	Dismiss	Show
Substantiate	Dispel	Trace
	Disprove*	
Praise	Imply skepticism	**Indicate**
	Question	
Celebrate	Undermine*	Identify
		Point out
Acknowledge		Reveal
	Warn	
Propose		**Introduce**
	Raise concern	
Imply		**Shift**
Suggest	**Make fun of**	
		Change
Emphasize	Mock*	Digress*
	Satirize	
Call attention to	Scoff at*	**Restate**
Focus on		
Highlight	**Concede**	Paraphrase
Reinforce		Summarize
Reiterate	Acknowledge	
Underscore	Recognize	**Hypothesize**
Explain	**Exaggerate**	Speculate
Account for	**Downplay**	**Analyze**
Articulate		
Clarify	Minimize*	Consider
Define		Describe
Explicate	**Lament***	Develop
Justify*		Explore
Qualify	Bemoan*	Reflect on
Specify		
		Attribute
Persuade		
		Cite
Advocate		Allude to
Encourage		
Promote		

*Signals an answer that is likely to be incorrect.

For a glossary of selected terms, see p. 230.

Reading for Function Exercises

1.   To understand what the new software—that is, analytics—can do that's different from more familiar software like spreadsheets, word processing, and graphics, consider the lowly photograph. Here the
5   relevant facts aren't how many bytes constitute a digital photograph, or a billion of them. That's about as instructive as counting the silver halide molecules used to form a single old-fashioned print photo. The important feature of a digital image's bytes is that, unlike
10   crystalline molecules, they are uniquely easy to store, transport, and manipulate with software. In the first era of digital images, people were fascinated by the convenience and malleability (think PhotoShop) of capturing, storing, and sharing pictures. Now, instead of
15   using software to manage photos, we can mine features of the bytes that make up the digital image. Facebook can, without privacy invasion, track where and when, for example, vacationing is trending, since digital images reveal at least that much. But more importantly, those
20   data can be cross-correlated, even in real time, with seemingly unrelated data such as local weather, interest rates, crime figures, and so on. Such correlations associated with just one photograph aren't revealing. But imagine looking at billions of photos over weeks,
25   months, years, then correlating them with dozens of directly related data sets (vacation bookings, air traffic), tangential information (weather, interest rates, unemployment), or orthogonal information (social or political trends). With essentially free super-computing,
30   we can mine and usefully associate massive, formerly unrelated data sets and unveil all manner of economic, cultural, and social realities.
     For science fiction aficionados, Isaac Asimov anticipated the idea of using massive data sets to predict
35   human behavior, coining it "psychohistory" in his 1951 Foundation trilogy. The bigger the data set, Asimov said then, the more predictable the future. With big-data analytics, one can finally see the forest, instead of just the capillaries in the tree leaves. Or to put it in more
40   accurate terms, one can see beyond the apparently random motion of a few thousand molecules of air inside a balloon; one can see the balloon itself, and beyond that, that it is inflating, that it is yellow, and that it is part of a bunch of balloons en route to a birthday party. The
45   data/software world has, until now, been largely about looking at the molecules inside one balloon.

1

The reference to "capturing, storing, and sharing pictures" (line 14) primarily serves to

A) underscore a key difference between old and new technologies.

B) point out technological features that were once considered novel.

C) describe how digital images are preserved.

D) emphasize the rapid nature of technological change.

2

The references to local weather, interest rates, and crime figures (lines 21-22) primarily serve to

A) provide examples of disparate subjects that may have hidden connections.

B) emphasize the range of topics covered on news websites.

C) point out local issues that may be of broader interest.

D) call attention to the limits of data analysis.

3

The passage's discussion of Isaac Asimov primarily serves to

A) introduce the concept of science fiction.

B) call attention to an individual who foresaw recent developments.

C) describe the influence of science fiction fans on technological discoveries.

D) emphasize the differences between science fiction and science.

2. The following passage is adapted from a novel by Willa Cather, originally published in 1918. The protagonist has been sent to live with his grandparents in Nebraska.

All the years that have passed have not dimmed my memory of that first glorious autumn. The new country lay open before me: there were no fences in those days, and I could choose my own way over the grass uplands,
5 trusting the pony to get me home again. Sometimes I followed the sunflower-bordered roads.

I used to love to drift along the pale-yellow cornfields, looking for the damp spots one sometimes found at their edges, where the smartweed soon turned a rich copper
10 color and the narrow brown leaves hung curled like cocoons about the swollen joints of the stem. Sometimes I went south to visit our German neighbors and to admire their catalpa grove, or to see the big elm tree that grew up out of a deep crack in the earth and had a
15 hawk's nest in its branches. Trees were so rare in that country, and they had to make such a hard fight to grow, that we used to feel anxious about them, and visit them as if they were persons. It must have been the scarcity of detail in that tawny landscape that made detail so
20 precious.

Sometimes I rode north to the big prairie-dog town to watch the brown earth-owls fly home in the late afternoon and go down to their nests underground with the dogs. Antonia Shimerda liked to go with me, and we used to
25 wonder a great deal about these birds of subterranean habit. We had to be on our guard there, for rattlesnakes were always lurking about. They came to pick up an easy living among the dogs and owls, which were quite defenseless against them; took possession of their
30 comfortable houses and ate the eggs and puppies. We felt sorry for the owls. It was always mournful to see them come flying home at sunset and disappear under the earth.

But, after all, we felt, winged things who would live
35 like that must be rather degraded creatures. The dog-town was a long way from any pond or creek. Otto Fuchs said he had seen populous dog-towns in the desert where there was no surface water for fifty miles; he insisted that some of the holes must go down to water—nearly two
40 hundred feet, hereabouts. Antonia said she didn't believe it; that the dogs probably lapped up the dew in the early morning, like the rabbits.

Antonia had opinions about everything, and she was soon able to make them known. Almost every day she
45 came running across the prairie to have her reading lesson with me. Mrs. Shimerda grumbled, but realized it was important that one member of the family should learn English. When the lesson was over, we used to go up to the watermelon patch behind the garden. I split the
50 melons with an old corn-knife, and we lifted out the hearts and ate them with the juice trickling through our fingers. The white melons we did not touch, but we watched them with curiosity. They were to be picked later, when the hard frosts had set in, and put away for
55 winter use. After weeks on the ocean, the Shimerdas were famished for fruit. The two girls would wander for miles along the edge of the cornfields, hunting for ground-cherries.

Antonia loved to help grandmother in the kitchen
60 and to learn about cooking and housekeeping. She would stand beside her, watching her every movement. We were willing to believe that Mrs. Shimerda was a good housewife in her own country, but she managed poorly under new conditions. I remember how horrified
65 we were at the sour, ashy-grey bread she gave her family to eat. She mixed her dough, we discovered, in an old tin peck-measure that had been used about the barn. When she took the paste out to bake it, she left smears of dough sticking to the sides of the measure, put
70 the measure on the shelf behind the stove, and let this residue ferment. The next time she made bread, she scraped this sour stuff down into the fresh dough to serve as yeast.

1

The reference to the catalpa grove and the elm tree (line 13) primarily serves to

A) illustrate the narrator's love of nature.

B) call attention to the diversity of the natural world.

C) emphasize the barrenness of the landscape.

D) explain why the narrator felt anxious about his new life.

2

The narrator's reference to ground-cherries
(line 58) primarily serves to

A) emphasize the wholesome quality of the
Shimerdas' new life.
B) demonstrate the difficulty of finding food in
the narrator's new home.
C) describe a food that the narrator was desperate
to eat.
D) suggest the limited range of foods to which
the Shimerdas previously had access.

3

The narrator's statement that Mrs. Shimerda "was a
good housewife in her own country" (lines 62-63)
primarily serves to

A) highlight a contrast.
B) criticize an injustice.
C) defend a decision.
D) explain a reaction.

3. The following passage is adapted from "Makerspaces, Hackerspaces, and Community Scale Production in Detroit and Beyond," © 2013 by Sean Ansanelli.

During the mid-1980s, spaces began to emerge across Europe where computer hackers could convene for mutual support and camaraderie. In the past few years, the idea of fostering such shared, physical spaces
5 has been rapidly adapted by the diverse and growing community of "makers," who seek to apply the idea of "hacking" to physical objects, processes, or anything else that can be deciphered and improved upon.

A hackerspace is described by hackerspaces.org as
10 a "community-operated physical space where people with common interests, often in computers, technology, science, digital art or electronic art, can meet, socialize, and/or collaborate." Such spaces can vary in size, available technology, and membership structure (some
15 being completely open), but generally share community-oriented characteristics. Indeed, while the term "hacker" can sometimes have negative connotations, modern hackerspaces thrive off of community, openness, and assimilating diverse viewpoints – these
20 often being the only guiding principles in otherwise informal organizational structures.

In recent years, the city of Detroit has emerged as a hotbed for hackerspaces and other DIY ("Do-It-Yourself") experiments. Several hackerspaces
25 can already be found throughout the city and several more are currently in formation. Of course, Detroit's attractiveness for such projects can be partially attributed to cheap real estate, which allows aspiring hackers to acquire ample space for experimentation.
30 Some observers have also described this kind of making and tinkering as embedded in the DNA of Detroit's residents, who are able to harness substantial intergenerational knowledge and attract like-minded individuals.
35 Hackerspaces (or "makerspaces") can be found in more commercial forms, but the vast majority of spaces are self-organized and not-for-profit. For example, the OmniCorp hackerspace operates off member fees to cover rent and new equipment, from laser cutters to
40 welding tools. OmniCorp also hosts an "open hack night" every Thursday in which the space is open to the general public. Potential members are required to attend at least one open hack night prior to a consensus vote by the existing members for admittance; no
45 prospective members have yet been denied.

A visit to one of OmniCorp's open hack nights reveals the vast variety of activity and energy existing in the space. In the main common room alone, activities range from experimenting with sound installations and
50 learning to program Arduino boards to building speculative "oloid" shapes – all just for the sake of it. With a general atmosphere of mutual support, participants in the space are continually encouraged to help others.
55 One of the most active community-focused initiatives in the city is the Mt. Elliot Makerspace. Jeff Sturges, former MIT Media Lab Fellow and Co-Founder of OmniCorp, started the Mt. Elliot project with the aim of replicating MIT's Fab Lab model on a smaller, cheaper
60 scale in Detroit. "Fab Labs" are production facilities that consist of a small collection of flexible computer-controlled tools that cover several different scales and various materials, with the aim to make "almost anything" (including other machines). The Mt. Elliot
65 Makerspace now offers youth-based skill development programs in eight areas: Transportation, Electronics, Digital Tools, Wearables, Design and Fabrication, Food, Music, and Arts. The range of activities is meant to provide not only something for everyone, but a well-
70 rounded base knowledge of making to all participants.

While the center receives some foundational support, the space also derives significant support from the local community. Makerspaces throughout the city connect the space's youth-based programming directly to
75 school curriculums.

The growing interest in and development of hacker/makerspaces has been explained, in part, as a result of the growing maker movement. Through the combination of cultural norms and communication
80 channels from open source production as well as increasingly available technologies for physical production, amateur maker communities have developed in virtual and physical spaces.

Publications such as *Wired* are noticing the
85 transformative potential of this emerging movement and have sought to devote significant attention to its development. Chief editor Chris Anderson recently published a book entitled *Makers*, in which he proclaims that the movement will become the next Industrial
90 Revolution. Anderson argues such developments will allow for a new wave of business opportunities by providing mass-customization rather than mass-production.

The transformative potential of these trends goes
95 beyond new business opportunities or competitive advantages for economic growth. Rather, these trends demonstrate the potential to actually transform economic development models entirely.

The passage's discussion of Europe in the 1980s primarily serves to

A) introduce the concept of hackerspaces.
B) call attention to Detroit's unique role in the hackerspace movement.
C) compare hackerspaces in the United States to foreign hackerspaces.
D) provide a description of a place where hackerspaces have been particularly popular.

The author's statement that "the term 'hacker' can sometimes have negative connotations" (lines 16-17) serves to

A) criticize a movement.
B) anticipate a potential criticism.
C) contrast past and present forms of technology.
D) emphasize the exclusive nature of an organization.

The primary function of the third paragraph (lines 22-34) is to

A) point out that the decline of certain industries can have unexpected benefits.
B) explain why hackerspaces have succeeded in some cities and failed in others.
C) indicate some of the reasons that hackerspaces have flourished in a particular city.
D) demonstrate the effects of geography on the economy.

4

The passage's discussion of OmniCorp (line 38) primarily serves to

A) call attention to hackerspaces' urgent need for funds.
B) suggest that money should not play a role in creative enterprises.
C) point out that non-profit hackerspaces are typically more successful than for-profit ones.
D) emphasize that hackerspaces are open and flexible organizations.

The references to *Wired* magazine and Chris Anderson primarily serve to

A) describe a key figure in the maker movement.
B) underscore the economic power of the maker movement.
C) trace the influence of the Industrial Revolution on the maker movement.
D) suggest that mass-production is incompatible with the modern economy.

4. This passage is from Barbara Jordan's keynote address at the 1976 Democratic National Convention. A Texas native, Jordan was the first African-American woman to represent the Deep South in Congress.

It was one hundred and forty-four years ago that members of the Democratic Party first met in convention to select a Presidential candidate. A lot of years passed since 1832, and during that time it would

5 have been most unusual for any national political party to ask a Barbara Jordan to deliver a keynote address. But tonight, here I am. And I feel that notwithstanding the past that my presence here is one additional bit of evidence that the American Dream need not forever be

10 deferred.

Now that I have this grand distinction, what in the world am I supposed to say? I could list the problems which cause people to feel cynical, angry, frustrated: problems which include lack of integrity in government;

15 the feeling that the individual no longer counts; feeling that the grand American experiment is failing or has failed. I could recite these problems, and then I could sit down and offer no solutions. But I don't choose to do that either. The citizens of America expect more.

20 We are a people in search of a national community. We are a people trying not only to solve the problems of the present, unemployment, inflation, but we are attempting on a larger scale to fulfill the promise of America. We are attempting to fulfill our national purpose,

25 to create and sustain a society in which all of us are equal.

And now we must look to the future. Let us heed the voice of the people and recognize their common sense. If we do not, we not only blaspheme our political heritage, we ignore the common ties that bind all

30 Americans. Many fear the future. Many are distrustful of their leaders, and believe that their voices are never heard. Many seek only to satisfy their private interests. But this is the great danger America faces – that we will cease to be one nation and become instead a collection

35 of interest groups: city against suburb, region against region, individual against individual; each seeking to satisfy private wants. If that happens, who then will speak for America? Who then will speak for the common good?

This is the question which must be answered in 1976:

40 Are we to be one people bound together by common spirit, sharing in a common endeavor; or will we become a divided nation? For all of its uncertainty, we cannot flee the future. We must address and master the future together. It can be done if we restore the belief that we

45 share a sense of national community, that we share a common national endeavor.

There is no executive order; there is no law that can require the American people to form a national community. This we must do as individuals, and if we

50 do it as individuals, there is no President of the United States who can veto that decision.

As a first step, we must restore our belief in ourselves. We are a generous people, so why can't we be generous with each other?

55 And now, what are those of us who are elected public officials supposed to do? We call ourselves "public servants" but I'll tell you this: We as public servants must set an example for the rest of the nation. It is hypocritical for the public official to admonish and

60 exhort the people to uphold the common good if we are derelict in upholding the common good. More is required of public officials than slogans and handshakes and press releases.

If we promise as public officials, we must deliver.

65 If we as public officials propose, we must produce. If we say to the American people, "It is time for you to be sacrificial" – sacrifice. And again, if we make mistakes, we must be willing to admit them. What we have to do is strike a balance between the idea that

70 government should do everything and the idea that government ought to do nothing.

Let there be no illusions about the difficulty of forming this kind of a national community. It's tough, difficult, not easy. But a spirit of harmony will survive

75 in America only if each of us remembers, when self-interest and bitterness seem to prevail, that we share a common destiny.

We cannot improve on the system of government handed down to us by the founders of the Republic.

80 There is no way to improve upon that. But what we can do is to find new ways to implement that system and realize our destiny.

1

The passage's discussion of problems facing the American people (lines 12-17) primarily serves to

A) demonstrate the importance of a national community.

B) indicate some attitudes that the author rejects.

C) explain that Americans are justified in fearing the future.

D) emphasize the importance of local communities.

2

The author's discussion of fear and distrust in lines 30-32 primarily serves to

A) call attention to the central role of confidence in effective leadership.

B) emphasize the importance of strong regional identities.

C) point out some factors that pose a threat to national cohesion.

D) demonstrate the necessity of electing powerful representatives.

3

The reference to interest groups in line 35 primarily serves to

A) defend an action.

B) call attention to a risk.

C) describe an unlikely scenario.

D) propose a course of action.

4

Jordan's reference to the future in line 43 serves to

A) refute a widely accepted claim.

B) justify a controversial belief.

C) propose a novel alternative.

D) point out an inevitable occurrence.

5

The function of the quotation marks in lines 55-57 is to

A) indicate some unexpected tasks associated with public office.

B) suggest that certain politicians are not living up to their responsibilities.

C) praise politicians for their commitment to to civic life.

D) implore the American people to consider the common good.

6

The reference to "slogans and handshakes and press releases" (lines 62-63) primarily serves to

A) point out superficial actions that fail to address underlying problems.

B) call attention to the public aspect of political office.

C) suggest that politicians should increase their interactions with constituents.

D) emphasize the importance of collaboration between politicians and citizens.

5. The following passage is adapted from Julian Jackson, "New Research Suggests Dinosaurs Were Warm-Blooded and Active" © 2011 by Julian Jackson.

New research from the University of Adelaide has added to the debate about whether dinosaurs were cold-blooded and sluggish or warm-blooded and active. Professor Roger Seymour from the University's School
5 of Earth & Environmental Sciences has applied the latest theories of human and animal anatomy and physiology to provide insight into the lives of dinosaurs.

Human thigh bones have tiny holes – known as the
10 "nutrient foramen" – on the shaft that supply blood to living bone cells inside. New research has shown that the size of those holes is related to the maximum rate that a person can be active during aerobic exercise. Professor Seymour has used this principle to evaluate
15 the activity levels of dinosaurs.

"Far from being lifeless, bone cells have a relatively high metabolic rate and they therefore require a large blood supply to deliver oxygen. On the inside of the bone, the blood supply comes usually from a single
20 artery and vein that pass through a hole on the shaft – the nutrient foramen," he says.

Professor Seymour wondered whether the size of the nutrient foramen might indicate how much blood was necessary to keep the bones in good repair. For
25 example, highly active animals might cause more bone 'microfractures,' requiring more frequent repairs by the bone cells and therefore a greater blood supply. "My aim was to see whether we could use fossil bones of dinosaurs to indicate the level of bone metabolic rate
30 and possibly extend it to the whole body's metabolic rate," he says. "One of the big controversies among paleobiologists is whether dinosaurs were cold-blooded and sluggish or warm-blooded and active. Could the size of the foramen be a possible gauge for dinosaur
35 metabolic rate?"

Comparisons were made with the sizes of the holes in living mammals and reptiles, and their metabolic rates. Measuring mammals ranging from mice to elephants, and reptiles from lizards to crocodiles, one
40 of Professor Seymour's Honors students, Sarah Smith, combed the collections of Australian museums, photographing and measuring hundreds of tiny holes in thigh bones.

"The results were unequivocal. The sizes of the holes
45 were related closely to the maximum metabolic rates during peak movement in mammals and reptiles," Professor Seymour says. "The holes found in mammals were about 10 times larger than those in reptiles."

These holes were compared to those of fossil
50 dinosaurs. Dr. Don Henderson, Curator of Dinosaurs from the Royal Tyrrell Museum in Alberta, Canada, and Daniela Schwarz-Wings from the Museum für Naturkunde Humboldt University Berlin, Germany measured the holes in 10 species of
55 dinosaurs from five different groups, including bipedal and quadrupedal carnivores and herbivores, weighing 50kg to 20,000kg.

"On a relative comparison to eliminate the differences in body size, all of the dinosaurs had
60 holes in their thigh bones larger than those of mammals," Professor Seymour says.

"The dinosaurs appeared to be even more active than the mammals. We certainly didn't expect to see that. These results provide additional weight to
65 theories that dinosaurs were warm-blooded and highly active creatures, rather than cold-blooded and sluggish."

Professor Seymour says following the results of this study, it's likely that a simple measurement of
70 foramen size could be used to evaluate maximum activity levels in other vertebrate animals.

1

The reference to the size of the foramen (line 34) primarily serves to

A) compare the metabolic rates of different dinosaur species.

B) point out that dinosaurs were able to survive in a range of climates.

C) indicate a means of resolving a scientific dispute.

D) suggest that mammals and reptiles were once closer in size than they are today.

2

The statement that the dinosaurs "appeared to be even more active than the mammals" (lines 62-63) serves to

A) emphasize a conventional belief.

B) defend a finding.

C) propose a controversial claim.

D) call attention to a surprising discovery.

6. The following passage is adapted from "Scientists Discover Salty Aquifer, Previously Unknown Microbial Habitat Under Antarctica," © 2015 by Dartmouth College.

Using an airborne imaging system for the first time in Antarctica, scientists have discovered a vast network of unfrozen salty groundwater that may support previously unknown microbial life deep under the coldest, driest
5 desert on our planet. The findings shed new light on ancient climate change on Earth and provide strong evidence that a similar briny aquifer could support microscopic life on Mars. The scientists used SkyTEM, an airborne electromagnetic sensor, to detect and map
10 otherwise inaccessible subterranean features.

The system uses an antennae suspended beneath a helicopter to create a magnetic field that reveals the subsurface to a depth of about 1,000 feet. Because a helicopter was used, large areas of rugged terrain could
15 be surveyed. The SkyTEM team was funded by the National Science Foundation and led by researchers from the University of Tennessee, Knoxville (UTK), and Dartmouth College, which oversees the NSF's SkyTEM project.

20 "These unfrozen materials appear to be relics of past surface ecosystems and our findings provide compelling evidence that they now provide deep subsurface habitats for microbial life despite extreme environmental conditions," says lead author Jill Mikucki,
25 an assistant professor at UTK. "These new below-ground visualization technologies can also provide insight on glacial dynamics and how Antarctica responds to climate change."

Co-author Dartmouth Professor Ross Virginia is
30 SkyTEM's co-principal investigator and director of Dartmouth's Institute of Arctic Studies. "This project is studying the past and present climate to, in part, understand how climate change in the future will affect biodiversity and ecosystem processes," Virginia says.
35 "This fantastic new view beneath the surface will help us sort out competing ideas about how the McMurdo Dry Valleys have changed with time and how this history influences what we see today."

The researchers found that the unfrozen brines form
40 extensive, interconnected aquifers deep beneath glaciers and lakes and within permanently frozen soils. The brines extend from the coast to at least 7.5 miles inland in the McMurdo Dry Valleys, the largest ice-free region in Antarctica. The brines could be due to freezing and/or
45 deposits. The findings show for the first time that the Dry Valleys' lakes are interconnected rather than isolated; connectivity between lakes and aquifers is important in sustaining ecosystems through drastic climate change, such as lake dry-down events. The findings also challenge
50 the assumption that parts of the ice sheets below the pressure melting point are devoid of liquid water. In addition to providing answers about the biological adaptations of previously unknown ecosystems that persist in the extreme cold and dark of the Antarctic
55 winter, the new study could help scientists to understand whether similar conditions might exist elsewhere in the solar system, specifically beneath the surface of Mars, which has many similarities to the Dry Valleys. Overall, the Dry Valleys ecosystem –
60 cold, vegetation-free and home only to microscopic animal and plant life – resembles, during the Antarctic summer, conditions on the surface on Mars.

SkyTEM produced images of Taylor Valley along the Ross Sea that suggest briny sediments exist at
65 subsurface temperatures down to perhaps -68°F, which is considered suitable for microbial life. One of the studied areas was lower Taylor Glacier, where the data suggest ancient brine still exists beneath the glacier. That conclusion is supported by the presence
70 of Blood Falls, an iron-rich brine that seeps out of the glacier and hosts an active microbial ecosystem.

Scientists' understanding of Antarctica's underground environment is changing dramatically as research reveals that subglacial lakes are widespread
75 and that at least half of the areas covered by the ice sheet are akin to wetlands on other continents. But groundwater in the ice-free regions and along the coastal margins remains poorly understood.

1

The reference to brines in line 44 primarily serves to

A) offer an explanation.

B) point out a misconception.

C) refute a hypothesis.

D) define a term.

In context of the passage, the function of the sixth paragraph (lines 52-62) is to

A) describe some characteristics of Antarctic ecosystems not found elsewhere on earth.

B) compare the development of ecosystems in Antarctica to the development of ecosystems on Mars.

C) indicate a possible outcome of the SkyTEM research in Antarctica.

D) explain how microscopic plants and animals survive in extreme conditions.

3

The reference to microscopic animal and plant life (lines 60-61) primarily serves to

A) emphasize the harshness of the Antarctic climate.

B) describe the effects of iron on microbial life.

C) indicate the importance of research on glaciers.

D) compare an environment on Earth to an environment on another planet.

Explanations: Reading for Function Exercises

1.1 B

What is the context for *capturing, storing, and sharing pictures*? They are all capabilities that people found fascinating when they were first introduced. In the next sentence, the transition *now* indicates that these things are no longer considered so impressive. In other words, they used to be considered "novel" (new and interesting). B) is thus correct.

1.2 A

This question can be answered using the main point: big data reveals hidden connections. That is essentially what A) says, so it is the answer. B) and C) are incorrect because the author's focus is on the uses of data, not on news. D) is incorrect because the passage focuses on the possibilities of data analysis, not its limits.

1.3 B

Why mention Asimov? Because he predicted the current use of mass data sets all the way back in the 1950s. In other word, Asimov "foresaw recent developments." That makes B) the answer.

2.1 C

Why does the narrator refer to the catalpa grove and elm tree? The answer is in the following sentences. The statements that *Trees were so <u>rare</u> in that country...* and *It must have been the <u>scarcity</u> of detail in that tawny landscape* emphasize that landscape was extremely bare, i.e., barren. C) is therefore the answer.

2.2 D

This is a very straightforward question if you remember to back up a sentence. Remember that the one thing you <u>don't</u> want to do when answering a function question is start at the line reference and keep reading from there. The previous sentence indicates that *the Shimerdas were famished for fruit after weeks on the ocean*, the implication being that they did not have access to fresh produce during their journey. That statement is most consistent with the idea of a "limited range of foods" in D).

2.3 A

The key to answering this question is to notice the contradictor *but* in line 63. This word indicates a difference (=contrast) between Mrs. Shimerda's housewifely abilities in her old life and her lack of those abilities in her new life.

3.1 A

Don't make this question out to be any more complicated than it actually is. If you don't remember where *Europe in the 1980s* is mentioned, start from the beginning of the passage. You'll find the reference immediately, in lines 1-2. Why mention that time and place? To introduce the topic of the passage: hackerspaces. That makes A) the answer. There is no mention of the United States in that paragraph, eliminating B) and C). D) can be eliminated as well because the author says nothing to indicate that hackerspaces enjoyed exceptional popularity in Europe; he simply states that they originated there.

3.2 B

Consider how the argument is presented in this section of the passage. The sentence that includes lines 16-17 is presented in "while *x*...in fact *y*" form: while the idea of hacking might have an iffy reputation, hackerspaces are actually pretty great places. Why would the author mention the first idea? To show that he knows that other people hold negative views of his topic. In other words, he's *anticipating a potential criticism*. That makes B) correct.

3.3. C

The line reference in the question is quite long, indicating that only a small part of it is likely to be relevant. Start by focusing on the first (topic) sentence of paragraph, since that's the place most likely to give you the answer: *In recent years, the city of Detroit has emerged as a hotbed for hackerspaces and other DIY ("Do-It-Yourself") experiments*. That sentence tells you that the paragraph will focus on Detroit. The only answer that corresponds to that fact is C), which rephrases Detroit as "a particular city." Indeed, if you continue to read the paragraph, you will find that it provides a number of reasons for hackerspaces' success in Detroit.

3.4 D

Consider the context of the OmniCorp discussion. The topic sentence of the paragraph states that *the vast majority of [hacker]spaces are self-organized and not-for-profit*. The transition *For example* at the beginning of the following sentence indicates that OmniCorp is mentioned to support that idea. Which answer corresponds most closely to the topic sentence? D). *Self-organized* = open and flexible. In addition, the author mentions that OmniCorp hosts an *open* hack night that is open to the general public, a statement that also supports D).

3.5 B

Shortcut: the main point – makerspaces could transform economy – corresponds directly to B).

If you don't remember where the reference to *Wired* magazine appears, scan the passage for that title, focusing on topic sentences. As a shortcut look for the italicized word. It appears in the topic sentence beginning in line 84 and indicates the makerspace movement has *transformative potential*. If you keep reading, the last sentence (main point) directly supports B). A) is incorrect because Chris Anderson is not a participant in the maker movement. C) is incorrect because the author only draws a parallel between the changes wrought by the Industrial Revolution and those that could result from the maker movement. D) is also incorrect because there is nothing to support the idea that mass-production cannot exist in the modern economy – the author states only that mass-customization will *allow for a new wave of business opportunities*.

4.1 B

The key to this question is the sentence begun by the transition *But* in line 18. There, Jordan indicates that she does <u>not</u> intend to focus on people's dissatisfaction with the government and with the state of the country in general. In other words, Jordan lists those problems specifically for the purpose of *rejecting* the idea that she should focus on them. That makes B) correct.

4.2 C

Like the answer to question 4.2, the answer to this question hinges on the transition *but* – in this case, the one that appears in line 33, immediately after the line reference. In that sentence, Jordan indicates that the *great danger* (=pose a threat) is that America will be torn apart by special interests and lose sight of collective goals (=national cohesion). That corresponds to C).

4.3 B

As in question 4.2, the key phrase is *great danger* (=a risk), which Jordan uses to "call attention to" the threat that Americans will be split apart by an excessive focus on special interests.

4.4 D

This question requires you to be as literal as possible; it also requires you to focus on the wording of the sentence in which the key word (*future*) appears. What does that sentence say? *We cannot flee the future.* In other words, the future is inevitable. That makes the answer D).

4.5 B

Why do authors typically use quotation marks? To imply skepticism, a connotation that is almost always negative. C) and D) are both positive, so they can be eliminated. Now, consider the context: Jordan is describing politicians' *hypocrisy* – that is, they behave in such a way that contradicts their official titles. That corresponds directly to B).

4.6 A

Like the previous question, this question involves a section of the passage in which Jordan contrasts politicians' positive public face with their incompetence in upholding the public good. In that context, *slogans and handshakes and press releases* serve as examples of good-looking but fundamentally meaningless gestures. The answer that corresponds directly to that idea is A).

5.1 C

The previous sentence states that the debate over whether dinosaurs were warm-blooded or cold-blooded is a *big controversy* (=scientific dispute). In that context, the foramen is a factor (=a means) that scientists can use to resolve that dispute. That corresponds directly to C).

5.2 D

This is a very straightforward question if you focus on the most relevant information. In this case, it's the sentence immediately following the line reference. The statement *We certainly didn't expect to see that* indicates that the findings came as a surprise, making the answer D).

6.1 A

This question is much simpler than it might initially seem. The key word is *could*, which indicates that the author is speculating about a possible cause for the brines. In other words, the author is proposing a possible explanation for how they were created, making A) the answer.

6.2 C

Like the answer to the previous question, the answer to this question also depends on the word *could*, this time in line 55. That word indicates that the author is again speculating about the consequences of the SkyTEM research (=indicate a possible outcome) and makes C) correct.

6.3 D

Make sure you read the entire sentence in which the line reference appears. In that context, the references to plant and animal life serve as examples of ways in which the Antarctic surface resembles the surface of Mars. That corresponds directly to D).

Glossary of Function Words

Account for – explain

Acknowledge (a point) – recognize the merit or validity of an idea

Advocate – synonym for *promote* and *encourage*

Bolster – support, provide additional evidence for an idea

Concede (a point) – recognize the merit or validity of an opposing idea

Discredit – disprove (literally, demonstrate a lack of credibility)

> SAT passages are typically concerned with weighing evidence, considering prevailing theories, and proposing new explanations. Although authors and various experts cited in passages may have strong opinions about what is and is not true, passages do not, as a rule, contain sufficient information or evidence to definitively prove or disprove anything. *Discredit* is therefore unlikely to appear as a correct answer.

Dismiss – deny the importance or validity of an idea

Downplay – deliberately understate, imply that something is unimportant

Evoke – summon, call up (a memory, impression, etc.), recreate through description

Explicate – explain in great detail

Highlight – emphasize, call attention to

Minimize – deliberately understate the importance of an idea. Synonym for *downplay* and *trivialize*.

Mock – make fun of

Qualify – provide more information about a statement in order to make it seem less strong or blunt, or to indicate the conditions under which it would be true.

> For example, a statement like, "The SAT is the worst test EVER" is extremely strong (not to mention a good example of a **hyperbole**).

> To **qualify** it, however, you could say something like, "At least that's what it feels like when you're a junior in high school." That sentence reduces the impact of the first sentence, clarifies when and for whom it would be true, and makes it seem less extreme.

> It can be helpful to know that qualifying phrases are sometimes **parenthetical** – that is, they are found within parentheses or dashes – and are almost like asides to the reader.

For example, consider the following sentence:

> In his discovery of the law of the gravity, which would transform the course of scientific thought, Newton was struck by **– if the story can be believed –** an apple that fell from a tree above the spot where he was reclining.

The phrase between the dashes is intended to suggest that this story may not in fact be true. In other words, it is intended to provide information about the truth of – to *qualify* – the idea that Newton was struck by an apple.

As discussed earlier, answer choices that contain familiar words used in unfamiliar ways are generally correct since the second meaning itself is being tested. Since *qualify* is not being used in its most common sense of "fulfill requirements for," it has a higher than average chance of being correct.

So here's a shortcut: If you have difficulty coming up with an answer on your own and see "qualify a statement" as an option, you should probably begin by taking a very close look at it. This is NOT to say that you should choose it without thinking, simply that you should consider it <u>first</u>, making sure to look back to the passage and see if it does in fact describe the function of the statement or phrase in question.

Satirize – make fun of by using irony, sarcasm, or parody

Scoff at – make fun of, suggest that something is unworthy of serious consideration

Substantiate – give evidence or support for, back up

Undermine – weaken or attack the foundation of

Underscore – call attention to. Synonym for *emphasize* and *highlight*

Tone and Attitude

Tone and attitude questions appear infrequently, but you can plan to encounter one or two of them on the exam. In most cases, they essentially require you to identify whether the attitude of the author, or an individual discussed in a passage, is positive, negative, or neutral. They may also ask you to identify the relationship between specific wording and the tone. These questions are typically phrased in the following ways:

- What main effect does the quotation by Gupta (lines x-y) have on the tone of the passage?

- The author would most likely view the events described in lines x-y as…

- The information in lines x-y suggests that Klein would view the "skeptics" with…

Most answers provided for tone questions are fairly moderate; however, you may occasionally encounter more "extreme" options, which are typically **incorrect**. If an author's attitude is positive, for example, the answer is more likely to be **approving** or **appreciative** than **excited**; if the author's attitude is negative, the answer is more likely to be **skeptical** than **alarmed**; and if an author uses strong language, the answer is more likely to be **emphatic** or **determined** than **melodramatic**.

There are several reasons for this pattern: first is that, with the exception of historical documents, passages tends to be relatively neutral in tone. Positive passages are slightly positive, and negative passages are slightly negative. The second reason is that many science passages concern arguments that have not yet been proven. As a result, authors are unlikely to say that a given piece of evidence *conclusively* proves a new theory. Instead, they use **qualifying statements** and say that evidence *suggests* a theory has some merit. The second statement is much more cautious than the first, and answers tend to reflect that fact.

Neutral Tone, Definite Opinion

While the terms "tone" and "attitude" are sometimes used interchangeably, they are not precisely the same thing. An author can present information about a topic in a tone that is relatively neutral but still have a distinct opinion about which ideas are correct and which ones incorrect. **A lack of strong language does not imply a neutral attitude.** The information necessary to figure out what the individual in question thinks will always be present, even though you may have to read closely to identify it.

232

When tackling science passages, you should be particularly careful not to confuse a dry or objective tone with an absence of opinion or point of view. SAT passages are, for all intents and purpose, not just recitations of factual information. Rather, they are chosen because they contain some sort of argument, or because they explain why a new theory is superior to the existing one. Although there will certainly be indications that the "old idea" has been rejected and the "new idea" accepted, the overall *tone* is likely to remain fairly neutral during discussions of both.

Note, however, that answers indicating a lack of interest, e.g., **indifferent**, **apathetic**, or **resigned**, are highly unlikely to be correct. The reason for this is simple. Authors (particularly paired-passage authors) as well as individuals discussed in passages tend to have distinct, often conflicting, points of view. If they didn't, there would be nothing to test. The only **exception** would involve a character in a **fiction passage** who demonstrated a clear sense of detachment in a particular situation.

Let's start with a straightforward example:

The so-called machine-learning approach...links several powerful software techniques that make it possible for the robot to learn new tasks rapidly with a relatively small amount of training. The new approach
5 includes a powerful artificial intelligence technique known as "deep learning," which has previously been used to achieve major advances in both computer vision and speech recognition. Now the researchers have found that it can also be used to improve the actions of
10 robots working in the physical world on tasks that require both machine vision and touch.

The author's **positive attitude** is indicated by a series of specific words and phrases:

- *make it possible*

- *powerful artificial intelligence technique*

- *major advances*

- *improve the actions*

The author's *tone*, however, remains relatively restrained throughout the passage. He does not, for example, say that that this technology is extraordinary, nor does he say that it is the most important invention ever.

Instead, he understates his enthusiasm by using **qualifying words** such as *relatively* small and *major* advance. His tone could therefore be characterized as **appreciative** or **approving**, but NOT **enthusiastic** or **excited**. It could also be described with more neutral terms such as **informative** or **analytical**.

The ability to distinguish between tone and attitude can become very important when you are asked about attitude alone. "Attitude" questions require you to focus on what an individual thinks rather than the words used to express a particular viewpoint.

Playing Positive/Negative with Tone and Attitude Questions

As is true for SAT Reading questions in general, considering answer choices to tone and attitude questions in terms of positive, negative, and neutral is a helpful and straightforward strategy for eliminating incorrect answers and identifying correct ones.

Sets of answers to these questions typically contain both positive and negative options – often two of each – so this is an overall reliable approach.

Let's look at an example:

The public has been worried about the safety of genetically modified (GM) foods since scientists at the University of Washington developed the first genetically modified tobacco plants in the 1970s. In the
5 mid-1990s, when the first GM crops reached the market, Greenpeace, the Sierra Club, Ralph Nader, Prince Charles and a number of celebrity chefs took highly visible stands against them. Consumers in Europe became particularly alarmed: a survey
10 conducted in 1997, for example, found that 69 percent of the Austrian public saw serious risks in GM foods, compared with only 14 percent of Americans.
But as medical researchers know, nothing can really be "proved safe." One can only fail to turn up
15 significant risk after trying hard to find it—as is the case with GM crops.
Although it might seem creepy to add virus DNA to a plant, doing so is, in fact, no big deal, proponents say. Viruses have been inserting their DNA into the
20 genomes of crops, as well as humans and all other organisms, for millions of years. They often deliver the genes of other species while they are at it, which is why our own genome is loaded with genetic sequences that originated in viruses and nonhuman species.
25   Could eating plants with altered genes allow new DNA to work its way into our own? It is theoretically possible but hugely improbable. Scientists have never found genetic material that could survive a trip through the human gut and make it into cells. Besides, we are
30 routinely exposed to—we even consume—the viruses and bacteria whose genes end up in GM foods. The bacterium B. thuringiensis, for example, which produces proteins fatal to insects, is sometimes enlisted as a natural pesticide in organic farming.
35   In any case, people have consumed as many as trillions of meals containing genetically modified ingredients over the past few decades. Not a single verified case of illness has ever been attributed to the genetic alterations.

40   Critics often disparage U.S. research on the safety of genetically modified foods, which is often funded or even conducted by GM companies, such as Monsanto. But much research on the subject comes from the European Commission, the administrative body of the
45 E.U., which cannot be so easily dismissed as an industry tool. The European Commission has funded 130 research projects, carried out by more than 500 independent teams on the safety of GM crops. None of those studies found any special risks from GM crops.

1

Which choice best reflects the perspective of the "proponents" (line 18) on genetically modified foods?

A) They are necessary to combat hunger but too costly to grow on a large scale.

B) They are an established part of the food supply and have no harmful effects.

C) They produce poor-tasting crops and may cause genetic alterations.

D) They damage the environment and leave people vulnerable to bacterial infection.

2

Which choice provides the best evidence for the answer to the previous question?

A) Lines 9-11 ("a survey…foods")
B) Lines 27-29 ("Scientists…cells")
C) Lines 35 -39 ("In any…alterations")
D) Lines 43-46 ("But…tool")

Before you start plugging in answers, think logically for a moment about the information provided for you.

The question asks what "proponents" of genetically modified foods are likely to think about these crops. By definition, a proponent is a person who is in favor of something, so the answer to Question #1 must be positive. (Conversely, a question that asks about "skeptics" will, by definition, almost certainly have a negative answer.)

You can of course go back to line 18 and check this out, in which case you'll find that "proponents" are people who believe modifying food genetically is *no big deal*, but it isn't actually necessary to do so.

Playing positive/negative, you can eliminate C) and D) right away because both answers are negative. A) is half-positive, half-negative, but the negative half is at odds with the idea of "proponents." If half of the answer is wrong, the whole answer is wrong. Still, if you're not fully comfortable crossing this answer out, you can leave it.

At this point, you can start plugging in the line references from Question #2, but again, think about how the passage is organized. The entire first paragraph talks about opposition to GM foods, so it's extremely unlikely that lines 9-11 are correct. You can skip A) for the moment. Likewise, the last paragraph starts off by mentioning *critics*. Lines 43-46 are located there, so it's a pretty safe assumption that D) isn't right either.

If you need a little more context for B), back up and read from the beginning of the paragraph. Lines 27-29 provide the answer to the question in the previous sentence: *Could eating plants with altered genes allow new DNA to seep into our own?* The answer to that question is not only "no," but it does not directly support either A) or B).

The biggest trap you could fall into here is to think that you might be missing something and either start rereading the passage for more context, or sitting and puzzling over the answers. But if a set of lines don't really fit, they don't really fit. When that is the case, spending time trying to find a relationship where there is none is just about the worst thing you could do.

Instead, move on and check lines 35-39, which clearly support C) in Question #1. *Trillions of meals containing genetically modified ingredients* = an established part of the food supply, and *not a single verifiable case of illness* = no harmful effects.

Inferring Attitude

Although answers to many attitude questions are indicated in the passage, some questions may ask you to move a step beyond what is literally stated and infer what the author of the passage or a person/group discussed in the passage would most likely think about a particular viewpoint or individual(s).

These types of questions are always present in Passage 1/Passage 2 sets (we'll look at some samples in Chapter 11), but they can also accompany single passages that discuss multiple points of view.

Let's look at an example:

Sometime near the end of the Pleistocene, a band of people left northeastern Asia, crossed the Bering land bridge when the sea level was low, entered Alaska and became the first Americans. Since the
5 1930s, archaeologists have thought these people were members of the Clovis culture. First discovered in New Mexico in the 1930s, the Clovis culture is known for its distinct stone tools, primarily fluted projectile points. For decades, Clovis artifacts were the oldest
10 known in the New World, dating to 13,000 years ago. But in recent years, researchers have found more and more evidence that people were living in North and South America before the Clovis.
     The most recently confirmed evidence comes from
15 Washington. During a dig conducted from 1977 to 1979, researchers uncovered a bone projectile point stuck in a mastodon rib. Since then, the age of the find has been debated, but recently anthropologist Michael Waters and his colleagues announced a new radiocarbon date
20 for the rib: 13,800 years ago, making it 800 years older than the oldest Clovis artifact. Other pre-Clovis evidence comes from a variety of locations across the New World.

1

The "researchers" (line 11) would most likely view the theory described in lines 4-6 with

A) admiration because they offer a novel perspective.

B) skepticism because it does not take important new evidence into account.

C) hostility because it threatens to overturn decades of research.

D) suspicion because it is based on an unreliable methodology.

2

Which choice provides the best evidence for the answer to the previous question?

A) Lines 1-4 ("Sometime...Americans)

B) Lines 6-9 ("First...points")

C) Lines 9-10 ("For...ago")

D) Lines 17-21 ("Since...artifact")

As discussed earlier, the passage follows a predictable pattern: it discusses an established theory (the Clovis people were the first people to inhabit North America) and a new theory that challenges it (a group of people inhabited North America before the Clovis arrived).

The author's *tone*, however, remains relatively neutral throughout the discussion of both theories. For example, instead of saying that the theory that the Clovis were the first inhabitants of North America is *absolutely* wrong, the author simply states that *more evidence* suggests that this is not the case.

Despite this restrained language, the **attitude** toward the "old idea" is negative, whereas the attitude toward the "new idea" is positive. We're going to use that information to answer both questions. Because we have line references for the first question, we're going to answer them in order.

1) What's the theory in lines 4-6?

The Clovis were the first people in North America.

2) What do the researchers believe?

People were living in North and South America before the Clovis. (The Clovis were NOT the first people in North America.)

3) What's the relationship?

The information in steps 1 and 2 indicates opposing ideas, so the researchers are going to disagree with the theory. That means we're going to look for a negative answer.

Now, we're going to consider just the first word of each option.

A) Admiration: positive. Cross out.

B) Skepticism: negative, relatively neutral. Keep it.

C) Hostility: negative, too strong. Assume it's wrong.

D) Suspicion: negative, relatively neutral. Keep it.

Working this way, we're left with B) and D). B) makes sense because someone who believed that the Clovis were the first people in North America would be overlooking the evidence described in the second paragraph. D) doesn't fit because there's no information in the passage to suggest that the advocates' methods are unreliable. So the correct answer is B).

Now for the second question. You could go through and check each option individually, but there's a much faster way to find the answer. We're looking for lines that support the idea that the Clovis were the first people in the Americas, which is part of the "old idea."

Because the passage is arranged so that the "old idea" comprises most of the first paragraph and the "new idea" comprises the second paragraph, the correct lines must be in the second paragraph. D) is the only option that contains lines in the second paragraph, so it must be the answer. And indeed, those lines discuss evidence for the theory that the Clovis were not the first people in the Americas.

Simplifying "Tone" Answers

Instead of just asking you to identify the author's tone, tone questions will generally ask you to identify *how* the use of specific words or phrases contributes to the tone. Although these questions may appear very complicated, their answers can be simplified considerably.

Let's look at an example. Just read the passage – don't try to answer the question yet.

The sharing economy is a little like online shopping, which started in America 15 years ago. At first, people were worried about security. But having made a successful purchase from, say, Amazon, they
5 felt safe buying elsewhere. Similarly, using Airbnb or a car-hire service for the first time encourages people to try other offerings. Next, consider eBay. Having started out as a peer-to-peer marketplace, it is now dominated by professional "power sellers" (many of whom started
10 out as ordinary eBay users). The same may happen with the sharing economy, which also provides new opportunities for enterprise. Some people have bought cars solely to rent them out, for example. Incumbents are getting involved too. Avis, a car-hire firm, has a share
15 in a sharing rival. So do GM and Daimler, two carmakers. In the future, companies may develop hybrid models, listing excess capacity (whether vehicles, equipment or office space) on peer-to-peer rental sites. In the past, new ways of doing things online have not displaced the
20 old ways entirely. But they have often changed them. Just as internet shopping forced Walmart and Tesco to adapt, so online sharing will shake up transport, tourism, equipment-hire and more.
The main worry is regulatory uncertainty. Will
25 room-4-renters be subject to hotel taxes, for example? In Amsterdam officials are using Airbnb listings to track down unlicensed hotels. In some American cities,

peer-to-peer taxi services have been banned after lobbying by traditional taxi firms. The danger is that
30 although some rules need to be updated to protect consumers from harm, incumbents will try to destroy competition. People who rent out rooms should pay tax, of course, but they should not be regulated like a Ritz-Carlton hotel. The lighter rules that typically govern
35 bed-and-breakfasts are more than adequate. The sharing economy is the latest example of the internet's value to consumers. This emerging model is now big and disruptive enough for regulators and companies to have woken up to it. That is a sign of its immense potential. It
40 is time to start caring about sharing.

1

What main effect do the author's statements about the sharing economy in lines 35-40 have on the tone of the passage?

A) They create an emphatic tone, conveying the strength of the author's convictions.

B) They create a resigned tone, focusing on the inevitability of economic change.

C) They create a celebratory tone, praising regulators for adapting.

D) They create a personal tone, describing the author's involvement in the sharing economy.

The answer choices include a lot of information, so it's easy to feel overwhelmed.

One strategy for simplifying things is to just focus on the tone word in each answer and ignore the rest of the information. You can think of the question as asking this:

1

What is the tone in lines 35-40?

A) Emphatic

B) Resigned

C) Celebratory

D) Personal

238

Approaching tone questions this way has both benefits and drawbacks. On one hand, you have less information to deal with, and thus less potential for confusion. On the other hand, you can't rely on the information in the second part of each answer choice to help you figure things out. If you can play positive/negative without too much difficulty, though, there's a very good chance you can find your way to the answer.

Some questions may be best approached with a **combination of strategies**: you can play positive/negative with the "tone" word to eliminate a couple of options, then consider the full answers to decide between the remaining choices.

That said, let's keep working through the simplified version:

35   … The sharing economy is the latest example of the internet's value to consumers. This emerging model is now big and disruptive enough for regulators and companies to have woken up to it. That is a sign of its immense potential. It
40 is time to start caring about sharing.

1

What is the tone in lines 35-40?

A) Emphatic
B) Resigned
C) Celebratory
D) Personal

The next thing we're going to do is ignore the options provided and answer the question in our own words.

When we look at the section in question, we can notice that it's positive. Phrases such as *the internet's value to consumers*, *immense potential*, and *It is time to start caring* indicate that the author thinks that the sharing economy is a pretty great thing. *Resigned* (accepting of a bad situation) is negative, so B) can be crossed out. The word *I*, which would indicate a *personal* tone does not appear, so D) can be eliminated as well.

That leaves A) and C). The fact that *celebratory* is pretty strong while *emphatic* is more neutral suggests that A) is probably correct. In fact, the lines in question – especially the last sentence – do consist mostly of short, strong statements, which support A). Still, we don't have quite enough information to decide, so we're going to check out the full answers.

35   … The sharing economy is the latest example of the internet's value to consumers. This emerging model is now big and disruptive enough for regulators and companies to have woken up to it. That is a sign of its immense potential. It
40 is time to start caring about sharing.

1

What main effect do the author's statements about the sharing economy in lines 35-40 have on the tone of the passage?

A) They create an emphatic tone, conveying the strength of the author's convictions.
B) They create a resigned tone, focusing on the inevitability of economic change.
C) They create a celebratory tone, praising regulators for adapting.
D) They create a personal tone, describing the author's involvement in the sharing economy.

239

Shortcut: A) contains the word *convictions*, which is used in its second meaning. When most students hear the word *conviction*, they picture a courtroom with a judge announcing "Guilty!" But *conviction* is also the noun form of *convinced*. In this definition, convictions are simply strong beliefs, and that's the only use that makes sense. That alone is enough to suggest that A) is the answer. And when you go back to the passage, it's pretty clear that the author strongly believes that the sharing economy is a big deal. So A) works.

The slightly longer way: Remember that when you're stuck between two answers, you want to pick the most specific part of one answer to check. If the passage supports it, that answer is right; if the passage doesn't support it, the other answer must be correct by default.

In this case, C) provides more specific information: it indicates that the passage *[praises] regulators for adapting*. When we go back to the passage, though, the only information we find about regulators is that the author thinks they should have *woken up to* the sharing economy. It does not actually say that they have adapted. So C) doesn't fit, again leaving A).

Register: Formal vs. Informal

Register refers to a text's level of formality or informality. Many students assume because the SAT is a Very Serious Test, all the passages must therefore be written in a Very Serious Manner. But while it is true that many historical texts will be quite formal, some contemporary passages may contain less serious parts.

For example, compare the following two excerpts. Passage 1 is taken from Daniel Webster's 1850 speech *The Union and the Constitution*. Passage 2 is from a 2013 newspaper editorial.

Passage 1

I wish to speak to-day, not as a Massachusetts man, nor as a Northern man, but as an American, and a member of the Senate of the United States. It is fortunate that there is a Senate of the United States; a
5 body not yet moved from its propriety, not lost to a just sense of its own dignity and its own high responsibilities, and a body to which the country looks, with confidence, for wise, moderate, patriotic, and healing counsels. It is not to be denied that we live in the midst of strong
10 agitations, and are surrounded by very considerable dangers to our institutions and government. The imprisoned winds are let loose. The East, the North, and the stormy South combine to throw the whole sea into commotion, to toss its billows to the skies, and
15 disclose its profoundest depths.

Passage 2

Yogi Berra, the former Major League baseball catcher and coach, once remarked that you can't hit and think at the same time. Of course, since he also reportedly said, "I really didn't say everything I said,"
5 it is not clear we should take his statements at face value. Nonetheless, a widespread view—in both academic journals and the popular press—is that thinking about what you are doing, as you are doing it, interferes with performance. The idea is that once
10 you have developed the ability to play an arpeggio on the piano, putt a golf ball or parallel park, attention to what you are doing leads to inaccuracies, blunders and sometimes even utter paralysis. As the great choreographer George Balanchine would say to his
15 dancers, "Don't think, dear; just do."
Perhaps you have experienced this destructive force yourself. Start thinking about just how to carry a full glass of water without spilling, and you'll end up drenched. How, exactly, do you initiate a telephone
20 conversation? Begin wondering, and before long, the recipient of your call will notice the heavy breathing and hang up.

The first passage is undoubtedly very **formal**. It contains extremely long sentences with multiple clauses, sophisticated, abstract vocabulary and phrasing (*propriety, agitations, disclose its profoundest depths*), and is filled with metaphorical language (*imprisoned winds, toss its billows to the skies*). The tone could thus be described as **elevated** or **lofty**. Because Webster uses the **first person** (*I*) throughout the passage, the tone could also be characterized as **personal**.

In terms of tone and style, the second passage is the complete opposite of the first. The sentences are far shorter and employ a much more **casual** or **colloquial** level of vocabulary (*blunders, end up drenched*). It contains allusions (references) to popular culture, e.g., Yogi Berra and baseball, and the author frequently uses the second person (*you*) to address the reader directly.

In addition, it includes several humorous quotations, including one at the beginning that is patently absurd (*I really didn't say everything I said*), and a rhetorical question (*How, exactly do you initiate a telephone conversation?*) that is used to give the impression that the author is thinking things over as she writes. Taken together, these elements create a tone that is **informal** or **conversational**.

Now, consider this excerpt from a passage we looked at earlier:

The sharing economy is a little like online
shopping, which started in America 15 years ago. At
first, people were worried about security. But having
made a successful purchase from, say, Amazon, they
5 felt safe buying elsewhere. Similarly, using Airbnb or
a car-hire service for the first time encourages people to
try other offerings. Next, consider eBay. Having started
out as a peer-to-peer marketplace, it is now dominated
by professional "power sellers" (many of whom started
10 out as ordinary eBay users). The same may happen with
the sharing economy, which also provides new
opportunities for enterprise. Some people have bought
cars solely to rent them out, for example. Incumbents
are getting involved too. Avis, a car-hire firm, has a share
15 in a sharing rival. So do GM and Daimler, two carmakers.
In the future, companies may develop hybrid models,
listing excess capacity (whether vehicles, equipment or
office space) on peer-to-peer rental sites.

In comparison to the examples we just looked at, this one falls somewhere in the middle.

It doesn't contain the sophisticated vocabulary and complex syntax (word order) of the first passage, but neither does it include the casual, humorous aspects of the second passage. It simply presents an argument – people are initially nervous about the sharing economy, but their concerns disappear when they participate in it – and supports it with various pieces of evidence. The tone is straightforward and moderately serious.

Even though the author clearly has a positive attitude toward the sharing economy, the tone could also be described as **informative, analytical,** or **objective**. These tones are associated with a **third person point of view** (*he/she/it*).

Certainty and Uncertainty

While SAT authors are rarely over-the-top extreme, they do sometimes voice some very strong opinions. Writing that is **emphatic**, **decisive**, **vehement**, **resolute**, or full of **conviction** tends to have some pronounced characteristics:

- It contains short, blunt declarations, e.g., *There is no compelling proof that it's true.*

- It contains strong words and phrases, e.g., *there is no doubt, certainly, only,* and *most.*

- It lacks qualifying words or phrases such as *sometimes, frequently,* or *might* that would soften its meaning.

For example, compare the following two statements:

1) Technology changes everything.

2) In some circumstances, technology has the potential to change things.

The two sentences focus on the same subject, but they do so in very different ways.

The first sentence is striking because it is so short and to-the-point. It simply says what it has to say, and that's that. Its tone could thus be described as **emphatic** or **decisive**.

The second sentence, on the other hand, is filled with **qualifying phrases** (*some, has the potential to be*) that tell us that the author wants to avoid making an overly strong statement. Its tone could be described as **tentative**, **hesitant**, or **cautious**.

On the SAT, you are likely to encounter many instances of **speculative** tones. In such cases, the author will discuss hypothetical situations – ones that have not actually occurred but that could occur – and will use words such as *could, might, probably,* and *perhaps.*

For example:

A better understanding of archaea's lifestyle and role in nitrogen cycles not only would rewrite ecology textbooks. It **<u>could also have practical applications</u>**, such as devising natural ways to boost a soil's nitrogen
5 content without needing to use chemical fertilizers, or designing sewage treatment plants that employ microbes to remove nitrogenous waste more efficiently, or understanding which microbes produce global-warming gases such as nitrous oxide.

In this passage, the word *could* indicates a **speculative** or **hypothetical** tone. The author is discussing the potential applications of knowledge regarding archaea's lifestyle and role in nitrogen cycles – knowledge and applications that do not currently exist but that might exist in the future.

In some cases, **rhetorical questions** can also indicate a lack of certainty:

Most of us are very familiar with the idea that our planet is nothing more than a tiny speck orbiting a typical star, somewhere near the edge of an otherwise un-noteworthy galaxy. In the midst of a universe
5 populated by billions of galaxies that stretch out to our cosmic horizon, we are led to believe that there is nothing special or unique about our location.
But what is the evidence for this cosmic humility? And how would we be able to tell if we
10 **were in a special place?** Astronomers typically gloss over these questions, assuming our own typicality sufficiently obvious to warrant no further discussion. To entertain the notion that we may, in fact, have a special location in the universe is, for many,
15 unthinkable. Nevertheless, that is exactly what some small groups of physicists around the world have recently been considering.

The questions at the beginning of the second paragraph are intended to cast doubt on the statement that *we are led to believe that there is nothing special or unique about our location.* They indicate that the author does not truly believe the usual answers to these questions, which *astronomers typically gloss over* (treat superficially). We can therefore describe both his tone and his attitude as **uncertain** or **tentative**. Alternately, the fact that he is mulling these questions over gives his writing a **reflective** tone as well.

Note: One common point of confusion stems from the presence of counterarguments – that is, ideas that contradict or weaken arguments presented in the passage. In some cases, as in the example above, authors will be genuinely uncertain about answers to questions, or about where they stand on particular issues. In most instances, however, they will come firmly down on one side. You should therefore be careful with the word **ambivalent** if you ever encounter it in an answer choice. To date, this word – a staple of the old SAT – has not appeared on any released exams, but you should be aware of this pitfall just in case.

If you are asked to consider the big picture and find yourself confused about what the author thinks, you should refer back to the **end of the conclusion** because that is where the author is most likely to reaffirm the main point. You can also scan the passage for contradictors such as *but* and *however* since "new ideas" usually appear after them.

Humor, Sarcasm, and Irony

Given the rarity with which tone questions appear, as well as the SAT's focus on testing relatively straightforward concepts such as informality and approval, the chances of your being asked about a genuinely humorous or sarcastic portion of a passage is extremely low. If they do appear, answers involving humor, mockery, and sarcasm are unlikely to be correct for the simple reason that they are inconsistent with the relatively moderate, neutral tone of most passages. That said, these are concepts that students frequently find confusing, and I am discussing them here for the sake of thoroughness.

If you do ever encounter humor in an SAT passage, it will almost certainly not be the obvious, over-the-top, laugh-out-loud type of humor that you probably associate with that word. Rather, it will be based on **wordplay** that either involves **punning** on alternate meanings of words, or using words to mean the **opposite** of what they normally mean (the literary equivalent of a kid who rolls his eyes and says "great" when he's asked to stop playing video games and take out the trash). It is up to the reader to recognize that meanings are being flipped *based on the context of the passage*.

For example:

The ethics of eating red meat have been **grilled** recently by critics who question its consequences for environmental health and animal welfare. But if you want to minimize animal suffering and promote more
5 sustainable agriculture, adopting a vegetarian diet might be the worst possible thing you could do.

In the first line, the author puns on the word *grilled* by using it in its second meaning ("question intensely") while simultaneously associating it with its first meaning ("cooking food on a grill"). The play on words creates a **humorous** tone.

In context of the unexpected assertion that the author makes in the next sentence (being a vegetarian is *bad* for animals and agriculture) the wordplay also creates a tone of **mockery** and **sarcasm** toward people who believe that eating meat is unethical.

Let's look at another example:

...To their senses, are women made slaves, because it is by their sensibility that they obtain present power. And will moralists pretend to assert, that this is the condition in which one half of the human race should
5 be encouraged to remain with listless inactivity and stupid acquiescence? **Kind instructors!** what were we created for? To remain, it may be said, innocent; they mean in a state of childhood. We might as well never have been born, unless it were necessary that we should
10 be created to enable man to acquire the noble privilege of reason, the power of discerning good from evil, whilst we lie down in the dust from whence we were taken, never to rise again.

If you are ever directly tested on a sarcastic or mocking tone, there is a significant possibility that it will appear in the context of a historical document. Because authors of these passages tend to hold very strong views, they are more likely to use emotionally charged language.

In the passage above, for example, the author (Mary Wollstonecraft) rails against the fact that women are kept in a state of perpetual childhood and not permitted to develop their powers of reason the way men are. In that context, her reference to *kind instructors* in line 6 cannot be taken literally. Instead, she is implying that these people are exactly the opposite of kind. Her tone can thus be described as **ironic**, **sarcastic**, or **mocking**.

Common Tone and Attitude Words

	Positive	Negative	Neutral
Moderate	Agreement Appreciative Approving Confident Informal Proud Sympathetic	Ambivalent Critical Disagreement Doubtful Skeptical Tentative Uncertain	Analytical Informative Neutral Objective Personal
Extreme	Amused Awed/Awestruck Excited Humorous	Angry Disdainful Fearful Furious Hostile Jeering Mocking Melodramatic Sarcastic	Academic Apathetic Indifferent Resigned

Tone and Attitude Exercises

1. Citrus greening, the plague that could wipe out Florida's $9 billion orange industry, begins with the touch of a jumpy brown bug on a sun-kissed leaf. From there, the bacterial disease incubates in the
5 tree's roots, then moves back up the trunk in full force, causing nutrient flows to seize up. Leaves turn yellow, and the oranges, deprived of sugars from the leaves, remain green, sour, and hard. Many fall before harvest, brown necrotic flesh ringing failed stems.

10 For the past decade, Florida's oranges have been literally starving. Since it first appeared in 2005, citrus greening, also known by its Chinese name, huanglongbing, has swept across Florida's groves like a flood. With no hills to block it, the Asian citrus
15 psyllid—the invasive aphid relative that carries the disease—has infected nearly every orchard in the state. By one estimate, 80 percent of Florida's citrus trees are infected and declining.

20 The disease has spread beyond Florida to nearly every orange-growing region in the United States.

Despite many generations of breeding by humanity, no citrus plant resists greening; it afflicts lemons, grapefruits, and other citrus species as well. Once a
25 tree is infected, it will die. Yet in a few select Floridian orchards, there are now trees that, thanks to innovative technology, can fight the greening tide.

1

The use of the phrases "jumpy brown bug" and "sun-kissed leaf" in the first sentence establishes a tone that is

A) critical.

B) mocking.

C) informal.

D) detached.

2. Chimps do it, birds do it, even you and I do it. Once you see someone yawn, you are compelled to do the same. Now it seems that wolves can be added to the list of animals known to spread yawns like a
5 contagion.

Among humans, even thinking about yawning can trigger the reflex, leading some to suspect that catching a yawn is linked to our ability to empathize with other humans. For instance, contagious yawning activates the
10 same parts of the brain that govern empathy and social know-how. And some studies have shown that humans with more fine-tuned social skills are more likely to catch a yawn.

Similarly, chimpanzees, baboons and bonobos
15 often yawn when they see other members of their species yawning. Chimps (Pan troglodytes) can catch yawns from humans, even virtual ones. At least in primates, contagious yawning seems to require an emotional connection and may function as a demonstration of
20 empathy. Beyond primates, though, the trends are less clear-cut. One study found evidence of contagious yawning in birds but didn't connect it to empathy. A 2008 study showed that dogs (Canis lupus familiaris) could catch yawns from humans, and another showed
25 that dogs were more likely to catch the yawn of a

familiar human rather than a stranger. But efforts to see if dogs catch yawns from each other and to replicate the results with humans have so far had no luck.

1

The author's attitude toward the possibility that yawning is a sign of empathy in non-primates is best described as one of

A) skepticism.

B) enthusiasm.

C) approval.

D) hostility.

2

Which lines provide the best evidence for the answer to the previous question?

A) Lines 2-3 ("Once…same")

B) Lines 6-9 ("Among…humans")

C) Lines 14-16 ("Similarly…yawning")

D) Lines 26-28 ("But…luck")

3. These are stimulating times for anyone interested in questions of animal consciousness. On what seems like a monthly basis, scientific teams announce the results of new experiments, adding to a preponderance
5 of evidence that we've been underestimating animal minds, even those of us who have rated them fairly highly. New animal behaviors and capacities are observed in the wild, often involving tool use—or at least object manipulation—the very kinds of activity
10 that led the distinguished zoologist Donald R. Griffin to found the field of cognitive ethology (animal thinking) in 1978: octopuses piling stones in front of their hideyholes, to name one recent example; or dolphins fitting marine sponges to their beaks in order to dig for
15 food on the seabed; or wasps using small stones to smooth the sand around their egg chambers, concealing them from predators. At the same time neurobiologists have been finding that the physical structures in our own brains most commonly held responsible for
20 consciousness are not as rare in the animal kingdom as had been assumed. Indeed they are common. All of this work and discovery appeared to reach a kind of crescendo last summer, when an international group of prominent neuroscientists meeting at the University of
25 Cambridge issued "The Cambridge Declaration on Consciousness in Non-Human Animals," a document stating that "humans are not unique in possessing the neurological substrates that generate consciousness." It goes further to conclude that numerous documented
30 animal behaviors must be considered "consistent with experienced feeling states."

1

The use of the phrases "stimulating times" (line 1), "what seems like a monthly basis" (lines 2-3), and "preponderance of evidence" (lines 4-5) in the first two sentences establishes a tone that is

A) dubious.

B) approving.

C) tentative.

D) disdainful.

---

4. Every time a car drives through a major intersection, it becomes a data point. Magnetic coils of wire lie just beneath the pavement, registering each passing car. This starts a cascade of information: Computers tally the
5 number and speed of cars, shoot the data through underground cables to a command center and finally translate it into the colors red, yellow and green. On the seventh floor of Boston City Hall, the three colors splash like paint across a wall-sized map.
10   To drivers, the color red means stop, but on the map it tells traffic engineers to leap into action. Traffic control centers like this one—a room cluttered with computer terminals and live video feeds of urban intersections— represent the brain of a traffic system. The city's network
15 of sensors, cables and signals are the nerves connected to the rest of the body. "Most people don't think there are eyes and ears keeping track of all this stuff," says John DeBenedictis, the center's engineering director. But in reality, engineers literally watch our every move,
20 making subtle changes that relieve and redirect traffic.
    The tactics and aims of traffic management are modest but powerful. Most intersections rely on a combination of pre-set timing and computer adaptation. For example, where a busy main road intersects with
25 a quiet residential street, the traffic signal might give 70 percent of "green time" to the main road, and 30 percent to the residential road. (Green lights last between a few seconds and a couple minutes, and tend to shorten at rush hour to help the traffic move
30 continuously.) But when traffic overwhelms the pre-set timing, engineers override the system and make changes.

1

What effect does the quotation by John DeBenedictis in lines 16-17 have on the tone of of the passage?

A) It creates a skeptical tone, implying that the power of computers to control traffic may be limited.

B) It creates an enthusiastic tone, emphasizing the power of technology to ensure safety.

C) It creates an ominous tone, suggesting the risks of unrestrained surveillance.

D) It creates a conversational tone, pointing out a common misconception in everyday language.

5.   To understand what the new software—that is,
analytics—can do that's different from more familiar
software like spreadsheets, word processing, and
graphics, consider the lowly photograph. Here the
5 relevant facts aren't how many bytes constitute a digital
photograph, or a billion of them. That's about as
instructive as counting the silver halide molecules used
to form a single old-fashioned print photo. The important
feature of a digital image's bytes is that, unlike
10 crystalline molecules, they are uniquely easy to store,
transport, and manipulate with software. In the first era
of digital images, people were fascinated by the
convenience and malleability (think PhotoShop) of
capturing, storing, and sharing pictures. Now, instead of
15 using software to manage photos, we can mine features
of the bytes that make up the digital image. Facebook
can, without privacy invasion, track where and when,
for example, vacationing is trending, since digital images
reveal at least that much. But more importantly, those
20 data can be cross-correlated, even in real time, with
seemingly unrelated data such as local weather, interest
rates, crime figures, and so on. Such correlations
associated with just one photograph aren't revealing.
But imagine looking at billions of photos over weeks,
25 months, years, then correlating them with dozens of
directly related data sets (vacation bookings, air traffic),
tangential information (weather, interest rates,
unemployment), or orthogonal information (social or
political trends). With essentially free super-computing,
30 we can mine and usefully associate massive, formerly
unrelated data sets and unveil all manner of economic,
cultural, and social realities.

   For science fiction aficionados, Isaac Asimov
anticipated the idea of using massive data sets to predict
35 human behavior, coining it "psychohistory" in his 1951
Foundation trilogy. The bigger the data set, Asimov said
then, the more predictable the future. With big-data
analytics, one can finally see the forest, instead of just
the capillaries in the tree leaves. Or to put it in more
40 accurate terms, one can see beyond the apparently
random motion of a few thousand molecules of air inside
a balloon; one can see the balloon itself, and beyond that,
that it is inflating, that it is yellow, and that it is part of a
bunch of balloons en route to a birthday party. The
45 data/software world has, until now, been largely about
looking at the molecules inside one balloon.

What effect does the word "imagine" (line 24)
have on the tone of the passage?

A) It creates a mysterious tone that suggests the
   unlimited potential of technology.

B) It creates a skeptical tone that suggests the
   necessity of resisting certain inventions.

C) It creates a speculative tone that encourages
   the reader to consider a scenario.

D) It creates a defiant tone that emphasizes the
   need to persevere in the face of adversity.

6. The following passage is adapted from Jane Austen, *Northanger Abbey*, originally published in 1817.

No one who had ever seen Catherine Morland in her infancy would have supposed her born to be an heroine. Her situation in life, the character of her father and mother, her own person and disposition, were all
5 equally against her.

Her father was a clergyman, without being neglected, or poor, and a very respectable man, though his name was Richard—and he had never been handsome. He had a considerable independence besides
10 two good livings—and he was not in the least addicted to locking up his daughters. Her mother was a woman of useful plain sense, with a good temper, and, what is more remarkable, with a good constitution. She had three sons before Catherine was born; and instead of
15 dying in bringing the latter into the world, as anybody might expect, she still lived on—lived to have six children more—to see them growing up around her, and to enjoy excellent health herself. A family of ten children will be always called a fine family, where there
20 are heads and arms and legs enough for the number; but the Morlands had little other right to the word, for they were in general very plain, and Catherine, for many years of her life, as plain as any. She had a thin awkward figure, a sallow skin without colour, dark lank
25 hair, and strong features—so much for her person; and not less unpropitious for heroism seemed her mind. She was fond of all boy's plays, and greatly preferred cricket not merely to dolls, but to the more heroic enjoyments of infancy, nursing a dormouse, feeding a
30 canary-bird, or watering a rose-bush. Indeed she had no taste for a garden; and if she gathered flowers at all, it was chiefly for the pleasure of mischief—at least so it was conjectured from her always preferring those which she was forbidden to take. Such were her
35 propensities—her abilities were quite as extraordinary. She never could learn or understand anything before she was taught; and sometimes not even then, for she was often inattentive, and occasionally stupid. Her mother was three months in teaching her only
40 to repeat the "Beggar's Petition"; and after all, her next sister, Sally, could say it better than she did. Not that Catherine was always stupid—by no means; she learnt the fable of "The Hare and Many Friends" as quickly as any girl in England. Her mother wished her
45 to learn music; and Catherine was sure she should like it, for she was very fond of tinkling the keys of the old forlorn spinner; so, at eight years old she began. She learnt a year, and could not bear it; and Mrs. Morland, who did not insist on her daughters being accomplished
50 in spite of incapacity or distaste, allowed her to leave off. The day which dismissed the music-master was one of the happiest of Catherine's life. Her taste for drawing was not superior; though whenever she could obtain the outside of a letter from her mother or seize
55 upon any other odd piece of paper, she did what she could in that way, by drawing houses and trees, hens and chickens, all very much like one another. Writing and accounts she was taught by her father; French by her mother: her proficiency in either was not
60 remarkable, and she shirked her lessons in both whenever she could. What a strange, unaccountable character!—for with all these symptoms of profligacy at ten years old, she had neither a bad heart nor a bad temper, was seldom stubborn, scarcely ever
65 quarrelsome, and very kind to the little ones, with few interruptions of tyranny; she was moreover noisy and wild, hated confinement and cleanliness, and loved nothing so well in the world as rolling down the green slope at the back of the house.

1

What effect does the phrase "What a strange, unaccountable character!" (lines 61-62) have on the tone of the passage?

A) It creates a harsh tone that suggests Catherine's parents are responsible for her educational deficiencies.

B) It creates a gently mocking tone that implies Catherine's shortcomings are not unusual in a young girl.

C) It creates a puzzled tone that emphasizes the inexplicable nature of Catherine's difficulties.

D) It creates a resigned tone that suggests Catherine's difficulties are irreversible.

7. This passage is adapted from Jamaica Kincaid, *Annie John*, © 1985 Farrar, Straus and Giroux. The protagonist is a girl growing up in the Caribbean.

It was the first day of a new term, Miss Nelson said, so we would not be attending to any of our usual subjects; instead, we were to spend the morning in contemplation and reflection and writing something she
5 described as an "autobiographical essay." In the afternoon, we would read aloud to each other our auto-biographical essays. (I knew quite well about "autobiography" and "essay," but reflection and contemplation! A day at school spent in such a way!
10 Of course, in most books all the good people were always contemplating and reflecting before they did anything. Perhaps in her mind's eye she could see our future and, against all prediction, we turned out to be good people.) On hearing this, a huge sigh went up
15 from the girls.

Half the sighs were in happiness at the thought of sitting and gazing off into clear space, the other half in unhappiness at the misdeeds that would have to go unaccomplished. I joined the happy half, because I
20 knew it would please Miss Nelson, and, my own selfish interest aside, I liked so much the way she wore her ironed hair and her long-sleeved blouse and box-pleated skirt that I wanted to please her.

The morning was uneventful enough: a girl
25 spilled ink from her inkwell all over her uniform; a girl broke her pen nib and then made a big to-do about replacing it; girls twisted and turned in their seats and pinched each other's bottoms; girls passed notes to each other. All this Miss Nelson must have seen and
30 heard, but she didn't say anything—only kept reading her book: an elaborately illustrated edition of *The Tempest*, as later, passing by her desk, I saw. Midway in the morning, we were told to go out and stretch our legs and breathe some fresh air for a few minutes;
35 when we returned, we were given glasses of cold lemonade and a slice of bun to refresh us.

As soon as the sun stood in the middle of the sky, we were sent home for lunch. The earth may have grown an inch or two larger between the time I had
40 walked to school that morning and the time I went home to lunch, for some girls made a small space for me in their little band. But I couldn't pay much attention to them; my mind was on my new surroundings, my new teacher, what I had written in my nice new
45 notebook with its black-all-mixed-up-with-white cover and smooth lined pages (so glad was I to get rid of my old notebooks, which had on their covers a picture of a wrinkled-up woman wearing a crown on her head and a neckful and armfuls of diamonds and pearls—their
50 pages so coarse, as if they were made of cornmeal).

I flew home. I must have eaten my food. By half past one, we were sitting under a flamboyant tree in a secluded part of our schoolyard, our auto-biographical essays in hand. We were about to read aloud what
55 we had written during our morning of contemplation and reflection. In response to Miss Nelson, each girl stood up and read her composition. One girl told of a much revered and loved aunt who now lived in England and of how much she looked forward to
60 one day moving to England to live with her aunt; one girl told of her brother studying medicine in Canada and the life she imagined he lived there (it seemed quite odd to me); one girl told of the fright she had when she dreamed she was dead, and of the matching
65 fright she had when she woke and found that she wasn't (everyone laughed at this, and Miss Nelson had to call us to order over and over); one girl told of how her oldest sister's best friend's cousin's best friend (it was a real rigmarole) had gone on a Girl Guide
70 jamboree held in Trinidad and met someone who millions of years ago had taken tea with Lady Baden-Powell; one girl told of an excursion she and her father had made to Redonda, and of how they had seen some booby birds tending their chicks. Things
75 went on in that way, all so playful, all so imaginative. I began to wonder about what I had written, for it was the opposite of playful and it was the opposite of imaginative. What I had written was heartfelt, and, except for the very end, it was all too true.

1 ▮▮▮▮▮▮▮▮▮▮▮▮▮▮▮▮▮▮▮▮▮▮▮▮▮▮▮▮▮▮▮▮

Over the course of the passage, the narrator's attitude shifts from

A) eagerness to begin an assignment to uncertainty about sharing her work.

B) disappointment about starting school to excitement about the future.

C) disdain for some of her classmates to admiration for her teacher.

D) doubt in her ability to keep up with her friends to pride in her accomplishments.

2 ▮▮▮▮▮▮▮▮▮▮▮▮▮▮▮▮▮▮▮▮▮▮▮▮▮▮▮▮▮▮▮▮

Which lines provide the best evidence for the answer to the previous question?

A) Lines 19-23 ("I joined hearing...her")

B) Lines 42-46 ("But...pages")

C) Lines 57-60 ("One girl...aunt")

D) Lines 76-78 ("I began...true")

8. This passage is adapted from Barry Schwartz, "More Isn't Always Better," © 2006 by *Harvard Business Review.*

Marketers assume that the more choices they offer, the more likely customers will be able to find just the right thing. They assume, for instance, that offering 50 styles of jeans instead of two increases the chances that
5 shoppers will find a pair they really like. Nevertheless, research now shows that there can be too much choice; when there is, consumers are less likely to buy anything at all, and if they do buy, they are less satisfied with their selection.
10 It all began with jam. In 2000, psychologists Sheena Iyengar and Mark Lepper published a remarkable study. On one day, shoppers at an upscale food market saw a display table with 24 varieties of gourmet jam. Those who sampled the spreads received a coupon for $1 off
15 any jam. On another day, shoppers saw a similar table, except that only six varieties of the jam were on display. The large display attracted more interest than the small one. But when the time came to purchase, people who saw the large display were one-tenth as likely to buy as
20 people who saw the small display.
Other studies have confirmed this result that more choice is not always better. As the variety of snacks, soft drinks, and beers offered at convenience stores increases, for instance, sales volume and customer
25 satisfaction decrease. Moreover, as the number of retirement investment options available to employees increases, the chance that they will choose any decreases. These studies and others have shown not only that excessive choice can produce "choice
30 paralysis," but also that it can reduce people's satisfaction with their decisions, even if they made good ones. My colleagues and I have found that increased choice decreases satisfaction with matters as trivial as ice cream flavors and as significant as jobs.
35 These results challenge what we think we know about human nature and the determinants of well-being. Both psychology and business have operated on the assumption that the relationship between choice and well-being is straightforward: The more choices people
40 have, the better off they are. In psychology, the benefits of choice have been tied to autonomy and control. In business, the benefits of choice have been tied to the benefits of free markets more generally. Added options make no one worse off, and they are bound to make
45 someone better off.
Choice *is* good for us, but its relationship to satisfaction appears to be more complicated than we had assumed. There is diminishing marginal utility in having alternatives; each new option subtracts a little
50 from the feeling of well-being, until the marginal benefits of added choice level off. What's more, psychologists and business academics alike have largely ignored another outcome of choice: More of it requires increased time and effort and can lead to
55 anxiety, regret, excessively high expectations, and self-blame if the choices don't work out. When the number of available options is small, these costs are negligible, but the costs grow with the number of options. Eventually, each new option makes us feel
60 worse off than we did before.
Without a doubt, having more options enables us, most of the time, to achieve better objective outcomes. Again, having 50 styles of jeans as opposed to two increases the likelihood that customers will find a pair
65 that fits. But the subjective outcome may be that shoppers will feel overwhelmed and dissatisfied. This dissociation between objective and subjective results creates a significant challenge for retailers and marketers that look to choice as a way to enhance the
70 perceived value of their goods and services.
Choice can no longer be used to justify a marketing strategy in and of itself. More isn't always better, either for the customer or for the retailer. Discovering how much assortment is warranted is a
75 considerable empirical challenge. But companies that get the balance right will be amply rewarded.

1

What effect does the author's reference to "My colleagues and I" (line 32) have on the tone of the passage?

A) It creates a dubious tone that conveys the author's skepticism toward Iyengar and Lepper's research.

B) It creates a reassuring tone that conveys the power of individual experience.

C) It creates a conversational tone that conveys potentially dry information in a personal manner.

D) It creates a distraught tone that conveys the uncertainty accompanying excessive choice.

2

The author's attitude toward Iyengar and Lepper's research is best described as one of

A) skepticism.
B) approval.
C) defensiveness.
D) indifference.

3

Which lines provide the best evidence for the answer to the previous question?

A) Lines 17-18 ("The large...one")
B) Lines 32-34 ("My...jobs")
C) Lines 40-41 ("In...control")
D) Lines 48-49 ("There is...alternatives")

4

The author would most likely consider the viewpoint in lines 39-40 ("The more...are")

A) an example of a belief with which he does not agree.
B) a potentially valid assertion that has not yet been conclusively proven.
C) a straightforward statement of fact.
D) a belief that has long been considered controversial.

5

Which lines provide the best evidence for the answer to the previous question?

A) Line 15 ("On...table")
B) Lines 40-43 ("In...generally")
C) Lines 61-62 ("Without...outcomes")
D) Lines 72-73 ("More...retailer")

Explanations: Tone and Attitude Exercises

1.1 C

Jumpy brown bug and *sun-kissed leaf* are both very descriptive phrases designed to draw the reader in and engage him or her in the problem of citrus greening. They're exactly the opposite of the type of dry, objective language normally associated with scientific topics; in fact, they're fairly casual. The author is trying to grab the reader's interest by explaining things by adopting a friendly, easily accessible manner. "Informal" is the only answer consistent with that goal.

2.1-2 A, D

The fastest way to answer this question is to recall that yawning in primates is discussed in the first half of the passage, whereas yawning in non-primates is discussed at the end. If you do not remember, the phrase *Beyond primates* in line 20 is a big clue to the section of the passage you need to focus on. What does that line indicate? That the relationship between empathy and yawning in animals other than primates is *less clear-cut*. That's negative, but not overly so. The only answer consistent with that language is "skeptical" – "hostility" is too strong. For 2.2, lines 26-28 are the only lines cited after line 20, so you can assume they are correct. Indeed, they support the idea that yawning may not be related to empathy in dogs (that is, non-primates) by indicating that these animals have not been shown to catch yawns from one another.

3.1 B

The three quotes provided are positive and support the idea that a lot of good research on animal consciousness is currently being conducted, so the correct answer must be positive. "Approving" is the only option that fits.

4.1 D

Start by focusing on the language of the quote itself: *Most people don't think there are eyes and ears keeping track of all this stuff.* The most striking feature is the use of the word *stuff* – it's a very casual word, not one that normally appears in formal writing. In fact, that word creates an informal or "conversational" tone, making the answer D). You do not even need to consider any of the other information in the answer.

5. C

Despite the seeming complexity of the answer choices, this question can be answered without consideration of any information in the passage – the only relevant piece of information is the word *imagine*. Why would an author use that word? To encourage a reason to consider a possible situation or result. In other words, to "speculate." That makes C) the answer.

6. B

Consider the context in which the phrase in question appears. The narrator has just finished describing Catherine's lack of perseverance in her music lessons and her attempts to avoid studying accounting and French – all perfectly normal behaviors for a mischievous young girl. The narrator, however, describes these behaviors as something astounding and perplexing. The key is to understand that the narrator's exaggerated description is deliberate; he or she understands full well that Catherine's behavior is normal and is poking fun at the conventional expectation of how a heroine should behave. The discrepancy between the behaviors themselves and the narrator's deliberately exaggerated surprise creates a "gently mocking" tone, making B) correct.

7.1-2 A, D

The easiest way to answer these questions is to use the following shortcut: the question asks how the narrator's attitude shifts "over the course of the passage" — that is, from the beginning of the passage to the end. As a result, the correct line reference can only appear in one of those two places. The only line reference that corresponds to either of those places is lines 76-78, so D) is the most likely answer to 7.2. It indicates that the narrator *began to wonder about what [she] had written.* In other words, she felt "uncertainty" about sharing her work. A) is thus the answer to 7.1.

8.1 C

The key word is *I.* Whenever an author or narrator refers to him/herself in the first person, look for an answer that includes the idea of personal, informal, or conversational. Those ideas are present in C), making it the correct answer.

8.2-3 B, B

If you use the main point (too much choice = bad), 8.2 can be a very straightforward question, and you are probably best off answering the questions in order. The discussion of Iyengar and Lepper indicates that they ran the pioneering experiment that demonstrated the negative effects of too much choice. Since the author agrees with Iyengar and Lepper, the correct choice must be positive; therefore, B) is the only possible answer to 8.2. Looking at the following question, you know that the correct set of lines must indicate that the author believes Iyengar and Lepper's research is accurate. You can also start by assuming that the correct lines are likely to be somewhere close to the spot where Iyengar and Lepper's names appear, making A) and B) top candidates for the correct answer. Be careful with A) – although lines 17-18 do appear as part of the discussion of Iyengar and Lepper's research, they don't discuss the results. In fact, they state what the conventional wisdom would predict: people spent more time looking at the table with more options. B) is the correct answer to 8.3 because it indicates that the author's own research has confirmed Iyengar and Lepper's findings.

8.4-5 A, D

Again, using the main point is the fastest way to answer this pair of questions. Start by defining the viewpoint in lines 39-40: *The more choices people have, the better off they are.* If you know that the author's point is that too much choice <u>isn't</u> good, you can jump to A) as the correct answer to 8.4. For 8.5, the main point is almost invariably reiterated at the end of a passage. D) cites lines at the end, so you can check that answer first. Sure enough, it reiterates the point that *more isn't always better.*

Rhetorical Strategy

Rhetorical strategy questions come in a variety of forms. They may ask about the point of view from which a passage is written; how paragraphs or passages are organized; or how counterarguments are presented. They are typically phrased in the following ways:

- This passage is written from the perspective of someone who is...

- Which choice best describes the structure of this passage?

- The statement in line x signals a shift from...

Point of View

There are several narrative points of view that you should be familiar with for the SAT. Some questions may ask you to identify them directly, but other questions may test them indirectly. In such cases, recognizing the point of view can provide an effective shortcut.

A **first-person** narrative is written from the perspective of the narrator. Usually the word *I* will appear (first-person singular), but occasionally *we* (first-person plural) may also be used. All personal anecdotes are, by definition, written in the first person.

For example, let's return to this excerpt from Daniel Webster's speech. Notice the repeated use of the word *I*:

I do not affect to regard myself, Mr. President, as holding, or as fit to hold, the helm in this combat with the political elements; but **I** have a duty to perform, and **I** mean to perform it with fidelity, not without a sense of existing dangers, but not without hope. **I** have a part to act, not for my own security or safety, for **I** am looking out for no fragment upon which to float away from the wreck, if wreck there must be, but for the good of the whole, and the preservation of all; and there is that which will keep **me** to my duty during this struggle, whether the sun and the stars shall appear, or shall not appear for many days. **I** speak to-day for the preservation of the Union.

A **third-person** narrative, on the other hand, is written from an objective or impersonal perspective and describes other people or things rather than the narrator him- or herself.

For example:

Every time a car drives through a major intersection, it becomes a data point. Magnetic coils of wire lie just beneath the pavement, registering each passing car. This starts a cascade of information: Computers tally the number and speed of cars, shoot the data through underground cables to a command center and finally translate it into the colors red, yellow and green. On the seventh floor of Boston City Hall, the three colors splash like paint across a wall-sized map.

Although this passage is highly descriptive, it focuses on events, not on the narrator. Unlike the first passage, its tone is much more neutral and detached. **The majority of SAT passages are written from a third-person perspective.**

Second person narrations are less common than either first- or third-person narrations, but you may encounter them from time to time. They can address the reader directly by using the word *you*, or indirectly by giving **commands**. For example, the following excerpt does both of these things:

… The idea is that once **you** have developed the ability to play an arpeggio on the piano, putt a golf ball or parallel park, attention to what you are doing leads to inaccuracies, blunders and sometimes even utter paralysis. As the great choreographer George Balanchine would say to his dancers, "Don't think, dear; just do."
Perhaps **you** have experienced this destructive force yourself. **Start thinking** about just how to carry a full glass of water without spilling, and **you'll** end up drenched. How, exactly, do **you** initiate a telephone conversation? **Begin wondering**, and before long, the recipient of **your** call will notice the heavy breathing and hang up. Our actions, the French philosopher Maurice Merleau-Ponty tells us, exhibit a "magical" efficacy, but when we focus on them, they degenerate into the absurd. A 13-time winner on the Professional Golfers Association Tour, Dave Hill, put it like this: "**You** can't be thinking about the mechanics of the sport while **you** are performing."

Noticing pronouns can also provide a very effective shortcut if you encounter questions asking you to identify where a **shift** occurs in the passage. To answer these questions, you must be able to recognize key places in the development of the argument: where new or contradictory information is introduced, where important ideas appear, and where "old ideas" shift to "new ideas." You should also pay close attention to changes in point of view.

For example, we're going to take another look at this excerpt from Barbara Jordan's 1976 National Democratic Convention speech:

It was one hundred and forty-four years ago that members of the Democratic Party first met in convention to select a Presidential candidate. A lot of years passed since 1832, and during that time it would
5 have been most unusual for any national political party to ask a Barbara Jordan to deliver a keynote address. But tonight, here **I** am. And **I** feel that notwithstanding the past that **my** presence here is one additional bit of evidence that the American Dream need not forever be
10 deferred.

Now that **I** have this grand distinction, what in the world am **I** supposed to say? **I** could list the problems which cause people to feel cynical, angry, frustrated: problems which include lack of integrity in government;
15 the feeling that the individual no longer counts; feeling that the grand American experiment is failing or has failed. **I** could recite these problems, and then **I** could sit down and offer no solutions. But **I** don't choose to do that either. The citizens of America expect more.
20 **We** are a people in search of a national community. **We** are a people trying not only to solve the problems of the present, unemployment, inflation, but **we** are attempting on a larger scale to fulfill the promise of America. **We** are attempting to fulfill our national
25 purpose, to create and sustain a society in which all of **us** are equal.

Which choice best describes the shift that occurs in line 20?

A) A criticism of a situation to an acknowledgment of its significance.

B) A discussion of a problem to a description of a solution.

C) A personal reaction to a discussion of a general concern.

D) A presentation of a claim to a questioning of that claim.

Like many SAT Reading questions, this one appears to be considerably more difficult than it actually is. The most important thing to understand is that the question is asking about the *shift* that occurs in line 20. By definition, a shift is a change from one thing to another, so to answer the question, we must look at the information before line 20 as well as line 20 itself.

If we just look at the previous paragraph as well as the paragraph that line 20 begins, we can notice that in the previous paragraph, the word *I* appears repeatedly, whereas the new paragraph refers to *we*. The shift is from personal to general, making C) correct.

Some point-of-view questions may ask about the author or narrator's **relationship** to the subject of the passage – that is, whether the author/narrator is **personally involved**, or whether he or she is merely an **interested observer**. In such cases, it is important that you notice the pronouns that the author uses throughout the passage. An author who is personally involved will use personal pronouns (*I, we*), while an author who is not directly involved will use impersonal pronouns (*he, she, it, they*).

Most authors of science and social science passages will be informed observers – people who are strongly interested in and highly knowledgeable about their subjects, but who do not actually participate in the events/research they describe. As a result, they will often demonstrate a positive attitude toward their subjects. (Again: if they weren't interested, they wouldn't bother to write about them in the first place.)

In contrast, authors of fiction passages and historical documents may be either directly involved or knowledgeable observers.

For example, let's return to this social science passage:

Every time a car drives through a major intersection, it becomes a data point. Magnetic coils of wire lie just beneath the pavement, registering each passing car. This starts a cascade of information: Computers tally the
5 number and speed of cars, shoot the data through underground cables to a command center and finally translate it into the colors red, yellow and green. On the seventh floor of Boston City Hall, the three colors splash like paint across a wall-sized map.
10 To drivers, the color red means stop, but on the map it tells traffic engineers to leap into action. Traffic control centers like this one—a room cluttered with computer terminals and live video feeds of urban intersections—represent the brain of a traffic system. The city's network
15 of sensors, cables and signals are the nerves connected to the rest of the body. "Most people don't think there are eyes and ears keeping track of all this stuff," says John DeBenedictis, the center's engineering director. But in reality, engineers literally watch our every move,
20 making subtle changes that relieve and redirect traffic.
The tactics and aims of traffic management are modest but powerful. Most intersections rely on a combination of pre-set timing and computer adaptation.

For example, where a busy main road intersects with
25 a quiet residential street, the traffic signal might give 70 percent of "green time" to the main road, and 30 percent to the residential road. (Green lights last between a few seconds and a couple minutes, and tend to shorten at rush hour to help the traffic move
30 continuously.) But when traffic overwhelms the pre-set timing, engineers override the system and make changes.

1

This passage is written from the perspective of someone who is

A) actively involved in promoting traffic safety throughout urban areas.
B) familiar with the activities of traffic engineers.
C) an employee of the traffic control center in Boston City Hall.
D) opposed to the intrusion of traffic engineers into everyday life.

This passage is descriptive or informative: it explains what traffic engineers do and how a traffic control center functions, from an outsider's perspective. The tone is neutral/positive. In addition to containing the most common description of a non-fiction writer, B) corresponds to this perspective: someone informed about a subject but not directly involved.

Both A) and C) indicate personal involvement, eliminating them. Although that is not the case for D), "opposed" is negative, and nothing in the passage suggests that the author disapproves of traffic engineers' role in everyday life. While you may be somewhat put off by the fact that traffic engineers are *literally watch[ing] our every move*, there is no evidence that the author feels that way, and you cannot project your own impressions onto the author.

Other point of view questions could ask about the narrator's perspective in terms of **age** (child vs. adult) or **time**. These questions tend to occur when passages discuss events that took place at different times, often earlier, or when the narrator is looking back on an event.

In such cases, you must pay attention to **tense** – that is, whether the passage is written in the **present** (*is, are*) or **past** (*was, were*). The action of a passage written in the present is taking place as the author describes it, while the action of a passage written in the past has already occurred.

On the next page, we're going to look at an example. Pay attention to the passage's point of view and tense.

The following passage is adapted from a novel by Willa Cather, originally published in 1918. The narrator has been sent to live with his grandparents in Nebraska.

On the afternoon of that Sunday I took my first long ride on my pony, under Otto's direction. After that Dude and I went twice a week to the post-office, six miles east of us, and I saved the men a good
5 deal of time by riding on errands to our neighbors. When we had to borrow anything, I was always the messenger.

All the years that have passed have not dimmed my memory of that first glorious autumn. The new country
10 lay open before me: there were no fences in those days, and I could choose my own way over the grass uplands, trusting the pony to get me home again. Sometimes I followed the sunflower-bordered roads.

I used to love to drift along the pale-yellow cornfields,
15 looking for the damp spots one sometimes found at their edges, where the smartweed soon turned a rich copper color and the narrow brown leaves hung curled like cocoons about the swollen joints of the stem. Sometimes I went south to visit our German neighbors and to
20 admire their catalpa grove, or to see the big elm tree that grew up out of a deep crack in the earth and had a hawk's nest in its branches. Trees were so rare in that country, and they had to make such a hard fight to grow, that we used to feel anxious about them, and visit them
25 as if they were persons. It must have been the scarcity of detail in that tawny landscape that made detail so precious.

Sometimes I rode north to the big prairie-dog town to watch the brown earth-owls fly home in the late afternoon
30 and go down to their nests underground with the dogs. Antonia Shimerda liked to go with me, and we used to wonder a great deal about these birds of subterranean habit. We had to be on our guard there, for rattlesnakes were always lurking about. They came to pick up an easy
35 living among the dogs and owls, which were quite defenseless against them; took possession of their comfortable houses and ate the eggs and puppies. We felt sorry for the owls. It was always mournful to see them come flying home at sunset and disappear under
40 the earth.

But, after all, we felt, winged things who would live like that must be rather degraded creatures. The dog-town was a long way from any pond or creek. Otto Fuchs said he had seen populous dog-towns in the desert where
45 there was no surface water for fifty miles; he insisted that some of the holes must go down to water—nearly two hundred feet, hereabouts. Antonia said she didn't believe it; that the dogs probably lapped up the dew in the early morning, like the rabbits.

50 Antonia had opinions about everything, and she was soon able to make them known. Almost every day she came running across the prairie to have her reading lesson with me. Mrs. Shimerda grumbled, but realized it was important that one member of the family should
55 learn English. When the lesson was over, we used to go up to the watermelon patch behind the garden. I split the melons with an old corn-knife, and we lifted out the hearts and ate them with the juice trickling through our fingers. The white melons we did not touch, but we
60 watched them with curiosity. They were to be picked later, when the hard frosts had set in, and put away for winter use. After weeks on the ocean, the Shimerdas were famished for fruit. The two girls would wander for miles along the edge of the cornfields, hunting for
65 ground-cherries.

Antonia loved to help grandmother in the kitchen and to learn about cooking and housekeeping. She would stand beside her, watching her every movement. We were willing to believe that Mrs. Shimerda was a
70 good housewife in her own country, but she managed poorly under new conditions. I remember how horrified we were at the sour, ashy-grey bread she gave her family to eat. She mixed her dough, we discovered, in an old tin peck-measure that had been used about the
75 barn. When she took the paste out to bake it, she left smears of dough sticking to the sides of the measure, put the measure on the shelf behind the stove, and let this residue ferment. The next time she made bread, she scraped this sour stuff down into the fresh dough to
80 serve as yeast.

1

This passage is written from the perspective of

A) an adult recalling a memorable experience that occurred earlier in his adult life.

B) an adult recounting a significant childhood memory.

C) a child describing the development of a friendship.

D) a narrator analyzing a story told to him by an acquaintance.

The key to answering this question is the line *All the years that have passed have not dimmed my memory of that first glorious autumn.* The narrator is looking back on an event that occurred earlier in his life. Even though he's describing what happened when he was a boy, the phrase *All the years that have passed* indicates he's no longer a boy at the time he's telling the story. Which answer does that correspond to? B).

If you didn't notice that phrase and played process of elimination, you could eliminate D) immediately because the passage is written in the first person, as indicated by the repeated use of the word *I*.

Now we need to think carefully about the other answers. Let's start with A). Yes, the passage is told by an adult recounting a significant memory, but be careful – it's not an *adult* memory. The key phrase *All the years that have passed* (line 8) indicates that the narrator is recounting events that occurred much earlier in his life. We can also reasonably infer that the narrator was young at the time of the passage from the fact that he and Antonia were having reading lessons (lines 51-53).

To eliminate C), think about the tense in which the passage is written. All of the verbs are in the past tense (*went, rode, grumbled, followed*), indicating that the action took place in the past.

Paragraph and Passage Organization

Paragraph and passage organization questions test your understanding of rhetorical strategies on a large scale. Occasionally, they may also be paired with supporting evidence questions. To answer these questions correctly and quickly, you must be able to identify places where key ideas and arguments are introduced, as well as transition words that indicate the relationships between those ideas.

If a question asks about the **organization of a paragraph**, you should begin by skimming for important transitions within that paragraph. Then, consider the functions of those transitions (compare/contrast, indicate sequence of events, etc.) and what sorts of relationships between ideas they convey.

If a question asks about the **overall organization of a passage**, you should focus on the end of the introduction and the first sentence of each subsequent paragraph.

While you should be able to recognize how paragraphs and passages are organized, you should not take the time to label each section of a passage as you read it. If you are comfortable determining organization, you can most likely figure it out on the spot when necessary. As a preparation strategy, however, you may find it helpful to label the various parts of a passage (e.g., historical context, supporting example, counterargument, etc.).

You should also be on the lookout for changes in point of view, especially those involving first-person narrations (*I*), because this information can provide an important shortcut for both identifying correct answers and eliminating incorrect ones.

In some cases, you may also be able to **simplify** some questions by **focusing on one part of an answer choice** and checking it against the corresponding part of the passage.

Starting on the next page, we're going to look at some examples.

The sharing economy is a little like online shopping, which started in America 15 years ago. At first, people were worried about security. But having made a successful purchase from, say, Amazon, they
5 felt safe buying elsewhere. Similarly, using Airbnb or a car-hire service for the first time encourages people to try other offerings. Next, consider eBay. Having started out as a peer-to-peer marketplace, it is now dominated by professional "power sellers" (many of whom started
10 out as ordinary eBay users). The same may happen with the sharing economy, which also provides new opportunities for enterprise. Some people have bought cars solely to rent them out, for example. Incumbents are getting involved too. Avis, a car-hire firm, has a share
15 in a sharing rival. So do GM and Daimler, two carmakers. In the future, companies may develop hybrid models, listing excess capacity (whether vehicles, equipment or office space) on peer-to-peer rental sites. In the past, new ways of doing things online have not displaced the
20 old ways entirely. But they have often changed them. Just as internet shopping forced Walmart and Tesco to adapt, so online sharing will shake up transport, tourism, equipment-hire and more.

The main worry is regulatory uncertainty. Will
25 room-4-renters be subject to hotel taxes, for example? In Amsterdam officials are using Airbnb listings to track down unlicensed hotels. In some American cities, peer-to-peer taxi services have been banned after lobbying by traditional taxi firms. The danger is that
30 although some rules need to be updated to protect consumers from harm, incumbents will try to destroy competition. People who rent out rooms should pay tax, of course, but they should not be regulated like a Ritz-Carlton hotel. The lighter rules that typically govern
35 bed-and-breakfasts are more than adequate. The sharing economy is the latest example of the internet's value to consumers. This emerging model is now big and disruptive enough for regulators and companies to have woken up to it. That is a sign of its immense potential. It
40 is time to start caring about sharing.

1

Which choice best describes the structure of the first paragraph (lines 1-23)?

A) A comparison is presented and developed through supporting examples.

B) A principle is described, and an opposing principle is then introduced.

C) The strengths and weaknesses of several competing explanations are discussed.

D) A personal account of an experience is provided, followed by a reflection on that experience.

Before we start working carefully through the answers, we can eliminate D). A quick glance at the passage reveals that the word *I* does not appear anywhere, so the passage cannot be "personal."

The next thing we want to do is simplify the question and the answers. The question asks about the entire first paragraph – that's 23 lines. **Remember, however, that a long line reference usually indicates that it is <u>not</u> necessary to reread the entire section carefully.** So instead, we're going to focus on the beginning of the passage, say lines 1-7. The beginning of the correct answer must describe what's happening in those lines.

The sharing economy is **a little like** online shopping, which started in America 15 years ago. At first, people were worried about security. But having made a successful purchase from, say, Amazon, they
5 felt safe buying elsewhere. Similarly, using Airbnb or a car-hire service for the first time encourages people to try other offerings.

1

Which choice best describes the structure of the first paragraph (lines 1-23)?

A) A comparison is presented and developed through supporting examples.

B) A principle is described, and an opposing principle is then introduced.

C) The strengths and weaknesses of several competing explanations are discussed.

D) A personal account of an experience is provided, followed by a reflection on that experience.

What is happening at the beginning of the passage? Well, the first sentence presents a comparison, as indicated by the phrase *a little like*. If we focus on just the start of each answer choice, we can see that A) is the only option that begins with the word *comparison*, suggesting that it is correct. When we read a little further, we can see that the following lines do in fact develop that comparison, as indicated by the transition *similarly*. A) is thus correct.

The answer choices could, however, be written in a manner less conducive to this type of shortcut. What if they were presented like this?

The sharing economy is a little like online shopping, which started in America 15 years ago. **At first**, people were worried about security. **But** having made a successful purchase from, say, Amazon, they
5 felt safe buying elsewhere. **Similarly**, using Airbnb or a car-hire service for the first time encourages people to try other offerings. **Next**, consider eBay. Having started out as a peer-to-peer marketplace, it is now dominated by professional "power sellers" (many of whom started
10 out as ordinary eBay users). **The same** may happen with the sharing economy, which **also** provides new opportunities for enterprise.

1

Which choice best describes the structure of the first paragraph (lines 1-23)?

A) An assertion is presented, and supporting examples are provided.

B) A principle is described, and an opposing principle is then introduced.

C) The strengths and weaknesses of several competing explanations are discussed.

D) A personal account of an experience is presented, followed by a reflection on that experience.

Although we can no longer use the word "comparison" in A) as a shortcut we can still get important information by focusing on pronouns and transitions. The word *I* does not appear, so D) can be eliminated right away. An "opposing principle" or "competing explanations" would almost certainly be signaled by contradictors such as *but* or *however*, but no such transitions appear here, eliminating B).

Again, that leaves A). In addition to expressing a comparison, the first sentence also conveys an argument, i.e., an assertion. And when we look at the transitions, we can see that they are mostly continuers that introduce information supporting that assertion.

Now let's look at a full-length example.

The following passage is adapted from Michael Anft, "Solving the Mystery of Death Valley's Walking Rocks," © 2011 by *Johns Hopkins Magazine*.

For six decades, observers have been <u>confounded</u> by the movement of large rocks across a dry lake bed in California's Death Valley National Park. Leaving flat trails behind them, rocks that weigh up to 100

5 pounds seemingly do Michael Jackson's moonwalk across the valley's sere, cracked surface, sometimes traveling more than 100 yards. Without a body of water to pick them up and move them, the rocks at Racetrack Playa, a flat space between the valley's high cliffs,

10 have been the subject of much speculation, including whether they have been relocated by human pranksters or space aliens. The rocks have become the desert equivalent of Midwestern crop circles. "They really are a curiosity," says Ralph Lorenz, a planetary scientist at

15 the Applied Physics Laboratory. "Some [people] have mentioned UFOs. But I've always believed that this is something science could solve."

It has tried. **One theory** holds that the rocks are blown along by powerful winds. **Another** posits that

20 the wind pushes thin sheets of ice, created when the desert's temperatures dip low enough to freeze water from a rare rainstorm, and the rocks go along for the ride. But neither theory is rock solid. Winds at the playa aren't strong enough—some scientists believe that

25 they'd have to be 100 miles per hour or more—to blow the rocks across the valley. And rocks subject to the "ice sailing theory" wouldn't create trails as they moved.

Lorenz and a team of investigators believe that a

30 **combination of forces may work to rearrange Racetrack Playa's rocks.** "We saw that it would take a lot of wind to move these rocks, which are larger than you'd expect wind to move," Lorenz explains. "That led us to this idea that ice might be picking up the

35 rocks and floating them." As they explained in the January issue of *The American Journal of Physics*, instead of moving along with wind-driven sheets of ice, the rocks may instead be lifted by the ice, making them more subject to the wind's force. The key, Lorenz

40 says, is that the lifting by an "ice collar" reduces friction with the ground, to the point that the wind now has enough force to move the rock. The rock moves, the ice doesn't, and because part of the rock juts through the ice, it marks the territory it has covered.

45 Lorenz's team came to its conclusion through a combination of intuition, lab work, and observation— not that the last part was easy. Watching the rocks travel is a bit like witnessing the rusting of a hubcap. Instances of movement are rare and last for only a few

50 seconds. Lorenz's team placed low-resolution cameras on the cliffs (which are about 30 miles from the nearest paved road) to take pictures once per hour. For the past three winters, the researchers have weathered extreme temperatures and several flat tires to measure how

55 often the thermometer dips below freezing, how often the playa gets rain and floods, and the strength of the winds. "The measurements seem to back up our hypothesis," he says. "Any of the theories may be true at any one time, but ice rafting may be the best explan-

60 ation for the trails we've been seeing. We've seen trails like this documented in Arctic coastal areas, and the mechanism is somewhat similar. A belt of ice surrounds a boulder during high tide, picks it up, and then drops it elsewhere." His "ice raft theory" was also

65 borne out by an experiment that used the ingenuity of a high school science fair. Lorenz placed a basalt pebble in a Tupperware container with water so that the pebble projected just above the surface. He then turned the container upside down in a baking tray filled with a

70 layer of coarse sand at its base, and put the whole thing in his home freezer. The rock's "keel" (its protruding part) projected downward into the sand, which simulated the cracked surface of the playa (which scientists call "Special K" because of its resemblance to cereal

75 flakes). A gentle push or slight puff of air caused the Tupperware container to move, just as an ice raft would under the right conditions. The pebble made a trail in the soft sand. "It was primitive but effective," Lorenz says of the experiment. Lorenz has spent the

80 last 20 years studying Titan, a moon of Saturn. He says that Racetrack Playa's surface mirrors that of a dried lakebed on Titan. Observations and experiments on Earth may yield clues to that moon's geology. "We also may get some idea of how climate affects

85 geology—particularly as the climate changes here on Earth," Lorenz says. "When we study other planets and their moons, we're forced to use Occam's razor – sometimes the simplest answer is best, which means you look to Earth for some answers. Once you get out

90 there on Earth, you realize how strange so much of its surface is. So, you have to figure there's weird stuff to be found on Titan as well." Whether that's true or not will take much more investigation. He adds: "One day, we'll figure all this out. For the moment, the moving

95 rock present a wonderful problem to study in a beautiful place."

Which choice best describes the structure of this passage?

A) A theory is presented, and evidence to refute it is provided.

B) A mystery is described, explanations are considered, and a synthesis is proposed.

C) A hypothesis is introduced, and its strengths and weaknesses are analyzed.

D) A new technology is described, its application is discussed, and its implications are considered.

It's understandable that you might get a little nervous (or more than a little nervous) about having to boil 96 lines worth of information down into a single statement, but here again, you can actually answer the question using only the first sentence.

What do we learn from it? That observers have been *confounded* (utterly baffled) by the movement of the Racetrack Playa rocks – in other words, there's a mystery going on. Based on that piece of information alone, you can identify B) as the answer most likely to be correct.

If you want to check the answer further, you can focus on the beginnings of subsequent paragraphs. The words *One theory* and *another [theory]* at the beginning of the second paragraph correspond to "explanations," and the phrase *a combination of forces* corresponds to "synthesis." So B) is correct.

Counterarguments

One important component of the "old idea/new" structure is the counterargument. Simply put, a counterargument is an argument that weakens an idea – most often the "new idea" – and that supports an opposing idea. It could represent a viewpoint held by real people, but it could also describe objections that are **hypothetical** – ones that represent what someone arguing the opposite point of view *might* say.

The following types of phrases are tipoffs that an author is introducing a counterargument:

- Some people/researchers have argued that...
- It might/could be argued that...
- A possible objection/concern is that...
- On the other hand, one could argue that...
- Of course, it is true that...

Although it may seem contradictory to you, authors use counterarguments in order to *strengthen* their own claims. By addressing – and refuting or **rebutting** – possible objections, they can explain why those objections do not outweigh their own argument and thus demonstrate that their own argument is stronger than the other side's.

Some counterarguments will appear near the beginning of a passage – remember that authors often begin with "old ideas" – but they can also show up closer to the end. Having finished explaining their argument, authors will sometimes then turn to potential objections.

It is important to understand that counterarguments will sometimes be presented in indirect ways. Instead of asserting that anyone who disagrees with them is wrong, authors may make **concessions**, acknowledging that some of the objections to their argument are valid. They may also agree with part of the objection while disagreeing with other parts. In such cases, you must read very carefully to determine which idea the author agrees/disagrees with. In the following passage, the counterargument is in bold, and the rebuttal is italicized.

The sharing economy is a little like online shopping, which started in America 15 years ago. At first, people were worried about security. But having made a successful purchase from, say, Amazon, they
5 felt safe buying elsewhere. Similarly, using Airbnb or a car-hire service for the first time encourages people to try other offerings. Next, consider eBay. Having started out as a peer-to-peer marketplace, it is now dominated by professional "power sellers" (many of whom started
10 out as ordinary eBay users). The same may happen with the sharing economy, which also provides new opportunities for enterprise. Some people have bought cars solely to rent them out, for example. Incumbents are getting involved too. Avis, a car-hire firm, has a share
15 in a sharing rival. So do GM and Daimler, two carmakers. In the future, companies may develop hybrid models, listing excess capacity (whether vehicles, equipment or office space) on peer-to-peer rental sites. In the past, new ways of doing things online have not displaced the
20 old ways entirely. But they have often changed them. Just as internet shopping forced Walmart and Tesco to adapt, so online sharing will shake up transport, tourism, equipment-hire and more.
The main worry is regulatory uncertainty. Will
25 **room-4-renters be subject to hotel taxes, for example?**
In Amsterdam officials are using Airbnb listings to
track down unlicensed hotels. In some American cities,
peer-to-peer taxi services have been banned after
lobbying by traditional taxi firms. *The danger is that*
30 *although some rules need to be updated to protect consumers from harm, incumbents will try to destroy competition. People who rent out rooms should pay tax, of course, but they should not be regulated like a Ritz-Carlton hotel. The lighter rules that typically govern*
35 *bed-and-breakfasts are more than adequate. The sharing economy is the latest example of the internet's value to consumers. This emerging model is now big and disruptive enough for regulators and companies to have woken up to it. That is a sign of its immense potential. It*
40 *is time to start caring about sharing.*

This passage contains an excellent example of a counterargument that is presented somewhat subtly. The author introduces a potential **drawback** (*the main worry, regulatory uncertainty*), poses a **rhetorical question** (*Will room-4-renters be subject to hotel taxes, for example?*), and then provides examples of how different places (*Amsterdam, some American cities*) have responded in different ways. Finally, he states his opinion: although some regulation is necessary to protect consumers, it must not stifle competition. The sharing economy is too big to go back now.

Notice that the parts of the counterargument are separated from one another. First, the author presents the counterargument, and only after he is done expanding on it does he respond with his own assertion. He does not flip between viewpoints; once he has discussed an idea, he leaves it and moves on.

Sometimes, however, authors may weave elements of the counterargument into their own arguments, flipping back and forth within the same section or even within the same sentence. The presence of contradictors such as *although, while,* and *whereas* often signals this structure. When this is the case, the information that follows the contradictor will correspond to the "new idea."

In the passage below, for instance, the author repeatedly alternates between opposing viewpoints within sentences or pairs of sentences. Again, the counterarguments are in bold, whereas the author's arguments are italicized.

The world is complex and interconnected, and the evolution of our communications system from a broadcast model to a networked one has added a new dimension to the mix. **The Internet has made us all less**
5 **dependent on professional journalists and editors for information about the wider world, allowing us to seek out information directly via online search or to receive it from friends through social media.** *But this enhanced convenience comes with a considerable risk: that we*
10 *will be exposed to what we want to know at the expense of what we need to know.* **While we can find virtual communities that correspond to our every curiosity,** *there's little pushing us beyond our comfort zones to or into the unknown, even if the unknown may have*
15 *serious implications for our lives.* There are things we should probably know more about—like political and religious conflicts in Russia or basic geography. But even if we knew more than we do, there's no guarantee that the knowledge gained would prompt us to act in a
20 particularly admirable fashion.

Here, the author develops his counterargument primarily by considering one of the main downsides of the Internet: namely, that people do not pay attention to important information about the world because they are intensely focused on their own interests and have little incentive to move beyond their comfort zones.

Effect of a Rhetorical Strategy

The final type of rhetorical strategy question asks you to identify the effect of a particular rhetorical strategy, such as repetition or word choice. Although these questions are phrased differently, they are more or less identical to certain function or main point questions – they are essentially asking you why information is presented in a particular way (i.e., its purpose) or what point it is used to support.

For example, let's return to this excerpt from Barbara Jordan's 1976 speech:

...And now we must look to the future. Let us heed the voice of the people and recognize their common sense. If we do not, we not only blaspheme our political heritage, we ignore the common ties that bind all
30 Americans. Many fear the future. Many are distrustful of their leaders, and believe that their voices are never heard. Many seek only to satisfy their private interests. But this is the great danger America faces – that we will cease to be one nation and become instead a collection
35 of interest groups: city against suburb, region against region, individual against individual; each seeking to satisfy private wants. If that happens, who then will speak for America? Who then will speak for the common good?
  This is the question which must be answered in 1976:
40 Are we to be one people bound together by common spirit, sharing in a common endeavor; or will we become a divided nation? For all of its uncertainty, we cannot flee the future. We must address and master the future together. It can be done if we restore the belief that we
45 share a sense of national community, that we share a common national endeavor.

1

What is the effect of the repetition of the word "we" in the fifth paragraph (lines 39-46)?

A) It evokes a sense of danger, calling attention to the dangers posed by political corruption.

B) It creates a sense of unity, emphasizing the connection between the author and the reader.

C) It reveals a need for sociability, pointing out the risks of excessive solitude.

D) It underscores the longstanding nature of a problem faced by citizens in the United States.

Although there is a lot of information packed into the answer choices, the question is much simpler than it appears. In fact, it's almost unnecessary to even look at the passage.

There is one main reason that authors choose to write in the first person plural (*we*): to create a sense of solidarity, i.e., unity. This stylistic choice implies that a particular situation applies to everyone and that the author is as involved as the reader. With that information, you can immediately identify B) as the correct answer.

Rhetorical Strategy Exercises

1.   These are stimulating times for anyone interested in questions of animal consciousness. On what seems like a monthly basis, scientific teams announce the results of new experiments, adding to a preponderance
5 of evidence that we've been underestimating animal minds, even those of us who have rated them fairly highly. New animal behaviors and capacities are observed in the wild, often involving tool use—or at least object manipulation—the very kinds of activity
10 that led the distinguished zoologist Donald R. Griffin to found the field of cognitive ethology (animal thinking) in 1978: octopuses piling stones in front of their hideyholes, to name one recent example; or dolphins fitting marine sponges to their beaks in order to dig for
15 food on the seabed; or wasps using small stones to smooth the sand around their egg chambers, concealing them from predators. At the same time neurobiologists have been finding that the physical structures in our own brains most commonly held responsible for
20 consciousness are not as rare in the animal kingdom as had been assumed. Indeed they are common. All of this work and discovery appeared to reach a kind of crescendo last summer, when an international group of prominent neuroscientists meeting at the University of
25 Cambridge issued "The Cambridge Declaration on Consciousness in Non-Human Animals," a document stating that "humans are not unique in possessing the neurological substrates that generate consciousness." It goes further to conclude that numerous documented
30 animal behaviors must be considered "consistent with experienced feeling states."

1

Which choice best describes the organization of this passage?

A) A theory is offered, an experiment is presented, and a critique is offered.

B) An existing model is discussed, its flaws are examined, and a new model is proposed.

C) Several examples of animal behavior are presented, and their significance is analyzed.

D) An assertion is made, and specific examples are provided to support it.

2

In line 21, the author's focus shifts from

A) a series of examples to a description of an outcome.

B) focus on an individual to a consideration of a group.

C) an examination of a problem to a proposal of a solution.

D) a discussion of a claim to a questioning of that claim.

2. The following passage is adapted from Jane Austen, *Northanger Abbey*, originally published in 1817.

No one who had ever seen Catherine Morland in her infancy would have supposed her born to be an heroine. Her situation in life, the character of her father and mother, her own person and disposition, were all
5 equally against her.

Her father was a clergyman, without being neglected, or poor, and a very respectable man, though his name was Richard—and he had never been handsome. He had a considerable independence besides
10 two good livings—and he was not in the least addicted to locking up his daughters. Her mother was a woman of useful plain sense, with a good temper, and, what is more remarkable, with a good constitution. She had three sons before Catherine was born; and instead of
15 dying in bringing the latter into the world, as anybody might expect, she still lived on—lived to have six children more—to see them growing up around her, and to enjoy excellent health herself. A family of ten children will be always called a fine family, where there
20 are heads and arms and legs enough for the number; but the Morlands had little other right to the word, for they were in general very plain, and Catherine, for many years of her life, as plain as any. She had a thin awkward figure, a sallow skin without colour, dark lank
25 hair, and strong features—so much for her person; and not less unpropitious for heroism seemed her mind. She was fond of all boy's plays, and greatly preferred cricket not merely to dolls, but to the more heroic enjoyments of infancy, nursing a dormouse, feeding a
30 canary-bird, or watering a rose-bush. Indeed she had no taste for a garden; and if she gathered flowers at all, it was chiefly for the pleasure of mischief— at least so it was conjectured from her always preferring those which she was forbidden to take.
35 Such were her propensities—her abilities were quite as extraordinary. She never could learn or understand anything before she was taught; and sometimes not even then, for she was often inattentive, and occasionally stupid. Her mother was three months in teaching her
40 only to repeat the "Beggar's Petition"; and after all, her next sister, Sally, could say it better than she did. Not that Catherine was always stupid—by no means; she learnt the fable of "The Hare and Many Friends" as quickly as any girl in England. Her mother wished her
45 to learn music; and Catherine was sure she should like it, for she was very fond of tinkling the keys of the old forlorn spinner; so, at eight years old she began. She learnt a year, and could not bear it; and Mrs. Morland, who did not insist on her daughters being accomplished in

50 spite of incapacity or distaste, allowed her to leave off. The day which dismissed the music-master was one of the happiest of Catherine's life. Her taste for drawing was not superior; though whenever she could obtain the outside of a letter from her mother or seize
55 upon any other odd piece of paper, she did what she could in that way, by drawing houses and trees, hens and chickens, all very much like one another. Writing and accounts she was taught by her father; French by her mother: her proficiency in either was not
60 remarkable, and she shirked her lessons in both whenever she could. What a strange, unaccountable character!—for with all these symptoms of profligacy at ten years old, she had neither a bad heart nor a bad temper, was seldom stubborn, scarcely ever
65 quarrelsome, and very kind to the little ones, with few interruptions of tyranny; she was moreover noisy and wild, hated confinement and cleanliness, and loved nothing so well in the world as rolling down the green slope at the back of the house.

1

This passage is written from the perspective of

A) a member of Catherine's family who is critical of Catherine's upbringing.

B) an observer familiar with Catherine and her family.

C) a character who finds herself at odds with her family.

D) a character who is puzzled by the constraints placed on her by society.

2

The words "never," "not even," and "inattentive" (lines 36-38) mainly have the effect of

A) rebuking Catherine's mother for her excessive demands on her daughter.

B) pointing out Catherine's contrary nature.

C) calling attention to Catherine's lack of precociousness.

D) provoking a sense of sympathy for Catherine's misbehavior.

3. This passage is adapted from Barry Schwartz, "More Isn't Always Better," © 2006 by *Harvard Business Review.*

Marketers assume that the more choices they offer, the more likely customers will be able to find just the right thing. They assume, for instance, that offering 50 styles of jeans instead of two increases the chances that
5 shoppers will find a pair they really like. Nevertheless, research now shows that there can be too much choice; when there is, consumers are less likely to buy anything at all, and if they do buy, they are less satisfied with their selection.
10 It all began with jam. In 2000, psychologists Sheena Iyengar and Mark Lepper published a remarkable study. On one day, shoppers at an upscale food market saw a display table with 24 varieties of gourmet jam. Those who sampled the spreads received a coupon for $1 off
15 any jam. On another day, shoppers saw a similar table, except that only six varieties of the jam were on display. The large display attracted more interest than the small one. But when the time came to purchase, people who saw the large display were one-tenth as likely to buy as
20 people who saw the small display.

Other studies have confirmed this result that more choice is not always better. As the variety of snacks, soft drinks, and beers offered at convenience stores increases, for instance, sales volume and customer
25 satisfaction decrease. Moreover, as the number of retirement investment options available to employees increases, the chance that they will choose any decreases. These studies and others have shown not only that excessive choice can produce "choice
30 paralysis," but also that it can reduce people's satisfaction with their decisions, even if they made good ones. My colleagues and I have found that increased choice decreases satisfaction with matters as trivial as ice cream flavors and as significant as jobs.
35 These results challenge what we think we know about human nature and the determinants of well-being. Both psychology and business have operated on the assumption that the relationship between choice and well-being is straightforward: The more choices people
40 have, the better off they are. In psychology, the benefits of choice have been tied to autonomy and control. In business, the benefits of choice have been tied to the benefits of free markets more generally. Added options make no one worse off, and they are bound to make
45 someone better off.

Choice *is* good for us, but its relationship to satisfaction appears to be more complicated than we had assumed. There is diminishing marginal utility in having alternatives; each new option subtracts a little
50 from the feeling of well-being, until the marginal benefits of added choice level off. What's more, psychologists and business academics alike have largely ignored another outcome of choice: More of it requires increased time and effort and can lead to
55 anxiety, regret, excessively high expectations, and self-blame if the choices don't work out. When the number of available options is small, these costs are negligible, but the costs grow with the number of options. Eventually, each new option makes us feel
60 worse off than we did before.

Without a doubt, having more options enables us, most of the time, to achieve better objective outcomes. Again, having 50 styles of jeans as opposed to two increases the likelihood that customers will find a pair
65 that fits. But the subjective outcome may be that shoppers will feel overwhelmed and dissatisfied. This dissociation between objective and subjective results creates a significant challenge for retailers and marketers that look to choice as a way to enhance the
70 perceived value of their goods and services.

Choice can no longer be used to justify a marketing strategy in and of itself. More isn't always better, either for the customer or for the retailer. Discovering how much assortment is warranted is a
75 considerable empirical challenge. But companies that get the balance right will be amply rewarded.

1

This passage is written from the perspective of

A) an interested observer who believes that customers should be offered as many choices as possible.

B) a person who is knowledgeable about economic theory but who lacks practical experience.

C) a researcher actively engaged in studying the effects of choice on consumer behavior.

D) a marketing expert who wants to advertise products more effectively.

Which of the following best describes the
organization of the first two paragraphs
(lines 1-20)?

A) A claim is presented, an opposing claim is
offered, and evidence is provided.

B) An unexpected finding is described, and an
attempt to dismiss the finding is made.

C) A hypothesis is proposed, an experiment is
carried out, and the results are analyzed.

D) Competing explanations for a phenomenon
are discussed, and the results of a study
designed to test them are evaluated.

4. The following passage is adapted from Olympe de Gouges, *Declaration of the Rights of Women*. It was initially published in 1791, during the French Revolution, and was written in response to the *Declaration of the Rights of Man* (1789).

Woman, wake up; the toxin of reason is being heard throughout the whole universe; discover your rights. The powerful empire of nature is no longer surrounded by prejudice, fanaticism, superstition, and
5 lies. The flame of truth has dispersed all the clouds of folly and usurpation. Enslaved man has multiplied his strength and needs recourse to yours to break his chains. Having become free, he has become unjust to his companion. Oh, women, women! When will you cease
10 to be blind? What advantage have you received from the Revolution? A more pronounced scorn, a more marked disdain. In the centuries of corruption you ruled only over the weakness of men. The reclamation of your patrimony, based on the wise decrees of nature –
15 what have you to dread from such a fine undertaking? Do you fear that our legislators, correctors of that morality, long ensnared by political practices now out of date, will only say again to you: women, what is there in common between you and us? Everything, you
20 will have to answer. If they persist in their weakness in putting this hypocrisy in contradiction to their principles, courageously oppose the force of reason to the empty pretensions of superiority; unite yourselves beneath the standards of philosophy; deploy all the
25 energy of your character. Regardless of what barriers confront you, it is in your power to free yourselves; you have only to want to. Let us pass not to the shocking tableau of what you have been in society; and since national education is in question at this moment, let us
30 see whether our wise legislators will think judiciously about the education of women.
  Women have done more harm than good. Constraint and dissimulation have been their lot. What force has robbed them of, ruse returned to them; they had recourse
35 to all the resources of their charms, and the most irreproachable persons did not resist them. Poison and the sword were both subject to them; they commanded in crime as in fortune. The French government, especially, depended throughout the centuries on the nocturnal
40 administrations of women; the cabinet could keep no secrets as a result of their indiscretions; all have been subject to the cupidity and ambition of this sex, formerly contemptible and respected, and since the revolution, respectable and scorned.

45   In this sort of contradictory situation, what remarks could I not make! I have but a moment to make them, but this moment will fix the attention of the remotest posterity. Under the Old Regime, all was vicious, all was guilty; but could not the amelioration of
50 conditions be perceived even in the substance of vices? A woman only had to be beautiful or amiable; when she possessed these two advantages, she saw a hundred fortunes at her feet. If she did not profit from them, she had a bizarre character or a rare philosophy
55 which made her scorn wealth; then she was deemed to be like a crazy woman. A young, inexperienced woman, seduced by a man whom she loves, will abandon her parents to follow him; the ingrate will leave her after a few years, and the older she has
60 become with him, the more inhuman is his inconstancy; if she has children, he will likewise abandon them. If he is rich, he will consider himself excused from sharing his fortune with his noble victims. If some involvement binds him to his duties, he will
65 deny them, trusting that the laws will support him. If he is married, any other obligation loses its rights. Then what laws remain to extirpate vice all the way to its root? The law of dividing wealth and public administration between men and women. It can easily
70 be seen that one who is born into a rich family gains very much from such equal sharing. But the one born into a poor family with merit and virtue – what is her lot? Poverty and opprobrium. If she does not precisely excel in music or painting, she cannot be admitted to
75 any public function when she has all the capacity for it.

1

Which of the following best characterizes the narrator's shift in focus in lines 45-46?

A) She shifts from criticizing a group of people to praising that group.

B) She shifts from discussing political affairs to discussing artistic affairs.

C) She shifts from discussing opposing views to attempting to reconcile those views.

D) She shifts from describing a problem to offering a personal opinion.

5. The following passage is adapted from "Scientists Discover Salty Aquifer, Previously Unknown Microbial Habitat Under Antarctica," © 2015 by Dartmouth College.

Using an airborne imaging system for the first time in Antarctica, scientists have discovered a vast network of unfrozen salty groundwater that may support previously unknown microbial life deep under the coldest, driest
5 desert on our planet. The findings shed new light on ancient climate change on Earth and provide strong evidence that a similar briny aquifer could support microscopic life on Mars. The scientists used SkyTEM, an airborne electromagnetic sensor, to detect and map
10 otherwise inaccessible subterranean features.

The system uses an antennae suspended beneath a helicopter to create a magnetic field that reveals the subsurface to a depth of about 1,000 feet. Because a helicopter was used, large areas of rugged terrain could
15 be surveyed. The SkyTEM team was funded by the National Science Foundation and led by researchers from the University of Tennessee, Knoxville (UTK), and Dartmouth College, which oversees the NSF's SkyTEM project.

20 "These unfrozen materials appear to be relics of past surface ecosystems and our findings provide compelling evidence that they now provide deep subsurface habitats for microbial life despite extreme environmental conditions," says lead author Jill Mikucki,
25 an assistant professor at UTK. "These new below-ground visualization technologies can also provide insight on glacial dynamics and how Antarctica responds to climate change."

Co-author Dartmouth Professor Ross Virginia is
30 SkyTEM's co-principal investigator and director of Dartmouth's Institute of Arctic Studies. "This project is studying the past and present climate to, in part, understand how climate change in the future will affect biodiversity and ecosystem processes," Virginia says.
35 "This fantastic new view beneath the surface will help us sort out competing ideas about how the McMurdo Dry Valleys have changed with time and how this history influences what we see today."

The researchers found that the unfrozen brines form
40 extensive, interconnected aquifers deep beneath glaciers and lakes and within permanently frozen soils. The brines extend from the coast to at least 7.5 miles inland in the McMurdo Dry Valleys, the largest ice-free region in Antarctica. The brines could be due to freezing and/or
45 deposits. The findings show for the first time that the Dry Valleys' lakes are interconnected rather than isolated; connectivity between lakes and aquifers is important in sustaining ecosystems through drastic climate change, such as lake dry-down events. The findings also challenge

50 the assumption that parts of the ice sheets below the pressure melting point are devoid of liquid water. In addition to providing answers about the biological adaptations of previously unknown ecosystems that persist in the extreme cold and dark of the Antarctic
55 winter, the new study could help scientists to understand whether similar conditions might exist elsewhere in the solar system, specifically beneath the surface of Mars, which has many similarities to the Dry Valleys. Overall, the Dry Valleys ecosystem –
60 cold, vegetation-free and home only to microscopic animal and plant life – resembles, during the Antarctic summer, conditions on the surface on Mars.

SkyTEM produced images of Taylor Valley along the Ross Sea that suggest briny sediments exist at
65 subsurface temperatures down to perhaps -68°F, which is considered suitable for microbial life. One of the studied areas was lower Taylor Glacier, where the data suggest ancient brine still exists beneath the glacier. That conclusion is supported by the presence
70 of Blood Falls, an iron-rich brine that seeps out of the glacier and hosts an active microbial ecosystem.

Scientists' understanding of Antarctica's underground environment is changing dramatically as research reveals that subglacial lakes are widespread
75 and that at least half of the areas covered by the ice sheet are akin to wetlands on other continents. But groundwater in the ice-free regions and along the coastal margins remains poorly understood.

1

Which choice best describes the organization of this passage?

A) An experiment is discussed, and several interpretations of its results are analyzed.

B) A finding is described, and the implications of that finding are considered.

C) A hypothesis is presented, an attempt to validate it using new technology is described, and the resulting data are evaluated.

D) An ecosystem on Earth is compared to an an ecosystem on Mars, and the origin of each is discussed.

Explanations: Rhetorical Strategy Exercises

1.1 D

Don't get distracted by the lengthy answer choices. In reality, all you need is the first sentence of the passage: *These are stimulating times for anyone interested in questions of animal consciousness.* That is a subjective statement, i.e., an assertion. That points right to D). The rest of the passage consists of details supporting the claim: first, the findings that animals exhibit sophisticated behaviors, and then the description of the "Cambridge Declaration."

1.2 A

What sort of information precedes line 21? A series of examples illustrating the idea that animals are likely capable of conscious thought. What happens in line 21? The author begins to describe the meeting of neuroscientists at Cambridge – the phrase *All of this work and discovery appeared to reach a kind of crescendo last summer* indicates that the meeting was the result of the discoveries described in the previous section of the passage. The shift from examples to result (=outcome) corresponds to A).

2.1 B

The passage is written from an objective, third-person point of view: Catherine and her family members are referred to as *she*, *he*, and *they*. Furthermore, the narration is purely descriptive. The narrator knows a lot about Catherine and her family but is not directly involved in the action. That eliminates C) and D). Choosing between A) and B), you might run into trouble if you don't realize that the description of Catherine's faults is ironic. The narrator is not actually criticizing Catherine but rather poking fun at the convention of a too-good-to-be-true heroine. That eliminates A). B) is correct because the narrator is simply an observer who is very familiar with the lives of Catherine and her family.

2.2 C

To simplify this question, rephrase it as, "what point are the words *never, not even,* and *inattentive* used to make?" Essentially, they are intended to emphasize the fact that Catherine's abilities aren't particularly extraordinary for a girl of her age. In other words, she lack precociousness (exceptional maturity). That makes C) the answer.

3.1 C

This question throws an awful lot of information at you, but in fact it can be answered very quickly using only one tiny section of the passage. The use of the first person in the phrase *My colleagues and I* indicates that the writer is personally involved ("actively engaged") in the type of research he describes. The answer is therefore C).

3.2 A

To simplify this question, match the beginning of the passage to the beginning of an answer choice. The repetition of the word *assume* (lines 1 and 3), followed by the phrase *Nevertheless, research now shows* indicates "old idea/new idea," or claim and opposing claim. That corresponds directly to A).

4.1 D

The easiest way to answer this question is to recognize that the word *I* appears for the first time in line 46, indicating a shift to a first-person (personal) point of view. That corresponds to D).

5.1 B

The easiest way to answer this question is to match the beginning of the passage to the beginning of an answer choice. The first sentence of the passage refers to the fact that scientists have *discovered* something. Discovery = finding, making B) correct.

Paired Passages

Not surprisingly, paired passages are many people's least favorite part of SAT Reading. They often hit you just when you're starting to tire, and they demand a level of focus that goes even beyond that required for the rest of the section. Moreover, they are often filled with antiquated language and complex syntax, making literal comprehension a less straightforward matter than it is on the rest of the Reading Test. Although there is no simple way to make these passages and questions easy, breaking them down carefully can go a long way toward making them more manageable.

If you are taking APUSH or another challenging U.S. History class that makes substantial use of primary sources, this type of writing will probably be familiar to you. It is even possible that you will encounter documents you've studied in class – or, if not the exact documents, then very similar ones. If you are unaccustomed to reading old-fashioned prose, however, these passages may represent a more significant challenge.

If you are a strong reader who handles this type of writing well, you can probably approach paired passages much as you approach the other type of passages. If, however, you find relationship questions consistently too confusing or time consuming, you should consider skipping them entirely (filling in your favorite letter) in order to spend more time on the questions that ask about each passage individually. Typically you will encounter only three or four relationship questions per test, so skipping them does not represent a major sacrifice of points. **In fact, if you are not aiming for a very high score and struggle disproportionately with these questions, you are probably better off using the time you would have spent on them to answer other, more straightforward questions.**

Alternately, you may want to skim through the relationship questions to see whether any of them seem manageable. If you find one(s), you can do it/them and skip the others.

Or, if paired passages take you noticeably longer than the other passages but you are still able to answer the questions given enough time, you can always plan to leave them for last, regardless of where they appear. That way, you will not risk spending more time on a smaller number of questions mid-way through the section, forcing yourself to rush through a greater number of questions later on.

Regardless of what option you choose, if you find paired passages in any way problematic, you should have a clear strategy for managing them before you walk into the test.

Overview of Paired Passages

The College Board refers to paired passages as "The Great Global Conversation," but in reality this title is somewhat exaggerated. Based on the exams released thus far, the "conversation" consists primarily of excerpts from nineteenth-century American documents presenting **conflicting views** on some aspect of equality or social/political rights – most frequently involving the status of women and African Americans. An occasional European writer might be thrown in for variety, as might a set of passages written in the late eighteenth- or early twentieth century, but the majority of passage sets stay within a fairly restricted set of time periods and themes.

Both passages will *always* discuss the same idea or event, and thus far they appear to conform to a fairly predictable pattern: **Passage 1** expresses the **"anti-" argument or less radical position** (e.g., women should not be granted the same rights as men; people should not violate unjust laws but rather work to change them) and is more **negative** in tone. **Passage 2**, in contrast, typically **celebrates inclusion and full equality** for all groups, and is more **positive**. The College Board shows a clear preference for ending on a good note.

While the relationship between the passages is typically the same from test to test, the way in which the College Board asks about that relationship is not. Instead of asking you to identify a "contrast" or "disagreement," questions may instead use more abstract or confusing language, requiring you to identify the "central tension" or "conflict" between the passages. Do not let the phrasing fool you into thinking that you are being asked to do something very complicated! Instead, stay focused on the fact that you are simply being asked to recognize what major point the authors of the passages disagree about.

As you read, you should also make sure to note any major stylistic differences between the passages. For example, is one written from a first-person perspective (*I*) while the other is written from an objective, third-person (*he, she, it*) stance? If so, then the first passage is by definition more personal than the second, and the second one is by definition more detached/neutral/objective than the first – prime fodder for relationship questions.

All that said, you should keep in mind that **these patterns may shift as the test evolves,** and not assume that the passages in the *Official Guide* are fully representative of what could appear on future exams. It is possible, for example, that a handful of other, subtler relationships (which regularly appeared on the old SAT) may become more relevant:

- Passage 1 and Passage 2 agree but have different (not necessarily opposing) focuses or stylistic differences.

- Passage 1 and Passage 2 discuss different aspects of the same event or idea.

- Passage 2 provides an example of an idea described generally in Passage 1.

- Passage 2 provides an explanation for a phenomenon discussed in Passage 1.

Also: If you look through the *Official Guide*, you'll notice that the first test includes a science-themed pair, whereas the other seven tests use historical documents. Although it seems reasonable to assume that many future tests will include paired historical documents as well, it is also possible that other types of passages will be used. I am therefore including a science example among the exercises for the sake of thoroughness.

How to Read Paired Passages

As a general rule, **your goal should be to deal with the smallest amount of information possible at any given time.** The more work you do in terms of determining arguments upfront, the less work you'll need to do later. And when you break questions down and work through them methodically, you greatly reduce the chance of confusion.

So in a nutshell:

1. Clearly mark the questions that ask about Passage 1 only; the ones that ask about Passage 2 only; and the ones that ask about both passages.

2. Read Passage 1: write main point + tone

3. Answer Passage 1 questions

4. Read Passage 2: write main point + tone AND relationship to Passage 1

5. Answer Passage 2 questions

6. Answer Passage 1/Passage 2 relationship questions

It is important to determine the relationship between the passages upfront because you will always encounter questions that test your understanding of that relationship. Some of these questions will be worded very directly ("Which choice best describes the relationship between the passages?"), while others will be more roundabout, asking you to infer how the author of one passage would most likely respond to a statement made in the other passage.

Either way, if you've already defined the topic and the relationship, you've essentially answered some of these questions before you've even looked at them. If the authors of the two passages disagree – which, as we've seen, they usually will – correct answers to relationship questions will usually be negative. You can thus eliminate positive and neutral options, which can often be identified from the first few words of the answer. Furthermore, when answers include more detailed information about the passages, you may sometimes be able to use the main points themselves. (For a good example, see Test 8, #39.)

If you choose to skip some of the questions, or you leave the paired passages for last and start to run short on time, you can also use your knowledge of the test's structure to help you make educated guesses. For example, take a look at the following question. We don't even need a set of passages here – our only concern is how to use the framework of the test to predict the most probable answer.

1

Compared with Douglass's view in Passage 1 of "America," King's view in Passage 2 of "the American people" is more

A) objective.
B) despondent.
C) uplifting.
D) doubtful.

The key to predicting the most likely answer lies in the question, which asks what quality Passage 2 has "more" of. Based on the most common pattern, you can assume that Passage 2 is more positive than Passage 1, and that the correct answer is positive as well.

B) and D) are negative, and A) is neutral, leaving C) as the only positive option. Note, by the way, that it does not matter whether you know what *despondent* means as long as you can recognize that *uplifting* fits. The prefix DE- also suggests that B) is negative.

To be very clear: If you are answering the questions for real, you can assume that there will sometimes be exceptions to the usual pattern, and you should <u>always</u> go back to the passage for confirmation. You can, however, save time by checking the most likely answer first. For a question like the one above, you could work from the assumption that C) was correct and then reread the appropriate lines to double-check. If you recognized that C) fit, you could choose it and move on; if you didn't, you could then consider the other answers.

You should also be aware that some questions will ask you to identify a statement with which both authors would agree, even when the passages clearly convey conflicting opinions. In such cases, you must proceed very carefully. Answers to these questions may depend on an easily overlooked detail in one or both of the passages. Sometimes that detail will be located in a key place (introduction, last sentence, a topic sentence, close to a major transition or a dash/colon), but sometimes it will not. Because it is very unlikely that you will remember the information necessary to answer the question, you should always plan to return to the passages as necessary. You should also make sure not to eliminate any answer you're uncertain about until you have confirmed that it is incorrect.

I repeat: Do not even attempt to rely on your memory. Just read.

Relationship Questions are Inference Questions

Because there is absolutely no difference between questions that ask about one passage in a paired passage set, and questions that ask about single passages elsewhere on the test, there is absolutely no difference in how you should approach questions that ask about Passage 1 or Passage 2 only.

For most students, the real challenge is the relationship questions, which ask you to infer how one author would likely react to the other's ideas. When you encounter these questions, you must take the time to break them down, defining each idea separately and clearly before attempting to determine the relationship between the two perspectives.

Relationship questions should be broken down in the following way:

1. Reread the lines in question and sum up the idea in your own words.

2. Reiterate the main point of the other passage.

3. Determine whether the authors would agree or disagree.

4. Look at the answers: if the authors would agree, eliminate all negative options; if the authors would disagree, eliminate all positive options.

5. Check the remaining answers against the passage, focusing on the most specific part of each answer.

It is extremely important that you take a moment and write or underline the main point of each passage because if an answer to a Passage 1/Passage 2 relationship question restates the main point of the appropriate passage, that answer will almost certainly be correct.

This guideline becomes exceedingly important when questions are phrased in a roundabout or complex manner. As long as you know which passage is being asked about and what the point of that passage is, you can probably find your way to the answer. For an excellent example of how this applies to a real SAT question, see Test 7, #41: the question is phrased in an exceptionally complicated way, but the correct answer, A), merely restates the point of Passage 2 (which appears in the last sentence).

In addition, note that if you ever encounter an answer to a relationship question indicating that one author would lack interest in the other author's argument (e.g., *apathetic, indifferent*), that answer will almost certainly be incorrect. Passages are chosen precisely because there is a clear relationship between the authors' ideas, so these words are inconsistent with the framework of the test.

Beginning on the next page, we're going to look at a sample set of passages along with some questions.

Passage 1 is adapted from J.B. Sanford, *Argument Against Senate Constitutional Amendment No. 8*. Passage 2 is adapted from Susan B. Anthony, *Woman's Rights to the Suffrage*. Anthony delivered this speech in 1873, after being arrested for voting in the 1872 presidential election. Sanford was the Chairman of the 1911 California Democratic Caucus.

Passage 1

Suffrage is not a right. It is a privilege that may or may not be granted. Politics is no place for a woman; consequently the privilege should not be granted to her.

The mother's influence is needed in the home. She
5 can do little good by gadding the streets and neglecting her children. Let her teach her daughters that modesty, patience, and gentleness are the charms of women... The mothers of this country can shape the destinies of the nation by keeping in their places and attending to
10 those duties that God Almighty intended for them. The kindly, gentle influence of the mother in the home and the dignified influence of the teacher in the school will far outweigh all the influence of all the mannish female politicians on earth.

15 Do women have to vote in order to receive the protection of man? Why, men have gone to war, endured every privation and death itself in defense of woman. To man, woman is the dearest creature on earth, and there is no extreme to which he would not go
20 for his mother or sister. By keeping woman in her exalted position man can be induced to do more for her than he could by having her mix up in affairs that will cause him to lose respect and regard for her. Woman does not have to vote to secure her rights. Man will go
25 to any extreme to protect and elevate her now. As long as woman is woman and keeps her place she will get more protection and more consideration than man gets. When she abdicates her throne she throws down the scepter of her power and loses her influence.

30 Woman is woman. She can not unsex herself or change her sphere. Let her be content with her lot and perform those high duties intended for her by the Great Creator, and she will accomplish far more in governmental affairs than she can ever accomplish by
35 mixing up in the dirty pool of politics. Keep the home pure and all will be well with the Republic. Let not the sanctity of the home be invaded by every little politician that may be running up and down the highway for office. Let the manly men and the
40 womanly women defeat this amendment and keep woman where she belongs in order that she may retain the respect of all mankind.

Passage 2

Friends and Fellow Citizens: I stand before you tonight under indictment for the alleged crime of
45 having voted at the last presidential election, without having a lawful right to vote. It shall be my work this evening to prove to you that in thus voting, I not only committed no crime, but, instead, simply exercised my citizen's rights, guaranteed to me and all United
50 States citizens by the National Constitution, beyond the power of any State to deny.

The preamble of the Federal Constitution says: "We, the people of the United States, in order to form a more perfect union, establish justice, insure
55 domestic tranquility, provide for the common defense, promote the general welfare, and secure the blessings of liberty to ourselves and our posterity, do ordain and establish this Constitution for the United States of America..."

60 **For any State to make sex a qualification that must ever result in the disfranchisement of one entire half of the people is therefore a violation of the supreme law of the land.** By it the blessings of liberty are for ever withheld from women and their
65 female posterity. To them this government has no just powers derived from the consent of the governed. To them this government is not a democracy. It is not a republic. It is an odious aristocracy; a hateful oligarchy of sex; the most hateful aristocracy ever
70 established on the face of the globe...

It was we, the people; not we, the white male citizens; nor yet we, the male citizens; but we, the whole people, who formed the Union. And we formed it, not to give the blessings of liberty, but to secure
75 them; not to the half of ourselves and the half of our posterity, but to the whole people—women as well as men. And it is a downright mockery to talk to women of their enjoyment of the blessings of liberty while they are denied the use of the only means of securing
80 them provided by this democratic-republican government—the ballot.

The only question left to be settled now is: Are women persons? And I hardly believe any of our opponents will have the hardihood to say they are not.
85 Being persons, then, women are citizens; and no State has a right to make any law, or to enforce any old law, that shall abridge their privileges or immunities. Hence, every discrimination against women in the constitutions and laws of the several States is today
90 null and void, precisely as in every one against Negroes.

Let's start by breaking things down:

Passage 1

Main point: women shouldn't vote
Tone: negative (condescending)

Passage 2

Main point: women should vote
Tone: positive (determined)

Relationship: Disagree

Notice that although both passages contain a fair amount of information, they do not contain a lot of different ideas. Unlike science passages, which tend to detail the various stages of an experiment, both passages here remain focused on supporting a single point. This is important because it means that if you get the gist, you don't have to struggle through every last turn of phrase.

Luckily, Passage 1 gives you the point in the first three lines. The rest of the passage serves only to elaborate on it. Passage 2 doesn't directly state the point right away, but Anthony's first-paragraph discussion of her illegal decision to vote provides a pretty good clue about where things are headed. Besides, you can pretty much infer what Passage 2 will be about just from reading Passage 1: the College Board would never permit Sanford's view to stand unchallenged, and a response from a well-known suffragist (Anthony, Elizabeth Cady Stanton, Carrie Chapman Catt, or Lucretia Mott) is the logical choice for Passage 2.

At the same time, however, you should notice that neither author's argument is entirely one-dimensional. Instead, they are both positive and negative in turn. Sanford in Passage 1, for example, is opposed to women acquiring the right to vote, but he is quite positive toward women themselves. Phrases such as *dearest creature on earth* (lines 18-19) and *exalted* (lofty, elevated) *position* (line 21) convey that attitude. Likewise, Anthony (Passage 2) clearly has a positive attitude toward the Constitution, which promises full rights to all citizens, and a negative attitude toward the fact that women are prohibited from exercising those rights.

All that considered, let's start by looking at a straightforward relationship question:

1

Which choice best states the relationship between the two passages?

A) Passage 2 proposes an alternate explanation for a phenomenon presented in Passage 1.

B) Passage 2 discredits the results of an undertaking discussed in Passage 1.

C) Passage 2 considers the implications of a belief alluded to in Passage 1.

D) Passage 2 denounces an idea that is defended in Passage 1.

We know that the authors of the two passages disagree, so we can assume that the correct answer will be negative. If we start by looking at the beginning of each answer choice, we can see that only B) and D) are negative, suggesting that we should check them first.

"Discredits" is almost certainly too strong – 40 lines aren't enough to discredit anything – but "denounces" is a bit more moderate. And indeed, D) is consistent with the fact that Anthony takes serious issue with the notion that women should be denied the full rights of citizenship on the grounds of gender – an idea that the author of Passage 1 clearly defends.

Another type of relationship question essentially asks you to identify the main point of each passage:

1

Which choice best states describes the way that the two authors conceive of women's proper role in society?

A) Sanford believes that women's role should be confined to the domestic sphere, while Anthony believes that women should participate fully in public life.

B) Sanford believes that women should be dependent on their husbands, while Anthony believes that women should seek their own sources of income.

C) Sanford believes that women are emotionally unsuited to holding office while Anthony believes that they are superior politicians.

D) Sanford believes that women should place the needs of their families above their own desires, while Anthony believes that women should focus on their own interests.

Don't be put off by the fact that the answer choices give you so much information to wade through. In reality, the question is much simpler than it appears.

What is the topic of both passages? Whether women should vote. That's it. There is no mention of whether women should work outside the home, so B) can be eliminated. There is also no discussion of whether women should place their own needs or those of their families first, eliminating D).

Now, be careful with C). The passages do have a political theme, but there is no explicit discussion of whether women should hold office, or of whether they are better politicians than men. So C) can be eliminated as well.

That leaves A), which phrases the topic more abstractly ("public life") but accurately captures the contrast between the views in the two passages: Sanford thinks that women should focus on home and family ("the domestic sphere"), whereas Anthony believes that women should enjoy all of the rights of citizenship.

You could also be asked to identify a difference involving style or point of view. Such questions do not appear frequently, but they are fair game for the test.

1

In comparison to the author of Passage 1, the author of Passage 2 is more

A) doubtful.
B) decisive.
C) personal.
D) detached.

If you notice that the word *I* appears in Passage 2 but not Passage 1, you can jump to C). A passage in the first person is by definition more *personal* than one in the third person.

Another way in which the SAT tests relationships between passages involves asking how the author of one passage would likely respond to the author of the other passage. **Every exam typically includes at least one of these questions.**

1

Anthony would most likely have reacted to lines 25-29 ("As…influence") of Passage 2 with

A) agreement, because she believes that women can achieve equality in a variety of ways.
B) appreciation, because she believes that and health could lead to new therapies.
C) disapproval, because she believes that political rights are necessary for full participation in society.
D) skepticism, because she believes that differences between men and women have been exaggerated.

The shortest way to answer this question is to use the relationship between the passages. The authors disagree very strongly, so the correct answer will almost certainly be negative. You can skim the line reference for confirmation; then, look at only the first word of each answer. *Agreement* and *appreciation* are both positive, so you can eliminate A) and B) right away.

Now, be careful with D). You might find it logical to assume that someone who holds such strong views about equality would also think that differences between men and women have been overblown. But Anthony never discusses that idea directly. Her focus is on the rights that the Constitution ensures to women as *people*. She makes no mention of the differences between men and women, or how large those differences are.

In contrast, C) pretty much sums up the main point of Passage 2: women are entitled to full citizenship, and that includes the right to vote. So C) is correct.

Otherwise, you can ignore the choices provided and answer the question on your own. Although this may seem like a more time-consuming approach, it can actually save you time by allowing you to jump to the correct answer and bypass any potential distractors.

1) Reread the lines in question and summarize them.

As long as woman is woman and keeps her place she will get more protection and more consideration than man gets. When she abdicates [steps down from] her throne she throws down the scepter of her power and loses her influence. Basically, women can only have power by not having power.

2) Restate the point of the <u>other</u> passage. (In this case, Passage 2)

P2: Women are entitled to all of the rights of full citizens.

3) Determine what the author of the other passage would think.

It's pretty clear that the authors would disagree. Why? Because Anthony believes that women must have the same political rights as men in order to truly be free – which is pretty much what C) says. Working this way allows you bypass the temptation of D).

You will also encounter relationship questions whose answers are less obviously phrased in terms of positive and negative. To be sure, you can still use this technique to eliminate answers – you just have to read a bit more closely to do so.

1

Sanford in Passage 1 would most likely characterize the position taken by Anthony in lines 47-51 ("I not...deny") in Passage 2 as

A) overly ambitious in comparison to the goals of moderate suffragists.

B) incompatible with women's natural role in society.

C) a compelling example of the democratic process in action.

D) consistent with the Constitutional ideals of liberty and equality.

Lines 47-50: *I not only committed no crime, but, instead, simply exercised my citizen's rights, guaranteed to me and all United States citizens by the National Constitution, beyond the power of any State to deny.*

That is a position that Sanford would clearly reject, so the answer must be negative.

Again, focus on the beginning of each answer. "Overly ambitious" and "incompatible" are negative, so A) and B) both stay. "Compelling" and "consistent" are positive, so C) and D) can be eliminated.

Upon closer inspection, A) can be crossed out as well because Sanford does not even mention moderate suffragists. Based on Passage 1, he appears to be opposed to *all* suffragists. That leaves B), which accurately states his position.

Paired Passages and Supporting Evidence Questions

Although you can assume that questions asking about only Passage 1 or Passage 2 will sometimes be followed by supporting evidence questions, the appearance of these questions in relation to paired passage *relationship* questions is unfortunately somewhat unclear. If you look at the first four tests in the *Official Guide*, you'll notice that some questions asking about the relationship between the two passages are followed by questions asking you to identify the lines that support the previous question. In later (administered) tests, however, such questions no longer appear. Given that, it seems unlikely you will encounter one when you take the exam; however, I am including an example below for the sake of caution.

The question we just looked at on the previous page could, for example, be asked this way:

1

Sanford in Passage 1 would most likely characterize the position taken by Anthony in lines 47-51 ("I not...deny") in Passage 2 as

A) overly ambitious in comparison to the goals of moderate suffragists.

B) incompatible with women's natural role in society.

C) a compelling example of the democratic process in action.

D) consistent with the Constitutional ideals of liberty and equality.

2

Which choice provides the best evidence for the answer to the previous question?

A) Lines 16-18 ("Why, men...woman")

B) Lines 18-19 ("To man...earth")

C) Lines 24-25 ("Man...now")

D) Lines 30-31 ("Woman...sphere")

As we've seen, the most efficient way to solve supporting evidence pairs is often to plug the answers to the second question into the first question and work from there. When supporting evidence questions are coupled with paired passage relationship questions, however, a bit more flexibility is required.

If you are able to answer the first question quickly using the main point, you should answer the questions in order. Then, you can simply check each line reference in the second question to see if it supports the correct idea.

If, on the other hand, the answer is based on a detail not directly related to the main point, you may be better served by plugging the line references in the second question into the first question.

It's fairly easy to answer Question #1 by using the main point of Passage 1: B) effectively sums up Sanford's argument. However, that information alone is unlikely to give you the answer to Question #2 since pretty much all of Passage 1 is devoted to the idea that women should not have the right to vote. As a result, you need to get a little more specific about what you're looking for when you go to check the line references.

The answer to Question #1 actually provides an important clue when it refers to women's "natural" role in society. The correct set of lines in Passage 2 must therefore be consistent with the belief that women's subordinate status is innate.

One by one, we're going to check the answers against that requirement.

A) **Why, men have gone to war, endured every privation and death itself in defense of woman.**

No, this answer focuses on men instead of women. The fact that men have suffered to defend women has nothing to do with the fact that Sanford views women's secondary status as "natural."

B) **To man, woman is the dearest creature on earth.**

No, this focuses on men as well. It's completely off-topic.

C) **Man will go to any extreme to protect or elevate her now.**

No. Same problem as A) and B).

D) **Woman is woman. She can not unsex herself or change her sphere.**

This works. The statement that woman *can not unsex herself or change her sphere* is consistent with the idea that her position is fixed by nature itself.

So D) is the correct answer to Question #2.

Agreement Questions

As mentioned earlier in this chapter, passages with conflicting viewpoints typically include a question asking you to identify a point that the authors would *agree* on. These questions are intended to test your understanding of the complexities of the relationship between the passages – more specifically, the fact that an author can recognize the validity of part of an argument while (strongly) disagreeing with almost everything else.

As a result, knowing the general relationship between the passages is *not* sufficient to answer all of the questions. While the information necessary to answer an agreement question may be located in a key place (intro, conclusion, after a major transition) in one or both of the passages, it is also possible that the answer will hinge on information in the middle of a paragraph.

Let's look at an example, still using the "Sanford vs. Anthony" passage from p. 281.

1

Which idea is supported by the authors of both passages?

A) Women are deserving of respect and esteem.
B) Men are responsible for ensuring women's protection.
C) The moral obligations of women are often ignored.
D) It is inevitable that women will obtain the same rights as men.

If you're trying to answer the question using only the simplest main points, you might eliminate D) immediately. After all, Sanford in Passage 1 believes that it is only natural for women not to vote, and so he would undoubtedly reject the idea that there was anything "inevitable" about women obtaining that right.

This, however, is where most people start to get lost and try to rely on their memories. If you've only thought about the main point of Passage 1 in the simplest terms – that is, "women shouldn't vote" – then it's entirely possible that none of the remaining answers would look particularly appealing to you. There's a reasonable chance you'd be able to eliminate D), but then you might get thrown off and pick C) (the confusing answer) because A) seemed too positive.

The problem is that Sanford, while clearly negative toward the idea of women voting, is just as clearly positive toward women themselves. He makes it clear that they hold an *exalted* position (line 21), and that men hold them in extremely high regard. So in fact, he would agree with Anthony that women are *deserving of respect and esteem*, making the answer A).

You could also be asked about the primary purpose of both passages:

The primary purpose of each passage is to

A) distinguish between a natural right and an individual preference.

B) advance an argument about whether a particular action should be considered a right.

C) explain the role of a specific principle within a democratic system.

D) discuss the process by which rights and privileges are determined.

You can treat this type of question much as you would any other function question. To avoid getting distracted by the abstract language in the answer choices, keep your focus as concrete and specific as possible.

To reiterate: what is the topic of the passages? Whether women should have the right to vote. That's one right, singular.

On that basis, you can eliminate D) because it refers to *rights and privileges*, plural. It's outside the scope of the passage.

Now we're going to think very carefully about the other answers. All of them are fairly neutral, so unfortunately positive/negative isn't an option here.

A) doesn't fit because both authors are discussing whether something is a right or a privilege; the idea that voting might be a "preference" (as opposed to a privilege, which Sanford does mention) is not discussed at all.

B) works. Voting = a particular action, and both passages are essentially devoted to discussing whether voting is a right and for whom. Sanford states in the first line that it is a privilege (that is, not a right), whereas Anthony makes clear that she believes the opposite.

C) is off-topic and too broad. The passages aren't devoted to explaining "the role of a specific principle within a democratic system" at all. They're arguments about who gets to vote and why.

The answer is therefore B).

Note that if a question states that a particular feature of both passages is the same, (e.g., "The purpose of **both** passages is to…"), you may sometimes be able to answer it by reading only one of the passages. If the feature in question is true for one passage, it must automatically be true for the other.

For example, consider the following question:

In context of each passage as a whole, the questions in lines 15-16 of Passage 1 and lines 82-83 of Passage 2 primarily serve to

A) criticize a procedure.
B) defend an action.
C) sympathize with a perspective.
D) underscore a point.

To simplify things, you can start by reading lines 15-16 of Passage 1: *Do women have to vote in order to receive the protection of man?* (Alternately, if you prefer to use Passage 2, you can read lines 82-83: *The only question left to be settled now is: Are women persons?*)

Why does Sanford pose this question? It's a rhetorical question, so he already knows what the answer is. (*No, women don't need to vote in order to receive man's protection.*) Why bother to ask a question then? For stylistic flair that serves to emphasize, i.e., *underscore*, his point. None of the other answers makes sense.

Because the question itself tells you that whatever is true for Passage 1 must also be true for Passage 2, you can – if you feel comfortable doing so, or if you are pressed for time – skip reading the relevant lines in Passage 2 entirely.

If you'd like to test out this strategy in an *Official Guide* question, you can see Test 5, #41.

Paired Passage Exercises

2. Passage 1 is adapted from a 1774 speech to Congress by Joseph Galloway. Passage 2 is adapted from Alexander Hamilton," A Full Vindication of the Measures of the Congress." Both were written in 1774. As the British imposed a series of taxes on the American colonists, tensions grew between those who wished to remain loyal to Britain and those who wanted greater independence.

Passage 1

The discovery of the Colonies was made under a commission granted by the supreme authority of the British State, that they have been settled under that authority, and therefore are truly the property of that
5 State. Parliamentary jurisdiction has been constantly exercised over them from their first settlement; its executive authority has ever run through all their inferior political systems: the Colonists have ever sworn allegiance to the British State, and have been
10 considered, both by the State and by themselves, as subjects of the British Government. Protection and allegiance are reciprocal duties; the one cannot exist without the other. The Colonies cannot claim the protection of Britain upon any principle of reason or
15 law, while they deny its supreme authority. Upon this ground the authority of Parliament stands too firm to be shaken by any arguments whatever; and therefore to deny that authority, and at the same time to declare their incapacity to be represented, amounts to a full
20 and explicit declaration of independence.

As to the tax, it is neither unjust or oppressive, it being rather a relief than a burthen*; but it is want of constitutional principle in the authority that passed it, which is the ground for complaint. This, and this only,
25 is the source of American grievances…

If we do not approve of a representation in Parliament, let us ask for a participation in the freedom and power of the English constitution in some other mode of incorporation…I therefore bescech you, by the
30 respect you are bound to pay to the instructions of your constituents, by the regard you have for the honor and safety of your country, and as you wish to avoid a war with Great-Britain, which must terminate, at all events in the ruin of America, not to rely on a denial of the
35 authority of Parliament, a refusal to be represented… because whatever protestations, in that case, may be made to the contrary, it will prove to the world that we intend to throw off our allegiance to the State, and to involve the two countries in all the horrors of a civil
40 war.

*a burden

Passage 2

That Americans are entitled to freedom, is incontrovertible upon every rational principle. All men have one common original: they participate in one common nature, and consequently have one common
45 right. No reason can be assigned why one man should exercise any power, or preeminence over his fellow creatures more than another; unless they have voluntarily veiled him with it. Since then, Americans have not by any act of theirs empowered the British
50 Parliament to make laws for them, it follows they can have no just authority to do it.

Besides the clear voice of natural justice in this respect, the fundamental principles of the English constitution are in our favor. It has been repeatedly
55 demonstrated, that the idea of legislation, or taxation, when the subject is not represented, is inconsistent with that. Nor is this all, our charters, the express conditions on which our progenitors relinquished their native countries, and came to settle in this,
60 preclude every claim of ruling and taxing us without our assent.

Every subterfuge that sophistry has been able to invent, to evade or obscure this truth, has been refuted by the most conclusive reasonings; so that we may
65 pronounce it a matter of undeniable certainty, that the pretensions of Parliament are contradictory to the law of nature, subversive of the British constitution, and destructive of the faith of the most solemn compacts.

What then is the subject of our controversy with
70 the mother country? It is this, whether we shall preserve that security to our lives and properties, which the law of nature, the genius of the British constitution, and our charters afford us or whether we shall resign them into the hands of the British House of Commons,
75 which is no more privileged to dispose of them than the Grand Mogul? What can actuate those men, who labor to delude any of us into an opinion, that the object of contention between the parents and the colonies is only three pence duty upon tea? or that the
80 commotions in America originate in a plan, formed by some turbulent men to erect it into a republican government? The parliament claims a right to tax us in all cases whatsoever; its late laws are in virtue of that claim. How ridiculous then is it to affirm, that we
85 are quarrelling for the trifling Aim of three pence a pound on tea; when it is evidently the principle against which we contend.

1

Which choice best describes the relationship between the two passages?

A) Passage 2 presents a personal account of a conflict that Passage 1 discusses objectively.

B) Passage 2 rejects a line of reasoning that Passage 1 advances.

C) Passage 2 takes a practical view of a reaction that Passage 1 approaches idealistically.

D) Passage 2 provides an example of an idea described in Passage 1.

2

Both passages discuss the tensions between Britain and the Colonies in terms of

A) financial matters.

B) moral obligations.

C) religious freedom.

D) historical conflicts.

3

The author of Passage 2 would most likely respond to the statement in lines 13-17 of Passage 1 ("The Colonies...whatever") with

A) approval, because levying taxes is a central purpose of government.

B) skepticism, because the actions of Parliament are at odds with natural and British law.

C) scorn, because no individual has the inherent authority to rule over others.

D) acceptance, because the Colonies must reaffirm their allegiance to Britain.

4

Galloway in Passage 1 would most likely characterize Hamilton's statement in lines 48-51 of Passage 2 ("Americans...do it") as

A) too radical to be taken seriously by the majority of citizens.

B) inconsistent with the need to establish reliable systems of trade.

C) a principled defense of national sovereignty.

D) a troubling misconception of an established relationship.

5

Galloway in Passage 1 and Hamilton in Passage 2 would be most likely to agree with which of the following statements?

A) The English constitution is worthy of great respect.

B) Regulations that conflict with the laws of nature must be overturned.

C) Historical ties between nations should be preserved at all cost.

D) Individuals should only be taxed in proportion to their incomes.

2. Passage 1 is adapted from the "Atlanta Compromise" speech by W.E.B. DuBois, delivered in 1895. Passage 2 is adapted from a 1903 essay by Booker T. Washington. DuBois and Washington were among the most influential leaders in the African American community during the late nineteenth and early twentieth century.

Passage 1

Ignorant and inexperienced, it is not strange that in the first years of our new life we began at the top instead of at the bottom; that a seat in Congress or the state legislature was more sought than real estate or
5 industrial skill; that the political convention or stump speaking had more attractions than starting a dairy farm or truck garden. A ship lost at sea for many days suddenly sighted a friendly vessel. From the mast of the unfortunate vessel was seen a signal, "Water,
10 water; we die of thirst!" The answer from the friendly vessel at once came back, "Cast down your bucket where you are." A second time the signal, "Water, water; send us water!" ran up from the distressed vessel, and was answered, "Cast down your bucket
15 where you are." And a third and fourth signal for water was answered, "Cast down your bucket where you are." The captain of the distressed vessel, at last heeding the injunction, cast down his bucket, and it came up full of fresh, sparkling water from the mouth of the
20 Amazon River. To those of my race who depend on bettering their condition in a foreign land or who underestimate the importance of cultivating friendly relations with the Southern white man, who is their next-door neighbor, I would say: "Cast down your
25 bucket where you are" — cast it down in making friends in every manly way of the people of all races by whom we are surrounded...

No race can prosper till it learns that there is as much dignity in tilling a field as in writing a poem. It is
30 at the bottom of life we must begin, and not at the top. To those of the white race who look to the incoming of those of foreign birth and strange tongue and habits for the prosperity of the South, were I permitted I would repeat what I say to my own race, "Cast down
35 your bucket where you are." Cast it down among the eight millions of Negroes whose habits you know, whose fidelity and love you have tested...As we have proved our loyalty to you in the past, in nursing your children, watching by the sick-bed of your mothers
40 and fathers, and often following them with tear-dimmed eyes to their graves, so in the future, in our humble way, we shall stand by you with a devotion that no foreigner can approach, ready to lay down our lives,

if need be, in defense of yours, interlacing our
45 industrial, commercial, civil, and religious life with yours in a way that shall make the interests of both races one. In all things that are purely social we can be as separate as the fingers, yet one as the hand in all things essential to mutual progress.

Passage 2

50 The Negro race, like all races, is going to be saved by its exceptional men. The problem of education, then, among Negroes must first of all deal with the Talented Tenth; it is the problem of developing the Best of this race that they may guide the Mass away
55 from the contamination and death of the Worst, in their own and other races. Now the training of men is a difficult and intricate task. Its technique is a matter for educational experts, but its object is for the vision of seers. If we make money the objects of
60 man-training, we shall develop money-makers but not necessarily men; if we make technical skill the object of education, we may possess artisans but not, in nature, men....

I am an earnest advocate of manual training and
65 trade teaching for black boys, and for white boys, too. I believe that next to the founding of Negro colleges the most valuable addition to Negro education since the war, has been industrial training for black boys. Nevertheless, I insist that the object
70 of all true education is not to make men carpenters, it is to make carpenters men; there are two means of making the carpenter a man, each equally important: the first is to give the group and community in which he works, liberally trained teachers and leaders to
75 teach him and his family what life means; the second is to give him sufficient intelligence and technical skill to make him an efficient workman; the first object demands the Negro college and college-bred men—not a quantity of such colleges, but a few of
80 excellent quality; not too many college-bred men, but enough to leaven the lump, to inspire the masses, to raise the Talented Tenth to leadership; the second object demands a good system of common schools, well-taught, conveniently located and properly
85 equipped.

1

Which idea is supported by the authors of both passages?

A) The primary goal of education is to ensure skill and efficiency.

B) It is possible to find fulfillment in a wide range of occupations.

C) Formal education should be reserved for only the most talented students.

D) Individuals can most effectively improve their lives through education.

2

Which statement identifies a central conflict between the two passages?

A) DuBois proposes a broad system of education, while Washington rejects that approach as impractical.

B) DuBois adopts an international perspective, while Washington focuses on domestic interests.

C) DuBois focuses on improving the prospects of a group as a whole, while Washington advocates the elevation of a narrow elite.

D) DuBois describes the nature of a problem, while Washington emphasizes a possible solution.

3

Washington in Passage 2 would most likely have responded to lines 29-30 ("It is...top") of Passage 1 with

A) appreciation, because citizens of a democracy should not have to demonstrate their loyalty.

B) sympathy, because citizens of a democracy should play an active role in their communities.

C) disagreement, because true freedom cannot be attained without education.

D) skepticism, because it ignores the capabilities of certain individuals.

4

Based on Passage 1, DuBois would most likely characterize the viewpoint described by Washington in lines 78-85 of Passage 2 ("the first... equipped") as

A) economically impractical.

B) generally persuasive.

C) overly ambitious.

D) beyond reproach.

3. Passage 1 is adapted from the website locavores.com, © 2010. Passage 2 is adapted from Ronald Bailey, "The Food Miles Mistake," © 2008 *Reason* magazine.

Passage 1

Our food now travels an average of 1,500 miles before ending up on our plates. This globalization of the food supply has serious consequences for the environment, our health, our communities and our
5 tastebuds. Much of the food grown in the breadbasket surrounding us must be shipped across the country to distribution centers before it makes its way back to our supermarket shelves. Because uncounted costs of this long distance journey (air pollution and global
10 warming, the ecological costs of large scale monoculture, the loss of family farms and local community dollars) are not paid for at the checkout counter, many of us do not think about them at all.

What is eaten by the great majority of North
15 Americans comes from a global everywhere, yet from nowhere that we know in particular. How many of our children even know what a chicken eats or how an onion grows? The distance from which our food comes represents our separation from the
20 knowledge of how and by whom what we consume is produced, processed, and transported. And yet, the quality of a food is derived not merely from its genes and the greens that fed it, but from how it is prepared and cared for all the way until it reaches our mouths.
25 If the production, processing, and transport of what we eat is destructive of the land and of human community — as it very often is — how can we understand the implications of our own participation in the global food system when those processes are
30 located elsewhere and so are obscured from us? How can we act responsibly and effectively for change if we do not understand how the food system works and our own role within it.

Corporations, which are the principal beneficiaries
35 of a global food system, now dominate the production, processing, distribution, and consumption of food, but alternatives are emerging which together could form the basis for foodshed development. Just as many farmers are recognizing the social and
40 environmental advantages to sustainable agriculture, so are many consumers coming to appreciate the benefits of fresh and sustainably produced food. Such producers and consumers are being linked through such innovative arrangements as community supported
45 agriculture and farmers' markets. Alternative producers, alternative consumers, and alternative small entrepreneurs are rediscovering community and finding common ground.

Passage 2

In their recent policy primer for the Mercatus
50 Center at George Mason University, economic geographer Pierre Desrochers and economic consultant Hiroko Shimizu challenge the notion that food miles – the distance food travels from farm to plate – are a good sustainability indicator. As
55 Desrochers and Shimizu point out, the food trade has been historically driven by urbanization. As agriculture became more efficient, people were liberated from farms and able to develop other skills that helped raise general living standards. People
60 freed from having to scrabble for food, for instance, could work in factories, write software, or become physicians. Modernization is a process in which people get further and further away from the farm.

Modern technologies like canning and refrigeration
65 made it possible to extend the food trade from staple grains and spices to fruits, vegetables, and meats. As a result, world trade in fruits and vegetables—fresh and processed—doubled in the 1980s and increased by 30 percent between 1990 and 2001. Fruits and
70 vegetables accounted for 22 percent of the exports of developing economies in 2001. If farmers, processors, shippers, and retailers did not profit from providing distant consumers with these foods, the foods wouldn't be on store shelves. And consumers, of
75 course, benefit from being able to buy fresh foods year around.

So just how much carbon dioxide is emitted by transporting food from farm to fork? Desrochers and Shimizu cite a comprehensive study done by the
80 United Kingdom's Department of Environment, Food and Rural Affairs (DEFRA) which reported that 82 percent of food miles were generated within the U.K. Consumer shopping trips accounted for 48 percent and trucking for 31 percent of British
85 miles. Air freight amounted to less than 1 percent of food miles. In total, food transportation accounted for only 1.8 percent of Britain's carbon dioxide emissions.

1

Which choice best describes the relationship between the two passages?

A) Passage 2 offers an alternative explanation for a phenomenon that Passage 1 describes.

B) Passage 2 proposes a solution to a problem that Passage 1 presents.

C) Passage 2 expresses doubt about the benefits of a practice that Passage 1 advocates.

D) Passage 2 provides historical context for a tradition that Passage 1 discusses.

2

The authors of both passages would most likely agree with which of the following statements about food?

A) People must understand the food production system in order to make informed choices about their health.

B) A significant amount of the food consumed today is not produced locally.

C) Transporting food over long distances may reduce its quality.

D) The corporate model of food production is a necessary aspect of urbanization.

3

How would the author of Passage 2 most likely respond to the discussion in lines 8-14 of Passage 1 ("Because...all")?

A) He would claim that most pollution comes from sources other than food transportation.

B) He would assert that access to foods grown far away has led more people to adopt healthful diets.

C) He would argue that transporting food over long distances is the best way to feed an increasingly urban population.

D) He would point out that most family farms today exist by choice rather than necessity.

4

Which choice provides the best evidence for the answer to the previous question?

A) Lines 64-66 ("Modern...meats")

B) Lines 74-76 ("And...around")

C) Lines 82-83 ("82 percent...UK")

D) Lines 86-87 ("In...emissions")

5

How would the author of Passage 1 most likely respond to the authors of Passage 2's claim about "fresh foods" (line 75)?

A) With skepticism, because the nutritional value of food transported over long distances may be compromised.

B) With approval, because people should consume locally produced food whenever possible.

C) With disdain, because the corporate model of food production cannot be altered.

D) With interest, because new technologies may preserve foods for longer periods.

6

Which choice provides the best evidence for the answer to the previous question?

A) Lines 5-6 ("Much...country")

B) Lines 14-15 ("What...everywhere")

C) Lines 21-24 ("And...mouths")

D) Lines 37-38 ("alternatives...development")

Explanations: Paired Passage Exercises

1.1 B

The passages express opposing viewpoints, so the correct answer must convey disagreement B) is correct because it is most consistent with that relationship: the author of Passage 2 rejects the idea that the Colonies must go along with Parliament's demands because they are fully ruled by Britain (=a line of reasoning), and instead states that Parliament's laws must be rejected because they are unjust. Although both passages are at times written in the first-person plural (*we*), neither is actually personal, eliminating A). An argument could be made that the author of Passage 2 is somewhat idealistic in his insistence on freedom and his appeals to the law of nature, but C) states exactly the opposite – that the more practical, cautious author of Passage 1 is too idealistic. D) is incorrect because the passages only present conflicting arguments; Passage 2 does not provide an example of any idea discussed in Passage 1.

1.2 A

Both passages discuss the conflict between Britain and the Colonies in terms of taxation, which is another way of saying "financial matters." Passage 1 does so in lines 21-25, and Passage 2 does so in line 55 and again in lines 76-87.

1.3 B

Lines 13-17 of Passage 1 essentially state Galloway's point: because the Colonies are subject to British protection and rule, they have no grounds for attacking any decision made by Parliament. Clearly, that's a statement with which Hamilton in Passage 2 would disagree, so you can assume that the correct answer will be negative. "Approval" and "acceptance" are both positive, so A) and D) can be eliminated. Now, why would Hamilton disagree? The key lines are 64-76, where Hamilton makes a clear distinction between the law of nature and the genius of the British constitution, which guarantee the Colonists' freedom, and the unjust laws of Parliament, which contradict both. That is directly consistent with B). C) is too broad and off-topic: Hamilton says nothing about whether "any individual" is innately qualified to rule. He is only concerned with specific, unjust acts of Parliament.

1.4 D

Because the passages contain opposing arguments, you can assume that the answer to this question is negative. C), the only positive answer, can thus be eliminated. A) might sound plausible, but Galloway does not discuss rebellion against Britain in terms of how "the majority of citizens" would perceive it. He only discusses the potential outcome (war). B) is completely off-topic: Galloway refers to the issue of taxation but says nothing about trade, reliable or otherwise. That leaves D), which accurately captures Galloway's concern: the current relationship between Britain and the Colonies has existed since the Colonies were founded (=an established relationship), and the Colonists' rejection of it would lead to war (=troubling).

1.5 A

This is an example of a question in which relying too heavily on general points can get you in trouble. If your first instinct when you read A) was to eliminate that answer, you fell into the trap. Clearly, Galloway in Passage 1 is favorable toward the British constitution. And, based on Hamilton's insistence on the injustices committed by the British (Passage 2), you might assume that Hamilton is opposed to the British constitution as well. In reality, however, his argument is subtler than that: he makes a clear distinction between the acts of Parliament, which he opposes, and the British constitution, which he views as *genius* (line 72). A) is thus correct. B) is supported by Passage 2 but not Passage 1. C), while somewhat consistent with Passage 1, is far too extreme. Galloway believes that the dispute over taxation is relatively minor; there is nothing to suggest that he believes ties should be preserved at all cost. D) is completely off-topic: neither author discusses how individuals should be taxed, only whether Britain has the right to tax the Colonies in the way that it has done.

2.1 B

Although DuBois and Washington disagree about the best way for African Americans to improve their status, both authors are clear about the fact that both professional and manual jobs (= a wide range of occupations) can offer rewards. DuBois states that *No race can prosper till it learns that there is as much dignity in tilling a field as in writing a poem* (lines 28-29), and Washington makes clear that he is an earnest advocate for manual training. Washington also makes clear throughout Passage 2 that he only considers traditional education and preparation for middle/upper-class careers appropriate for exceptional men, but that the rest can find fulfillment in manual labor.

2.2 C

The easiest way to answer this question is to use the main points. Passage 1: African Americans should start @ bottom, work up; Passage 2: Focus on "talented tenth." The phrase *talented tenth* refers to the cultivation of a small group of elites, whereas DuBois in Passage 1 is primarily concerned with raising the prospects of African Americans as a whole. C) is thus correct. A) does not fit because Washington in Passage 2 proposes a system of education, not DuBois in Passage 1. For B), Passage 1 does include references to *a foreign land* and *those of foreign birth*, but DuBois' principle concern is the situation in the United States. It is far too big of a stretch to describe his perspective as "international." D) is incorrect because each passage focuses on presenting a different solution to the same problem.

2.3 D

Because the authors disagree in their approach to improving the prospects of African Americans, you can assume that the correct answer to this question is negative. "Appreciation" and "sympathy" are positive, so A) and B) can be eliminated. C) is off-topic: the issue is not whether education is necessary for freedom, but whether it is necessary for economic (and, to a lesser degree, social) advancement. That leaves D), which is consistent with the main point of Passage 2: Washington is in favor of cultivating an elite that would start "at the top." From that perspective, DuBois' attitude fails to take into account ("ignores") the fact that certain individuals are exceptionally capable and should be singled out as such.

2.4 C

What is the viewpoint expressed in lines 78-85? That education should be used to create an African-American elite ("the Talented Tenth") who, it can be assumed, would seek prestigious jobs and titles. What would DuBois think of that? Given his focus on bringing everyone up from the bottom, he would probably have a somewhat negative attitude toward that idea. B) is straightforwardly positive and can be eliminated. Be careful with D), however: *beyond reproach* means "beyond criticism," i.e., perfect, so this answer is actually extremely positive and can be eliminated as well. A) is off-topic: DuBois does not discuss the disadvantages of trying to raise people too far beyond their existing position in economic terms. That leaves C), which is correct. If DuBois believes that African Americans as a whole should start at the bottom and focus on practical, manual labor only, then the idea of creating a substantial group of elites who would jump straight to the top would likely strike him as excessively ambitious.

3.1 C

The easiest way to answer this question is to use the main points. Main point of Passage 1: industrial food = bad, buy local (=a practice). Main point of Passage 2: buying local doesn't help the environment (=expresses doubt). Relationship: negative. The only answer with negative wording is C), making it the answer.

3.2 B

Lines 5-8 of Passage 1 state that *Much of the food grown in the breadbasket surrounding us must be shipped across the country to distribution centers before it makes its way back to our supermarket shelves.* The author of Passage 2 does not make the point nearly as explicitly, but he does state in lines 67-69 that *world trade in fruits, vegetables – fresh and processed – doubled in the 1980s and increased by 30 percent between 1990 and 2001.* These lines directly suggest that people consume an enormous amount of food produced far away, an idea consistent with B). Only the author of Passage 1 would agree with A) and C), and only the author of Passage 2 would agree with D).

3.3-4 A, D

Start by defining "the discussion" in lines 8-14 of Passage 1: transporting food is bad for the environment. What would the author of Passage 2 think of that idea? If you paid close attention to the conclusion, the answer should be fairly straightforward: the environmental impact has been overstated. In addition, the end of Passage 2 gives you the answer to the following question. If you don't remember what it says, the fact that D) in 3.4 provides a line reference at the end of passage – where the main point is usually located – suggests that you should check that answer first. In the conclusion of Passage 2, the author is pretty clear that food miles account for only a small portion (1.8 percent) of Britain's carbon-dioxide emissions. Therefore, most carbon-dioxide emissions (98.2 percent, to be exact) must come from "other sources." That makes A) the answer to 3.3 and D) the answer to 3.4.

3.5-6 A, C

The biggest danger with this question is that you will take it at face value. You might reason that because the authors of Passage 1 are in favor of fresh food, they would obviously have a positive attitude toward it. The problem, however, is that the author of Passage 2 is talking about fresh food that has been transported long distances – exactly what the author of Passage 1 is against. So the correct answer must indicate opposition, narrowing your options for 3.5 to A) and C). "Disdain" is on the strong side, however, and lines 39-48 indicate that the author of Passage 1 believes that the corporate food model <u>can</u> be altered. C) can thus be eliminated. The correct lines in 3.6 must therefore convey the idea that food transported over long distances isn't quite so healthy. A) is correct because in context of the author of Passage 1's argument, the statement that *the quality of a food is derived...from how it is prepared and cared for all the way until it reaches our mouths* implies that food transported halfway around the world might not be so fresh and high-quality after all.

Graphics and Data Analysis

If you're not accustomed to working with graphs and tables, data analysis questions can be intimidating. Without a doubt, shifting from sentences and paragraphs to lines and numbers can be jarring. You're solidly in reading mode, then wham! You have to answer a question about a...pie chart? It's a change that can easily leave you feeling off-balance.

The good news, however, is that graphic-based questions are rarely as complicated as they appear. No matter how unfamiliar the terminology may be, all of the information you need to answer these questions will be right in front of you. In fact, they are set up precisely so that you can figure them without outside knowledge. If you stay calm and consider things carefully, there's a good chance you'll be fine.

In fact, questions that involve graphics are often simpler than they initially appear. Although graphics are always related in some way to the passages they accompany, **many data analysis questions can be answered on the basis of the graphics alone – you do not need to take the passage into account at all.**

Data analysis questions can be divided into three main types:

1) Questions that require the graphic only.

2) Questions that refer to both the graphic and the passage, but that can be answered using only one or the other.

3) Questions that require both the graphic and the passage.

While the first and third types are fairly straightforward in terms of what information you need to base your answer on, the second type can be somewhat trickier. Because these questions refer to the passage as well as the graphic, it is very easy to think that you must look at both. In many cases, however, doing so can be unnecessarily time consuming and confusing. In this chapter, we're going to break down examples of all three types so that you can understand what you need to consider and when.

Before we get started, though, one **note**: If you are uncomfortable working with graphs but are otherwise a strong reader, you should consider planning to glance through the graph questions and leaving any ones that you cannot answer quickly until the end of the test. It is not worth wasting three or four minutes going back and forth between a passage and a graphic for the sake of a single question when you could be answering several text-based questions in the same amount of time.

Reading Graphs: Finding the Point and Skimming

Although graphs and passages might strike you as two completely different entities, reading a text and interpreting a graph have more in common than you might suspect. One simply conveys information in words while the other conveys it in bars and numbers.

Like passages, most graphs have a "point" to convey, and they are often much more efficient at conveying it than written words. In fact, that's precisely why they are used. (Ever heard the expression "a picture is worth a thousand words"?) Rather than resort to lengthy explanations, science and social-science writers often choose to represent data visually in order to help readers quickly obtain a big-picture understanding of complex situations.

Just as you can skim passages to get a general idea of what they are saying, you can also "skim" graphs visually to get a general sense of the information they convey. And again, your goal is to avoid getting caught in the details for as long as possible.

Here are some questions to consider:

- What is the shape of the graph? Does it go up, down, or both?

- Are changes steady; or is there a big jump somewhere? If so, where?

- Is there an "outlier" point with a value very different from that of the other points?

- Are there items whose values don't change at all?

- If there are multiple lines, do the lines ever meet?

If you approach data analysis questions with a general understanding of what the graphic conveys, you can often identify correct answers or eliminate multiple incorrect answers quickly.

For example, consider the following graph:

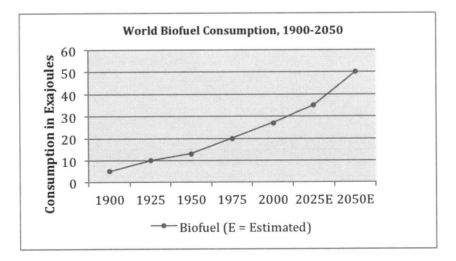

The first thing to notice is that this graph displays a unit of measurement – the exajoule (title of the y-axis) – that very few non-scientists will be familiar with. That's the type of wording that makes these questions *seem* so difficult. In reality, the terminology is **completely irrelevant**. As long as you understand that an exajoule is a unit of measurement, you can ignore it.

So what you're looking at is this:

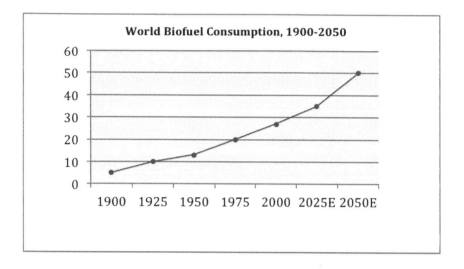

With the terminology taken away, you can focus on the essential: the graph represents a steady increase over time. In addition, values increase by about the same amount (5-10 points) during most of the intervals, except for the period from 2025 to 2050, which is larger (about 15 points). At no point do values fall, and no two values are ever the same.

Now, let's consider the title of the graph: World Biofuel Consumption, 1900-2050. The point of a title is to tell you what something is about, and graphs are no different. In this case, the title combined with what we've already determined tells us that biofuel use rose steadily throughout the twentieth century and will continue to rise steadily into the twenty-first.

The "main point" could thus be something along the lines of "BF use ↑ 20-21C." Using that information, we can infer that the correct answer to any accompanying question must be consistent with that idea.

We can also infer that answer choices indicating any of the following would be **incorrect**:

- Biofuel consumption peaked in a year prior to 2050.

- Biofuel consumption decreased at any point.

- Biofuel consumption in the 20th century was greater than it will be in the 21st.

- The largest rise in biofuel consumption occurred at a point other than 2025-2050.

To be clear, you do not need to figure all of this out before looking at the answers. Your goal is simply to get the gist so that you can eliminate any answer that is inconsistent with it.

Reading Between the Lines

Some questions may ask you to read between the lines of the graph – literally. That is, they will ask you to determine information about points that are not directly represented on the graph but that can be determined from the information provided.

For example, take a look at this graph:

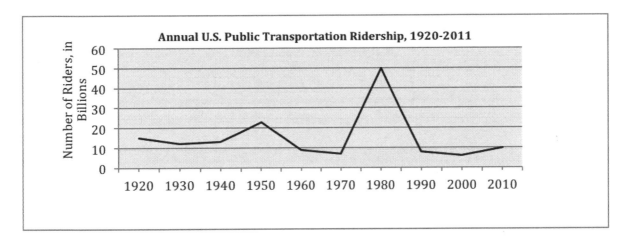

Annual U.S. Public Transportation Ridership, 1920-2011

All of the years listed along the *x*-axis are in multiples of 10 (1920, 1930, etc.); however, there are also tick marks halfway *between* each set of years. You could therefore encounter a question that looks like this:

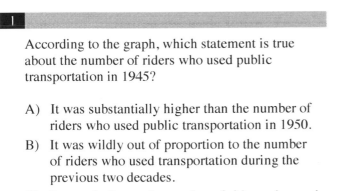

According to the graph, which statement is true about the number of riders who used public transportation in 1945?

A) It was substantially higher than the number of riders who used public transportation in 1950.

B) It was wildly out of proportion to the number of riders who used transportation during the previous two decades.

C) It was similar to the number of riders who used public transportation a decade later.

D) It was lower than the number of riders who used public transportation in 2010.

When you look at the graph, you will of course notice that 1945 does not appear. Both 1940 and 1950 do appear, though, so the tick mark between them logically represents 1945.

What does the graph tell us about the number of public transportation riders in 1945? Drawing a line from the tick mark, we can see that it was a little under 20 billion. (Remember that the numbers represent billions; the zeroes are omitted for the sake of readability.) It's a little lower than in 1950 but otherwise around the same as it was during the surrounding decades.

Now that we've figured out some basics, we're going to look at the answers:

A) No. Remember we just said that the number in 1945 was *lower* than it was in 1950.

B) The extreme phrase *wildly out of proportion* immediately suggests that this answer is wrong. Besides, the only part of the graph that's really out of proportion to the rest is the part representing 1980. So we're going to assume this answer is incorrect.

C) A decade later was 1955. If we look at the tick mark between 1950 and 1960 and trace a line up (or just compare visually), we end up with a point in roughly the same range as that for 1945. So C) works. Just to be safe, though, we're going to check D).

D) No, this is backwards. Ridership in 2010 was lower. That means ridership in 1945 was *higher*.

So the answer is C).

Multiple Variables

The graphs we've looked at so far have contained only one variable – that is, they have only charted the rise and/or fall of a single factor. Unfortunately, many of the graphs you are asked to work with on the SAT will contain more than one variable. When this is the case, you should **always start by noting the key difference between the lines** (or sectors, in the case of a bar graph or pie chart).

The biggest difference (or similarity) between the lines is the point of the graph.

Here are some questions to consider:

- Do the lines move in a similar way, or do they move in different ways? (e.g., do both lines rise or fall, or does one line rise while the other falls?)

- Is one line consistently high and the other consistently low?

- Do both lines ever pass through the same point?

- If there is a large increase/decrease, does it occur in the same place for both lines, or does it occur in different places?

I cannot stress how important this step is. While it may seem as if these questions are asking you to process an enormous amount of information, the reality is that only a small portion of what you see will actually be relevant.

Furthermore, the questions will almost invariably target the most significant differences between the lines or sectors. If you've already established those differences upfront, you're already most of the way to the answer.

Let's consider this somewhat altered version of a graph we examined a little while ago:

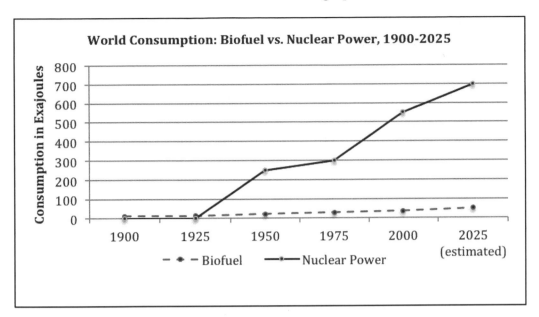

When we look at the graph, the difference between the two energy sources is striking: biofuel use rose slightly and gradually throughout the twentieth century and will continue its slow, steady increase in the twenty-first century. In contrast, nuclear power use rose sharply and significantly beginning in the mid-twentieth century and will continue to increase substantially in the twenty-first century.

Our "main point" could therefore be something like "NP way up, BF up slowly" (nuclear power use is going way up, while biofuel use is rising slowly).

We could even be asked to deal with three variables:

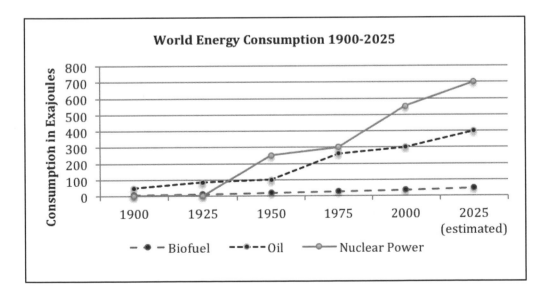

Here, the main thing to notice is that biofuel use rose slightly and slowly; nuclear power use rose significantly and quickly; and oil use was somewhere in the middle.

Now let's look at a few more graph-only questions. The most straightforward of these will simply ask you to identify the answer best supported by the graph. Often, you will be able to answer these questions just by keeping the big picture in mind.

Let's consider the second version of the graph on the previous page, the one with the three variables. (Note that on the SAT, the actual questions frequently appear on different pages from the graphs themselves, so you must be comfortable flipping back and forth.)

Remember the big picture: nuclear energy – high; oil – medium; biofuel – low. In addition, the lines for oil and nuclear power are about equal at 1975.

1

Which choice is supported by data in the graph?

A) The amount of oil and the amount of nuclear power used in 1950 were roughly the same.

B) By 2025, more energy will be obtained from nuclear energy than from oil or biofuel.

C) The use of biofuels is predicted to decline between 2000 and 2025.

D) Oil use rose at a dramatically higher rate than did biofuel use between 1975 and 2000.

We could work through these answers one by one (and in fact we're going to do so in a moment), but first let's consider the **shortcut**. The overall point of the graph is that nuclear energy has been way outstripping biofuel and oil for more than a century and will continue to do so in the immediate future.

Which answer comes closest to saying that? B). It simply states what the graph shows most obviously – by 2025, nuclear energy will be far ahead.

Or, playing process of elimination:

A) is incorrect because oil and biofuel use were about the same in 1975, not 1950.

C) is incorrect because the use of biofuel is expected to increase slightly, not decrease.

D) is incorrect because although oil use did rise at a higher rate than biofuel use between 1975 and 2000, it did so at a *slightly* higher rate, not a *dramatically* higher rate. Don't forget that it only takes one wrong word to make an answer wrong.

Now we're going to try something a little bit more challenging.

"Backwards" Graphs and "Trick" Answers

In all of the graphs we've looked at so far, one thing was pretty straightforward: a line going up indicated that values were rising, and a line going down indicated that values were falling. Simple...right? Well, maybe not always.

We're going to try an experiment. Look at the graph below, and do your best to answer the question that follows.

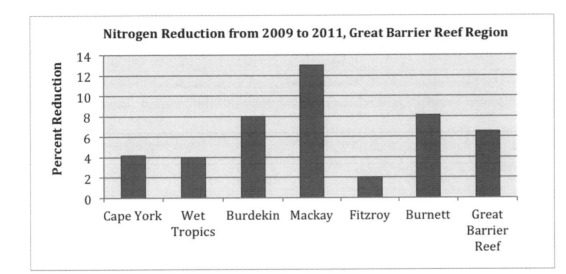

1

Which choice about nitrogen levels in 2011 is supported by data in the graph?

A) The amount of nitrogen in the water was highest at Mackay.
B) Nitrogen levels at Fitzroy were lower than than those at Cape York.
C) The amount of nitrogen in the water at Mackay declined by the largest percentage.
D) The amount of nitrogen in the water was generally comparable at Cape York and Wet Tropics.

If you picked A) or thought that there was more than one correct answer, congratulations – you've just fallen into the trap designed to ensnare all but the savviest graph readers.

The key to this question is to pay very close attention to its title. The title tells us that the bars indicate nitrogen *reduction*. The higher the bar, the larger the reduction, i.e., the amount by which nitrogen decreased. So higher bars = *lower* levels of nitrogen. In other words, up = down.

If you miss that very important fact, you risk misinterpreting the graph entirely.

Let's work through the answer choices to see how that misunderstanding can play out.

A) is a classic "trick" answer, placed first to sidetrack you. It plays on the assumption that you'll see the highest bar in A) and leap to assume it indicates nitrogen *levels* were highest at that point. But of course it's not nitrogen levels that increased, but rather nitrogen reduction. Moral of the story: if you see an answer that looks too easy when you haven't actually thought about the question, there's a pretty good chance it's wrong.

B) has a similar problem. It assumes that you'll see that the bar for Fitzroy is lower than that for Cape York and leap to what seems to be a logical conclusion. The problem is that the graph actually tells us that nitrogen levels decreased less at Fitzroy than they did at Cape York. Furthermore, we know nothing about the original amount of nitrogen at either place – it's entirely possible that nitrogen levels at Fitzroy were higher than those at Cape York.

C) is correct because it states the point of the graph: nitrogen levels declined by a greater percentage at Mackay than they did at any of the other regions shown. Remember: in this case, a high bar = a large **decrease**.

D) is incorrect for the same reason as B) – we know nothing about the nitrogen amounts themselves. The graph only tells us that nitrogen levels at Cape York and Wet Tropics declined by similar percentages.

Another potential "trick" the SAT could throw at you involves not graphs but the wording of the questions. It is important to understand that although graphic-based questions may look very different from other questions, they are still reading questions. As a result, you must pay careful attention to how they are phrased. **Some incorrect answers may accurately convey the information represented in the graph but not answer the particular question being asked.**

One factor that you must consider is **scope** – that is, whether the question asks about a **specific feature** or piece of data in the graph, or whether it asks you to **provide an overview** or understand a **general trend**. If, for example, a question asks you which answer best summarizes the information in the graph, you could see an option that correctly describes a specific aspect of that graph. Although that answer may be factually correct, it will still be wrong because it does not answer the question at hand.

For example, consider this graph:

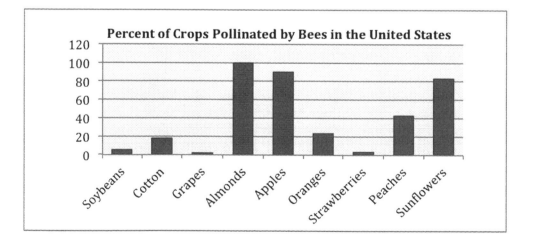

Which information best summarizes the information presented in the graph?

A) Every crop grown in the United States relies on bees for at least 20 percent of its pollination.

B) Bees are responsible for pollinating about 90 percent of apples around the world.

C) The percent of peaches pollinated by bees is more than double the percent of cotton.

D) The percent of United States crops pollinated by bees varies significantly.

The question tells us that we are looking for an answer that provides an **overview** of the information represented in the graph. **Answers that contain specific facts and/or figures are thus likely to be wrong**.

Let's start by considering the big picture of the graph. One striking feature is how **varied** the bars are. A few of the bars are clustered near the top, a few are near the bottom, and only one is right in the middle. If we wanted to write a main point, we could say something like "percent/bee poll. varies, but mostly very high/low."

While we could check out the answers one by one, we're actually going to apply that information to create a **shortcut**.

Three of the answers contain specific amounts: A) contains 20 percent, B) contains 90 percent, and C) contains *double*. Only D) does not contain a specific amount, and sure enough, it is consistent with our summary: the percent of US crops pollinated by bees ranges from just above zero all the way up to 100. So D) is the correct answer.

If you had checked the answers out one at a time, you could have gotten into some trouble.

A) is pretty obviously wrong. Some of the bars are much lower than 20 percent.

B) is a little trickier – it's half-right, half wrong. The title of the graph tells us that we're only dealing with crops in the United States, but this answer refers to the *world*. So even though the graph does in fact indicate that bees pollinate around 90% of apples in the U.S., this answer is beyond the scope of the passage. It could be true, but we don't know.

C) is the answer you really need to be careful with. The bar for peaches is indeed a little more than twice as high as it is for cotton, but this answer choice only deals with **two specific crops**, whereas the question asks us to **summarize**. So even though this answer is true, it's still wrong. If you checked the answers in order, though, there's a reasonable chance you'd get fooled and never even look at D).

Tables

Some questions will not use graphs at all but rather tables. For example, in a science passage discussing the antibiotic-resistant bacteria, you could see something like the table below. MRSA is a type of bacteria that is especially resistant to common antibiotics.

Antibiotic	General Effectiveness %	General Resistance %	MRSA Effectiveness %	MRSA Resistance %
Erithromycin	31.94	68.06	26.92	73.08
Vancomycin	100	0	100	0
Mupirocin	90.28	9.72	73.08	26.92
Penicillin	5	95	0	100
Clindamicin	83.33	16.67	69.23	30.77
Rifampicin	86.11	13.89	61.54	38.46

Don't let the complicated names distract you. Focus on the numbers, and compare the similar columns: effective vs. effective, resistant vs. resistant.

The main thing to notice is that the "General Effectiveness" numbers are always higher than the "MRSA Effectiveness" numbers. Basically, the chart is telling us that antibiotics that are generally effective are a lot less effective against MRSA. That makes sense: as stated above, MRSA is a particularly antibiotic-resistant type of bacteria.

1

Based on the table, which antibiotic showed the greatest discrepancy between its general effectiveness and its effectiveness against MRSA?

A) Erithryomycin
B) Vancomycin
C) Penicillin
D) Rifampicin

This question doesn't need to be hard – remember, all the information you need is right in front of you – but it does have the potential to be confusing.

The first thing to do is to make sure you're clear on what the question is asking and do some basic work upfront to determine what sort of information the correct answer must contain.

In this case, the key word is "discrepancy" – the question is asking which antibiotic shows the greatest **difference** between its general effectiveness and its effectiveness against MRSA.

The correct answer will therefore have a much higher number in the "general effectiveness" column than in the "MRSA effectiveness" column. One by one, we're going to check each answer. We're going to round the numbers to make things easy.

A) 32 vs. 27. That's pretty close. We'll leave it but assume it's wrong.

B) 100 vs. 100. There's no difference. Eliminate it.

C) 5 vs. 0. Pretty much the same as A). That leaves…

D) 86 vs. 62. That's a significant difference. So D) is correct.

Paired Graphics

Another potential twist the SAT could throw at you is to pair two graphics and ask about the relationship between them.

Once again, while these questions may look enormously complicated, the reality is that they will almost certainly focus on the graphics' most striking features. Only a few key pieces of information will actually be relevant.

For example, consider the charts below:

Figure 1   **Figure 2**

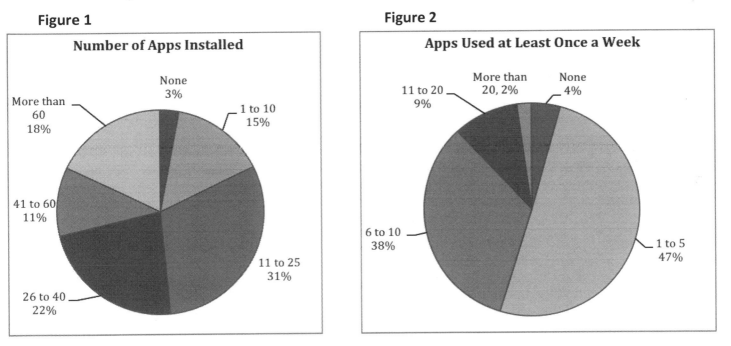

Adapted from "People Love Their Smartphones, but…" *Scientific American*.

Taken together, the graphs most directly support the idea that

A) the number of apps people install has risen significantly.
B) Most people use more than 10 different apps at least one time per week.
C) people download many more apps than they actually use.
D) people's social networks strongly influence their choice of apps.

Which statement most accurately describes a major difference in the type of data represented in the two graphs?

A) Figure 1 emphasizes the preferences of individual users, whereas Figure 2 emphasizes the preferences of groups.
B) Figure 1 focuses on the quantity of technology accessed, whereas Figure 2 focuses on the frequency of its use.
C) Figure 1 depicts a theoretical outcome, whereas Figure 2 depicts an actual result.
D) Figure 1 conveys the habits of new app users, whereas Figure 2 conveys the habits of longtime users.

Question #1: When you look at a pair of charts like this, the first thing you want to notice is whether any of the sectors are particularly large or small. Figure 2 should grab your attention because one of its sectors is so large – almost 50%. In contrast, the sectors in Figure 1 are distributed a bit more evenly. You can assume that difference will be significant.

Next, consider what information the charts reveal.

Figure 1 shows the number of apps that people install. When you add up the relevant sectors, you'll find that 53% of people have between 11 and 40 apps, and 51% of people have more than 25 apps. So basically, the point of the chart is that most people have a lot of apps.

Figure 2 shows how many apps people actually use on a regular basis. This is where that huge sector becomes important. It indicates that a significant number of people (47%) use only 1-5 apps once a week or more. Furthermore, the next-largest sector indicates that an additional 38% use only 6-10 apps that often. We know from Figure 1, however, that most people have more than 11 apps installed, and many of them have more than 25 apps.

The difference between the number of apps people install and the number of apps they regularly use suggests that people install many apps they don't use. And that is what C) says.

A) is off-topic: the charts show nothing about how the number of apps installed has changed over time. B) is incorrect because Figure 2 shows that most people (51%) use either no apps (4%) or 1-5 apps (47%) weekly. D) is off-topic as well: neither chart includes information about social networks. So that again leaves C).

Question #2: This question is far easier than it might initially seem. In fact, you can determine the answer from the titles of the charts alone. *Number of apps* = quantity (Figure 1); *at least once a week* = frequency of use (Figure 2). If you can make those relationships, you can jump directly to the correct answer, B).

To Synthesize...Or Not

Now that we've looked at bunch of graphics-only questions, we're going to add in a passage.

As discussed earlier in this chapter, questions that refer to both the graphic and the passage come in two varieties. The first type requires you to take both sources into account. These questions tend to be the most difficult, but there is also no "trick" to them. They simply tell you what information to obtain to answer the question.

The other type refers to both sources but can actually be answered using only one source. You can check the other source for confirmation, but you don't necessarily need to do so. Let's start with a relatively straightforward question of this type.

We're going to come back to this graph:

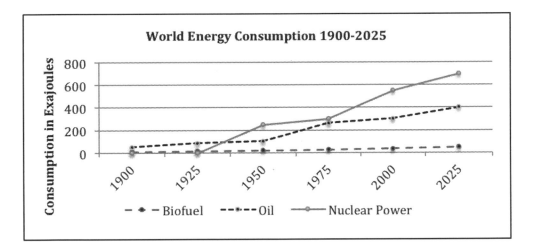

1

The passage and the graph are in agreement that in the twenty-first century, nuclear power will

A) constitute a significant source of energy.
B) lag behind other major energy sources.
C) eliminate the reliance on biofuel and oil.
D) allow for the creation of new technologies.

There's a reason we're looking at this question without a passage – we don't actually need one. The question *tells* us that the passage and the question are in agreement, so if it's true for one, it must be true for the other. The question is so specific and the graph sufficiently basic that it would be almost impossible to create answers true for the graph but not the passage.

So once again, what's the point of this graph? The use of nuclear power has been rising, and nuclear power will provide a lot of energy in the 21st century. That's what A) says.

Now let's look at a graph paired with a passage.

This passage is adapted from Sharon Tregaskis, "What Bees Tell Us About Global Climate Change," © 2010 by *Johns Hopkins Magazine*.

Standing in the apiary on the grounds of the U.S. Department of Agriculture's Bee Research Laboratory in Beltsville, Maryland, Wayne Esaias digs through the canvas shoulder bag leaning against his leg in search of
5 the cable he uses to download data. It's dusk as he runs the cord from his laptop—precariously perched on the beam of a cast-iron platform scale—to a small, battery-operated data logger attached to the spring inside the scale's steel column. In the 1800s, a scale like this
10 would have weighed sacks of grain or crates of apples, peaches, and melons. Since arriving at the USDA's bee lab in January 2007, this scale has been loaded with a single item: a colony of *Apis mellifera*, the fuzzy, black-and-yellow honey bee. An attached, 12-bit
15 recorder captures the hive's weight to within a 10th of a pound, along with a daily register of relative ambient humidity and temperature.

On this late January afternoon, during a comparatively balmy respite between the blizzards that
20 dumped several feet of snow on the Middle Atlantic states, the bees, their honey, and the wooden boxes in which they live weigh 94.5 pounds. In mid-July, as last year's unusually long nectar flow finally ebbed, the whole contraption topped out at 275 pounds, including
25 nearly 150 pounds of honey. "Right now, the colony is in a cluster about the size of a soccer ball," says Esaias, who's kept bees for nearly two decades and knows without lifting the lid what's going on inside this hive. "The center of the cluster is where the queen is, and
30 they're keeping her at 93 degrees—the rest are just hanging there, tensing their flight muscles to generate heat." Provided that they have enough calories to fuel their winter workout, a healthy colony can survive as far north as Anchorage, Alaska. "They slowly eat their
35 way up through the winter," he says. "It's a race: Will they eat all their honey before the nectar flows, or not?" To make sure their charges win that race, apiarists have long relied on scale hives for vital management clues. By tracking daily weight variations, a beekeeper can
40 discern when the colony needs a nutritional boost to carry it through lean times, whether to add extra combs for honey storage and even detect incursions by marauding robber bees—all without disturbing the colony. A graph of the hive's weight—which can

45 increase by as much as 35 pounds a day in some parts of the United States during peak nectar flow—reveals the date on which the bees' foraging was most productive and provides a direct record of successful pollination. "Around here, the bees make
50 their living in the month of May," says Esaias, noting that his bees often achieve daily spikes of 25 pounds, the maximum in Maryland. "There's almost no nectar coming in for the rest of the year." A scientist by training and career oceanographer at NASA, Esaias
55 established the Mink Hollow Apiary in his Highland, Maryland, backyard in 1992 with a trio of hand-me-down hives and an antique platform scale much like the one at the Beltsville bee lab. Ever since, he's maintained a meticulous record of the bees' daily
60 weight, as well as weather patterns and such details as his efforts to keep them healthy. In late 2006, honey bees nationwide began disappearing in an ongoing syndrome dubbed colony collapse disorder (CCD). Entire hives went empty as bees inexplicably
65 abandoned their young and their honey. Commercial beekeepers reported losses up to 90 percent, and the large-scale farmers who rely on honey bees to ensure rich harvests of almonds, apples, and sunflowers became very, very nervous. Looking for clues, Esaias
70 turned to his own records. While the resulting graphs threw no light on the cause of CCD, a staggering trend emerged: In the span of just 15 seasons, the date on which his Mink Hollow bees brought home the most nectar had shifted by two weeks—from late May
75 to the middle of the month. "I was shocked when I plotted this up," he says. "It was right under my nose, going on the whole time." The epiphany would lead Esaias to launch a series of research collaborations, featuring honey bees and other pollinators, to
80 investigate the relationships among plants, pollinators, and weather patterns. Already, the work has begun to reveal insights into the often unintended consequences of human interventions in natural and agricultural ecosystems, and exposed significant
85 gaps in how we understand the effect climate change will have on everything from food production to terrestrial ecology.

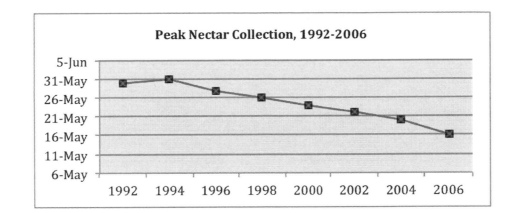

Peak Nectar Collection, 1992-2006

1

Data in the graph provide the most direct support for which idea in the passage?

OR:

Which concept is supported by the passage and by the information in the graph?

A) Human intervention in agriculture can have unintended consequences.
B) Peak nectar collection now occurs earlier than it did in recent years.
C) Bees that consume sufficient nutrients during the winter can survive in northern regions.
D) Bees collect the largest amount of honey during the month of May.

Let's start by considering how the question is constructed. **All of the answers restate points that are mentioned in the passage, so you don't need to look at the passage to check whether a particular answer is present.**

Your only job is to figure out which one of the points the graph supports. The simplest way to do that is figure out the point of the graph. By definition, it must be the same point as the point presented in the passage.

How do you figure out the point of the graph? Start by looking at the title and the data in each of the axes. The title indicates the graph represents when peak nectar collection occurred (when the highest amount of nectar was collected). The x-axis shows years, and the y-axis shows dates in May, with high bars representing dates in late May and low bars representing dates in early May.

The bars get progressively shorter, indicating that peak nectar collection occurred steadily earlier in May between 1992 and 2006. That's exactly what B) says.

The question could also be asked this way:

1

Do the data in the graph provide support for Wayne Esaias's claim that the time when his bees were collecting the most nectar had shifted by two weeks?

A) Yes, because the data provide evidence that peak collection moved from late May to mid-May.

B) Yes, because in each year, peak collection occurred during the month of May.

C) No, because the graph indicates that peak collection shifted from the beginning of June to the beginning of May.

D) No, because peak collection time did not move earlier in every two-year period.

Once again, the question itself states the claim you need to check, namely that Esaias claimed that his bees were collecting the most honey two weeks earlier than they used to. As a result, you do not need to consult the passage at all.

And once again, the easiest way to approach this question is to answer it for real upfront so that you do not become confused by the answer choices.

As discussed before, the graph shows that peak nectar production declined from late May to mid-May between 1992 and 2006. That's a period of two weeks, so yes, the graph does support Esaias's claim. That makes A) the correct answer.

Note: Answer choices may sometimes include terminology that is slightly different from the terminology used in the passage or the question. When this is the case, you must be able to connect the original idea to the rephrased version. Here, for instance, the question refers to the time when bees are "collecting the most nectar," whereas the graph refers to "peak nectar production." It's the same concept, just rephrased in the graph. The principle of "same idea, different words" applies here too.

Now, we're going to look at a question that actually requires you to work with both a graph and a passage. We're going to keep the same passage but use this graph:

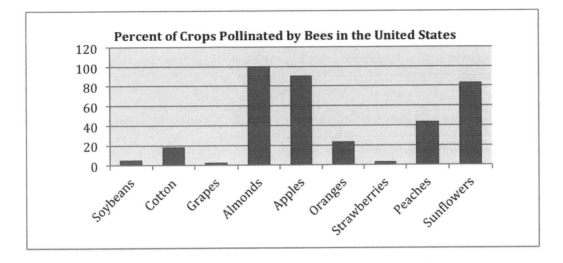

1

What purpose does the graph serve in relation to the passage as a whole?

A) It places the discussion of the bees' disappearance into a larger scientific context.
B) It illustrates which crops are most affected by bees' disappearance.
C) It indicates which crops are most profitable to cultivate in the bees' absence.
D) It demonstrates the consequences of human interference on bee populations.

Start by summing up what information the graph conveys: essentially, it shows how much pollination by bees various crops require. The high bars represent crops that are pollinated primarily or even exclusively by bees, while the low bars represent crops that receive a far lower percentage of their pollination from bees. How does that fit into the passage? Logically, the crops that receive the highest percentage of their pollination from bees will be most affected by the bees' disappearance – which is exactly what B) says.

Let's look at another question:

1

The information in the graph best supports which idea in the passage?

A) Lines 9-11 ("In the 1800s…melons")
B) Lines 44-49 ("A graph…pollination")
C) Lines 65-69 ("Commercial…nervous")
D) Lines 72-75 ("In…month")

317

In this case, the line-reference construction of the answer choices leaves you no choice but to go back to the passage; however, you still need to figure out some basic things beforehand.

First, we're going to take a moment and summarize the information presented in the graph. Let's reiterate the main point: percent/bee poll. varies, but mostly very high/low.

How does the graph relate to the passage? The passage discusses the decline in the bee population, and the graph shows the percentage of pollination from bees that each crop receives.

The graph thus allows us to make some reasonable inferences about how different crops would be affected by the bees' disappearance. Crops that received most of their pollination from bees (high bars) would be strongly affected, while crops that received less of their pollination from bees (low bars) would be less affected.

Now that we've figured out the basics, we're going to look at the answer choices:

A) **In the 1800s, a scale like this would have weighed sacks of grain or crates of apples, peaches, and melons.**

Apples and peaches are *included* in the graph, but this answer is otherwise off-topic. The graph shows the percent of each crop pollinated by bees; weight has nothing to do with that.

B) **A graph of the hive's weight — which can increase by as much as 35 pounds a day in some parts of the United States during peak nectar flow – reveals the date on which the bees' foraging was most productive and provides a direct record of successful pollination.**

Don't be fooled by the word *graph*. This answer has the same problem as A): the lines are about the relationship between weight and foraging, but the graph is about pollination.

C) **Commercial beekeepers reported losses up to 90 percent, and the large-scale farmers who rely on honey bees to ensure rich harvests of almonds, apples, and sunflowers became very, very nervous.**

The graph doesn't depict losses, but it does depict almonds, apples, and sunflowers. In fact, those are the crops that get the highest percentage of their pollination from bees (highest bars). It follows logically that the bees' disappearance would affect those crops the most severely, making beekeepers nervous. So C) works.

D) **In the span of just 15 seasons, the date on which his Mink Hollow bees brought home the most nectar had shifted by two weeks — from late May to the middle of the month.**

Once again, completely off-topic. The graph tells us absolutely nothing about dates, or when the change in nectar production occurred.

So the answer is C).

Alternately, you could be asked to use both the passage and the graph to make a small leap of logic. For example, the question we just looked at could also be asked this way:

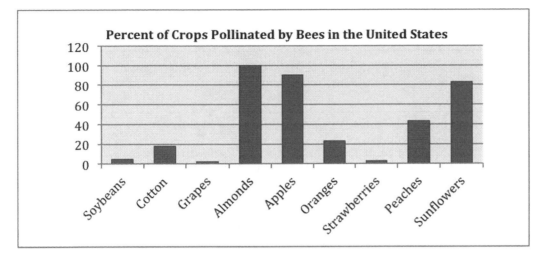

Percent of Crops Pollinated by Bees in the United States

1

Based on information in the passage and the graph, which crop is most likely to remain profitable for large-scale farmers?

A) Peaches
B) Almonds
C) Oranges
D) Sunflowers

The passage indicates that large-scale farmers who grow almonds, apples, and sunflowers have become *very nervous* (lines 68-69) as a result of declining bee populations. The graph supports that statement by showing how dependent these crops are on bees for pollination. Logically, the crops that are **less** dependent on bee pollination (=lower bars) will continue to grow more normally and thus remain profitable. The bar for oranges is lowest, so C) is correct. Although oranges are never mentioned in the passage, you can still make a reasonable inference.

Some questions may also ask you to infer the author's probable attitude toward the graphic:

1

The author of the passage would most likely consider the information in the graph to be

A) questionable data that could reasonably be disputed.
B) intriguing but unsupported by personal observations.
C) an accurate illustration of why some farmers are concerned.
D) more accurate for some regions than for others.

Initially, it might look as if the answer could be anywhere. The question is very general, and there are no line references. If you think carefully, though, you can narrow things down.

The title of the graph provides some very important information. It tells you that the graph is about *crops*. Logically, then, the necessary section of the passage must relate to crops in some way. Based on that information, the mention of "farmers" in C) and "some regions" in D) suggests that the answer is located around one of those words/phrases, with C) the more likely option. You don't know for sure, of course, but these answers are worth checking first.

If you scan for the word *farmers*, you'll discover it appears in one place: line 67. And if you read the entire sentence in which it appears, you'll see that large-scale farmers are particularly concerned because they rely on almonds, apples, and sunflowers – exactly the crops that are most dependent on bee pollination and thus most likely to be affected by the bees' disappearance. So the answer is in fact C).

In another twist, this question could be paired with a supporting evidence question:

2

Which lines from the passage provide the best evidence for the previous question?

A) Lines 49-50 ("Around…May")
B) Lines 65-69 ("Commercial…nervous")
C) Lines 72-75 ("In…month")
D) Lines 81-84 ("Already…ecosystems")

In this case, the process for answering Question #1 is similar. Although the paired structure looks more complicated, it actually gives you some help by providing specific possibilities for where the answer is located.

You still need to start by reiterating the big picture of the graph. If you know that it focuses on specific crops, you can check each set of lines for references to crops. Then, simply plug the line references into the first question, just as you would for any other supporting evidence pair:

1

The author of the passage would most likely consider the information in the graph to be

A) Lines 49-50 ("Around…May")
B) Lines 65-69 ("Commercial…nervous")
C) Lines 72-75 ("In…month")
D) Lines 81-84 ("Already…ecosystems")

When you get to B), the content overlap with the graph should be clear. Even if you don't immediately make the connection between the bars of the graph and the relative vulnerability of various crops, the fact that both the graph and this section of the passage have the same focus provides an important clue that B) is the correct answer.

Graphics and Extended Reasoning

Like extended reasoning questions that accompany text-only passages, some graphic-based questions may ask you to step beyond the words and images that appear in the passage/graphic and identify information that would support or provide a better understanding of a statement in the passage.

For example, we're going to come back to our original graph:

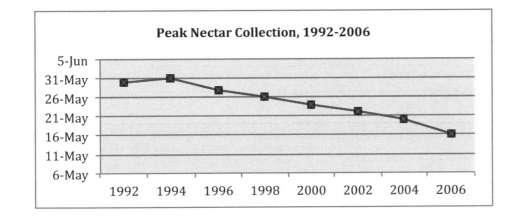

1

What information, if presented in the graph, would be most useful in developing the "insights" referred to in line 82?

A) The types of pesticides used to treat crops pollinated by bees.

B) Crop varieties pollinated by bees at different times of the year.

C) Plant species from which bees collect the greatest amount of nectar.

D) The average number of bees associated with a hive between 1992 and 2006.

Start by defining the "insights" mentioned in line 82: *Already, the work has begun to reveal insights into the <u>often unintended consequences of human interventions in natural and agricultural ecosystems</u> and exposed significant gaps in how we understand the effect climate change will have on everything from food production to terrestrial ecology.*

Based on this statement, you can infer that the correct answer must have something to do with *the unintended consequences of human interventions.*

Now, look at the answers. Only one option is in any way related to *human intervention* in the environment: A). Pesticides are created by humans, and information about which types are used could help shed light on how they might inadvertently affect crop growth – that is, their *unintended consequences* (lines 82-83). All of the other answers involve naturally occurring phenomena unrelated to human intervention.

Graphics and Data Analysis Exercises

Note: Some of the graphs in this exercise refer to a passage when none is provided. This is a deliberate strategy intended to reinforce the point that many questions can be answered using the graph alone, even when the passage is mentioned in the question.

1.

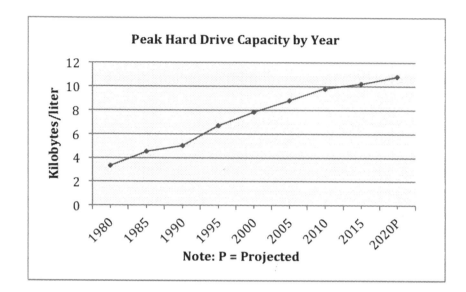

1

According to the graph, which statement is true about peak hard drive capacity in 2005?

A) It was double the peak hard drive capacity of a decade earlier.

B) It was around one kilobyte/liter higher than it had been five years earlier.

C) It was higher than peak hard drive capacity in 2010.

D) It was nine kilobytes/liter lower than it was in 2010.

2

Which choice best summarizes the information presented in the graph?

A) Hard drive capacity is expected to peak sometime before 2020.

B) Peak hard drive capacity was slightly higher in 2000 than in 1995.

C) Expanding peak hard drive capacity has led to a large increase in computer sales.

D) Peak hard drive capacity has increased dramatically since 1980.

2.

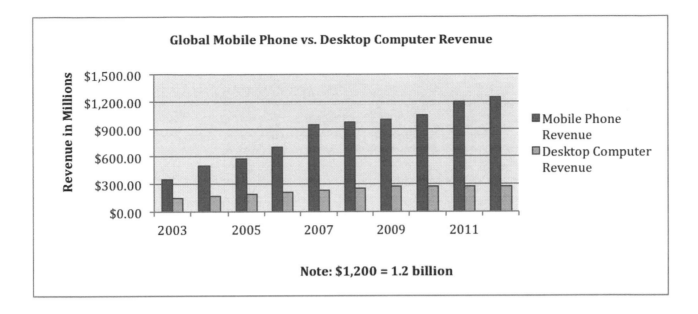

1

According to the graph, which statement is true about the amount of revenue from mobile phone sales in 2008?

A) It was slightly higher than the amount of revenue from PC sales in 2008.

B) It was similar to the amount of revenue from PC sales in 2009.

C) It was similar to the amount of revenue from mobile phone sales in 2009.

D) It was wildly out of proportion to the amount of revenue from mobiles phone sales the previous year.

2

Which information best summarizes the information presented in the graph?

A) The gap between revenue from mobile phone sales and PC sales has increased significantly.

B) Revenue from PC sales increased more rapidly than did revenue from mobile phone sales.

C) Revenue from tablet sales may soon overtake revenue from mobile phone sales.

D) Revenue from mobile phone sales has risen steadily, while revenue from PC sales has declined.

3

Data in the graph provide most direct support for which idea in the passage?

A) People increasingly prefer mobile devices for common tasks.

B) Consumers prefer to buy from companies whose products are already familiar to them.

C) Mobile sales in new markets are substantially higher than are mobile sales in established markets.

D) Tablets can now perform many of the same functions as mobile phones.

3.

Figure 1

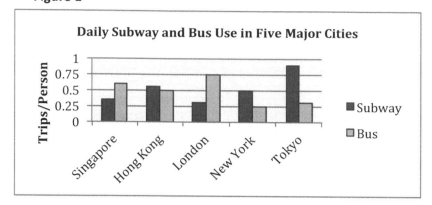

Figure 2

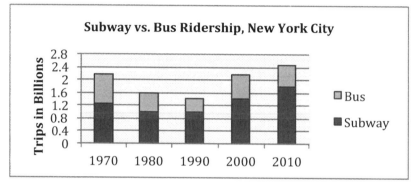

1

Information in figure 1 suggests that public transportation users in London

A) take subways and buses at similar rates.
B) are unusually reliant on buses.
C) take at least one subway trip daily.
D) take subways at about the same rate as people in New York.

2

Which of the following statements about bus use in New York City is best supported by information in figure 2?

A) It reached its highest point in 2010.
B) It was lower in 1980 than it was in 1990.
C) It began to rebound after 1990.
D) It declined in every decade.

3

Information in Figure 1 supports the author's point that buses are growing in popularity as a means of urban transport by indicating that

A) many people around the world take at least one bus trip every day.
B) bus ridership surpasses subway ridership in some major cities.
C) people in Tokyo make far more trips by bus daily than they do trips by subway.
D) the number of bus trips taken by people in major cities has substantially increased.

4

Taken together, the graphs suggest that public transit users in New York City

A) use buses more often today than they did in previous decades.
B) use buses about as often as they use the subway.
C) rely more heavily on buses than do public transit users in other cities.
D) increasingly prefer to travel by subway.

4. The following passage is adapted from Michael Anft, "Solving the Mystery of Death Valley's Walking Rocks," © 2011 by *Johns Hopkins Magazine*.

For six decades, observers have been confounded by the movement of large rocks across a dry lake bed in California's Death Valley National Park. Leaving flat trails behind them, rocks that weigh up to 100
5 pounds seemingly do Michael Jackson's moonwalk across the valley's sere, cracked surface, sometimes traveling more than 100 yards. Without a body of water to pick them up and move them, the rocks at Racetrack Playa, a flat space between the valley's high cliffs,
10 have been the subject of much speculation, including whether they have been relocated by human pranksters or space aliens. The rocks have become the desert equivalent of Midwestern crop circles. "They really are a curiosity," says Ralph Lorenz, a planetary scientist at
15 the Applied Physics Laboratory. "Some [people] have mentioned UFOs. But I've always believed that this is something science could solve."
It has tried. One theory holds that the rocks are blown along by powerful winds. Another posits that
20 the wind pushes thin sheets of ice, created when the desert's temperatures dip low enough to freeze water from a rare rainstorm, and the rocks go along for the ride. But neither theory is rock solid. Winds at the playa aren't strong enough—some scientists believe that
25 they'd have to be 100 miles per hour or more—to blow the rocks across the valley. And rocks subject to the "ice sailing theory" wouldn't create trails as they moved.
Lorenz and a team of investigators believe that a
30 combination of forces may work to rearrange Racetrack Playa's rocks. "We saw that it would take a lot of wind to move these rocks, which are larger than you'd expect wind to move," Lorenz explains. "That led us to this idea that ice might be picking up the
35 rocks and floating them." As they explained in the January issue of *The American Journal of Physics*, instead of moving along with wind-driven sheets of ice, the rocks may instead be lifted by the ice, making them more subject to the wind's force. The key, Lorenz
40 says, is that the lifting by an "ice collar" reduces friction with the ground, to the point that the wind now has enough force to move the rock. The rock moves, the ice doesn't, and because part of the rock juts through the ice, it marks the territory it has covered.
45 Lorenz's team came to its conclusion through a combination of intuition, lab work, and observation— not that the last part was easy. Watching the rocks travel is a bit like witnessing the rusting of a hubcap. Instances of movement are rare and last for only a few

50 seconds. Lorenz's team placed low-resolution cameras on the cliffs (which are about 30 miles from the nearest paved road) to take pictures once per hour. For the past three winters, the researchers have weathered extreme temperatures and several flat tires to measure how
55 often the thermometer dips below freezing, how often the playa gets rain and floods, and the strength of the winds. "The measurements seem to back up our hypothesis," he says. "Any of the theories may be true at any one time, but ice rafting may be the best explan-
60 ation for the trails we've been seeing. We've seen trails like this documented in Arctic coastal areas, and the mechanism is somewhat similar. A belt of ice sur- rounds a boulder during high tide, picks it up, and then drops it elsewhere." His "ice raft theory" was also
65 borne out by an experiment that used the ingenuity of a high school science fair. Lorenz placed a basalt pebble in a Tupperware container with water so that the pebble projected just above the surface. He then turned the container upside down in a baking tray filled with a
70 layer of coarse sand at its base, and put the whole thing in his home freezer. The rock's "keel" (its protruding part) projected downward into the sand, which simu- lated the cracked surface of the playa (which scientists call "Special K" because of its resemblance to cereal
75 flakes). A gentle push or slight puff of air caused the Tupperware container to move, just as an ice raft would under the right conditions. The pebble made a trail in the soft sand. "It was primitive but effective," Lorenz says of the experiment. Lorenz has spent the
80 last 20 years studying Titan, a moon of Saturn. He says that Racetrack Playa's surface mirrors that of a dried lakebed on Titan. Observations and experiments on Earth may yield clues to that moon's geology. "We also may get some idea of how climate affects
85 geology—particularly as the climate changes here on Earth," Lorenz says. "When we study other planets and their moons, we're forced to use Occam's razor – sometimes the simplest answer is best, which means you look to Earth for some answers. Once you get out
90 there on Earth, you realize how strange so much of its surface is. So, you have to figure there's weird stuff to be found on Titan as well." Whether that's true or not will take much more investigation. He adds: "One day, we'll figure all this out. For the moment, the moving
95 rock present a wonderful problem to study in a beautiful place."

Racetrack Playa Average vs. Maximum Wind Speed

	Average Wind Speed (miles/hour)	Peak Wind Speed (miles/hour)
2008		
November	20	67
December	19	72
January	21	78
February	23	92
March	25	87
2009		
November	19	69
December	21	71
January	20	76
February	22	90
March	24	89

1

According to the graph, which statement is true about wind speeds at Racketrack Playa in 2009?

A) Peak wind speeds increased during every month between November and March.

B) Average wind speeds increased during every month between November and March.

C) Average wind speed in February was substantially higher than it was in December.

D) The lowest peak wind speed occurred in November.

2

Which choice is best supported by the information in the chart?

A) Peak wind speeds in 2009 were higher in every month than they were in 2008.

B) Average wind speeds in some months exceeded peak wind speeds in others.

C) The windiest months at Racetrack Playa were February and March.

D) Peak wind speed in February 2009 was higher than peak wind speed in February 2008.

3

Which of the following statements from the passage is represented by the chart?

A) Lines 16-17 ("But...solve")

B) Lines 23-26 ("Winds...valley")

C) Lines 39-42 ("The key...rock")

D) Lines 58-60 ("Any...seeing")

5. The following passage is adapted from "Makerspaces, Hackerspaces, and Community Scale Production in Detroit and Beyond," © 2013 by Sean Ansanelli.

During the mid-1980s, spaces began to emerge across Europe where computer hackers could convene for mutual support and camaraderie. In the past few years, the idea of fostering such shared, physical spaces
5 has been rapidly adapted by the diverse and growing community of "makers," who seek to apply the idea of "hacking" to physical objects, processes, or anything else that can be deciphered and improved upon.

A hackerspace is described by hackerspaces.org as
10 a "community-operated physical space where people with common interests, often in computers, technology, science, digital art or electronic art, can meet, socialize, and/or collaborate." Such spaces can vary in size, available technology, and membership structure (some
15 being completely open), but generally share community-oriented characteristics. Indeed, while the term "hacker" can sometimes have negative connotations, modern hackerspaces thrive off of community, openness, and assimilating diverse viewpoints – these
20 often being the only guiding principles in otherwise informal organizational structures.

In recent years, the city of Detroit has emerged as a hotbed for hackerspaces and other DIY ("Do-It-Yourself") experiments. Several hackerspaces
25 can already be found throughout the city and several more are currently in formation. Of course, Detroit's attractiveness for such projects can be partially attributed to cheap real estate, which allows aspiring hackers to acquire ample space for experimentation.
30 Some observers have also described this kind of making and tinkering as embedded in the DNA of Detroit's residents, who are able to harness substantial intergenerational knowledge and attract like-minded individuals.
35 Hackerspaces (or "makerspaces") can be found in more commercial forms, but the vast majority of spaces are self-organized and not-for-profit. For example, the OmniCorp hackerspace operates off member fees to cover rent and new equipment, from laser cutters to
40 welding tools. OmniCorp also hosts an "open hack night" every Thursday in which the space is open to the general public. Potential members are required to attend at least one open hack night prior to a consensus vote by the existing members for admittance; no
45 prospective members have yet been denied.

A visit to one of OmniCorp's open hack nights reveals the vast variety of activity and energy existing in the space. In the main common room alone, activities range from experimenting with sound installations and
50 learning to program Arduino boards to building speculative "oloid" shapes – all just for the sake of it. With a general atmosphere of mutual support, participants in the space are continually encouraged to help others.
55 One of the most active community-focused initiatives in the city is the Mt. Elliot Makerspace. Jeff Sturges, former MIT Media Lab Fellow and Co-Founder of OmniCorp, started the Mt. Elliot project with the aim of replicating MIT's Fab Lab model on a smaller, cheaper
60 scale in Detroit. "Fab Labs" are production facilities that consist of a small collection of flexible computer-controlled tools that cover several different scales and various materials, with the aim to make "almost anything" (including other machines). The Mt. Elliot
65 Makerspace now offers youth-based skill development programs in eight areas: Transportation, Electronics, Digital Tools, Wearables, Design and Fabrication, Food, Music, and Arts. The range of activities is meant to provide not only something for everyone, but a well-
70 rounded base knowledge of making to all participants.

While the center receives some foundational support, the space also derives significant support from the local community. Makerspaces throughout the city connect the space's youth-based programming directly to
75 school curriculums.

The growing interest in and development of hacker/makerspaces has been explained, in part, as a result of the growing maker movement. Through the combination of cultural norms and communication
80 channels from open source production as well as increasingly available technologies for physical production, amateur maker communities have developed in virtual and physical spaces.

Publications such as *Wired* are noticing the
85 transformative potential of this emerging movement and have sought to devote significant attention to its development. Chief editor Chris Anderson recently published a book entitled *Makers*, in which he proclaims that the movement will become the next Industrial
90 Revolution. Anderson argues such developments will allow for a new wave of business opportunities by providing mass-customization rather than mass-production.

The transformative potential of these trends goes
95 beyond new business opportunities or competitive advantages for economic growth. Rather, these trends demonstrate the potential to actually transform economic development models entirely.

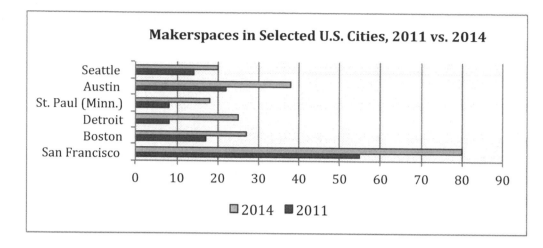

Makerspaces in Selected U.S. Cities, 2011 vs. 2014

■ 2014 ■ 2011

6. The following passage is adapted from Julian Jackson, "New Research Suggests Dinosaurs Were Warm-Blooded and Active" © 2011 by Julian Jackson.

New research from the University of Adelaide has added to the debate about whether dinosaurs were cold-blooded and sluggish or warm-blooded and active. Professor Roger Seymour from the University's School
5   of Earth & Environmental Sciences has applied the latest theories of human and animal anatomy and physiology to provide insight into the lives of dinosaurs.

Human thigh bones have tiny holes – known as the
10 "nutrient foramen" – on the shaft that supply blood to living bone cells inside. New research has shown that the size of those holes is related to the maximum rate that a person can be active during aerobic exercise. Professor Seymour has used this principle to evaluate
15 the activity levels of dinosaurs.

"Far from being lifeless, bone cells have a relatively high metabolic rate and they therefore require a large blood supply to deliver oxygen. On the inside of the bone, the blood supply comes usually from a single
20 artery and vein that pass through a hole on the shaft – the nutrient foramen," he says.

Professor Seymour wondered whether the size of the nutrient foramen might indicate how much blood was necessary to keep the bones in good repair. For
25 example, highly active animals might cause more bone 'microfractures,' requiring more frequent repairs by the bone cells and therefore a greater blood supply. "My aim was to see whether we could use fossil bones of dinosaurs to indicate the level of bone metabolic rate
30 and possibly extend it to the whole body's metabolic rate," he says. "One of the big controversies among paleobiologists is whether dinosaurs were cold-blooded and sluggish or warm-blooded and active. Could the size of the foramen be a possible gauge for dinosaur
35 metabolic rate?"

Comparisons were made with the sizes of the holes in living mammals and reptiles, and their metabolic rates. Measuring mammals ranging from mice to elephants, and reptiles from lizards to crocodiles, one
40 of Professor Seymour's Honors students, Sarah Smith, combed the collections of Australian museums, photographing and measuring hundreds of tiny holes in thigh bones.

"The results were unequivocal. The sizes of the holes
45 were related closely to the maximum metabolic rates during peak movement in mammals and reptiles," Professor Seymour says. "The holes found in mammals were about 10 times larger than those in reptiles."

These holes were compared to those of fossil
50 dinosaurs. Dr. Don Henderson, Curator of Dinosaurs from the Royal Tyrrell Museum in Alberta, Canada, and Daniela Schwarz-Wings from the Museum für Naturkunde Humboldt University Berlin, Germany measured the holes in 10 species of
55 dinosaurs from five different groups, including bipedal and quadrupedal carnivores and herbivores, weighing 50kg to 20,000kg.

"On a relative comparison to eliminate the differences in body size, all of the dinosaurs had
60 holes in their thigh bones larger than those of mammals," Professor Seymour says.

"The dinosaurs appeared to be even more active than the mammals. We certainly didn't expect to see that. These results provide additional weight to
65 theories that dinosaurs were warm-blooded and highly active creatures, rather than cold-blooded and sluggish."

Professor Seymour says following the results of this study, it's likely that a simple measurement of
70 foramen size could be used to evaluate maximum activity levels in other vertebrate animals.

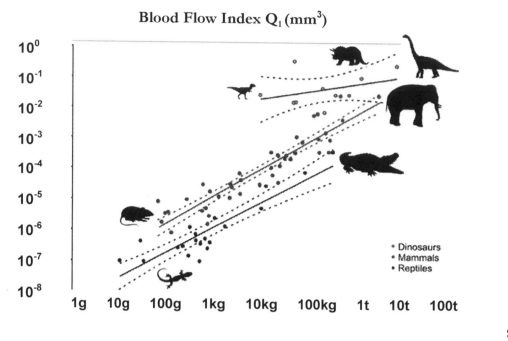

Blood Flow Index Q₁ (mm³)

Seymour et al 2011

1

Which statement is best supported by data in the graph?

A) Light reptiles have higher blood flow than heavier reptiles.

B) Heavy mammals have lower blood flow than heavy reptiles.

C) Blood flow in the heaviest mammals is slightly higher than in light dinosaurs.

D) Blood flow is fairly uniform in dinosaurs at a wide range of weights.

2

The author of the passage would most likely consider the information in the graph to be

A) a compelling piece of evidence in support of Professor Seymour's theory.

B) a potentially interesting but premature finding.

C) conclusive proof that dinosaurs were active and warm-blooded.

D) suggestive of a point of view towards which the author is skeptical.

3

Do the data in the table provide support for Professor Seymour's claim that dinosaurs were warm-blooded and highly active?

A) Yes, because they indicate that dinosaurs had foramens larger than the foramens of the largest mammals.

B) Yes, because they suggest that dinosaurs had even higher metabolic rates than animals known to be warm-blooded.

C) No, because they show that dinosaurs had lower blood flow than reptiles.

D) No, because they reveal only minimal changes in metabolic rate between small and large dinosaurs.

Explanations: Graphics and Data Analysis Exercises

1.1 B

B) is correct because the point for 2005 indicates that peak hard drive capacity was approximately 9 kilobytes/liter. Even though that number does not appear on the graph, you can infer that this is the case because 8 and 10 do appear, and the point for 2005 is situated between them. If you look back to 2000, you can see that the graph indicates a peak capacity of 8 kilobytes/liter, or one less than in 2005. Note that this question can be tricky if you forget that each line on the graph represents *two* kilobytes/liter. A point halfway between two lines therefore equals one kilobyte/liter.

A) is incorrect because peak hard drive capacity in 1995 (a decade earlier) was 7 – only 2 kilobytes less, not half (that would be 4). C) is incorrect because peak hard drive capacity in 2010 was higher than in 2005; you can tell just by looking at the graph. D) is incorrect for the same reason as C) – don't get thrown off by the mention of the number nine. In this case, it indicates the peak hard drive capacity was 9 kilobytes/liter, not that it was 9 kilobytes/liter *less*.

1.2 D

Remember that this question is asking you to **summarize** the graph, not just to identify which statement it supports. The point of the graph is that peak hard drive capacity has increased enormously since 1980 and is predicted to continue increasing. Based on that information alone, you should be able to identify D) as the answer.

Playing process of elimination, A) is incorrect because the graph indicates that peak hard drive capacity will keep increasing through 2020; it will not peak before then. For B), it is true that the peak hard drive capacity was slightly higher in 2000 than in 1995, but that statement only describes a small portion of the graph, and the question asks for the big picture. C) is incorrect because the graph provides no information at all about computer sales; this answer is beyond the bounds of what can be inferred.

2.1 C

If you look at the graph as a whole, you should notice that mobile phone revenue has gone up very substantially, whereas PC revenue has been much lower and has grown much more slowly. Furthermore, mobile phone revenue has been consistently much higher than PC revenue. Using that information, you can assume both A) and B) are wrong – at no point was mobile phone revenue only *slightly* higher than PC revenue, nor was it ever similar to PC revenue. In D), the phrase "wildly out of proportion" should also give you pause. Indeed the graph indicates that mobile phone revenue leveled off beginning in 2007. In 2008 (the tick mark between 2007 and 2009), it was only marginally higher than in 2007. That leaves C), which is correct: the mobile phone bars for 2008 and 2009 are almost the same.

2.2. A

Take a moment to reiterate the point of the graph: mobile phone revenue has gone way up, whereas PC revenue has increased much more slowly and stayed far below mobile phone revenue. By the most recent year indicated in the graph, the PC bars are only about a quarter as high as the mobile phone bars. In contrast, they are half as high during the first year plotted on the graph. That indicates a larger gap between mobile phone and PC sales, making A) correct. B) is incorrect because the graph indicates the opposite: revenue from PC sales increased more slowly than revenue from mobile phone sales. C) is incorrect because the graph shows nothing about tablets. D) is incorrect because PC revenue did not decline – it merely increased less than mobile phone revenue did.

2.3 A

Forget about the reference to the passage that isn't there – the question is really asking what the graph shows, i.e., its "point." What is that point? That mobile phone revenue is increasingly outstripping desktop computer revenue. What does that suggest? That mobile phones have become much, much more popular than desktop computers. Which answer is most consistent with that idea? A). Even though that answer does not mention anything about desktop computers, it is still generally consistent with the graph – if people increasingly prefer mobile "devices" (note the slight change of terminology from the graph) for "numerous common tasks," then revenue from sales of mobile devices would logically increase as well (and implicitly, sales of desktop computers, which were previously used for those tasks, would go down). B) is incorrect because the graph provides no information about companies, familiar to consumers or not. C) is incorrect because the graph likewise provides no information about established vs. un-established markets. D) is incorrect because the graph provides information about mobile phones only, not mobile devices in general. Note how this is different from A): correct answers may phrase information from the graph in a more general way ("mobile *phones*" in the graph vs. "mobile *devices*" in the correct answer), but they cannot replace specific information from a graph with something equally specific (e.g., tablets).

3.1 B

When you look at the bar for London on the graph, there are two things to notice: one is that the bar for buses is much higher than the bar for subways, and the other is that the bar for buses is higher than it is in any other city. That indicates that people in London take buses at a higher rate than people in other cities. In other words, they are "unusually reliant on buses." The answer is therefore B). A) is incorrect because, as stated, the bar for buses is much higher than that for subways. C) is incorrect because the graph indicates just over .25 trips/person daily. (Remember that the bars represent increments of .25, not one). D) is incorrect because the bar for subway use in New York is much higher than the bar for subway use in London.

3.2 C

Start by making sure that you're looking only at the top part of the bar (light gray), which shows bus use, not at the entire bar, which shows both bus and subway use. If you consider the graph as a whole, you can notice that the "bus" bars get smaller and then larger again. The correct answer is related to that fact. C) correctly states that bus use began to rebound (become larger) after 1990, which is precisely what the graph shows – there is a big leap from 1990 to 2000. A) is incorrect because the graph indicates that bus use was higher in 1970 than in 2010. B) is incorrect because the bar for bus use in 1990 is clearly *smaller* than the bar for 1980. D) is incorrect because bus use only declined until 1990, after which it began to increase.

3.3 B

This question is fairly complex, so start by simplifying it. First, don't get distracted by the reference to the (non-existent) passage. The question is only telling you that the graph supports a point in the passage, and that the point in the passage will be the point of the graph. So the question is really only asking you to determine the point of the graph. What is the point of the graph? Bus use is more common in some cities, and subway use is more common in others. That is consistent with B), which is the answer. If you think about the question carefully, that makes sense: the fact that people in some cities use buses more heavily than subways would indeed support the idea that buses are growing in popularity. A) is incorrect because the graph does not indicate that people take more than one bus trip per day in any city – remember that each bar represents .25 trips, not one. C) is incorrect because it states the opposite of what the graph shows – people in Tokyo take far more *subway* trips than bus trips. D) is incorrect because the graph indicates nothing about whether bus trips have increased or not – it only gives us a snapshot of how many trips people take on average at one point in time.

3.4 D

The question is essentially telling you that the graphs depict similar phenomena, so start by figuring out what one graph reveals, then use the other graph to confirm that idea. If you look at Figure 1, you can see that subway ridership is a lot higher than bus ridership, so the correct answer must be related to that idea. That is essentially what D) says, so you can assume that it is right. If you look at Figure 2, you'll see that subway use has risen significantly since 1990, indicating that people in New York *increasingly* prefer the subway. A) is incorrect because the graph shows the opposite – bus use has declined, suggesting that preference for it has declined; B) is incorrect because the graphs show that subway use is much higher than bus use. C) is incorrect because Figure 1 shows that bus use is higher in London and Singapore than in New York. Figure 2 also shows nothing about bus use in cities other than New York.

4.1 D

A) is incorrect because peak wind speed was lower in March than in February (89 vs. 90). B) is incorrect because average wind speed was higher in December than in January (21 vs. 20). C) is incorrect because average wind speed in February was only 1 mph higher than in December (22 vs. 21), not *substantially* higher. D) is correct because 69 mph is the lowest peak wind speed provided for any month in 2009.

4.2 C

Unlike a graph, from which you can get a very quick overview of a situation, a chart isn't nearly as easy to get the big picture from. For that reason, you are better off working through the answers one by one rather than trying to get an overview of the chart as a whole. A) can be eliminated easily if you start from November and compare peak wind speeds in 2008 to those in 2009: peak speed in December 2008 was higher than in December 2009. B) is phrased in a general way, but that answer can be eliminated easily as well: all of the values for average speed are clearly far below all of the values for peak speed. C) is correct because the values for both average and peak wind speeds are higher than they are in any other month. D) is incorrect because peak wind speed in February 2009 (90) was lower than peak wind speed in February 2008 (92).

4.3 B

Before you start hunting through the passage, figure out what sort of statement you're looking for. The chart indicates various wind speeds, so the correct section of the passage must focus on wind speeds as well. A) is off-topic – those lines have nothing to do with wind speeds. B) is correct because those lines indicate that the winds at Racetrack Playa would have needed to blow more than 100 mph to move the rocks, and the chart indicates that their highest speed was 92 mph. Be careful with C) – lines 39-40 do refer to the wind, but the chart shows nothing about "ice collars" or rock movement. D) is likewise incorrect because the chart reveals nothing directly about ice rafting, only wind speed.

5.1 B

This is a straightforward detail question, so you don't need to worry about the point of the graph. A) is incorrect because there were more makerspaces in Austin in 2014 than in Detroit the same year. Be careful not to get confused by the fact that there were fewer makerspaces in Austin in 2011 than in Detroit in 2014. B) is correct because the number of makerspaces is Austin in 2014 was just under 40, while the number in San Francisco was 80 – that's almost half. C) is incorrect because the number of makerspaces in Austin grew from 2011 to 2014. D) is incorrect because the 2014 bar for Austin is longer than the 2014 bar for Boston.

5.2 C

What is the point of the graph? Basically, that there were far more makerspaces in various U.S. cities in 2014 than in 2011. What is the point of the passage? That makerspaces are a major, growing phenomenon that could transform the economy. Would the author's attitude toward the graph be positive or negative? Positive. Eliminate B) and D). Now, look at A) and C). Be very careful with A). The author does state that makerspaces will revolutionize the economy, but the graph provides no information whatsoever about the economy. A) can thus be eliminated, leaving C). The author would likely approve of the fact that makerspaces are proliferating so rapidly across the United States.

5.3 A

If you keep the point of the passage in mind, this question is fairly straightforward. You're looking for the lines that indicate that makerspaces are sprouting up all over the place. That's big-picture information, so the answer is probably located at the beginning or the end of the passage. A) or D) are thus most likely to be correct. If you work in order, you'll hit the answer quickly: lines 3-6 state that *the idea of fostering such shared, physical spaces has been rapidly adapted by the diverse and growing community of "makers,"* which corresponds to the growth of makerspaces depicted in the graph.

6.1 D

Since the question is phrased so generally, you can assume that the answer will be related to the point of the graph. The graph has a lot going on, but if you had to pick out the most important information, it would probably have something to do with the fact that dinosaurs are way up at the top (indicating very high blood flow), above both mammals and reptiles. Keeping that in mind, you can check the answers. A) is incorrect because the relationship between weight and blood flow is linear – heavy reptiles have higher blood flow than light reptiles. B) is incorrect because the line for heavy mammals is clearly well above the line for heavy reptiles. You can use the point to eliminate C) – all of the dinosaurs are heavier than even the heaviest mammals. D) is correct because the graph indicates that blood flow is similarly high (=relatively uniform) in dinosaurs at weights ranging from 1 kilogram to 10 tons.

6.2 A

What does the author think? He has a pretty positive attitude toward Professor Seymour's theory – the passage indicates that there's a fair amount of evidence to suggest it's accurate. What is that theory? That dinosaurs were warm-blooded and active, as indicated by their high maximum blood flow (i.e., their metabolic rate). What does the graph show? That dinosaurs had extremely high blood flow, indicating extremely high metabolism. So logically, the author would have a positive attitude toward the graph. That eliminates B) and D). Now consider A) and C). The wording of C) should make you immediately suspicious; a single graph isn't enough to "conclusively prove" anything. The graph does, however, provide excellent "support" for Seymour's theory, making A) correct.

6.3 B

Although the question alludes to the passage, you don't actually need it. The question itself tells you the relevant piece of information: Professor Seymour claims that dinosaurs are warm-blooded and active. Your only job is to determine whether the graph supports that claim. What does the graph show? That dinosaurs had extremely high blood flow, which is consistent with Professor Seymour's theory (high maximum blood flow = high metabolic rate = warm-bloodedness). That eliminates C) and D). A) can also be eliminated because the graph provides no information about foramen size, leaving B). That answer is correct because the graph indicates that blood flow is higher in all dinosaurs than in even the heaviest mammals, which are known to be warm-blooded.

Appendix A: 2018 <u>Official Guide</u> Questions by Category

Test	Question #

Vocabulary in Context

Test	Question #
Test 1	3
Test 1	8
Test 1	12
Test 1	18
Test 1	40
Test 1	45
Test 1	48
Test 2	14
Test 2	16
Test 2	25
Test 2	37
Test 2	39
Test 2	43
Test 2	47
Test 3	2
Test 3	6
Test 3	16
Test 3	17
Test 3	22
Test 3	28
Test 3	31
Test 3	35
Test 3	47
Test 4	3
Test 4	9
Test 4	10
Test 4	13
Test 4	18
Test 4	24
Test 4	33
Test 4	34
Test 5	10
Test 5	14
Test 5	15
Test 5	22
Test 5	29
Test 5	37
Test 5	38
Test 5	44
Test 5	47
Test 6	2
Test 6	14
Test 6	18
Test 6	26
Test 6	35
Test 6	37
Test 6	44
Test 7	10
Test 7	15
Test 7	18
Test 7	31
Test 7	32
Test 7	35
Test 7	49
Test 8	8
Test 8	12
Test 8	13
Test 8	25
Test 8	27
Test 8	35
Test 8	38
Test 8	49

The Big Picture

Test	Question #	
Test 1	1	Summary of a passage
Test 1	32	Purpose of a passage
Test 1	33	Main point
Test 2	1	Summary
Test 2	11	Purpose of a passage
Test 2	29	Purpose of a passage
Test 2	33	Main point
Test 3	1	Summary
Test 3	14	Point of a paragraph
Test 3	48	Purpose of a paragraph
Test 4	11	Summary of a paragraph
Test 4	22	Purpose of a passage
Test 4	41	Purpose of a passage
Test 4	42	Purpose of a passage
Test 5	8	Main idea of paragraph
Test 5	11	Point of a passage
Test 5	16	Central claim
Test 5	17	Point of a passage

Non-Paired "Support/Contradict" Questions

Literal Comprehension

Test 6 34 Evidence
Test 6 38 No line reference
Test 6 39 Evidence
Test 6 47 No line reference
Test 6 48 Evidence
Test 7 2
Test 7 5 No line reference
Test 7 6 Evidence
Test 7 8 No line reference
Test 7 9 Evidence
Test 7 12 No line reference
Test 7 13 Evidence
Test 7 46 No line reference
Test 7 47 Evidence
Test 8 7
Test 8 10
Test 8 14 No line reference
Test 8 15 Evidence
Test 8 26
Test 8 28 No line reference
Test 8 29 Evidence
Test 8 43 No line reference
Test 8 44 Evidence
Test 8 47
Test 8 48
Test 8 52

Inference

Test 1 15 Attitude
Test 1 21 Main point
Test 1 26
Test 2 26
Test 2 38
Test 2 48 No line reference
Test 2 49 Evidence
Test 3 3 No line reference
Test 3 4 Evidence
Test 3 8
Test 3 23 Assumption
Test 3 29 No line reference
Test 3 30 Evidence
Test 3 32 No line reference
Test 3 33 Evidence
Test 3 43 Line reference
Test 3 44 Evidence
Test 3 45 No line reference
Test 3 46 Evidence
Test 3 49 Assumption

Test 4 8
Test 4 16 No line reference
Test 4 17 Evidence
Test 4 25 No line reference
Test 4 26 Evidence
Test 4 31
Test 4 35
Test 4 48
Test 5 3
Test 5 13
Test 5 33 No line reference
Test 5 34 Evidence
Test 5 50 No line reference
Test 5 51 Evidence
Test 6 7 No line reference
Test 6 8 Evidence
Test 6 24
Test 6 30
Test 6 45 No line reference
Test 6 46 Evidence
Test 7 24 No line reference
Test 7 25 Evidence
Test 7 27 No line reference
Test 7 28 Evidence
Test 7 33 No line reference
Test 7 34 Evidence
Test 7 36 No line reference
Test 7 37 Evidence
Test 7 44 No line reference
Test 7 45 Evidence
Test 8 5 No line reference
Test 8 6 Evidence
Test 8 33 No line reference
Test 8 34 Evidence

Extended Reasoning/Analogy

Test 5 36
Test 7 21
Test 7 52 Analogy
Test 8 3
Test 8 16
Test 8 36
Test 8 50

Function/Purpose

Test 1	19
Test 1	22
Test 1	25
Test 1	27
Test 1	32
Test 1	34
Test 1	42
Test 1	46
Test 2	2
Test 2	4
Test 2	8
Test 2	11
Test 2	15
Test 2	28
Test 2	29
Test 2	34
Test 3	5
Test 3	11
Test 3	25
Test 4	4
Test 4	22
Test 4	30
Test 4	41
Test 4	42
Test 4	45
Test 5	2
Test 5	48
Test 5	52
Test 6	1
Test 6	3
Test 6	5
Test 6	6
Test 6	11
Test 6	15
Test 6	22
Test 6	29
Test 6	36
Test 6	40
Test 6	50
Test 7	4
Test 7	7
Test 7	11
Test 7	14
Test 7	22
Test 7	23
Test 7	26
Test 7	30
Test 7	43
Test 8	2
Test 8	9
Test 8	11
Test 8	18
Test 8	32
Test 8	41
Test 8	42
Test 8	46

Tone and Attitude

Test 1	6	Attitude
Test 1	15	Attitude
Test 3	42	Tone
Test 4	1	No line reference
Test 4	2	Evidence
Test 4	19	Graphic
Test 4	23	Attitude
Test 5	24	Attitude/Line reference
Test 5	25	Evidence
Test 7	16	Attitude/Line reference
Test 7	17	Evidence
Test 8	45	Tone

Rhetorical Strategy and Passage Organization

Test 1	2	Passage structure
Test 1	34	
Test 2	3	Point of view
Test 2	12	Counterargument
Test 3	21	Passage organization
Test 4	43	Passage organization
Test 4	44	Evidence
Test 5	32	Shift of focus
Test 6	43	Point of view
Test 7	3	
Test 7	42	
Test 7	48	
Test 8	1	
Test 8	43	

Paired Passages

Test 1	49	
Test 1	50	
Test 1	51	
Test 1	52	Evidence
Test 2	30	
Test 2	31	
Test 2	32	
Test 3	38	Function
Test 3	39	
Test 3	40	Agree
Test 3	41	
Test 4	36	
Test 4	37	Evidence
Test 4	38	
Test 4	39	Evidence
Test 4	40	
Test 5	19	
Test 5	20	
Test 5	21	
Test 6	41	
Test 6	42	Agree
Test 7	38	
Test 7	39	
Test 7	40	
Test 7	41	
Test 8	39	
Test 8	40	
Test 8	41	Function

Graphics and Data Analysis

Test 1	28	Graphic only
Test 1	29	Graphic + passage
Test 1	30	Graphic only
Test 1	31	Graphic + passage
Test 2	50	Graphic only
Test 2	51	Graphic + passage
Test 2	52	Graphic only
Test 3	50	Graphic only
Test 3	51	Graphic only
Test 3	52	Graphic only
Test 4	50	Graphic only
Test 4	51	Graphic + passage
Test 4	52	Graphic only
Test 5	30	Graphic only
Test 5	31	Graphic only
Test 5	39	Graphic only
Test 5	40	Graphic only
Test 5	41	Graphic + passage
Test 6	19	Graphic only
Test 6	20	Graphic only
Test 6	21	Graphic + passage
Test 6	51	Graphic only
Test 6	52	Graphic only
Test 7	19	Graphic only
Test 7	20	Graphic only
Test 7	21	Graphic + passage (extended reasoning)
Test 7	50	Graphic + passage (function of a graphic)
Test 7	51	Graphic only
Test 8	19	Graphic only
Test 8	20	Graphic only
Test 8	21	Graphic + passage
Test 8	30	Graphic only
Test 8	31	Graphic + passage

Appendix B: 2018 Official Guide Questions by Test

Test 1

#	Category	Sub-Category
1	Big Picture	Summary
2	Rhetorical Strategy	Passage Structure
3	Vocabulary	
4	Literal Comp.	No line reference
5	Evidence	
6	Attitude	
7	Function	Paragraph
8	Vocabulary	
9	Literal Comp.	Line reference
10	Evidence	
11	Main Point	Examples
12	Vocabulary	
13	Literal Comp.	No line reference
14	Evidence	
15	Attitude	Inference
16	Literal Comp.	Line reference
17	Evidence	
18	Vocabulary	
19	Function	
20	Data Analysis	
21	Inference	Main point
22	Function	Word
23	Support/Contradict	Contradict
24	Literal Comp.	Line reference
25	Function	
26	Inference	
27	Function	
28	Data Analysis	Graphic only
29	Data Analysis	Graphic + passage
30	Evidence	Graphic only
31	Data Analysis	Graphic + passage
32	Big Picture	Purpose of a passage
33	Big Picture	Main point
34	Function	Rhetorical strategy
35	Literal Comp.	
36	Literal Comp.	No line reference
37	Evidence	
38	Literal Comp.	Line reference
39	Evidence	
40	Vocabulary	
41	Function	Main point
42	Function	
43	Literal Comp.	No line reference
44	Evidence	
45	Vocabulary	
46	Function	
47	Literal Comp.	No line reference
48	Vocabulary	
49	P1/P2 Relationship	
50	P1/P2 Relationship	Line reference
51	Support	
52	P1/P2 Relationship	

Test 2

#	Category	Sub-Category
1	Big Picture	Summary
2	Function	
3	Rhetorical Strategy	Point of view
4	Function	
5	Literal Comp.	No line reference
6	Literal Comp.	No line reference
7	Support	
8	Function	
9	Literal Comp.	No line reference
10	Evidence	
11	Big Picture	Purpose of a passage
12	Rhetorical Strategy	Counterargument
13	Support	
14	Vocabulary	
15	Function	
16	Vocabulary	
17	Support/Undermine	Support
18	Main Point	
19	Data Analysis	Graphic only
20	Data Analysis	Graphic only
21	Data Analysis	Graphic + passage
22	Literal Comp.	No line reference
23	Evidence	
24	Literal Comp.	
25	Vocabulary	
26	Inference	
27	Literal Comp.	
28	Function	
29	Big Picture	Purpose of a passage
30	P1/P2 Relationship	
31	P1/P2 Relationship	Agree
32	P1/P2 Relationship	
33	Big Picture	Main point
34	Function	
35	Literal Comp.	No line reference
36	Evidence	
37	Vocabulary	
38	Inference	
39	Vocabulary	

40	Literal Comp.	No line reference
41	Evidence	
42	Literal Comp.	Line reference
43	Function	Purpose of a paragraph
44	Vocabulary	
45	Literal Comp.	No line reference
46	Evidence	
47	Vocabulary	
48	Inference	No line reference
49	Evidence	
50	Data Analysis	Graphic only
51	Data Analysis	Graphic + passage
52	Data Analysis	Graphic only

Test 3

1	Big Picture	Summary
2	Vocabulary	
3	Inference	No line reference
4	Evidence	
5	Function	
6	Vocabulary	
7	Literal Comp.	No line reference
8	Inference	
9	Literal Comp.	No line reference
10	Evidence	
11	Function	
12	Literal Comp.	No line reference
13	Evidence	
14	Big Picture	Point of a paragraph
15	Evidence	
16	Vocabulary	
17	Vocabulary	
18	Support/Contradict	Support
19	Data Analysis	Graphic only
20	Data Analysis	Graphic only
21	Rhetorical Strategy	Passage organization
22	Vocabulary	
23	Inference	Assumption
24	Evidence	
25	Function	
26	Literal Comp.	Line reference
27	Literal Comp.	No line reference
28	Vocabulary	
29	Inference	No line reference
30	Evidence	
31	Vocabulary	
32	Inference	No line reference
33	Evidence	
34	Literal Comp.	No line reference
35	Vocabulary	

36	Literal Comp.	No line reference
37	Evidence	
38	P1/P2 Relationship	Function
39	P1/P2 Relationship	
40	P1/P2 Relationship	Agree
41	P1/P2 Relationship	
42	Tone	
43	Inference	Line reference
44	Evidence	
45	Inference	No line reference
46	Evidence	
47	Vocabulary	
48	Big Picture	Purpose of a paragraph
49	Inference	Assumption
50	Data Analysis	Graphic only
51	Data Analysis	Graphic only
52	Data Analysis	Graphic only

Test 4

1	Attitude	No line reference
2	Evidence	
3	Vocabulary	
4	Function	
5	Literal Comp.	No line reference
6	Evidence	
7	Literal Comp.	No line reference
8	Inference	
9	Vocabulary	
10	Vocabulary	
11	Big Picture	Summary of a paragraph
12	Literal Comp.	No line reference
13	Vocabulary	
14	Literal Comp.	No line reference
15	Evidence	
16	Inference	No line reference
17	Evidence	
18	Vocabulary	
19	Attitude	Graphic
20	Data Analysis	Graphic only
21	Data Analysis	Graphic only
22	Big Picture	Purpose of a passage
23	Attitude	
24	Vocabulary	
25	Inference	No line reference
26	Evidence	
27	Literal Comp.	No line reference
28	Evidence	
29	Inference	
30	Function	Punctuation
31	Inference	

32	Literal Comp.	No line reference
33	Vocabulary	
34	Vocabulary	
35	Inference	
36	P1/P2 Relationship	Line Reference
37	Evidence	
38	P1/P2 Relationship	Line Reference
39	Evidence	
40	P1/P2 Relationship	
41	Big Picture	Purpose of a passage
42	Big Picture	Purpose of a passage
43	Rhetorical Strategy	Passage organization
44	Evidence	
45	Function	
46	Literal Comp.	No line reference
47	Evidence	
48	Inference	
49	Support/Contradict	Support
50	Data Analysis	Graphic only
51	Data Analysis	Graphic + passage
52	Data Analysis	Graphic only

Test 5

1	Rhetorical Strategy	Organization/focus
2	Function	Purpose of a paragraph
3	Inference	
4	Literal Comp.	Line reference
5	Evidence	
6	Literal Comp.	
7	Literal Comp.	
8	Big Picture	Main idea/paragraph
9	Support/Contradict	Support
10	Vocabulary	
11	Big picture	Point of a passage
12	Support	
13	Inference	
14	Vocabulary	
15	Vocabulary	
16	Big Picture	Central claim
17	Big Picture	Point of a passage
18	Evidence	
19	P1/P2 Relationship	
20	P1/P2 Relationship	
21	P1/P2 Relationship	
22	Vocabulary	
23	Literal Comp.	
24	Attitude	Line reference
25	Evidence	
26	Literal Comp.	No line reference
27	Evidence	

28	Literal Comp.	
29	Vocabulary	
30	Data Analysis	Graphic only
31	Data Analysis	Graphic only
32	Rhetorical Strategy	Organization/focus
33	Inference	No line reference
34	Evidence	
35	Support/Contradict	Support
36	Extended Reasoning	
37	Vocabulary	
38	Vocabulary	
39	Data Analysis	Graphic only
40	Data Analysis	Graphic only
41	Data Analysis	Graphic + passage
42	Literal Comp.	No line reference
43	Evidence	
44	Vocabulary	
45	Literal Comp.	No line reference
46	Evidence	
47	Vocabulary	
48	Function	Purpose of a paragraph
49	Literal Comp.	
50	Inference	No line reference
51	Evidence	
52	Function	Purpose of a question

Test 6

1	Function	Purpose of a paragraph
2	Vocabulary	
3	Function	
4	Support/Contradict	Support
5	Function	
6	Function	Purpose of a word
7	Inference	No line reference
8	Evidence	
9	Literal Comp.	Attitude
10	Literal Comp.	
11	Big Picture/Function	Purpose of a passage
12	Literal Comp.	No line reference
13	Evidence	
14	Vocabulary	
15	Function	
16	Literal Comp.	No line reference
17	Evidence	
18	Vocabulary	
19	Data Analysis	Graphic only
20	Data Analysis	Graphic only
21	Data Analysis	Graphic + passage
22	Big Picture/Function	Purpose of a passage
23	Literal Comp.	

24	Inference	
25	Literal Comp.	
26	Vocabulary	
27	Literal Comp.	Line reference
28	Evidence	
29	Function	Purpose of a paragraph
30	Inference	
31	Literal Comp.	No line reference
32	Evidence	
33	Literal Comp.	No line reference
34	Evidence	
35	Vocabulary	
36	Function	
37	Vocabulary	
38	Literal Comp.	No line reference
39	Evidence	
40	Big Picture/Function	Purpose of a passage
41	P1/P2 Relationship	
42	P1/P2 Relationship	Agree
43	Rhetorical Strategy	Point of view
44	Vocabulary	
45	Inference	No line reference
46	Evidence	
47	Literal Comp.	No line reference
48	Evidence	
49	Vocabulary	
50	Function	
51	Data Analysis	Graphic only
52	Data Analysis	Graph only

Test 7

1	Big Picture	Major Theme
2	Literal Comp.	
3	Rhetorical Strategy	
4	Function	
5	Literal Comp.	No line reference
6	Evidence	
7	Function	
8	Literal Comp.	No line reference
9	Evidence	
10	Vocabulary	
11	Big Picture/Function	Purpose of a passage
12	Literal Comp.	No line reference
13	Evidence	
14	Function	"Vague" answers
15	Vocabulary	
16	Attitude	Line reference
17	Evidence	
18	Vocabulary	
19	Data Analysis	Graphic only

20	Data Analysis	Graphic only
21	Data Analysis	Extended reasoning
22	Big Picture/Function	Purpose of a passage
23	Function	
24	Inference	No line reference
25	Evidence	
26	Function	
27	Inference	No line reference
28	Evidence	
29	Big Picture	Main idea
30	Function	
31	Vocabulary	
32	Vocabulary	
33	Inference	No line reference
34	Evidence	
35	Vocabulary	
36	Inference	No line reference
37	Evidence	
38	P1/P2 Relationship	Agree
39	P1/P2 Relationship	
40	P1/P2 Relationship	
41	P1/P2 Relationship	
42	Rhetorical Strategy	Shift in focus
43	Function	
44	Inference	No line reference
45	Evidence	
46	Literal Comp.	No line reference
47	Evidence	
48	Rhetorical Strategy	
49	Vocabulary	
50	Data Analysis	Function of a graph
51	Data Analysis	Graphic only
52	Analogy	

Test 8

1	Rhetorical Strategy	Shift in focus
2	Function	
3	Extended reasoning	No line reference
4	Evidence	
5	Inference	No line reference
6	Evidence	
7	Literal Comp.	
8	Vocabulary	
9	Function	
10	Literal Comp.	
11	Function/Big Picture	Purpose of a passage
12	Vocabulary	
13	Vocabulary	
14	Literal Comp.	No line reference
15	Evidence	

16	Extended reasoning	No line reference
17	Evidence	
18	Function	
19	Data Analysis	
20	Data Analysis	
21	Data Analysis	Graphic + passage
22	Big Picture	Central idea of a passage
23	Rhetorical Strategy	Structure of passage
24	Evidence	No prior question
25	Vocabulary	
26	Literal Comp.	
27	Vocabulary	
28	Literal Comp.	No line reference
29	Evidence	
30	Data Analysis	
31	Data Analysis	Graphic + passage
32	Function	
33	Inference	No line reference
34	Evidence	
35	Vocabulary	
36	Extended reasoning	No line reference
37	Evidence	
38	Vocabulary	
39	P1/P2 Relationship	
40	P1/P2 Relationship	Agree
41	Function	
42	Big Picture/Function	Purpose of a passage
43	Literal Comp.	No line reference
44	Evidence	
45	Tone	
46	Function	
47	Literal Comp.	
48	Literal Comp.	
49	Vocabulary	
50	Extended reasoning	No line reference
51	Evidence	
52	Literal Comp.	

Reprints and Permissions

Acheson, Dean. From "Speech at Berkeley, California, March 16, 1950. http://teachingamericanhistory.org/library/document/speech-at-berkeley-california/

Adee, Sally. From "Roughnecks in Space: Moon Mining in Science Fiction," *New Scientist*, 27 April 2012. http://www.newscientist.com/gallery/moon-mining

Anft, Michael. "Solving the Mystery of Death Valley's Walking Rocks," *Johns Hopkins Magazine*, 6/1/11. Reprinted by permission of *Johns Hopkins Magazine*. http://archive.magazine.jhu.edu/2011/06/solving-the-mystery-of-death-valley's-walking-rocks/

Ansanelli, Sean. "Makerspaces, Hackerspaces and Community-Scale Production in Detroit and Beyond," *Urban Magazine*, Spring 2013, p. 31. Reprinted by permission of the author. http://blogs.cuit.columbia.edu/urbanmagazine/files/2015/02/URBAN_Spring2013_WEB.pdf

Archer, Mike. From "Ordering the vegetarian meal? There's more animal blood on your hands," *The Conversation*, 16 December 2011. http://theconversation.edu.au/ordering-the-vegetarian-meal-theres-more-animal-blood-on-your-hands-4659

Austen, Jane. *Northanger Abbey*. Originally published 1803. Excerpted from Chapter 1 through Project Gutenberg, http://www.gutenberg.org/files/121/121-h/121-h.htm

Ball, Philip. From "The Trouble With Scientists," *Nautilus*, 5/14/15. http://nautil.us/issue/24/error/the-trouble-with-scientists

Brauer, Wiebke. Adapted from "The Miracle of Space," *Smart Magazine*, 10/31/14. Reprinted by permission of *Smart Magazine*. *http://smart-magazine.com/space/the-miracle-of-space/*

de Gouges, Olympe. Adapted from *The Declaration of the Rights of Woman*, 1791. https://chnm.gmu.edu/revolution/d/293/

Douglass, Frederick. Adapted from "Self-Made Men," 1872. http://www.frederick-douglass-heritage.org/self-made-men/

DuBois, W.E.B. Adapted from "Atlanta Compromise Speech," 1895. http://historymatters.gmu.edu/d/39/

Freedman, David. Adapted from"The Truth About Genetically Modified Food," Scientificamerican.com (Nature, Inc.), September 1, 2013. https://www.scientificamerican.com/article/the-truth-about-genetically-modified-food/

Gholipour, Bahar. Adapted from "Sleep Shrinks the Brain's Synapses to Make Room for New Learning," Scientificamerican.com (Nature, Inc.), May 1, 2017. https://www.scientificamerican.com/article/sleep-shrinks-the-brain-rsquo-s-synapses-to-make-room-for-new-learning/

Gompers, Samuel. From "What Does the Working Man Want?" Address to Workers in Louisville, Kentucky, 1890. http://jackiewhiting.net/HonorsUS/Labor/gompers.pdf

Gross, Daniel. From "Will We Ever Be Able to Make Traffic Disappear?" Smithsonian.com, 5/7/2015. http://www.smithsonianmag.com/innovation/will-we-ever-be-able-to-make-traffic-disappear-180955164/

Jackson, Julian. "New Research Suggests that Dinosaurs Were Active and Warm-Blooded." *Earth Times*, 7/12/11. http://www.earthtimes.org/nature/new-research-suggests-dinosaurs-warm-blooded-active/1138/. Reprinted by permission of the author.

Jordan, Barbara. Adapted from the Keynote Speech, Democratic National Convention, delivered July 12, 1976. http://www.americanrhetoric.com/speeches/barbarajordan1976dnc.html

Kelemen, Peter B. From "The Origin of the Ocean Floor," *Scientific American*, February 2009. **Reproduced with permission, © 2009, Scientific American, Inc. All rights reserved.** http://www.scientificamerican.com/article/the-origin-of-the-ocean-floor/

Kincaid, Jamaica. Excerpt from "Gwen" from ANNIE JOHN by Jamaica Kincaid. Copyright © 1985 by Jamaica Kincaid. Reprinted by permission of Farrar, Straus and Giroux, LLC.

Koerth-Baker, Maggie: From "The Power of Positive Thinking, Truth or Myth?" *Live Science*, 8/29/08. http://www.livescience.com/2814-power-positive-thinking-truth-myth.html

Leech, Kirk: From "Why Moralism Spoils the Appetite," *Spiked Review of Books*. No. 53, February 2012. http://www.spiked-online.com/review_of_books/article/12154#.VaV2PFoT-fQ

Lehrer, Jonah. Adapted from "Under Pressure: The Search for Stress Vaccine," *Wired*, 7/28/10, 2:00 p.m. http://www.wired.com/2010/07/ff_stress_cure/

Lincoln, Abraham. Adapted from "First Inaugural Address," March 4, 1861. http://avalon.law.yale.edu/19th_century/lincoln1.asp

McConnell, David. From "Playing with Infinity on Riker's Island," *Prospect*, February 2012. http://www.prospectmagazine.co.uk/science-and-technology/playing-with-infinity-on-rikers-island

Miller, Greg. From "How Our Brains Make Memories," Smithsonian.com, May 2010. http://www.smithsonianmag.com/science-nature/how-our-brains-make-memories-14466850/

Mills, Mark. From "Every Breath You Take," *City Journal*, 7/2/13. http://www.city-journal.org/2013/bc0702mm.html

Montero, Barbara Gail. From "The Myth of 'Just Do It,'" *The New York Times*, 6/9/13. http://opinionator.blogs.nytimes.com/author/barbara-gail-montero/

Nuwer, Rachel. "What is a Species?" Smithsonian.com, 11/6/13. http://www.smithsonianmag.com/science-nature/what-is-a-species-insight-from-dolphins-and-humans-180947580/?no-ist

Orwell, George. Adapted from "Keep the Apidastra Flying," originally published 1936. Accessed from Project Gutenberg, http://gutenberg.net.au/ebooks02/0200021.txt

Panko, Ben. "What Does it Mean to Be a Species? Genetics is Changing the Answer," Smithsonian.com, May 19, 2017. http://www.smithsonianmag.com/science-nature/what-does-it-mean-be-species-genetics-changing-answer-180963380/

Riggio, Ronald. Excerpted from "Why Certain Smells Trigger Positive Memories," *Psychology Today*, May 1, 2012. Reprinted by permission of the author.

"The Rise of the Sharing Economy," *The Economist*, 3/9/2013. http://www.economist.com/news/leaders/21573104-internet-everything-hire-rise-sharing-economy

Rousseau, Jean-Jacques. From *The Social Contract*, 1762, trans. GDH Cole. http://www.gutenberg.org/files/46333/46333-h/46333-h.htm

Rupp, Rebecca. From "Surviving the Sneaky Psychology of Supermarkets," *National Geographic*, 6/15/15. http://theplate.nationalgeographic.com/2015/06/15/surviving-the-sneaky-psychology-of-supermarkets/

Sainani, Kristin. Adapted from "What, Me Worry?" *Stanford Magazine*, May/June 2014. https://alumni.stanford.edu/get/page/magazine/article/?article_id=70134. Reprinted by permission of the author.

Schwartz, Barry. "More Isn't Always Better," *Harvard Business Review*, June 2006. Reprinted by permission of Harvard Business Publishing. https://hbr.org/2006/06/more-isnt-always-better

"Scientists Discover Salty Aquifer, Previously Unknown Microbial Habitat Under Antarctica," © 2015, Dartmouth College. http://www.sciencenewsline.com/articles/2015042815560014.html

Sullivan, John Jeremiah. "One of Us," *Lapham's Quarterly*, Spring 2013. http://www.laphamsquarterly.org/animals/one-us

Taylor, Astra. "A Small World After All," *Bookforum*, June/July/August 2013. http://www.bookforum.com/inprint/020_02/11685

Thompson, Helen. "Yawning Spreads Like a Plague in Wolves," Smithsonian.com, 8/27/14, http://www.smithsonianmag.com/science-nature/yawning-spread-plague-wolves-180952484/

Tregaskis, Sharon. "The Buzz: What Bees Tell Us About Global Climate Change, *Johns Hopkins Magazine*. 6/2/2010. Reprinted by permission by *Johns Hopkins Magazine*. http://archive.magazine.jhu.edu/2010/06/the-buzz-what-bees-tell-us-about-global-climate-change/

Washington, Booker T. "The Talented Tenth," 1903. http://teachingamericanhistory.org/library/document/the-talented-tenth/

Wayman, Erin. "The First Americans," Smithsonian.com, 11/28/11. http://www.smithsonianmag.com/science-nature/the-first-americans-889302/

Wharton, Edith. *Summer*, originally published 1917. Excerpted from Chapter 1 through Project Gutenberg, http://www.gutenberg.org/files/166/166-h/166-h.htm

Webster, Daniel. Adapted from the "Seventh of March Speech to the Senate," 1850. https://www.dartmouth.edu/~dwebster/speeches/seventh-march.html

"Why Eat Locally?" *The Regal Vegan*, http://www.regalvegan.com/site/local-yokels/

ABOUT THE AUTHOR

Erica Meltzer earned her B.A. from Wellesley College and spent more than a decade tutoring privately in Boston and New York City, as well as nationally and internationally via Skype. Her experience working with students from a wide range of educational backgrounds and virtually every score level, from the third percentile to the 99th, gave her unique insight into the types of stumbling blocks students often encounter when preparing for standardized reading and writing tests.

She was inspired to begin writing her own test-prep materials in 2007, after visiting a local bookstore in search of additional practice questions for an SAT Writing student. Unable to find material that replicated the contents of the exam with sufficient accuracy, she decided to write her own. What started as a handful of exercises jotted down on a piece of paper became the basis for her first book, the original *Ultimate Guide to SAT Grammar*, published in 2011. Since that time, she has authored guides for SAT reading and vocabulary, as well as verbal guides for the ACT®, GRE®, and GMAT®. Her books have sold more than 100,000 copies and are used around the world. She lives in New York City, and you can visit her online at www.thecriticalreader.com.

Made in the USA
Middletown, DE
12 September 2017